Jewelry From

Sarah Coventry®
and *Emmons*®

Kay Oshel

4880 Lower Valley Road, Atglen, PA 19310 USA

Courtesy Olan Mills.

Dedication

My dedication for this book has to be to my husband, who has been the most supportive person in the world. Taking several weeks off in the summer, over his birthday no less, and driving to Newark, New York has to be true dedication. Although the lights went out while we were there, Alan stands as a beacon for my every endeavor and was the encouragement for my getting involved in the new Sarah Coventry company, even though he knew it would mean buying more jewelry.

Library of Congress Cataloging-in-Publication Data:

Oshel, Kay.
  Jewelry from Sarah Coventry and Emmons / by Kay Oshel.
    p. cm.
  ISBN 0-7643-2128-5 (pbk.)
1. Sarah Coventry, Inc.—Catalogs. 2. Emmons Jewelry (Firm)—Catalogs. 3. Costume jewelry—New York (State)—Newark—History—20th century—Catalogs. 4. Costume jewelry—Collectors and collecting—United States—Catalogs. I. Title.

NK7398.S275A4 2004
688'.2'0973075—dc22

2004015491

Designed by John P. Cheek
Cover design by Bruce M. Waters
Type set in Van Dijk/Humanist 521 BT

ISBN: 0-7643-2128-5
Printed in China
1 2 3 4

Published by Schiffer Publishing Ltd.
4880 Lower Valley Road
Atglen, PA 19310
Phone: (610) 593-1777; Fax: (610) 593-2002
E-mail: Info@schifferbooks.com

For the largest selection of fine reference books on this and related subjects, please visit our web site at
www.schifferbooks.com
We are always looking for people to write books on new and related subjects. If you have an idea for a book please contact us at the above address.

This book may be purchased from the publisher.
Include $3.95 for shipping.
Please try your bookstore first.
You may write for a free catalog.

In Europe, Schiffer books are distributed by
Bushwood Books
6 Marksbury Ave.
Kew Gardens
Surrey TW9 4JF England
Phone: 44 (0) 20 8392-8585; Fax: 44 (0) 20 8392-9876
E-mail: info@bushwoodbooks.co.uk
Free postage in the U.K., Europe; air mail at cost.

Contents

Acknowledgments 4

Chapter One: Overview 5

    Introduction 5

    The Company 5

    The Parties and the Driving Force 7

    The Jewelry 10

    Versatility 12

    Becoming A Collector 12

    Update on Unidentified Pieces From First Book 13

    Using This Book 14

    Sarah is "Home Again" 14

    You Are Invited 15

Chapter Two: Sarah Coventry (USA) 16

    Sets 19

    Brooches 33

    Earrings 37

    Necklaces 42

    Rings 66

    Bracelets 72

    Lady Coventry and New Sarah 77

    Miscellaneous – Watches, Accessories, Men's Items, Christmas Items 78

    Advertising and Catalogs 82

Chapter Three: Sarah Coventry International 85

    Sets 85

    Brooches 87

    Necklaces 90

    Rings, Bracelets, Accessories 93

    Catalogs from Canada (Early 1970s, 1973, 1980) 95

    Catalog from Scotland (1979) 105

    Catalog from Australia (1972) 108

Chapter Four: Emmons Jewelry 110

    Sets 116

    Brooches 132

    Earrings 137

    Necklaces 142

    Rings and Bracelets 151

    Miscellaneous 156

    1969 Catalog 158

    1970 Fall and Christmas Catalog 162

    1974 Catalog 166

    Caroline Emmons 1977– Companion Collection 170

Epilogue 171

Glossary 172

Bibliography 172

Appendix: Personal Collection Sheets Sample 173

Index 174

Acknowledgments

As with my first book, this project would not have been possible without a great deal of effort on the part of many people. The first name to be mentioned is Chris Davis, executive director of the Arcadia Historical Society in Newark, New York. Without his generosity and knowledge of the company and the people in the area, I would not have been able to document as many of the pieces. Chris also led me to making contact with many former employees, listed here alphabetically: Brenda Bruzee, Sandy DeValder, Jim and Allie Doyle, Tom Healy, Gilbert Lewis, Norma Miles, Nina Mooney, Mary Sanders, Bill and Carol Scheetz, Mary Elizabeth Snawder, Aileen Van Tyle, and Ginny Williams. Many collectors in the area also were very helpful – special thanks to Marjory Ritter, Arlena Jordan, Marlene McIlwain, Dorothy De May, and Virginia Minutolo.

A special thank you again to Dawn Michael for providing additional pieces of jewelry to be photographed and to Mary Beth Coffman for instigating this project with her challenge of researching and adding Emmons.

Many other dealers and collectors have also scoured the countryside searching for this jewelry – for me and for their own collections. No doubt Pat and Gary Wyatt get the prize for becoming real addicts in this collecting frenzy. They have surpassed me for numbers and have secured some very dynamic sets of both Sarah and Emmons. Other helpful people have been Abby Bellamy, Michelle Kernel, Lanell Peacock, Reba Thompson, and Jinny Wilson. I apologize to any who might have inadvertently been omitted.

And for the second time, I wish to thank my understanding and thought-provoking editor, Donna Baker. She has helped in making difficult tasks manageable. Thank you.

Chapter One

Overview

Welcome to my second contribution to the world of collectors' books. My first book, *Sarah Coventry Jewelry*, was published in 2003 and dealt strictly with the jewelry from that company. In researching that book, I discovered more accurate information about the related company of Emmons. Lots of misinformation has been published in other books about the existence of these two companies. Following publication of *Sarah Coventry Jewelry*, I met Mary Beth Coffman, a former Fashion Show Director with Emmons, who challenged me to write a second book that would include Emmons jewelry as well. So here, as in the first book, I will bring some of these past employees' words to you.

Introduction

Despite having been an educator and guidance counselor, one who has taught others about decision making and noted repeatedly how "our decisions affect our lives," I am totally and completely baffled by this process. In my first book, I contemplated the idea that I had missed out on being part of a company I would have enjoyed because I had chosen other paths. Today, I am amused as to how these decisions can "come full circle."

While conducting research for this book, I was overwhelmed again by stories of how wonderful the two companies had been to their employees – I envied the great memories of conventions, trips, cruises, and fabulous people. So, when I learned that a new company – Sarah Coventry – was starting with the party plan as before, I began to investigate further. To make a long story even longer, I ultimately became one of their Style Consultants. More information about this company will be found in a later section of the book.

As I embark on another accounting of this timeless jewelry, join me and envision your life as if you had been a representative of Sarah Coventry or Emmons, or an employee of the C. H. Stuart Company. Like many of those people, collecting these magnificent pieces of jewelry will likely become your passion. I invite you to accompany me on this journey – and to enjoy.

The Company

During my summer 2003 visit to Newark, New York – where the C.H. Stuart company was founded and based for over eighty years – I not only heard a lot about the company, I also viewed the building once housing Sarah Coventry, Emmons, and at least five other companies. Throughout the years, C. H. Stuart had over a dozen various divisions or subsidiaries.

The company actually began as a nursery under the name C.W. Stuart and Company, with Charles William Stuart at the helm. Charles W. had a jewelry company entitled Commercial Enterprises based in Syracuse. The following information is from an Open House brochure for that company in the late 1960s (*Courtesy of Arcadia Historical Society*).

"It all began when Charles W. Stuart gave up the jewelry business to purchase a farm on Willow Street in the village of Newark, New York. It wasn't much of a farm – as farms go – but it did boast a large number of young fruit trees.

And so, Charles W. Stuart became the owner of a farm – several hundred fruit trees – and a resident of Newark. However, having no desire to raise produce or the usual farm crops, young Stuart started to peddle his "growing assets" (fruit trees) to the neighboring farmers.

Success came slowly – but surely. This idea of taking the product to the consumer rather than having the consumer come to the producer proved to be well received – and one satisfied customer led to another – until finally the C. W. Stuart and Company was formed…more trees were grown and a thriving business had its beginning.

Salespeople were hired to see more farmers and to sell more trees. Like the "Yankee Peddlers" of Colonial Days, they traveled in wagons, from settlement to settlement, farm to farm, and door to door – bringing the inhabitants young trees from the farm on Willow Street.

The year 1895 marked a new era for the ever-expanding company. In this year a second company was formed to compete with the original company – this was Knight and Bostwick – another venture which proved highly successful and led to the formation of still another company in 1897 – EMMONS and COMPANY…and with this start, additional companies continued to be formed until a total of 13 were brought into being…later reduced to four.

Early in the present century, another young "Yankee Peddler" appeared on the scene. This was Charles H. Stuart – son of the founder but unlike his father – his likes and abilities were more in the direction of chemicals rather than growing of trees…young C.H. had studied chemistry at Cornell University and he was eager to make a niche for himself in this field of endeavor.

The idea of selling products door-to-door appealed to C.H. Stuart – and so he set out to develop one or more products which could be sold by the Nursery salesmen during the course of their calling on prospects.

One of the first, and always one of the most successful of the new products, was a highly concentrated flavoring extract – one drop being equal to a spoonful of liquid flavoring. This product was an instant success and was soon followed by a number of other food products such as tea, coffee, spices and puddings. Along with these items, such products as water softener, aspirin tablets and cough syrups became part of an ever expanding line. Many of these innovations gave way to cosmetics in later years and today Commercial Enterprises have three companies engaged in selling cosmetics on the "party plan."

The first silverware company was formed in 1930 – Home Decorators, Inc. This was followed a few years later by Empire Crafts Corporation. These two companies are the largest direct-selling distributors of silverware in America. Each of these companies have since expanded their product lines to include stainless steel flatware, plastic and china dinnerware.

For all practical purposes, our product lines seemed to be complete, however, there was still one more to be added – costume jewelry. In 1949 Emmons, Inc. was the first company in the nation to merchandise jewelry on a "direct to the consumer" basis. Later, Sarah Coventry, Inc. was formed to also merchandise jewelry through the party plan method proved so successful by the cosmetic companies.

To this imposing roster there were added two more companies – Hanover Fine China, Inc., having as their principal products fine chinaware, and Stuart-Christy, Inc., manufacturer of costume jewelry."

At this time, it was estimated that nearly eighteen thousand people were working as employees for the company through the sales force.

C.H. Stuart's son, Lyman, and grandson, C.W.(Bill), continued the leadership until the doors closed for the final time in the early 1980s.

These pictures depict the lineage of the Stuart family, starting at left with Charles William Stuart (1837-1923), who started the original company; Charles Henry Stuart; Lyman Stuart; and Charles William "Bill" Stuart, who started Sarah Coventry in 1949. *Courtesy of Arcadia Historical Society.*

The Stuart Coat of Arms is among many items on display in the Arcadia Historical Society Museum that chronicle a company in existence from 1852 to 1984. Most people in the community still have kind words for this company that employed many. *Courtesy of Arcadia Historical Society.*

Throughout the years, the residents of Newark, New York knew, loved, and supported this community-minded company. Many worked for the company right up to the end in 1984. It was known for its family oriented philosophy, which can be seen in a 1968 article from the local paper in which division heads provide information, rather than all the credit being taken by Bill Stuart. One motto repeated several times was "You Can't Do Business Sitting On Your Assets," which no doubt reflected the philosophy of the whole company as it continued trying new areas of business endeavor, expanding to other countries, developing new managers, and focusing on the many people involved in a family manner.

An article published in 1968 provides evidence of how much impact the C. H. Stuart Company had on the small community of Newark, New York. Each division of the company was highlighted, with its efforts toward this record sales year described. At the same time, groundbreaking had begun for the building of the complex later to be known as Stuart Park. *Courtesy of Arcadia Historical Society.*

Many former employees attended a presentation I had been asked to give during my visit to Newark. Although many of these people had lost their jobs, retirement benefits, or stock, they were still very positive in their comments about the company. One such person was Gilbert Lewis, who had worked for the company for forty-four years – from 1938 to 1982. As shown in the article displayed here, the company never overlooked a chance to promote, thank, or support any employee. Showers and/or parties were held for weddings, babies, and birthdays, and family picnics and activities were scheduled on a regular basis.

Many former employees spoke with me while I was visiting in Newark. One of those was Gilbert Lewis, pictured here as "Personality of the Month" in a C.W. Stuart publication. Gilbert worked in a variety of capacities during his forty-four years of employment, from the mailroom to office manager to bookkeeping. He was one of many who lost retirement benefits when the company went out of business. *Courtesy of Gilbert Lewis and Arcadia Historical Society.*

The new building was started in the late 1960s, but wasn't dedicated until 1977. The medallion pictured is just one of many commemorative items created from 1852 to 1984. Shown from both sides, it simply states: "The dreams and visions which find their culmination here are not the product of any one individual. Rather, they reflect the imagination and effort of thousands of employees, representatives, customers and associates. It is to them that this building is dedicated."

Stuart medallions were created in 1977 to commemorate 125 years of existence and the dedication of the company's new building in the Stuart Park complex. *Courtesy of Arcadia Historical Society.*

A name that should be mentioned here is that of Rex Wood. When Bill Stuart started the Sarah Coventry company in November of 1949, Rex became the first employee; in 1964, he became President of the subsidiary. Rex Wood's story is one of surprises and persistence. It was chronicled in 1967 in a book called *The Executive Breakthrough*, by Auren Uris. The chapter recounting his story was titled "Showroom in the Parlor," a very appropriate description. As a young man, Wood tried being a mechanic and owning a filling station before attending Cornell University. He briefly worked for Sears, Roebuck and as a life insurance salesman, successful at both but feeling restless. In 1949, he responded to an ad placed by Commercial Enterprises for a salesman but after taking a psychological test given all applicants and interviewing with the sales manager, he decided this wasn't for him. However, C.W.(Bill) Stuart realized by Rex's test scores that he was potentially an excellent salesman. Soon after, they ran into each other and Bill related his dream of starting a jewelry business with the home-party technique, a relatively new development in direct selling. Stuart, writes Uris, "picked up a pin and stuck it into a map of the United States. Wilkes-Barre, Pennsylvania, was punctured. 'That,' said Stuart, 'is your territory. Good luck.'"

Thus, at the age of thirty-three, Rex Wood began an adventure and journey none would have foreseen possible. Check out the book for the rest of his story. Needless, to say, he was a success and in 1964, as President of Sarah Coventry, Inc., he was able to create the ultimate direct sales company and be involved with tens of thousands of Fashion Show Directors across the country.

Rex Wood's talents were well documented in the area of business development and personnel; his abilities, however, ex-tended into the arena of fine arts as well, as portrayed by the drawing on Sarah Coventry's 25th Anniversary Year plate from 1974, entitled "Silver Memories and Golden Dreams."

Front and back of anniversary plate painted by Rex Wood, first employee and eventual President of Sarah Coventry, Inc. It commemorated Sarah Coventry's 25th Anniversary with a theme of "Silver Memories and Golden Dreams." This was a limited edition plate in 1974 so locating one of these plates is a real find. *Courtesy of Marjory Ritter.*

The Parties and the Driving Force

For both Sarah Coventry and Emmons, company growth can be attributed to several strategies. The main strategy was the two companies' workforce – the Fashion Show Directors and their ability to advance upward in the management system by becoming unit directors, branch, region and area managers. This workforce was mainly women who wished to be home with their families, yet bring in income and expand their social environment. However, there were many husband and wife teams.

Getting involved in either of the companies could be done at no cost. The jewelry demonstration kit and supplies were on loan to the Fashion Show Director (FSD), who could earn the right of keeping the kit by continuing to have parties. With Sarah Coventry, it was up to managers to collect the kits from FSDs not desiring to continue working, and this was also true for Emmons; therefore, it was important for managers to be close to their workforce. One inventory sheet dated 1962 stated at the bottom that if items weren't returned, the person agreed to pay the retail value of the items.

The main focus of both companies was for Fashion Show Directors to utilize the home party concept, allowing women to get together with other women for a social outing and to actually try on the pieces of jewelry before purchasing. This also gave the FSD a chance to encourage friends to host a party, thus receiving free jewelry and identifying others desiring to make some money. By helping others, advancement into management was possible. Hostesses, who were a valued part of the Sarah Coventry and Emmons success, were able to select unique items not available to the customers. Among those items in 1969 were wigs and wiglets.

Shown on this page are some of the original promotional flyers utilized in securing FSDs. These are from Sarah Coventry, with similar ones used for Emmons.

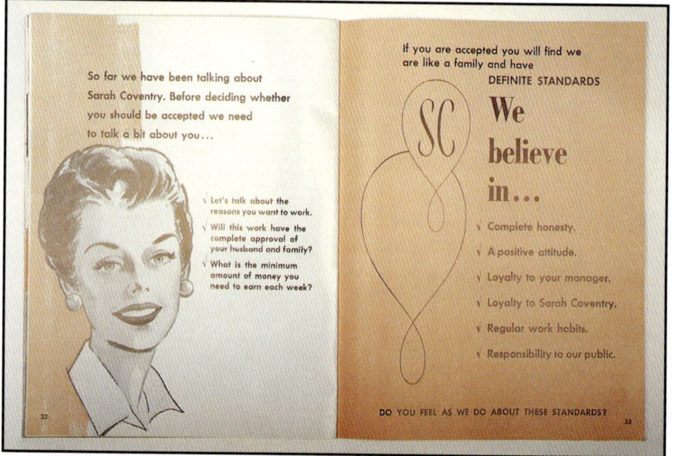

Left and Above:
Becoming a Fashion Show Director with Sarah Coventry and Emmons was one way for women in the 1950s and '60s to earn some extra money while raising a family. These pages are examples of the recruiting information that encouraged women to become FSDs. Many homes, boats, and vacations were paid for through earnings from this company. *Courtesy of Arcadia Historical Society.*

Much encouragement came from the Newark offices for employee advancement – this included meetings, scholarships, awards, trips, and jewelry, all paid for by the company. Newsletters, flyers, and brochures consistently supported the workforce, as evidenced by the following example.

The success of the Stuart companies, and especially Sarah Coventry, depended on the support and encouragement given to the sales force. Here is an example of a newsletter praising several individuals who had "climbed Sarah Coventry's ladder of success." *Courtesy of Arcadia Historical Society.*

One person we will hear more about later in the Emmons section is featured here. Meet Norma Miles, whose consistent efforts and winning smile created some memorable sales and who was rewarded in multiple ways – from being named "Miss Caroline Emmons" in 1974 to receiving numerous trophies, awards, jewelry, and pins.

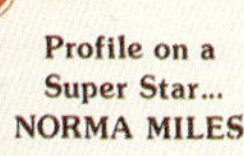

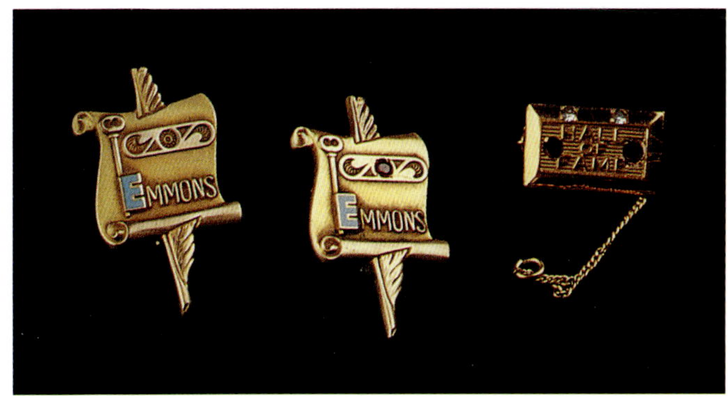

Emmons also created newsletters, pins, and awards to provide support for those with high achievement. Pictured here is Emmons FSD Norma Miles with some of her awards, pins, and "praisegrams." The award pins were given for recruiting, with the addition of ruby, sapphire, and diamonds up to a total of seventy recruits. *Courtesy of Norma Miles*

Profile on a Super Star... NORMA MILES

In Record Breaking Weeks 1979, NORMA MILES of the Ruth Hausman Region, Betty Hofmann Area, shattered the existing Fashion Leader Personal Sales Record with $12,500.90!

Together with her previous Record Setting accomplishments...as Top Unit in Total Sales ($16,263.00, set in 1975), and as Top Unit in Personal Sales ($10,758.60, set last year), Norma now holds the title to three RBW Records!

Norma joined Caroline during our seventh year in the jewelry direct selling business. Throughout these 23 years, she has won countless awards, trips, and honors for outstanding performance in the various levels she has held with the Company. In addition to excellence as a salesperson, Norma has also made a most significant contribution in recruiting. To this date, she has 149 personal, qualified Recruits to her credit!

As President Wayne stated in his congratulatory letter, "Norma Miles is not only a tribute to her Company, but a living reminder of our free enterprise system and a testimony of the greatness of women everywhere."

Because Norma's achievement is "not only a Company record, but a feat deserving of salutation and praise," as President Wayne continues in his letter, we felt that you would appreciate some insight on how she did the job. The following is adapted from a phone interview your editor had with this fine lady...

During the last days of September, or the first week of October, Norma plans her RBW strategy. She makes a list of previous year's RBW Hostesses, and calls her very top Hostess first, to give her the privilege of booking the first Show for Norma. Then, she calls her other former Hostesses to ask each one if they would book a Show during this special event. She books as many into the first week of RBW as possible, so bookings from these Shows can be fit into the other two weeks.

Throughout RBW, Norma devotes 18-hour days in carrying out her business. In addition to writing up all her own Shows, she does her own cooking, cleaning, laundry, and grocery shopping during these weeks.

Norma stresses the importance of her wonderful, loyal Hostesses and emphasizes the secret of her super success is thorough Hostess Coaching combined with the strength of self-determination. As a true competitor, she admits that she always wants to be Number One—and doesn't like anyone to beat her!

(continued on page 8)

7

The Jewelry

When I first began collecting, I focused on Sarah Coventry because it was easily identified on the back of each piece. However, I soon learned that not all of the jewelry or pieces of a set were marked. For both Sarah Coventry and Emmons, the selection process used in creating their highly successful costume jewelry was intense, with jewelry suppliers and the Stuart factory bringing prospective samples before a selection committee. Once the decision to produce a piece was made, the manufacturer would use a variety of identifying marks, including "SARAH COVENTRY," "SARAH COV," "SAC," "SC," and "COVENTRY." For Emmons, they stuck with "EMMONS" or "EmJ," even after adding the name Caroline to their company. Naming the piece of jewelry was important for both companies, as the jewelry could became personal to the prospective customer. Some names were used more than once throughout the years and some names were utilized by both companies on different items. This is very confusing when trying to match up earrings with a pin or necklace that has the same name but a different design. After the selected pieces had been produced and later discontinued from the collection, the molds were to be broken, thus preventing other companies from duplicating the design. However, I have located several items from other companies that are a match to some from Sarah Coventry or Emmons.

The C.H. Stuart company manufactured costume jewelry items for distribution. The following pages are some of the descriptive information given to FSDs about the process used in creating the jewelry.

MANUFACTURING CHARACTERISTICS			
	KARAT GOLD	**GOLD-FILLED & STERLING**	**COSTUME**
METAL	**10K GOLD** • 10/24 pure gold. **14K GOLD** • 14/24 pure gold. **18K GOLD** • 18/24 pure gold. **24K GOLD** • 24/24 pure (.999% pure)	**GOLD-FILLED** • (the same as overlay) 1/20th of weight of total piece is 14KT gold. **STERLING SILVER** • 92.5% pure silver.	**WHITE METAL** • 92% tin and other alloys. **BRASS** • 30% copper and 70% brass. **COPPER** • 92% copper and 8% other alloys.
ORIGINAL FORM	• bar • casting grain • sheet stock • wire tubing • tubing	**GOLD-FILLED** • bars • flat stock • tubing • wire **STERLING SILVER** • bars • casting grains • flat stock • tubing • wire	**WHITE METAL** • bars • casting grains **BRASS OR COPPER** • casting grains • flat stock • wire • tubing
MANUFACTURING METHODS	• lost wax casting • blanking, stamping • wire manipulation	**GOLD-FILLED** • blanking/stamping **STERLING SILVER** • casting • lost wax casting • blanking/stamping	**WHITE METAL AND BRASS:** • WHITE METAL CASTING - pouring metal into rubber molds. • BRASS or COPPER - Lost wax casting - put wax in plaster of Paris mold; melt wax out and pour metal into remaining plaster of Paris mold. • BLANKING/STAMPING • WIRE MANIPULATION

7

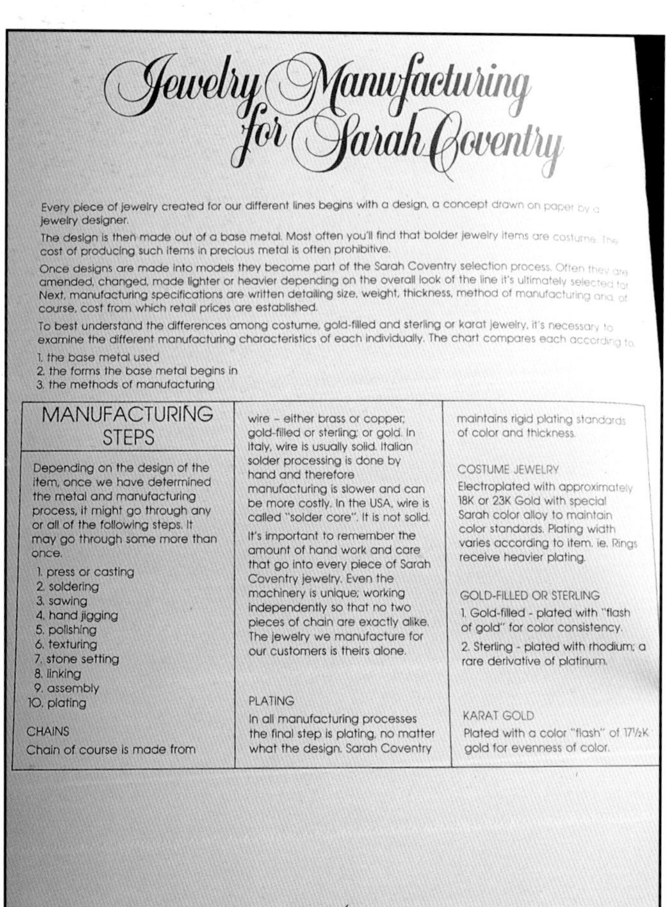

Jewelry Manufacturing for Sarah Coventry

Every piece of jewelry created for our different lines begins with a design, a concept drawn on paper by a jewelry designer.

The design is then made out of a base metal. Most often you'll find that bolder jewelry items are costume. The cost of producing such items in precious metal is often prohibitive.

Once designs are made into models they become part of the Sarah Coventry selection process. Often they are amended, changed, made lighter or heavier depending on the overall look of the line it's ultimately selected for. Next, manufacturing specifications are written detailing size, weight, thickness, method of manufacturing and, of course, cost from which retail prices are established.

To best understand the differences among costume, gold-filled and sterling or karat jewelry, it's necessary to examine the different manufacturing characteristics of each individually. The chart compares each according to.

1. the base metal used
2. the forms the base metal begins in
3. the methods of manufacturing

MANUFACTURING STEPS		
Depending on the design of the item, once we have determined the metal and manufacturing process, it might go through any or all of the following steps. It may go through some more than once. 1. press or casting 2. soldering 3. sawing 4. hand jigging 5. polishing 6. texturing 7. stone setting 8. linking 9. assembly 10. plating CHAINS Chain of course is made from	wire – either brass or copper; gold-filled or sterling; or gold. In Italy, wire is usually solid. Italian solder processing is done by hand and therefore manufacturing is slower and can be more costly. In the USA, wire is called "solder core". It is not solid. It's important to remember the amount of hand work and care that go into every piece of Sarah Coventry jewelry. Even the machinery is unique; working independently so that no two pieces of chain are exactly alike. The jewelry we manufacture for our customers is theirs alone. PLATING In all manufacturing processes the final step is plating, no matter what the design. Sarah Coventry	maintains rigid plating standards of color and thickness. COSTUME JEWELRY Electroplated with approximately 18K or 23K Gold with special Sarah color alloy to maintain color standards. Plating width varies according to item. ie. Rings receive heavier plating. GOLD-FILLED OR STERLING 1. Gold-filled - plated with "flash of gold" for color consistency. 2. Sterling - plated with rhodium; a rare derivative of platinum. KARAT GOLD Plated with a color "flash" of 17½K gold for evenness of color.

6

Fashion Jewelry

IT'S FUN

Fashion jewelry is fun, there's no doubt about it. No other type of jewelry can give you that styling combined with impact, at such reasonable prices! You can experiment - be bold - be subtle - be whatever you feel. Fashion jewelry is versatile, unique, able to stand up to all your fashion demands.

MORE ON HOW IT'S MADE

Part of fashion jewelry's ability to be so enduring is its physical composition. Much of Sarah Coventry's fashion jewelry is based upon a core of a tin alloy mixture of tin, zinc and lead (70% to 92% is tin). This base is poured into a rubber mold and allowed to harden. This is termed a white metal casting. From there, a layer of copper is applied for adhesion and sealing and a layer of nickel is applied for brightness. Finally, the item is coated with a goldentone or silvertone finish. White metal castings are commonly used for pavé (multi-stone set) items and those items that require an intricate design.

Another type of base used primarily for flat surfaced items, is a brass stamping. The base is composed of 70% brass and 30% copper which is rolled into a flat surface. A die, or etching of the design, is pressed onto the brass and you have a finished jewelry item. The same platings of metal are used with a brass stamping as with a white metal casting. A brass stamping is more durable than a white metal casting, but it is also heavier. It is the decision of the design and manufacturing departments as to which type of base a particular piece of jewelry will have.

The last metal layering that an item of fashion jewelry receives is a goldentone or silvertone finish. In a goldentone finish, a layer of approximately 18K Gold solution, totaling 4-7 millionths of an inch, is plated over the item. The nickel beneath determines the brightness.

In a silvertone finish, a layer of rhodium, totaling 2-4 millionths of an inch, is plated over the item. Rhodium is a stronger and more durable precious metal, a derivative of platinum, and therefore, a lesser plating of rhodium is needed to equal the durability of a gold plating. The nickel beneath again aids in brightness.

Fashion jewelry can have a variety of surface polishes. You will see a glossy high polish on many Sarah Coventry items although we also use a softer matte finish or a sandblasted finish. Fashion jewelry adapts to a variety of finishes that may be denied to precious metal designs because of size and boldness.

Indeed, boldness is one of the advantages open exclusively to fashion jewelry. Large or intricate designs can be manufactured in fashion jewelry without the prohibitive precious metal cost.

SPECIFICATIONS

Our superior reputation for quality has been established over the years because of the strict standards of manufacturing we enforce.

EARRINGS
All fashion line pierced earring posts and clutches are surgical steel. Earwires are 14K gold-filled or rolled gold plate.

All 14K gold pierced earrings have 14K gold posts and clutches. 14K gold-filled earrings. 14K gold-filled posts and clutches and sterling silver earrings have sterling silver posts and clutches.

CHAINS
Chains in Sarah's fashion line must undergo strict testing for strength, called a "pull test". Chains from 18" to 24" must withstand weight tests up to five pounds. 24" chains must pass a pull test of up to seven pounds. All men's lengths must meet the seven pound requirement as well. There is a four pound minimum for all fashion chains under 18".

It is adherence to these stringent requirements that gives you the confidence of knowing you're selling the very best.

CARE OF FASHION JEWELRY

Fashion jewelry can make many beautiful and unique fashion statements. It reflects who you are and how you feel while providing a much-needed assortment in basic styling. So even though it is not precious metal jewelry, it still deserves to be treated as such in order to preserve its beauty. Fashion jewelry is not made to be worn constantly. It should not be exposed to harsh detergents, dirt, grease or oil. It should not be soaked in water, however, an occasional "sponge bath" with a soft cloth dipped in mild detergent will erase any accumulated grime. Wiping your jewelry with a soft cloth after each use will also keep your jewelry looking brand new.

17

Jewelry manufacturing guidelines, information about Sarah Coventry jewelry, and information about the care of costume jewelry. *Courtesy of Dawn Michael.*

Many of the former employees mentioned the pictures that were displayed on the entrance wall of the corporate headquarters. The following pictures illustrate steps 13 and 22 in the process of creating a piece of jewelry that I showed but was unable to identify in my first book (see page 121). It is called **Timeless** and is also pictured on page 47 of this book.

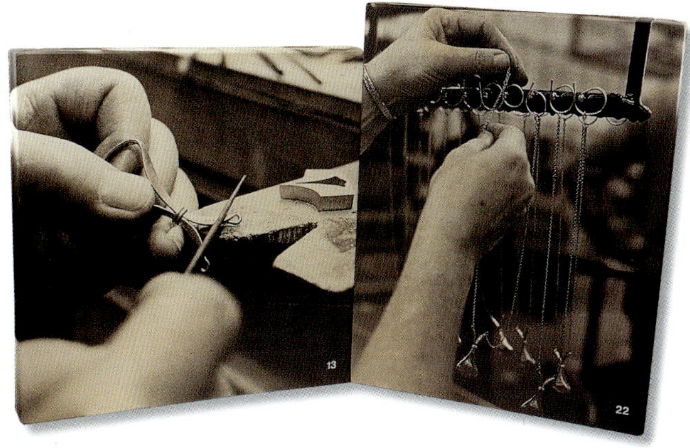

Here are two of the pictures originally displayed in the offices of C. H. Stuart depicting the over 22-step process for making by hand a piece of jewelry called **Timeless**. *Courtesy of Arcadia Historical Society.*

A variety of items were manufactured for both companies besides the usual jewelry. The pieces on the left are Sarah Coventry and those on the right are Emmons.

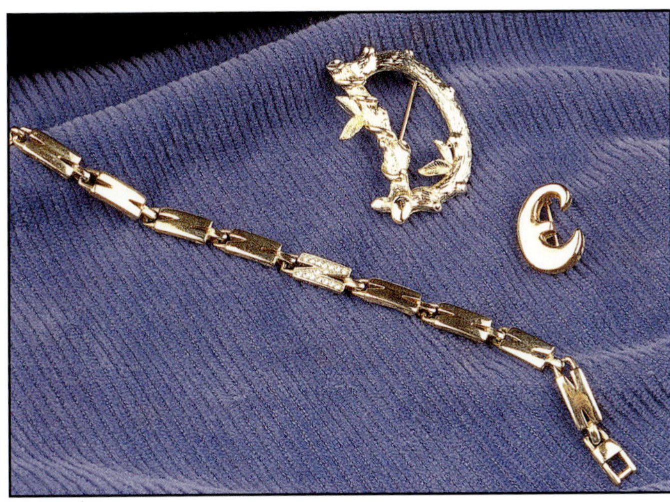

Initials were a common element used by Sarah Coventry designers. **Left to right:** **Identity Bracelet** (9163) with the initial 'N' linked to "create your own personal chain," the center initial paved with crystal chatons. D; $20-35. **Sarah's A. B. C.'s** (6960) are from the late 1960s and were continued for several years. "Sarah's designers really know their ABC's. Each of these 26 letters of the alphabet is an original and exclusive design of great beauty. Wear them in groups of three, a pair or even single – on your scarf, sweater, suit, or pocketbook." A; $8-15. **Sincerely Yours Initial Pin** (6065) is from a 1981 set. Throughout the Sarah Coventry years, there were nearly ten different kinds of initials available as pins or pendants for chains. B; $10-20. *Courtesy of Dawn Michael*

Top: **Twin-Key** (4855) **Key Chain** is from the mid 1960s. "Every man on your gift list will want one of these multi-purpose key chains. Handsomely attractive and sturdily functional, they'll prize its unique appointments. Really two key chains in one, the center has a 'take-apart' feature so house, desk and other valuable keys are on one – car keys on the other. A wonderful gift for any man!" A; $15-25. **Bottom row, left to right:** **Unidentified** pin is a cleverly designed mouse on ice skates and no doubt from the mid-1960s, perhaps from a winter catalog or Christmastime. $15-30. **Springtime** pin (1656) is from early 1960s. "Gay and full of promise as Springtime is this conversation piece which is as fresh and appealing as a morning in May… an attention-getter on your blouse, dress or suit, and one to lift your spirits any season of the year." B; $15-30. **Signature Pins B** (1585) dates from the mid-1960s. "Women love the 'personal' touch in their accessories. Now, you can wear your very own initials in jewelry. Emmons designers have completed a golden alphabet in a woven pattern of fancy script. They're perfect in size to wear 2, 3, even 4 initials at your shoulder…front and center…at the waist…or wherever it suits you." A; $10-20. *Courtesy of Mary Beth Coffman.*

In addition, at various times during its existence, the company was called upon to create custom designed jewelry for businesses, events, and celebrations. The pin and ring shown here, for example, were designed for the Lincoln-Rochester Bank, which at one time was located in Newark. Additional items shown were designed for Newark Country Club golf events.

Many custom items were made by the Stuart companies for various businesses in the area. This set of pin and ring was for the **Lincoln-Rochester Bank**, which had been based in Newark. *Courtesy of Arcadia Historical Society.*

Other custom requests were received from organizations in the area. These items – a key ring, bracelet, pin and cuff links, and tie bar – were created for the Newark Country Club golf events. This event was called the Silver Hat Tournament. These items are highly regarded and treasured by the local recipients. *Courtesy of Virginia and Peter Minutolo.*

Versatility

One of the main principles of Sarah Coventry and Emmons designers was to make the jewelry as versatile and adaptable as possible, in order to accommodate a variety of costumes, situations, and customers. This versatility could be seen in pins that also doubled as pendants; in pendants and necklaces that could be taken apart, worn together or separately; in bracelets that could be added to a necklace to lengthen it; and in earrings that could be worn as pendants or add-ons to pins. Some examples of this versatility with Emmons jewelry are shown in the accompanying photograph.

A bi-monthly newsletter called *Signet* was sent to FSDs of Sarah Coventry showing various ways to wear combinations of pieces. Emmons added these kind of ideas to their newsletters as well, and encouraged the versatility while showing pieces.

The versatility characteristic of Emmons jewelry is displayed by a bracelet with detachable balls and chain that could be attached to a pin, chain, or beads; a ball earring attached to a flower pin; and a necklace/belt tassel attached to make double loop and double tassel necklaces. *Courtesy of Mary Beth Coffman.*

Becoming a Collector

When I began my collection, there was little available knowledge regarding the names and other original information about the jewelry. The intent of my first book was to help new collectors or people who already had numerous pieces to become more knowledgeable about their items. I also decided to purchase duplicate items to have for trading or selling stock.

As I became more intent on securing Emmons pieces, I became glued to the Internet and to eBay. I learned to be careful, as one can easily become addicted to the process and also make some major mistakes. A word to the wise: know how to quickly change a bid that may have been entered incorrectly. I am a careful typist and never dreamt I would need to know this, however one day I made a maximum bid of $14.99. Later in the day, I noticed that in my record of bids, the price was listed not as $14.99 but as $1499.00! It's sure a good thing the other bidders can't see the amount entered. Time was running out so I didn't want to change the amount and perhaps not get back in. I won the item for only $34.00, which was great for me, but believe me I double-checked every bid from then on. This is what makes collecting so exciting.

Another note of warning is to be very careful of items that may be marked Sarah Coventry or Emmons but with different findings glued to them. I have also found some pieces that *looked* as if they have been painted – in this case, however, they were originally made that way. These items, called Golden Cluster, are shown on page 30.

I'd like to mention here that I have been in homes at Christmastime where I have seen wonderful trees created from old jewelry. Among the sparkling gems and metals are many Sarah and Emmons pieces. My first thought was "horrors," but then I was shown the following picture, which hung on the wall inside the front door of the Stuart offices. Someone, perhaps an employee or higher management FSD, created this wonderful "hot air balloon," no doubt from leftover pieces or broken findings. It totally changed my mind about using this jewelry for such decorator creations. It is truly another way of treasuring these wonderful pieces of jewelry – don't you agree?

This wonderful picture was created from broken pieces and leftover items by an employee during the 1970s, and was on display in the new building until the company closed in 1984. Luckily, it was retrieved from destruction and is treasured now by its owner. *Courtesy of Mary Sanders.*

Another issue I faced is that many items I saw were already ones I had, so I didn't bother looking at them. Ultimately I missed out on purchasing a bracelet marked Canada for $2. When I ultimately discovered it was a Canadian item, I paid for my mistake by shelling out $10. So be sure you look on the back…you might be missing an international piece.

Antique Rose bracelet is my WOOPS bracelet. Because I already had it, I didn't buy it for $1 or check the back. Then a friend offered it to me for $2, and again I didn't check it out. When I finally realized it said "Made in Canada" on the back (see example on left), the price was $10. So always check out the back!

This past year I have found that there are many younger women discovering the joys of picking up older pieces of jewelry rather than buying new pieces. Two such "thirty something" individuals have become hopefully life-long friends in South Texas. Susi and Letty were scouring the flea market for old Sarah Coventry jewelry and wandered over to our pizza business. In addition, Amanda, granddaughter of Pat and Gary Wyatt, not only became a model for her grandmother's rings in the pictures yet to come, she also became interested in the process of collecting and how beautiful the pieces were after many years of wearing or just being stored. So, whatever your age, you too can begin collecting.

Amanda Wyatt might be one of the youngest people interested in the idea of collecting. Of course, she may also be heir to the huge collection of her grandparents, Pat and Gary Wyatt, so liking the jewelry would be helpful. Amanda helped model some of their rings and bracelets for this book.

Update on Unidentified Pieces From First Book

Since publication of *Sarah Coventry Jewelry*, a number of other collectors have provided me with the names of several pieces listed as "Unidentified." Such was the case with Marjory Ritter, who identified *Timeless* (shown on page 121 in the first book and on page 47 of this book), as well as with Catherine Dippo, who identified the two sets shown in the following picture.

Left to right: *Celestial Spray* bracelet and pin from 1963. Matching earrings on page 75 of Oshel's Book I, *Sarah Coventry Jewelry*. *Contessa* pin and earrings are goldentone pieces with square faceted, red rhinestones and pearls. *Names are courtesy of Cathryn Dippo.*

Margie Burris identified the pendant on page 78 of the first book as a piece from another company and Janice Hess identified the earrings on page 153 (center photo, middle row, left side) as from that same other company. She also mentioned that on page 122, the *Granada* beads were gray, not blue, and were sold in conjunction with the Granada pin on page 100. Also, the *Moon-lites* pin on page 99 and matching earrings on page 106 are "vaseline glass," identified by Janell Peacock.

And on the very day I was getting ready to send off this manuscript, I received more information in the mail. A special thank you to Kenn and Grace Womack, who assisted with identification of the following items:

Page 14 (center photo): Left hand set is *Glamour Tones* necklace (8662) and bracelet (9662).

Page 19 (bottom photo): Top row, left set: *Futurama* earrings (not Jukebox, 7759).

Page 26: Necklace and bracelet on left are *Moonlight Serenade* from 1957. Center set is *Fiesta* from 1957 (bracelet 9596, and earrings 7596). On manikin is *Escapade* necklace from 1957. There was a white one, called *Frolic*.

Page 30 (top right photo): Bottom pin is *Vogue* (6797) and matching earrings are on page 43.

Page 33 (top photo): Far right pin is *Heritage*.

Page 33 (center photo): Far right pin is *Bit O'Fantasy*.

Page 42 (top photo): Top right earring are *Hidden Fire* (7731).

Page 43 (bottom photo): Left earrings are *Vogue* (7797).

Page 44 (top photo): Top right earrings are *Tailored Classic Earrings* (7512). Bottom right earrings are *First Lady*.

Page 51 (top photo): Second bracelet from left is *Tailored Classic* (9512).

Page 51 (center photo): Second bracelet from right is **First Lady**.

Page 54: **Moonlight Madness** had earrings the size of the necklace.

Page 55 (top photo): Right set is **Modern Design** necklace (8517) and earrings (7517).

Page 55 (center photo): Left set is **Contessa** necklace (8501) and earrings (7501), from the early 1960s.

Page 70 (bottom photo): Top left pin is **Aurora Lights** (6514).

Page 75 (bottom photo): Middle left earrings are **Aurora Lights** (7514).

Page 102 (top photo): Bottom left pin is **Crescent**.

Page 102 (center photo): Right hand pin is **Symphony** (6508) from the early 1960s.

Page 124 (top photo): Far right is **Ultra Fashion** necklace (8565); earrings are on page 37 of this book.

Page 129 (top photo): Far right bracelet matches pattern in barrettes called **Fashion Hold**.

Page 169 (bottom left photo): Top belt is **International** (9992-9993).

Another collector, Lillian Price, identified these pieces:

Page 125 (bottom photo): Two far right necklaces – orange/yellow/green is **Sun 'N Fun** (8685) and red/white/blue is **Pool Side** (8686) from 1967 flyer. Matching earrings on page 19, bottom photo (7685-7686).

Many thanks to all who have been able to assist in this process. I really appreciate everyone's help and dedication.

Using This Book

My intent in writing this second book is to further inform collectors about Sarah Coventry, as well as about Sarah International and Emmons. To provide additional insight regarding the pieces, I have included original prices and some of the original catalog descriptions (the latter identified by quotes). I have also included original company numbers (when known) following each piece name in parentheses. As you begin viewing the jewelry yet to come, you will notice the letters A, B, C, D, E, F, or G following each of the descriptions. These denote the original prices I was able to document: A=$1.00-4.99, B=$5.00-9.99, C=$10.00-14.99, D=$15.00-19.99, E=$20.00-24.99, F=$25.00-29.99, G=$30.00-34.99, H=over $35.00. Following this original pricing information is the current value for each item, expressed as a range from low to high. These values have been determined by considering several factors:

1) the quality of the jewelry – no missing sets, no discoloration of metal, no replacement of pin back, hooks, or sets;

2) the region where you locate the piece – coastal regions seem to be able to get more for items than the Midwest or southern areas;

3) where you are looking – flea-markets, antique shops, garage sales, etc., which can also affect how much variation there is in negotiating;

4) how badly you want the piece, to complete a set or just as an extraordinary piece or set;

5) and lastly, how available the item might be, i.e. Emmons pieces may be higher because not as many items were made and sold since the company was smaller.

Please use these prices only as a guide and not as absolute pricing, since there is a time lapse between my writing and your reading. Remember too, that collecting should be fun and exciting. Finding true buys can offset some of the more expensive prices you may pay on purpose or accidentally.

Sarah is "Home Again"

Nearly twenty years after the first Sarah Coventry company went out of business, another company has chosen to pursue the same path of the home party plans. This company is based in Rhode Island and has secured some of the same designers, manufacturers and previous Sarah Coventry and Emmons management personnel. As the catalog notes, the "combination of bringing today's fashion and style to you while maintaining the time honored tradition of integrity of design and service that made Sarah the most respected brand in the world, is what we are about today as Sarah comes home again."

One unique piece in the very first catalog is pictured here. It is titled Sarah's Original and replicates the **Evening Snowflake** pin first created in the early years of Sarah Coventry production. The pearl center is the main difference in what will become a present day collector's item. For more information about the new company, visit their website at www.sarahcoventry.com, call 1-866-88-SARAH (1-866-887-2724), or contact this author.

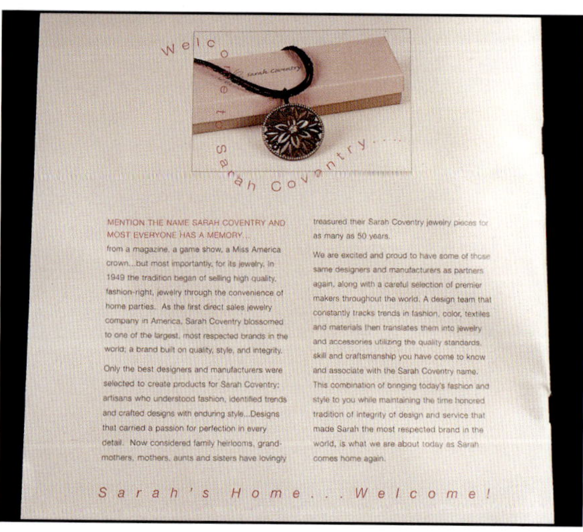

Cover and first inside page from catalog published by the new Sarah Coventry HPP, Inc., *Fine Fashion Accessories From Sarah Coventry™*, © 2003.

This page from the Sarah Coventry HPP catalog illustrates a beautiful piece patterned after the original *Evening Snowflake* pin, shown at right. The catalog copy reads: "Sprays of tiny leaves highlighted with Austrian crystals and centered with a simulated pearl is a timeless silver tone design from SARAH'S ORIGINAL collection." It retails for $55.00 in this catalog.

You Are Invited

At the end of this book, you will find examples of Collector Sheets on which to catalog your purchased items. I now invite each of you to begin your collection or to find more pieces to add to your treasured items from years past. I also invite you to write to me and share some of your experiences with Sarah Coventry, as well as to request one of the original charms given for recruiting. Little did I know that including this offer in my first book would bring such wonderful letters from people as far away as Great Britain, New York, California, Colorado and even a person I was looking for when researching that book. Small world! Send a self-addressed stamped envelope to me at the address below and I will send you one of the charms pictured here (as long as quantities last, but I do have quite a few). Send to:

Kay Oshel
1052 E. 345th Road
Flemington, Missouri 65650

As the original invitations to a fashion show read, "You Are Invited" to join the many collectors of Sarah Coventry and Emmons Jewelry and to enjoy this collection of information.

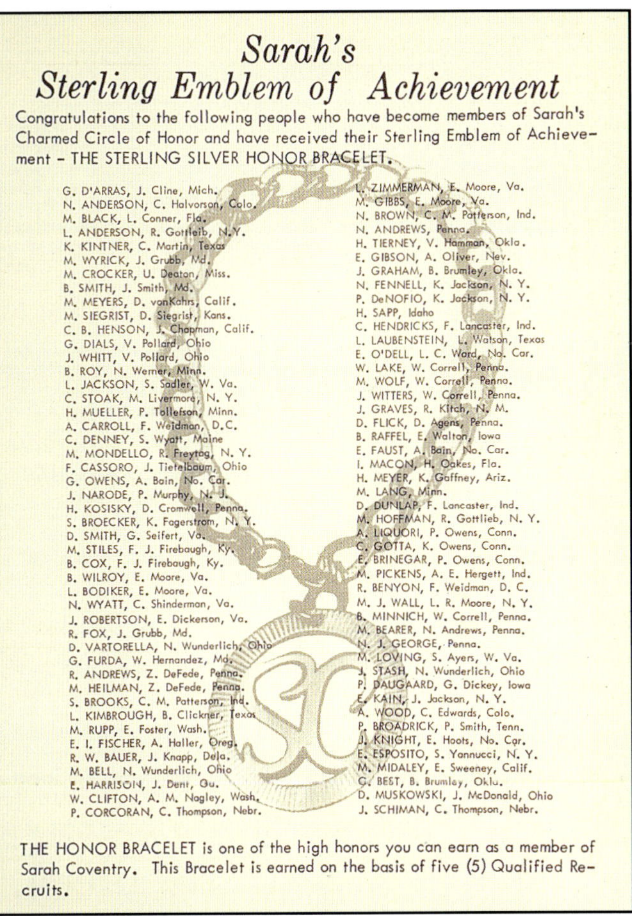

Sarah's
Sterling Emblem of Achievement

Congratulations to the following people who have become members of Sarah's Charmed Circle of Honor and have received their Sterling Emblem of Achievement – THE STERLING SILVER HONOR BRACELET.

G. D'ARRAS, J. Cline, Mich.	L. ZIMMERMAN, E. Moore, Va.
N. ANDERSON, C. Halvorson, Colo.	M. GIBBS, E. Moore, Va.
M. BLACK, L. Conner, Fla.	N. BROWN, C. M. Patterson, Ind.
L. ANDERSON, R. Gottleib, N.Y.	N. ANDREWS, Penna.
K. KINTNER, C. Martin, Texas	H. TIERNEY, V. Hamman, Okla.
M. WYRICK, J. Grubb, Md.	E. GIBSON, A. Oliver, Nev.
M. CROCKER, U. Deaton, Miss.	J. GRAHAM, B. Brumley, Okla.
B. SMITH, J. Smith, Md.	N. FENNELL, K. Jackson, N.Y.
M. MEYERS, D. vonKahrs, Calif.	P. DeNOFIO, K. Jackson, N.Y.
M. SIEGRIST, D. Siegrist, Kans.	H. SAPP, Idaho
C. B. HENSON, J. Chapman, Calif.	C. HENDRICKS, F. Lancaster, Ind.
G. DIALS, V. Pollard, Ohio	L. LAUBENSTEIN, L. Watson, Texas
J. WHITT, V. Pollard, Ohio	E. O'DELL, L. C. Ward, No. Car.
B. ROY, N. Werner, Minn.	W. LAKE, W. Correll, Penna.
L. JACKSON, S. Sadler, W. Va.	M. WOLF, W. Correll, Penna.
C. STOAK, M. Livermore, N.Y.	J. WITTERS, W. Correll, Penna.
H. MUELLER, P. Tollefson, Minn.	J. GRAVES, R. Kitch, N.M.
A. CARROLL, F. Weidman, D.C.	D. FLICK, D. Agens, Penna.
C. DENNEY, S. Wyatt, Maine	B. RAFFEL, E. Walton, Iowa
M. MONDELLO, R. Freytag, N.Y.	E. FAUST, A. Bain, No. Car.
F. CASSORO, J. Tietelbaum, Ohio	I. MACON, H. Oakes, Fla.
G. OWENS, A. Bain, No. Car.	H. MEYER, K. Gaffney, Ariz.
J. NARODE, P. Murphy, N.J.	M. LANG, Minn.
H. KOSISKY, D. Cromwell, Penna.	D. DUNLAP, F. Lancaster, Ind.
S. BROECKER, K. Fagerstrom, N.Y.	M. HOFFMAN, R. Gottlieb, N.Y.
D. SMITH, G. Seifert, Va.	A. LIQUORI, P. Owens, Conn.
M. STILES, F. J. Firebaugh, Ky.	C. GOTTA, K. Owens, Conn.
B. COX, F. J. Firebaugh, Ky.	E. BRINEGAR, P. Owens, Conn.
B. WILROY, E. Moore, Va.	M. PICKENS, A. E. Hergett, Ind.
L. BODIKER, E. Moore, Va.	R. BENYON, F. Weidman, D.C.
N. WYATT, C. Shinderman, Va.	M. J. WALL, L. R. Moore, N.Y.
J. ROBERTSON, E. Dickerson, Va.	B. MINNICH, W. Correll, Penna.
R. FOX, J. Grubb, Md.	M. BEARER, N. Andrews, Penna.
D. VARTORELLA, N. Wunderlich, Ohio	N. J. GEORGE, Penna.
G. FURDA, W. Hernandez, Md.	M. LOVING, S. Ayers, W. Va.
R. ANDREWS, Z. DeFede, Penna.	J. STASH, N. Wunderlich, Ohio
M. HEILMAN, Z. DeFede, Penna.	P. DAUGAARD, G. Dickey, Iowa
S. BROOKS, C. M. Patterson, Ind.	E. KAIN, J. Jackson, N.Y.
L. KIMBROUGH, B. Clickner, Texas	A. WOOD, C. Edwards, Colo.
M. RUPP, E. Foster, Wash.	P. BROADRICK, P. Smith, Tenn.
E. I. FISCHER, A. Haller, Oreg.	J. KNIGHT, E. Hoots, No. Car.
R. W. BAUER, J. Knapp, Dela.	E. ESPOSITO, S. Yannucci, N.Y.
M. BELL, N. Wunderlich, Ohio	M. MIDALEY, E. Sweeney, Calif.
E. HARRISON, J. Dent, Gu.	G. BEST, B. Brumley, Okla.
W. CLIFTON, A. M. Nagley, Wash.	D. MUSKOWSKI, J. McDonald, Ohio
P. CORCORAN, C. Thompson, Nebr.	J. SCHIMAN, C. Thompson, Nebr.

THE HONOR BRACELET is one of the high honors you can earn as a member of Sarah Coventry. This Bracelet is earned on the basis of five (5) Qualified Recruits.

Again, I invite everyone to send for one of these award charms, originally given to thank those who had obtained five qualified recruits for Fashion Show Directors. I had a lot when I began my project and still have quite a few left. When you write, be sure to let me know about *you*.

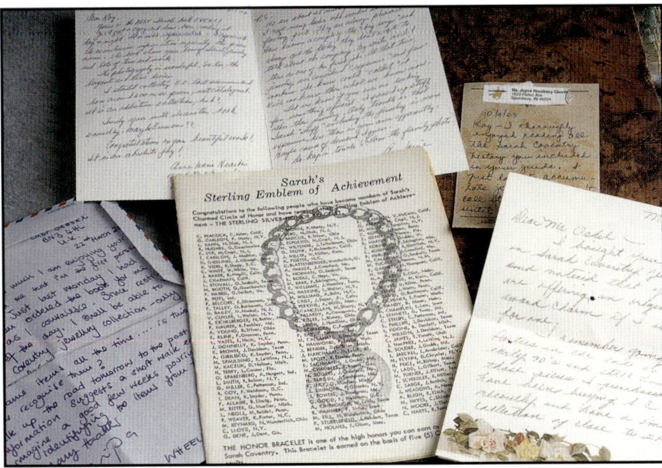

Little did I know that by offering this free Sarah Coventry charm, I would hear from so many wonderful people from so many diverse places, but that was the result. Thanks everyone.

Chapter Two

Sarah Coventry (USA)

From the very beginning, Sarah Coventry was destined to be a jewelry success. The combination of Bill Stuart and Rex Wood created a team dynamically capable of bringing together diversified, self-motivated Fashion Show Directors and magnificent costume jewelry. Rex Wood was able to create a system of presenting this jewelry to the housewife. At the company's ten year mark, sales were not continuing to increase. So Rex began looking at the advancement structure in the management system, which consisted of Fashion Show Director to District Manager to Division Manager. It occurred to him that perhaps many of the FSDs had advanced to the higher levels too rapidly, so he created another position. Now a Fashion Show Director moved to a Unit Manager, then to a Branch Manager and finally to a Division Manager. Later, Area Managers were added to structurally advance with the continued growth.

Through the years, many ways of recruiting were designed. One example was a looking glass theme, eventually used for one of the signature tags on Sarah's necklaces and bracelets. So as you are hunting for old Sarah Coventry pieces, there will be two identifying tags to look for – one is the diamond shaped tag < > and the other will have a hand mirror image similar to the one shown in the picture below. As noted earlier in the Introduction, several different identifying marks were used for Sarah Coventry through the years. The most common is "SARAH COV," while others are "SC," "SAC," "SARAH," "COVENTRY," and even the complete name of "SARAH COVENTRY." Note that some sellers on eBay have been trying to include "L.C." as a mark indicating Lady Coventry. I have asked several past employees about this and no one has concurred with it; in addition, none of the Lady Coventry pieces in my collection have this mark. Beware.

In addition to their use as recruitment tools, Sarah Coventry's promotional materials were used by the company for selling the idea of this remarkable costume jewelry and for keeping Fashion Show Directors updated and continually informed. Many of the employees wore articles of clothing such as blazers, scarves, t-shirts, or golf jackets to promote the company they were very proud to work for. In the 1960s, the company created a newsletter called the *Signet*, which featured employee accomplishments, new information, and ways of creating versatility with the pieces. Locating any of these items (as well as original Sarah Coventry catalogs) is important to the ardent collector, so be on the lookout for them. Managers were also kept apprised of corporate information through annual reports and, in the late 1970s and early 1980s, a "Manager's Digest." It was in some of these materials that a collector was able to identify some of my previously "unidentified" items so watch for them as well.

The management of Sarah Coventry, Inc. kept in contact with the sales force by continually sending out brochures, banners, story books, gift booklets (dream books), and *Signet* newsletters, in addition to clothing items such as jackets and scarves. Here are just a few examples. *Courtesy of Arcadia Historical Society and Dawn Michael.*

This looking glass idea used on Sarah Coventry promotional materials led to the hang tag found on many necklaces and bracelets.

Selection of jewelry for the upcoming catalogs and promotional materials was quite a process, with some six thousand pieces of jewelry brought from various manufacturers three times a year. Aileen VanTyle, fashion coordinator and one of the first women executives, indicated that the pieces chosen were then worn by employees for a testing period before being added to the line. The pieces not chosen were destroyed. It is amazing how this whole process was able to keep up with the trends and changing fashions from one season to the next. The process began in the late 1950s and continued throughout the rest of the Sarah Coventry years.

In the very early years, information about the jewelry pieces was passed from managers to the FSDs by word of mouth and via mimeographed "Phrase Books." The two examples pictured here were found in the Arcadia Historical Society Museum and were designated as belonging to C.W.(Bill) Stuart. One is dated 1949 and the other 1953. The top one is called "Inspirations" and gives very descriptive phrases about each of the pieces or sets of jewelry. Many are pictured, while some are described only and not shown. Since these pieces were very early in Sarah Coventry history, they may not be identified with a signature mark. *Frozen Lace* bracelet and earrings, shown on page 54 of my first book, were pictured in this early booklet.

Following these paper booklets, information was provided to the FSDs by means of a card file called a "cardex," first printed in black and white and later in color. These cards had the jewelry description on one side and a colorful photo on the other side. They were connected with a chain, and when an item was discontinued FSDs were asked to dispose of them. This they certainly did, so many items of that time period may not ever be identified. The cards were evidently continued through the early 1960s, as the first catalog I have been able to secure dates from 1966. A selection of catalogs are pictured at the end of this chapter.

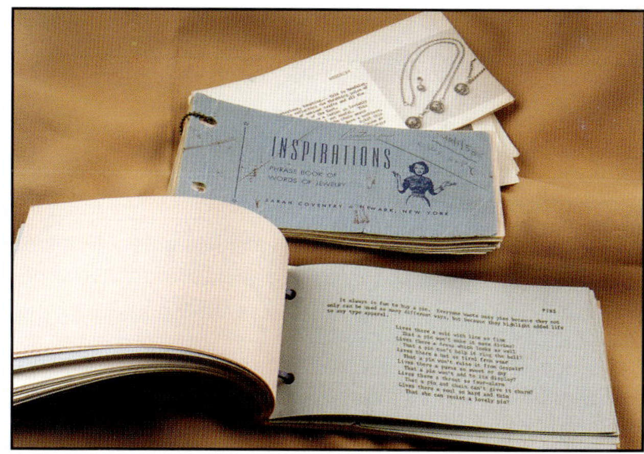

While visiting the Arcadia Historical Society Museum, I found many items of extreme interest. The booklets shown here, called "Phrase Book of Words of Jewelry," were used in the early 1950s to train FSDs on the company's products. The lower one is dated 1949, while the top one is annotated as belonging to "CWS" and dated 1953. *Courtesy of Arcadia Historical Society.*

Sample "cardex" files distributed to FSDs in the early years for use in describing and picturing new pieces of jewelry at the parties. *Courtesy of Helen Knapp and Sara Ayers.*

During Sarah Coventry's many productive years, a large variety of buttons, pins, charms, key rings, lighters, necklaces, earrings, and keys were also created and given as promotional awards. In the photo here, the second item from the left in the third row was issued in late 1979 to early 1980 in conjunction with an advertising campaign called "Direction 80." This was to promote the "New Sarah Coventry" and usher the company into a new decade with promising sales, a new direction, and continued costume jewelry. Unfortunately, however, the opposite effect was felt by the company – as was true for many businesses in the 1980s when the interest rate rocketed and people who had expanded on credit were doomed. This was the case with the Sarah Coventry company, as well as the whole of the Stuart Companies, as they sold out parts of the company and eventually went bankrupt and out of business in 1984.

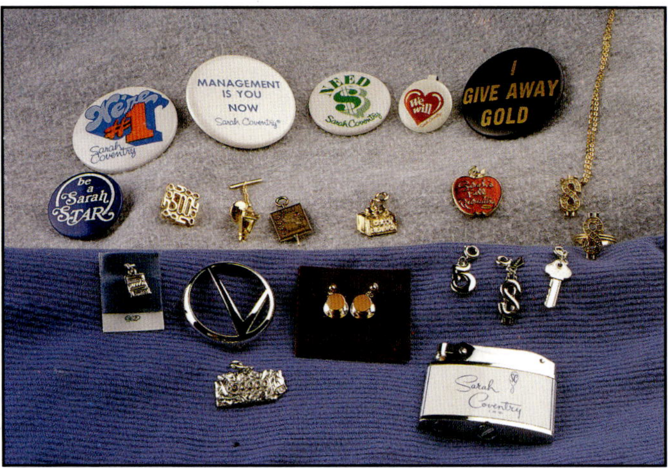

Buttons, pin, medallions, charms, lighters, key rings, and necklaces were some of the awards presented to the sales force – FSDs through management. The second item from the left in the third row is a pin representing "Direction 80," which eventually led to the downfall of the company. *Courtesy of Dawn Michael and Pat Wyatt.*

One of the most interesting items found at the Arcadia Historical Society Museum was a drawing of the Sarah Coventry Depot located in Des Moines, Iowa. Since I am originally from Iowa, this had special meaning for me – so of course it found its way into my picture taking. I have not been able to determine how many of these depots existed around the country. However, with the mother company located in the East, it would make sense to have one such distribution point located in the middle of the United States – and Des Moines would certainly qualify as a central location.

Sarah Coventry had depot locations in several areas throughout the United States. Since I am from Iowa, this painting depicting the depot in Des Moines, Iowa was of significant interest to me. *Courtesy of Arcadia Historical Society.*

It is now time to meet a very special friend I have acquired through my researching efforts. This is Dawn Michael. She was featured in my first book and came to my rescue again. Her collection has to be the largest I have ever encountered. Dawn began as a Fashion Show Director with Sarah Coventry in 1966 and rose into management, quickly becoming a Regional Manager in 1971. She continued with the company right to the end, so it is no wonder she has such a large collection of the jewelry. Dawn also kept a copy of all the catalogs from 1966 to 1984, which greatly assisted my endeavors to identify all of the pieces.

With her bubbly personality and quick smile, it is easy to see how Dawn was able to rise quickly by encouraging many FSDs on her team to strive for trips, awards, and numerous other gifts and trophies. She still remembers many of these team members and how inspiring their achievements were. While visiting with past employees in Newark or with FSDs around the country, I was constantly bombarded with conversation about "What Sarah Coventry Meant to Me." One FSD was asked this specific question. With Sarah Coventry supporting the ultimate achievement in her life, she said, it was the ability to build a new home. There are many houses "that Sarah built," to quote Helen Knapp of Delaware, who was featured in my first book.

Meet again Dawn Michael, who lives in Nashville, Tennessee. She was a great help with the first book and opened her home and jewelry boxes to me for the second time.

In her interview, Dawn identified some of the reasons for her success as having at least three parties a week herself and working closely with her team members. In 1983, one of her recruits became "Ms. Sarah Coventry," winning a trip to New York City and many other awards.

The newspaper article also shown here was published following my August 2003 presentation in Newark. Unknown to the over fifty people in attendance was a young lady by the name of Cathy Natale, who had just moved into the area. Cathy tearfully described how she and her two siblings lived with her grandmother, Beulah Johnson, in Michigan. During the day, Beulah was a line supervisor in a foundry where car parts were made and at night she was transformed into a Fashion Show Director with Sarah Coventry. Cathy spoke of the oppressively hot and dirty conditions in which her grandmother worked and how, when returning home, she would be transformed into a glamorous FSD by donning one of her few nice outfits, jewelry, and perfume.

Cathy recounted that it was the commission from her grandmother's jewelry sales dating from the late 1960s through the early 1980s that made the difference in the quality of their lives – such as being able to pay for school clothes and some of the extras. Cathy purchased one of my books to present to her grandmother at her 80th birthday in October, so I take this public opportunity to thank Cathy for her story and her grandmother for such dedication to her family and to a company she loved. No doubt every one of the thousands of FSDs has a story to tell about the benefits and support they received while working for Sarah Coventry, Inc.

Residents, collectors share stories

Book features former Newark jewelry company

By BRENDA PITTMAN
Times Correspondent

NEWARK — Years ago, Beulah "Boots" Johnson came home bone-tired and covered with soot each day from her job at a Michigan foundry where car parts were made.

A line supervisor, Johnson, like other employees, ran to her car the moment her shift was over to flee the oppressive 120-degree heat in her workplace.

Once at home, she would shower and make supper for the three grandchildren she helped raise in her home.

And on many nights, she'd then put on one of her few nice outfits, jewelry and perfume, and grab her blue Sarah Coventry jewelry kit and out the door she'd go — to sell it at home parties.

A Fashion Show Director during the 1960s, '70s and until the company was sold in 1981, Johnson was one of thousands of women and men around the world involved in direct sales of costume jewelry for the Sarah Coventry Inc. company that was headquartered in Newark.

The company was one of several divisions of the C.H. Stuart Co. In the late '80s, Lifestyle Brands, a division of Playboy Enterprises, purchased the Sarah Coventry name and is still making and selling jewelry under that name.

Johnson's granddaughter, 35-year-old Cathy Natale of Red Creek, tearfully recalled to more that 50 people gathered last week at the Arcadia Historical Society museum how her grandmother's jewelry sales made the difference in the quality of their lives. Natale's recollections followed a talk by Kay Oshel, of Springfield, Mo., a collector of Sarah Coventry and Emmons jewelry and the author of "Sarah Coventry Jewelry," published by Schiffer Publishing Ltd. of Atglen, Pa.

"The money from the foundry paid the bills. The money from Sarah Coventry paid for school clothes and all the extras," Natale told the audience.

She also said the sales job also brightened Johnson's days that began at 4 a.m., when she got up to make sure clothes and school lunches were ready for the children.

"She come home dirty and tired from working in the foundry, but then she's changed into a glamorous, confident sales woman.

"And with all that Sarah Coventry jewelry and perfume on, she felt pretty."

Natale said another benefit of her grandmother selling the jewelry was that she had some of the "cute jewelry" the company made for children.

"All my friends admired my jewelry collection," she said.

Natale bought a copy of Oshel's books, asked her to sign it, and said she plans to give it to Johnson at a surprise 80th birthday party in October in Michigan.

Oshel's talk sparked recollections from Natale and former employees of Sarah Coventry and other C.H. Stuart companies as well as questions from collectors about where best to sell or buy the jewelry, and current prices.

A retired guidance counselor and teacher, Oshel said she began collecting Sarah Coventry jewelry in 2000, when she and her husband, Alan, were selling pizza at a flea market in Canton, Texas.

"Once the vendors at the market knew I was interested, they would bring me boxes of the jewelry and I bought it," she said. "Fifteen hundred pieces later, I decided I had to catalog if I was going to continue collecting it.

"I had seen the other two Sarah Coventry books published by Schiffer and asked them if they were interested in me doing a third one, since my questions were not answered by the other two," she said.

In March of 2001, Oshel signed a contract to do the book and it came out in March 2003. Now she's working on a second one that will include the Emmons jewelry line, joking that "I'm a glutton for punishment."

"Since being in Newark, I've also been inspired to include Sarah Coventry's International line," Oshel said Friday, adding that her next book will also emphasize Newark people who worked at the factory, and area collectors.

The couple came to Newark this last week to do research.

"I'm very glad I did," she said. "I've never been in a community where the people were so kind and trustworthy, and willing to help me out. They cared so much about helping me to accurately chronicle these companies.

"My trip to Newark was successful and exceeded my expectations. I met wonderful people who will be lifelong friends."

Oshel met with executives of the former C.H. Stuart company who live in Newark, including Bill Scheetz, a president of Emmons Jewelry Inc.; Aileen VanTyle, a vice president of advertising and public relations of Sarah Coventry U.S.; and Jim Doyle, president of Sarah Coventry International.

Oshel and several area collectors brought their jewelry to historical society's museum, where she was photographing some of the collection for her next book.

Chris Davis, executive director of the Arcadia Historical Society, said he likes Oshel's book best because of the amount of information it contains.

The book includes about 350 color photographs of the jewelry, original prices and current value ranges, stories about the company, many actual jewelry catalog pages, and vignettes of three former fashion show directors.

"Sarah Coventry jewelry is extremely popular with today's collectors," Oshel told the audience. "I think Caroline Emmons Jewelry ... will be just as collectible." Schiffer, which publishes hundreds of collectors books and price guides for various collectible items as well as cookbooks and a variety of others, published two previous books about Sarah Coventry jewelry.

Oshel's book is available through Schiffer Publishing by calling (610) 593-1777 or at its Web site, www.schifferbooks.com. Oshel said Barnes and Noble also carries the book, as do other Internet firms.

These pictures depict some of the stories and experiences shared during employment with Sarah Coventry. "What Sarah Coventry Means to Me" conjures many varying memories I am sure, and of all the people I have spoken with, everyone has very positive comments. Cathy Natale's story in particular was very emotional. *Courtesy of Dawn Michael.*

Golden Brocade bracelet and earrings are from the early 1960s. Solid goldentone overlaid with vein-like goldentone enriches and embellishes, giving a brocade effect. Matching pin on page 32 of Oshel's Book I, *Sarah Coventry Jewelry*. B; $20-30. *Courtesy of Arlena Jordan.*

Left to right: This set is really pieces of two identical sets of different colors. ***Golden Scepter*** pin (5714) and ***Pink Radiance*** earrings (7715) from before 1966. "The grace and beauty of the rose in full bloom was captured by our designers in this rose ensemble. The unbreakable rose petals are imported from Austria, then they are hand painted and our own expert jewelry craftsman complete the design. Feminine loveliness in one of nature's loveliest designs, the rose, to give the touch of fashion to your favorite costume." There was no mark on either piece. B; $20-35. ***Unidentified*** set of goldentone filigree necklace and bracelet is from early years as there is no Sarah mark, but definitely identified as Sarah Coventry. $20-35. *Courtesy of Pat and Gary Wyatt.*

Cosmopolitan bracelet (9258) and belt (9650-9651, depending on size) are from 1966-1969. "A band of silvertone mesh to encircle your waist in fashion. Wear it with your favorite slacks or capris and for a dash of evening sparkle, wear it with your silks or brocades…at home anywhere." The bracelet was added in the late 60s. Set cost D; $8-15 each. *Courtesy of Arcadia Historical Society.*

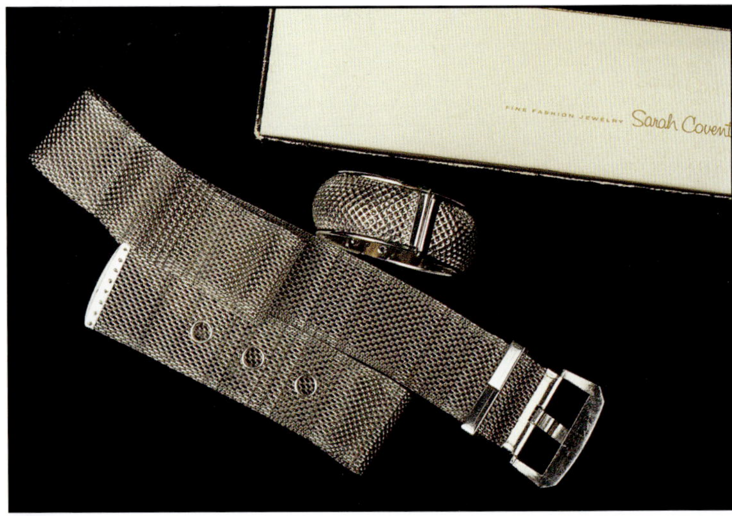

Left to right: *Rope of Fashion (jet)* necklace (8713) and earrings combine white opaque and jet black glass beads chain linked together and accented with goldentone cylinder spacers. "The latest in fashion is the jet and pearl rope" from the early 1960s. The earrings are a combination of the same opaque and black beads dangling from a goldentone mounting encasing a simulated pearl. There was an accompanying choker that could be worn with the necklace or as a bracelet. B; $30-45. *Shell-Cor* choker (8189) and *Shell* earrings (7117) are from 1981. The necklace came with a 15-17" peach cord and a 34" beige cord. "Our Sea 'n Sand jewelry reflects hazy blue waters, warming blends of sunset corals and glowing mother-of-pearl pinks. Gather the gentle tropics to your jewelry collection: subtle beauty that harmonizes with the splashy prints, crystal clear silks and wavy skirts of spring." Necklace G; $20-35. Earrings D; $15-25. *Courtesy of Dawn Michael.*

Left to right: *Unidentified* leaf pin and earrings are from the early 1960s. The outline of the leaves is gleaming silvertone with a sandpaper type finish inside the leaf. Unique and yet very simplistic. $15-30. *Tawny Shadows* bracelet and earrings are from the early years. The large dark brown and orange cabochon stones are nestled in swirls of goldentone and accented with clear smaller rhinestones. Matching necklace on page 55 of Oshel's Book I. $20-35. *Czarina* earrings (7404) and pendant (8404) are from 1971 and also had a matching ring. The dynamic turquoise cabochon sets captured in the antiqued goldentone mounting create a stunning yet simple ensemble. C; $20-35. *Courtesy of Pat and Gary Wyatt.*

Left to right: *Polonaise* pendant (8644) and earrings (7644) are from 1976. "Rhinestones permanently set through new methods in Austria." A similar necklace was created later and identified as New Polonaise on page 136 of Oshel's Book I. F; $15-30. *Debutante* necklace (8869) and earrings (7869) are SarahGlo goldentone from the early 1960s. "Dainty, delicate and delightfully attractive is this diamond-shaped pendant and earring set in textured and gleaming goldentone and boasting a 'pretend' pearl. Tiny enough to be worn on daughter's first date, so traditional in design that discriminating women of any age would enjoy wearing Debutante." B; $15-25.

Left to right are two sets from the late 1950s and early 1960s. *Fascination* pin (6712) and earrings (7507) set had dainty earrings as well as these daring ones. "The brightest of Sarah's fashion is this sun and star inspired pin and earring set. The brilliance of the sun, the design of the sun's rays and the romantic feeling of a starlit night are combined in a sunburst set to make you look and feel like a million dollars. The perfect fashion accent to that suit or dress that requires just the right piece of jewelry." This set is electro-plated gold. B; $15-25. *Cosmopolitan* necklace (8789), earrings (7789), and bracelet (9789) are SarahSheen goldentone. "Cosmopolitan is the name we chose for this classic ensemble in goldentone basket weave. The dictionary describes cosmopolitan as 'at home in any country, not local,' and that's how we feel about this exciting classic set of jewelry. At home, anywhere, town or city, morning, noon or night. Cosmopolitan is at home anywhere and knows no season." B; $20-35.

Left to right: *Turn-a-bout* earrings, bracelet, and necklace are a goldentone set designed in such a way as to let the necklace be worn with either side out by the unique snap clasp. The earring provide an example of both sides. This set is from the early 1960s. $35-50. *Courtesy of Pat and Gary Wyatt.* *Vienna* pin, earrings, and bracelet are from the late 1950s and early 1960s. This set is a glamorous combination of large navette black Austrian crystal rhinestones and tiny clear crystals, all set in silvertone. This is one of the most wonderful sets created by the Sarah Coventry company. (Note: in Oshel's Book I, these earrings were incorrectly identified on page 44 as Vienna Nights.) $65-80.

The Old and the New. Left to right: *Slim Line* earrings, necklace, and bracelet from the early 1960s. This set came in both silvertone and goldentone in a unique combination of textured and gleaming finish. The pendant is repeated for the earrings and reduced for the bracelet sections. A very striking ensemble from nearly fifty years ago and sought after even today. $35-50. *Sail Boat Charm* (3171) from 1984 is a brightly polished 14 Karat gold charm attached to a chain. The original price was $240 but most likely the item was purchased at half price. Today's value could be $50-75. *Courtesy of Pat Wyatt.*

Sweetheart Chatelaine pin (6574) and earrings (7574) are from the late 1950s and early 1960s. "Romantic pearlized hearts set in gleaming gold. An ensemble for the young in heart, 16 to 60. Charming left and right earrings with piercing arrows,…two tiny hearts bound together by a delicately woven chain. If you're in love, you'll want Sweetheart." There was also a matching necklace and none of the pieces are marked. Many of the items from the early years weren't identified, so may be difficult to recognize. These were identified by a Fashion Show Director from the very early years. B; $20-35. *Courtesy of Pat and Gary Wyatt.*

Left to right: *Fancy Free* necklace is from the early 1960s. The silvertone chain has attached drops of fancified feather design. Matching earrings on page 40 of Oshel's Book I. A; $15-30. *Caged Pearl* earrings (7320) and necklace (8320) are in goldentone with simulated pearls. There was a silvertone set also in 1970. B; $15-25.

Left to right: *Embraceable* necklace and bracelet is a herringbone style goldentone chain in a double to triple width. Its simplistic beauty makes it an attractive addition to any costume in the early 1960s or before. $15-30. *Unidentified* necklace, earrings, and ring are no doubt from the 1960s. The open-weave goldentone of the earrings and ring is repeated in the collar-like necklace with a golden tassel. $30-45. *Courtesy of Dawn Michael.*

Left clockwise: *Unidentified* pin and earrings is this striking goldentone feather or leaf with veined sections designed as if blowing in a breeze. No doubt from the early 1960s. $15-30. *Evening Comet* pin (6573) and earrings (7573) are from 1966. "Take the beauty of a star and combine it with all the animation and fire of a comet and you have a design of breathtaking beauty. A real after-five set is this pin and earring set." B; $25-40. *Americana* pin (6387) and earrings (7387) are from 1972 in a striking golden star shape with red, white, and blue cabochon beads. The earrings are three-pointed. C; $20-35.

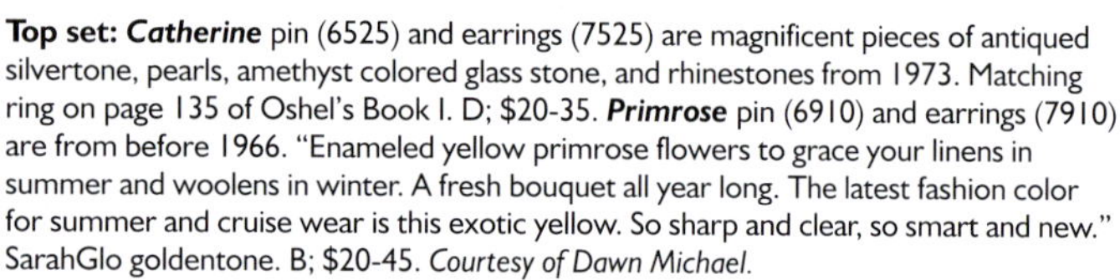

Top, left to right: *Fashion in Motion* pin (6251) and earrings (7251) are an artfully designed ensemble quite fashionable in 1969. This came only in silvertone. C; $15-25. *Sparkle Circle* pin (6540) and earrings (7540) are a special ensemble matching the Swan Lake Pendant on page 115 of Oshel's Book I. The double silvertone circles adorned with glass crystal rhinestones live up to the name. C; $10-20. **Bottom:** *Aquarius (Age of)* pin (6360), earrings (7360), and ring (5360) are straight from 1970 with their combination of small teal colored beads, tiny rhinestones, and pearl beads. E; $25-30.

Top set: *Catherine* pin (6525) and earrings (7525) are magnificent pieces of antiqued silvertone, pearls, amethyst colored glass stone, and rhinestones from 1973. Matching ring on page 135 of Oshel's Book I. D; $20-35. *Primrose* pin (6910) and earrings (7910) are from before 1966. "Enameled yellow primrose flowers to grace your linens in summer and woolens in winter. A fresh bouquet all year long. The latest fashion color for summer and cruise wear is this exotic yellow. So sharp and clear, so smart and new." SarahGlo goldentone. B; $20-45. *Courtesy of Dawn Michael.*

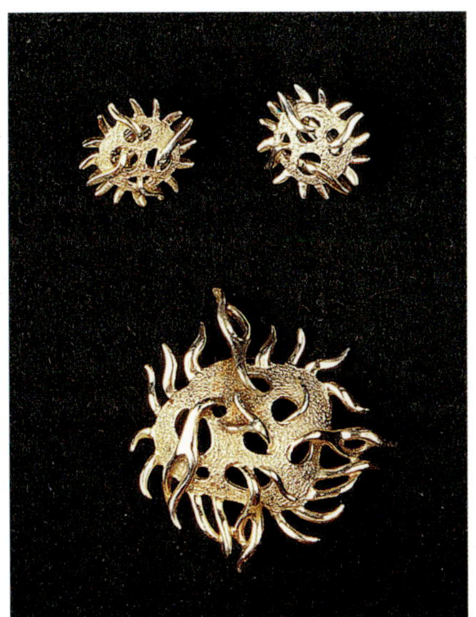

Sea Urchin pin (6316) and earrings (7316) are unique goldentone designs created for the early 1970s. The set came in silvertone as well. B; $12-25. *Courtesy of Arcadia Historical Society.*

Empress necklace (8515) attached to 18" adjustable chain and earrings (7515). "Designs from the Past Recreated for Today." The stones resemble fire opals but no mention of this was made. The tiny pearls surrounding the stones make for a very exquisite set. It was only available in 1972, so it will be difficult to locate. E; $25-45. *Courtesy of Arcadia Historical Society.*

Left to right: *Silvery Moon* necklace (8768) is a 30" necklace with stationed turquoise insets, coupled with a matching pendant and chain, the 16" *Blue Moon* choker (8769). Both were available in 1978. There were matching earrings not pictured here. E; $15-25. *Heritage* necklace/ pin (8383) and earrings (7383) are from 1976. Matching ring on page 69. E; $15-30. *Aztec* pendant (8470) and earrings (7470) are from 1972. This unique silvertone setting with turquoise sets was in only one catalog so may be hard to find. C; $15-30. *Courtesy of Dawn Michael.*

Left to right: *Golden Rope* necklace (8413) and earrings (7413) are from 1972. This is the brown stone background; there is also a white background set shown on page 31. E; $15-30. *Northern Lights* bracelet (9576), earrings (7576), and ring (5388) are a dynamic set with stones created to be iridescent in the light, giving multiple color rays set in sparkling silvertone mountings. One of my favorite sets and rather difficult to find. Produced in 1972-1974. E; $25-40. *Courtesy of Dawn Michael.*

Left to right: *Golden Ice* bracelet (9550) and earrings (7550) were part of the Holiday Collection in 1972. A very holiday ensemble of Austrian crystal rhinestones coupled with goldentone mountings. There was no necklace with this set and one was hardly needed with all the sparkle and glitter created by just the earrings and bracelet. F; $30-45. *Enchantress* necklace (8416) and earrings (7416) are from 1971. This ensemble was part of "Sarah's After-5 sparkling jewelry" collection. The rhinestones are Austrian crystals mounted into an exquisite design of goldentone swirls connected with channels of rhinestones. Truly marvelous then and highly sought after now. G; $35-50. *Courtesy of Dawn Michael.*

Cleopatra bracelet (9479), earrings (7479), and ring (5329) set is from 1972 and one of my favorite sets to wear, especially the bracelet. The stones are chipped stones inside an oval glass casing with iridescent shades ranging from purple to bright blue. Some sets have more of a purple hue – mine is all blue. A warning to the wearer is that the sets may fall out if they have been in a hot environment for a while, e.g., a vendor's showcase in the sun. The gleaming silvertone mountings are spectacular even thirty years later. E; $35-50.

Left to right: *Contessa* pendant/pin (6936), earrings (7936; also came in pierced), and bracelet (9936) are a very exquisite set from 1975 that was carried over several years. The large stone in the pendant and the smaller oval stones in the other pieces are similar to fire opals, however, no mention was made in any of the catalogs. G; $30-50. *Rustic Charmer* necklace (8880) and pierced earrings (7893) are from 1978. The rust colored beads are approximately 44" long with a removable button clip that matches the earrings in a textured goldentone finish. The necklace could be worn long or looped several times around the neck. D; $15-30. *Courtesy of Dawn Michael.*

Left to right: **White Charmer** necklace/belt (8248) and earrings (7248) are from 1975. The lariat style necklace/belt is 39" in length with white beads on the ends matching the earrings. D; $15-30. **Hi-Fashion** necklace (8898) and earrings (7898) is created from three white graduated size beads forming a tassel attached to a 24" chain from 1974. D; $15-30. **Perfection** necklace (8502) and **Anything Goes** clip earrings (7502) were from 1978. The necklace has no tag on it so may be missed as a Sarah Coventry piece. E; $20-35. **Summer Flirt** necklace (8604) and earrings (7604) are from 1974. The two chains are 22" and 29" with white engraved beads stationed along them. E; $18-25. *Courtesy of Dawn Michael.*

Left to right: **Taffee Tones** pendant (8179) and bracelet (9179) from 1975 are dazzling taffee colored beads suspended from an oriental design for the pendant and simply fashioned together for the colorful bracelet. E; $10-20. **Mini-Midi-Maxi** pendant (8405) and earrings (7405) are "The new mod look of 'in' jewelry" from 1971. This very modern silvertone design contrasting with the pendant on the left, shows the variety and styling range that made Sarah Coventry jewelry highly sought after. D; $10-20. *Courtesy of Dawn Michael.*

Venetian Treasure necklace (8939) and bracelet (9939) are from 1974. The necklace is 22" of linked and regular chain with an attached tassel and stationed hand-painted beads that coordinate with the bracelet and the matching earrings on page 107 of Oshel's Book I. E; $15-30. *Courtesy of Allie and Jim Doyle*

Moonlight pin (6851) and earrings (7841) are from 1974. This goldentone set of intricate design with pearls and clear crystals give the illusion of fine crochet. The pin was $10.50 and the earrings were $8.50. Current value: $15-30. *Courtesy of Jim and Allie Doyle.*

Operetta pin (6828) and bracelet (9828) are magnificent designs utilizing jet black stones and clear rhinestones. This set, including earrings, was only available in 1974 so finding one or all of these pieces will be a collector's dream. Original $26. Current value $20-50. *Courtesy of Arletta Jordan.*

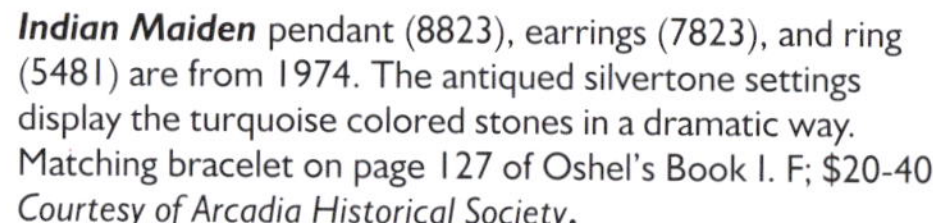

Indian Maiden pendant (8823), earrings (7823), and ring (5481) are from 1974. The antiqued silvertone settings display the turquoise colored stones in a dramatic way. Matching bracelet on page 127 of Oshel's Book I. F; $20-40. *Courtesy of Arcadia Historical Society.*

Left to right: *Sea Scroll* bracelet (9874) and earrings (7874) from 1974 imitate the effect of waves. This set was only in one catalog so may be difficult to locate. E; $25-35. *Coronation* necklace (8126) and bracelet (9126) are spectacular bright red glass rhinestones prong set in antiqued goldentone settings. There was also a matching ring (see page 68) found in 1975. G; $20-45. *Courtesy of Dawn Michael.*

Top left: *Duchess* necklace (6250) and earrings (7250) are identified as "Round the clock with Sarah." This textured and twisted look in goldentone could be worn for day or night, casual or fancy. F; $20-35. **Bottom:** *Bewitchery* necklace (8731) and earrings (7731) are identified as "All the fashion magic of Midnight black and gleaming silvertone…in this most unusual light weight chain with its matching swinging earrings." This set was carried over from the late 1960s into the early 70s because of the "tailored look for night or day." C; $10-20. *Courtesy of Dawn Michael.*

Left to right: *Matinee Elegance* necklace (8855) and earrings (7855) are from the late 1950s and early 60s. "A blend of high fashion and good taste. This new matinee length necklace is the very latest in fashion excitement and adds a look of elegance to any costume. The slim, svelte earrings complete the look of high fashion elegance. Any season is the right season for fine fashion jewelry." B; $10-20. *Coraline* pin (8924) and earrings (7924) are from the mid-70s and sport an oval shaped coral set in gleaming goldentone mounting. The pin has a hook to be used as a pendant on a chain. Very versatile and classy. Matching ring on pages 67 and 68. D; $20-35. *Courtesy of Dawn Michael.*

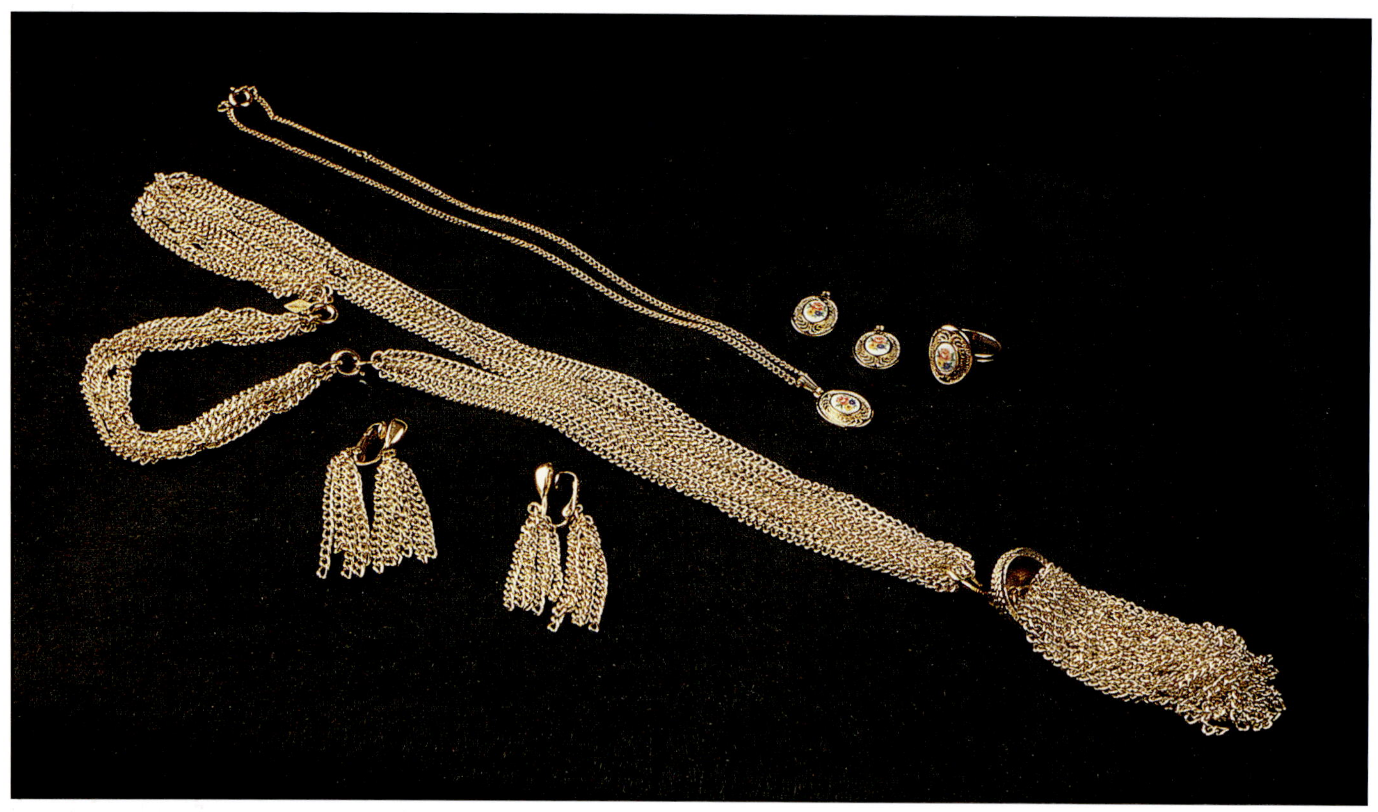

Left to right: *Tassel Magic* necklace/bracelet (8629) and earrings (7629) are from 1976. This set came in silvertone also. The necklace and bracelet together measure 30", or shorten the necklace and add a matching bracelet to the ensemble. Necklace $21.50 and earrings $9. Current value $10-18. *Victorian Bouquet* pendant (8111), earrings (7111), and ring (5603) are from 1975-76. A very dainty set in contrast to the Tassel Magic set. E; $15-25. *Courtesy of Pat and Gary Wyatt.*

Left to right: *Amethyst Oval Pin* (6518), bracelet (9518), and earrings (7518) are from the Lady Coventry set. There are no identifying marks on the pin or charm, but Sarah Cov is marked on the earrings. The set is goldentone with semi-precious stones from 1973 and was a part of the buy two at regular price and get the third at half price. D; $30-45. *Golden Cluster* bracelet and pin are from the early years, before 1966. At first glance, the goldentone grape design looked as if it had been painted black by a customer. However, that is not the case. B; $30-45. *Unidentified* salmon colored rose flower in bracelet, necklace, and earrings. This set is not marked on any of the pieces, but was identified as definitely an early set. Notice the unique mounting surrounding the roses. Very exquisite and a wonderful find. $50-65. *Courtesy of Pat and Gary Wyatt.*

Left to right: *Unidentified* bead necklace and dangle earrings are similar to several other sets, but not exactly the same. This bead set is thread strung in a creamy white with three decreasing in size beads dangling from a silvertone clip. $20-35. *Black Charmer* necklace/pin (8381) and earrings (7381) are from 1976. The black bead necklace can be removed from the pendant allowing it to be worn as a pin. The drop can also be removed. This is a very striking set to be worn day or night. E; $20-40. *Fashion-rite* necklace (8541) and earrings (7541) are from 1973. The versatile necklace can be worn with one strand or two, with the clasp in the back or as a pendant in front, or with the clasp taken off and used as a pin. The matching earrings are very dainty, giving just a hint of an ensemble. D; $15-30. *Courtesy of Dawn Michael.*

Left to right: *Golden Rope* pendant (8296) and earrings (7396) are from 1976. Also came with an amber background stone. E. $20-40. *Double Choice* pendant (8393) on a 24" chain and earrings (7393) were interchangeable with rose or eggshell drops. Sarah was interested in versatility and these exchangeable pieces were quite popular in 1976. Original pendant $17 and earrings $14. Current value: $10-20. *Courtesy of Dawn Michael.*

Left to right: *Fashion Mobile* necklace (8423) and earrings (7423) from 1971 are a combination of silver and goldentone metals designed for simplicity and fashion. C; $10-20. *Unidentified* necklace and earrings are a combination of amber, jet, and pearl-like beads combined on a goldentone chain. The mesh-like drop is removable and was repeated on the dangle earrings. It is believed the name contains "honey" and comes from the later years. $25-40. *Courtesy of Dawn Michael.*

Aqua Fleur(fler) pin (6502) and earrings (7502) are from before 1966. The aqua cabochon sets are highlighted by the white fresh-water pearl (simulated) in the center. B; $25-40. *Courtesy of Marjory Ritter.*

Left to right: *Windfall* necklace, earrings, and bracelet are from before 1966. The stylized solid and open leaves with textured and gleaming antiqued silvertone look like real sterling silver jewelry. B; $45-60. *Magic Spell* choker (8544) and pierced earrings (7544) were from 1979. The dainty and yet striking black and red sets contrast dramatically with the goldentone necklace and mountings. E; $10-20.

Left to right: *Debut* necklace (8407) is from 1979. The imported Austrian glass stones are set in a gleaming goldentone chain effect with solid gleaming rectangular pieces set at an angle from the stones. The 18" attached chain is created from metal sections secured with rings. There were matching earrings as well. E; $20-35. *Hong Kong* earrings (7362), necklace, and bracelet are from the late 1960s. The design is an oriental one utilizing Austrian crystals in a SarahSheen silvertone mounting. C; $40-60. *Courtesy of Dawn Michael.*

Left to right: *Chinese Modern* necklace (8938) and earrings (7938) are from before 1966 and were carried through the late 1960s. "The multi-color 'electra' stone centered in an unusual abstract Chinese modern motif makes a pendant and earring set so striking and unusual you'll feel it's a 'must' in your own jewelry wardrobe. A set to harmonize with any costume in your wardrobe for either daytime or evening wear." C; $15-30. *Gracious Lady* necklace (8906) and bracelet (9906) are from the early 1960s. The combination of a large goldentone chain and smaller chain combined with simulated pearls gives an elegant look coupled with a unique magnetic clasp. B; $15-25.

Left to right: *Safari* necklace (8984) had a bead section of 37" and a chain section of 29". There was a removable drop that could be attached to the chain or the dark brown bead section. This was a very versatile ensemble with matching earrings (7987) from 1978. G; $20-35. *Dynasty* pendant (8656) and earrings (7656) are from 1973. The red glass stones give the impression of an ostrich feather with the matching sets in the earrings. Very dynamic and only carried for one year. It might be hard to locate but will be a great addition to a collection. E; $20-35. *Centurion* pin/pendant (6342) and earrings (7342) are a unique ensemble from 1975 in goldentone. The cameo effect of the head in silvertone would make one think this was a part of men's collection, however, it is definitely for women. The tassel is removable as well. E; $20-35. *Courtesy of Dawn Michael.*

Top row, left to right: *Sea Star* bracelet (9349) and earrings (7349) are part of the Ecology collection from 1978. "The eternal mystery of the sea, the graceful starfish. Today, the 'Ecology Collection,' from Sarah Coventry. Finely crafted, exquisite in every detail, your starfish pieces are distinctively modern yet classically sophisticated, shimmering and warm, with the subtlety of the sea itself." Matching necklace on page 116 and ring on page 132 of Oshel's Book I. D; $18-35. *Tea Garden* enameled bracelet and glass pin (2183) are from 1982 and very different from other pieces of the time. Original pin price was $24. Because these will be difficult to find, the current value is $25-40. **Bottom:** *Sunburst* pin (6933), earrings (7933), bracelet (9686), and pendant/pin (8686) on a double chain are "So versatile, so Sarah" from 1976. The set had two sets of earrings; the other set matched the pendant. The goldentone styling is wearable today and very dramatic on solid colors. Original prices were earrings $9.50, pin $9, pendant/pin $16, and bracelet $14.50. However, with Sarah's purchase plan, buying two at the regular price allowed the third to be half price. $8-15 each piece. *Courtesy of Dawn Michael.*

Pins could be created for any event and season. These three were made throughout the years for wear during the Christmas holiday. The *Santa Claus* (6624), *Angel*, and *Holly Bell* (6625) pins are created from both textured and gleaming finish with touches of color through the enamel and rhinestone additions. A must for any collector. B; $10-20 each. *Courtesy of Dawn Michael.*

Brooches - Sarah Coventry Jewelry

Pins came in all shapes, sizes, and designs. Here are a few of the whimsical ones not identified by original name. They are in the shape of a bicycle built for two, eagle, guitar, bee, and hot air balloon. Some may have been custom made for a company or activity. *Courtesy of Dawn Michael.*

Left to right: *Silhouette* pin is from the early 1960s. This silvertone textured and gleaming round pin is artfully stenciled with flowers, leaves, and stems to create a fashion statement when worn on a dark coat or dress with that color peeking through. There were also matching earrings. A; $15-30. *Accent* pin (6200) is from 1968. The same name was used in earlier years. This goldentone, five leaf textured flower is very realistic with curved and waving petals. A; $10-20. *Nature's Pearl* pin (6318) from 1970 was found in only one catalog. The silvertone leaf and stem give the simulated pearl in the center an exquisite focus. There were also matching earrings. A; $20-35. *Tinsel Twist* pin (6603) is from 1976. This simple yet striking goldentone pin is highly textured. There were matching earrings. C; $15-30. **Top right, beside the tree:** *Ultima* pins (6211) came in pairs to be worn together or separately. In 1968, they could also be attached to pearls creating a magnificent necklace. There were matching earrings. The pin on the left is antiqued with a golden pearl center while the two on the right are shining silvertone with white cultured pearl centers. B; $10-20.

Back row: *Mother's Pin (Family Tree)* is from the early 1970s. The birth dates are designated by "fine Swarovski Austrian Rhinestones." Customers chose the sets to be included on the pin representing all members of the family. E; $15-30. **Front, left to right:** *Precious* pin (6857) from 1973 is a circular pin of leaves and a flower created with a simulated pearl in the center. A; $10-20. *Multiple Choice Pins – Sarah's ABC* (6298-6323) are from 1976 through the end of the 1970s. The gleaming silvertone letters are very simple cursive letters to be worn together or separately. B; $8-15. *Demi* (6577) is an open-weave donkey pin I found only in the Fall and Winter of 1972. It was a part of the children's section. A; $10-20. *Courtesy of Abby Bellamy.*

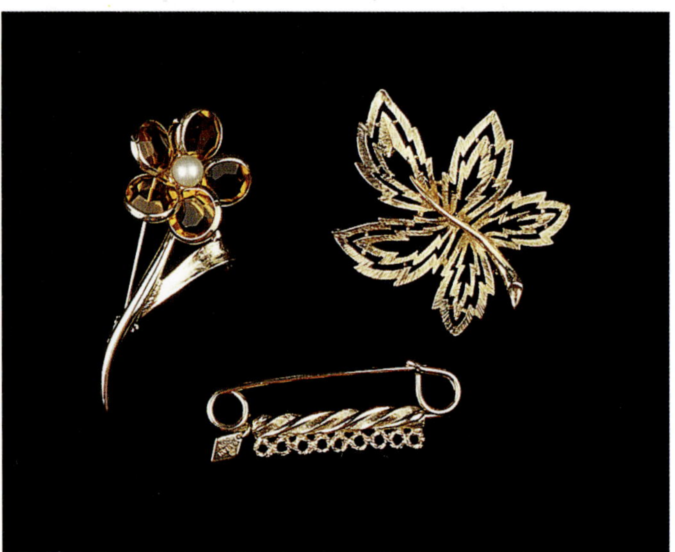

Clockwise, from top left: *Floral Delite* pin (6660) with imported Austrian glass stones is from the late 1970s, D; $12.50-25: *Windfall* pin (6547) is from the 1978 catalog and marked with SC. An unusual open maple leaf design in goldentone. B; $10-18: *Family Parade* pin (6154) features a unique safety pin shape that holds children's birthday charms. The pin included choice of nine dangles of boy or girl shapes. D; $10-20. The child shapes (6151) hang from pearls and came in packages of four. C; $3-5 each. These were featured in 1975 catalogs. *Courtesy of Arcadia Historical Society.*

Tic-Tac-Toe pins (6706) in goldentone from 1967. "What a happy trio, these three colorful little chick-a-dees. Each a different color and all boasting deep red eyes. Wear these colorful little charm-tacs singly, in pairs, or as a trio." These are pictured in a charming three compartment Sarah box called *Glamour Wardrobe Box*. B; $10-20. *Courtesy of Marjory Ritter.*

Top row, left to right: **"S"** pin (2013) is from 1981. The name says it all in this bold "soft textured" goldentone pin. D; $15-30 **Accent** pin (6640) is from the early 1960s. "The unusual abstract design of this pin makes it the ideal 'accent' piece for your suits and dresses. Loop your favorite silk scarf through its swirls to add a touch of color to your costume. Run matching ribbon through the earrings for that go together look." SarahSheen goldentone. The earrings were a miniature version of the pin. A; $20-35. *Silvery Maple* pin (6679) is from 1967. "A design from nature expertly crafted in textured silvertone makes a tailored pin…you'll never tire of. Silvery Maple is in bloom season after season." SarahSheen silvertone. B; $10-20. **Bottom row, left to right:** *Crescent* pin in gleaming silvertone is from the early 1960s. Matching earrings on page 38. A: $10-20. *Unidentified* feather pin in textured and gleaming silvertone is truly an artful design. Simple yet striking – no doubt from the early years. $20-35. *Flower of the Month* pin (6773) is similar to zodiac charms but features a specific flower for each month created from sterling silver in 1968. Dainty and yet uniquely striking is the rose for June. C; $10-20. *Changing Times* stick pin (6009) is from 1979. Each 2" stick pin included one heart, one initial, and one flower to be arranged in any order on the stick pin. The center of the flower is an imported Austrian glass stone. C; $10-20. *Courtesy of Pat and Gary Wyatt.*

Clockwise, from top left: *Fashion Rite* pin (8541) is from 1972. It can also be worn as a necklace with pearls attached in a single or double strand. The necklace is pictured in the International section on page 92. There were matching earrings as well. C; $10-20. *Victorian* pin (6528) is from 1972. This antiqued goldentone pin has opaque faceted stones in the center and smaller pearls on each outer section of the pin. B; $20-35. *Solitude* pin (6906) is from the early 1960s. "The tranquil beauty of a single flower is reflected in this white and goldentone flower pin. A slim goldentone stem supports the chalk white flower making a fashion pin that will bring many compliments your way when pinned to your suit, dress or coat." B; $30-45. *Courtesy of Marjory Ritter.*

Left to right: *Misty Morning* pin/pendant (6831) from 1981. "The flower motif will never fade. Warm weather calls for the portrayal of summer moments and cooler weather needs reminders of mellow breezes. The bouquet is delicate, matched with a soft, luminescent shade of grey, for a wonderful feeling of womanhood." C; $10-20. *Snow Blossom* pin (6559) is from 1973 and dynamically portrays the white effect and bold jewelry. B; $10-20. *Starburst* pin (6040) is a long pin created from glass stones in 1980. There was a dainty matching pendant and earrings. C; $8-18. **Bottom right:** *Crown* is one of the items upper management could order to give as an award to outstanding work done by their people. Sarah Coventry impressed me with the kind of support the company gave all of their people in providing some of these wonderful awards and outstanding specials. The person who received this award could not have put a monetary value on it. Today's current value may be more because of the scarcity of these items available. $15-30. *Courtesy of Dawn Michael.*

Left to right: *Moonmist* stick pin (6139) is from 1977 with a Hematite glass stone mounted in antiqued silvertone. There was also a matching ring. B; $10-20. *Elegance* stick pin (6677) is from 1979 with its pearlized glass stone set in goldentone mounting. B; $10-20. *Butterfly Scatter Tac* (6036) from 1981 is a hand-painted enamel pin to wear on coat, collar, or dress. B; $8-15. *Fan* bar pin (6054) from 1981 is described as "sweeping motion." It also came in goldentone. B; $10-20. **Lower right:** *Butterfly Duo* pin (6004) is actually two pins linked with a chain. This style was very popular in the late 1950s, but made a reappearance in 1981. B; $10-20. *Courtesy of Marlene McIlwain.*

Back row, left to right: *"Dogwood" Jet Black* pin (6223) from 1969 is "a colorful enamel flower pin to bloom from your lapel any season of the year." It also came in hot pink and white; the white pin can be seen on page 68 of Oshel's Book I. There were matching earrings. B; $10-20. *Feather* pin (6090) from 1981 is a goldentone gleaming and textured combination with a stylized feather design. C; $10-20. *Overture* pin/pendant (8367) is from 1981 "to answer the demands of today's woman." It was featured as a pendant and sold on a 30" dark brown cord but could be worn as a pin for lapel or scarves…very versatile. There were small matching earrings. C; $8-20. *Bold Gypsy* pin in burnt orange is from 1967. B; $8-15. **Front row, left to right:** *Oriental* pin (6443) is from 1971 in a striking goldentone and silvertone combination. Matching earrings on page 110 of Oshel's Book I. B; $8-20. *Waltz Time* pin (6770) from the 1950s and 60s "will always have the look of a family heirloom, worn perhaps by Grandmother to her first dance. A bit of romance from the past blended with modern workmanship and the results, a pin of lasting beauty." A; $15-30. *Bold Gypsy* pin in wedgewood blue is from 1967. B; $8-15.

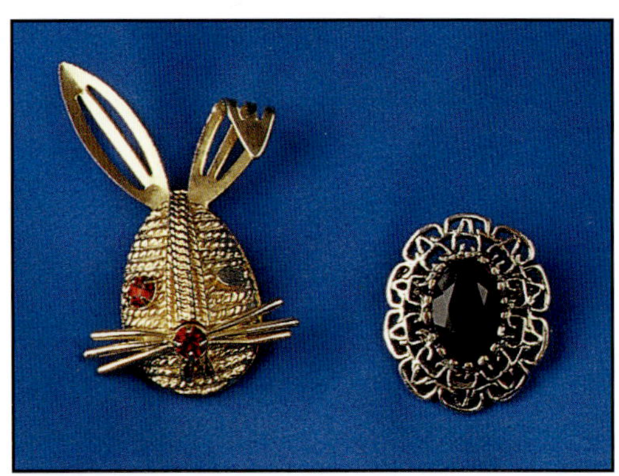

Left to right: *Unidentified* rabbit pin is a goldentone solid rabbit face with garnet rhinestones for one eye and nose. The flopping ear, winking eye, and whiskers make this whimsical pin an attention getter. The year is unknown, but I would guess earlier. $20-35. *First Lady* pin (6469) is from 1978. The black jet faceted center is an imported German glass stone. B; $20-35. *Courtesy of Pat and Gary Wyatt.*

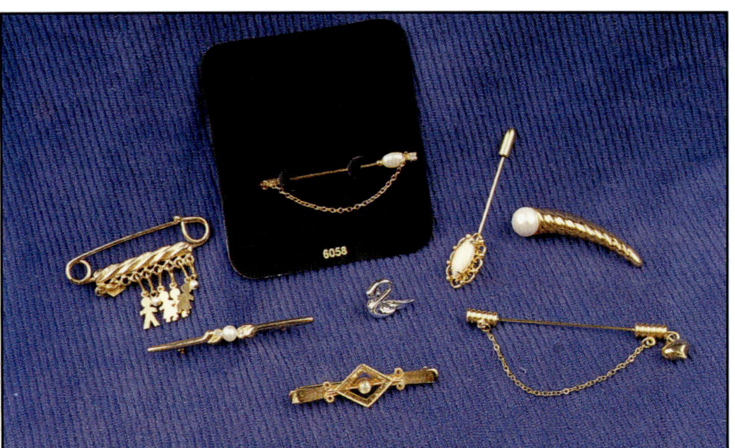

Back row, left to right: *Family Parade* pin (6154) is from 1975 and allowed the wearer to symbolize family by boy, girl, and pearl dangles. Four each of the three kinds of dangles were included with each pin. D; $10-20. *Sweetwater Magic* pin (6058) is a glass stone stick pin from a 1980 ensemble of choker, stick pin, and earrings. "Inspiration from the Far Eastern seas simulated pearls." B; $10-20. *Unidentified* stick pin has a mother-of-pearl navette shaped prong stone set in a goldentone filigree frame. $15-25. *Nova* pin (6097) in goldentone is from 1981. "Dramatic, dynamic clothing fashions need two things: that certain touch of jewelry class; that certain feeling of timelessness. Pearl fashions…there's no better way to have both especially when they're combined with smooth goldentone." C; $10-20. **Middle row, left to right:** *Jacqueline* pin (6056) from 1980 has glass stones on either side of the simulated pearl in this very simplistic bar pin. B; $10-20. *Swan Scatter Tac* (6042) from 1980 is one of many whimsical scatter pins created to wear together or separately. B; $8-15. *Heart Delight* stick pin (6049) is also from 1980. This bar pin has a hang chain and small heart charm to be worn on suits, dresses, or coats. C; $10-20. **Bottom row, center:** *Vintage* pin (6041) is from 1980, when bar pins and stick pins were very popular. This one features a clear glass stone. Below, you can see the same pin with a pink set, not clear. It is not known if the pin was actually sold this way (sometimes Fashion Show Directors were able to switch the stone for one that would be more appropriate to the customer's need.) B; $10-20. *Courtesy of Dawn Michael.*

Right:

Clockwise, from bottom left: *Unidentified* leaf with pearl pin is no doubt from the early years. The small simulated pearl gives it a classic look. $10-20. *Night Owl* pin from the 1950s and 60s is a unique goldentone owl with simulated small pearls for body, clear and dark blue crystal rhinestones for eyes, and a branch sporting a large simulated pearl. A; $15-30. *Vintage* pin (6041) is from 1980. The glass stone in the center is pictured either clear or pink. B; $10-20. *Unidentified* pin with a woman golfer has to have been a custom made piece for an award at a golfing event. $20-35. *Norwegian Ice* pin (6057) is from 1980 and part of an ensemble of ring and choker. "Cool and deep blue as the Norwegian Sea," it has a glass stone. B; $10-20. *Courtesy of Pat Wyatt.* *Unidentified* goldentone pin is a simple branch with leaves, highlighted with a white enamel flower centered by a clear glass rhinestone set. A matching stone is set on the branch. This must be from the late 1950s or early 1960s. $15-30. *Unidentified SC* pin is an intertwining S and C for Sarah Coventry. The S is from gleaming goldentone while the C is textured silvertone. This was no doubt an award or management bonus, or perhaps commemorated a special event of the company. Finding this pin would be a great addition to any collection. $20-35.

Back row, left to right: *Octagon* pin (6003) from 1979 features a modernistic design in goldentone. B; $10-20. *Unidentified* pin is a very striking and brightly gleaming goldentone overlay leaf. Delicate scalloping around the outer edge provides a unique fashion statement. $20-35. **Bottom row, left to right:** *The Sting* pin (6251) is a whimsical pin from 1975 featuring a bumble bee, one of "nature's friends." B; $10-20. *Anniversary* pin (6840) from 1974 has lapis stones and Austrian crystal rhinestones. A very outstanding and striking piece of jewelry sought after today because of its dynamic beauty and striking contrast silvertone. Matching earrings on page 40. D; $20-35. *Snowfall* pin (6450) is a striking snowflake pattern pin created in silvertone for the 1976 Holiday Jewelry Collection. "We at Sarah Coventry hope that the special selection of holiday jewelry which you see here will play a part in your holiday plans. Each item is brand new. So whether you select items for yourself or as gifts for friends or relatives, you are assured they are unique in every way. It's Sarah's way of saying 'Happy Holidays for 1976.' 'Tis the season to choose Sarah.'" B; $10-20. *Courtesy of Allie and Jim Doyle.*

Top row, left to right: *Squeaky* pin (6701) from 1976 is a charming mouse in goldentone with moveable eye. B; $8-15. *Lite Touch* pin (6836) is an elegantly enameled and goldentone butterfly from 1982. C; $10-20. *Gypsy* pin (6329) from 1978 is another butterfly, of very plain goldentone. B; $8-15. **Bottom row, left to right:** *Slow Poke* pin (6780) is, as its name suggests, a turtle from 1968. "Jewelry designed especially for the young in heart." A; $8-15. *Sultry* pin (2013) from 1972 is a stylized "S" shape in goldentone. D; $10-20. *Puppy Love* pin (6555) is an enameled and silvertone piece from the "young in heart" collection in 1973. B; $10-20. *Courtesy of Dawn Michael.*

Top set: *Nocturne* earrings (7614) are from 1966. "…a beautifully designed silvertone flower with its lustrous center pearl and petals edged with imitation marcasites…moon light glow." Matching pin on page 66 of Oshel's Book I. A; $15-25. **Bottom set**: *Carousel* earrings are from the late 1950s or early 1960s. This set was identified from a cardex. However, in Oshel's Book I, the name was given to another set very similar but different. These earrings match a bracelet which had various colored stones, so there may be earrings of varying colors as well. A; $20-35. *Courtesy of Pat and Gary Wyatt.*

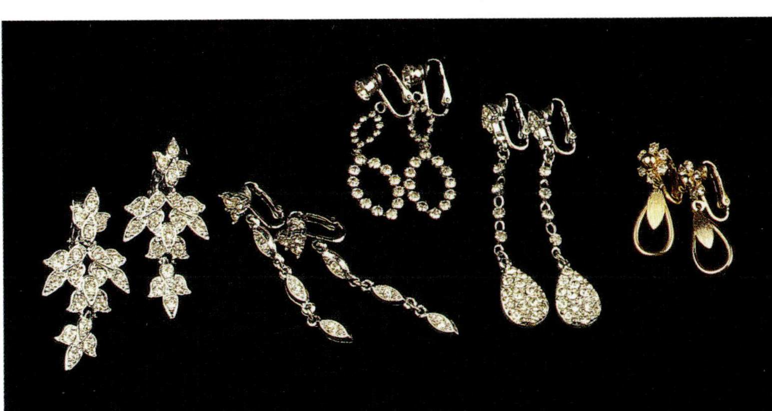

Left to right: *World's Fair* earrings (7947) from 1966. "The New York City World's Fair with all its glamour, gaiety, international flavor and romance, inspired this exclusive rhinestone creation which we have named 'World's Fair.' You'll feel like a woman of mystery and glamour in this sparkling ensemble inspired by the city lights and its world famous World's Fair." SarahSheen silvertone. Matching necklace on page 46 and bracelet on page 51 of Oshel's Book I. B; $15-25. *Unidentified* earrings are reminiscent of icicles in their gleaming silvertone paved with crystal clear rhinestones. $15-30. *Vienna* earrings (7376) are part of the Continental Sparkle collection from 1968. Matching necklace on page 84 of Oshel's Book I. B; $10-20. *Unidentified* earrings are no doubt from the early 1960s. The chain is also studded with rhinestones attached to a tear drop of rhinestones. Exquisite with the look of real jewelry. $20-35. *Chan-Di-Lites* earrings (7644) are from 1966. "As sparkling as a lighted crystal chandelier and equally as beautiful with its dazzling rhinestones and loops of goldentone." SarahGlo goldentone. Matching necklace on page 43. *Courtesy of Dawn Michael.*

Top row, left to right: *Portrait* earrings (7842) are before 1966. "The earring that can go anywhere you go and always feel at home is this lovely oval earring. The mixing of the textured finish with the gleaming goldentone finish is unusual and attractive." A; $12-25. *Military Brass* earrings (7754) are from 1968. "The latest look in fashion is the military look. Sarah's designers created this high fashion…and you don't have to be a general to wear stars wherever you want. Finished in glamorous goldentone." There was also a matching belt. A; $15-30. *Golden Swirl* earrings are from before 1966. This spiraling goldentone set of earrings give the illusion of spinning. Matching pin on page 32 of Oshel's Book I. A; $15-30. *Ultra Fashion* earrings (7565) are from before 1966. The design of spiraling textured goldentone is timeless and matches the necklace pendant on page 124 of Oshel's Book I. A; $10-20. **Bottom row, left to right:** *Touch of Elegance* earrings (7326) are from 1971. The original stone crystal was green, however, FSDs frequently mentioned how the stones could be changed upon request. These ember stones match lots of other ember necklaces and pins. B; $15-30. *Primrose* earrings (7075) are striking red dangle beads from 1979. Matching necklace on page 123 of Oshel's Book I. B; $15-30. *Courtesy of Dawn Michael.*

Top row, left to right: *Unidentified* earrings are small hoops in goldentone and black enamel. Very simple yet strikingly attractive with any dark costume. $10-20. *Unidentified* earrings are goldentone shapes like a cartoon star. The texturing starting out from the center gives more of a 3-D effect. $10-20. *Sabrina Fair* earrings (7699) are from the late 1950s and early 1960s. "You asked for it! Sarah's designers have created it!…Earrings made with the ever so popular Sabrina glass stone imported from Europe. A touch of delicate color…" Matching ring on page 53 and necklace on page 47 of Oshel's Book I. There was also a matching bracelet. A; $15-30. **Bottom row, left to right:** *Multi-Swirl* earrings (7930) are from before 1966. "Our current fashion sportswear calls for exotic colors and the look of bulk. Sarah achieves this look in this design made colorful with exotic colored glass stones centered in each swirl." Matching bracelet on page 50 of Oshel's Book I. A; $20-35. *Fashion In Motion* earrings (7261) are only pictured in 1969. The circle in textured silvertone holds five short chains with a textured silvertone bead at each end. Matching pin on page 68 of Oshel's Book I. B; $15-30. *Jet Flight* and *Pearl Flight* earrings (7684) are from the late 1950s and early 1960s. "Inspired by the design of a bird's wing…embodies an airyness and grace seldom, if ever, seen in a piece of costume jewelry. Its delicate wire work, contrasted by the boldness of the center set of simulated pearl or jet black." As shown by the back of the earring, there were two kinds of clasps, one to hold onto the lobe and the other to secure the back part of the earring to the back of the ear. These are the only ones I have seen like this. Matching pin on page 32 of Oshel's Book I. A; $15-30.

Clockwise, from far left: *Moonlight Madness* earrings are from the early 1960s or before. The slight curve of silvertone covered with rhinestones and simulated pearls makes an elegant complement to any evening wear. Shoe clips and matching pendant on page 54 of Oshel's Book I. A; $20-35. *Spanish Moss* earrings (7475) are goldentone geometric earrings. Matching necklace on page 118 of Oshel's Book I. They also came in antiqued silvertone in 1973. B; $10-20. *Indian Treasures* earrings (7888) are from before 1966. "The look of molded silver has been achieved through fine costume jewelry methods, the stones of turquoise color give you the feeling you've discovered Indian treasures." Matching bracelet on page 50 of Oshel's Book I. A; $20-35. *Delicious* earrings (7373) are from 1970. The golden glow peach colored glass stone with goldentone mounting truly gives a "delicious" look. Matching pin on page 99 of Oshel's Book I. B; $12-25. *Legend* earrings (7289) are pierced earrings from 1975. The scrimshaw-like carved ships match the necklace on page 114 of Oshel's Book I. C; $8-15. *Debutante* earrings (7869) are from before 1966. "Dainty, delicate and delightfully attractive is this diamond-shaped earrings set in textured and gleaming goldentone and boasting a 'pretend' pearl. Tiny enough to be worn on daughter's first date, so traditional in design that discriminating women of any age would enjoy wearing them." SarahGlo goldentone. There was a matching necklace. A; $10-20. *Scarlet Tears* earrings (7822) are from 1974. The magnificent red faceted glass tear drop stone is dramatically set off by the goldentone open frame. Matching necklace on page 122 of Oshel's Book I. B; $15-30. **Center:** *Coffee Break* earrings (7683) are from the early 1960s. "Coffee break, a time when women like to sit and gossip over the events of the day as they relax with a hot cup of coffee. A feeling of joy and pleasure is echoed in these smart pert ear bobs, filled to the top with their favorite brew." They are electro-plated gold making it possible for them to still look great forty years later. A; $15-30.

Top row, left to right: *Flower Flattery* earrings (7743) are a white enameled flower with textured/gleaming goldentone center. There were yellow and pink versions as well. "The magic of the daisy is captured in metals and hi-gloss enamel. Designed to grow on you any season of the year." Matching pin on page 69 of Oshel's Book I. B; $12-20. *Blue Note* earrings (7732) are from 1968. "Robin's egg blue stones nestled in gleaming silvertone that will hit a high note in fashion." Matching pin on page 29 of Oshel's Book I. A; $10-20. **Middle row, left to right:** *Stargazer* earrings (7092) were from 1980 and also available in pierced style. The goldentone mounting with glass stones creates a dressy accessory "For that very special woman…" C; $15-30. *Young and Gay* earrings (7733) are from the early 1960s and continued for several years along with the much loved bracelet on page 50 and necklace page 78 of Oshel's Book I. "Small women and teenage daughters will enjoy wearing the petite button earrings that repeat the delicate coin design of the necklace and bracelet." A; $10-20. **Bottom row, left to right:** *Simplicity* earrings (7612) are from 1966. "Simple and stunning is this golden tailored style…Simplicity is at home anywhere." Matching pin on page 69 of Oshel's Book I. A; $10-20. *Carved Tiger Eye* earrings (7694) from 1974 are from the Lady Coventry collection, which featured semi-precious stones. Matching pendant on page 87 of Oshel's Book I. D: $15-25.

Top row, left to right: *Unidentified* earrings representing double arrows are strikingly unique in textured and gleaming goldentone. They were marked "SC". $15-30. *Duchess* earrings (7250) are from 1976. Three circles of textured and twisted goldentone hang from a gleaming goldentone clasp for a magnificent pair of clip earrings. There was also a matching necklace. B; $10-20. **Bottom row, left to right:** *Madame Butterfly* earrings (7707) also came in goldentone. Matching pin on page 101 of Oshel's Book I. A; $8-15. *Colleen* earrings are clip style from before 1966. Heart shaped silvertone channeling with clear glass crystals frames the three emerald glass stones. Matching necklace on page 78 of Oshel's Book I. A; $20-35. *Courtesy of Arcadia Historical Society.*

Top row, left to right: *Tahitian Flower* earrings are salmon colored flowers artfully designed with goldentone stamens and dark green leaves cradling the petals. The design came in three colors. A; $10-20. *Coraline* earrings (7924) are from 1974. The flecked coral glass stone is mounted in gleaming and textured goldentone. Matching pin/pendant on page 29 and ring on pages 67 and 68. B; $10-20. **Middle row, left to right:** *Birds in Flight* earrings (7704) are from 1967. "What is lovelier or more graceful than birds in flight, and Sarah's designers have caught this beauty in a gleaming tailored silvertone earrings." Matching pin on page 69 of Oshel's Book I. A; $15-30. *Crescent* earrings are from the early 1960s. The gleaming silvertone shapes would accent any costume when worn in conjunction with the matching pin on page 34. $8-15. **Bottom row, left to right:** *Roman Coins* earrings (7399) are from 1971 in goldentone. They also came in silvertone. Matching scarf keeper on page 169 of Oshel's Book I. B; $10-20. *Unidentified* earrings are leaves of goldentone smartly designed with stem veins and a tiny simulated pearl. $10-20. *Courtesy of Pat and Gary Wyatt.*

Left to right: **Blue Champagne** earrings (7708) are from the early years. "Exciting, glamorous, outstandingly beautiful, exquisite, striking, and heavenly are only a few of the adjectives it would take to describe these sapphire blue earrings." Matching pin on page 32 and necklace on page 48 of Oshel's Book I. A; $20-35. **Two-Timer** earrings (7481) are from 1972. They were also made in goldentone. The top piece could be worn alone or with the bottom saddle-bag attachment. B; $10-20. **On Stage** earrings (7499) are from 1973. The baroque style pearl is capped with a gleaming silvertone mounting. Matching lariat necklace or belt attachments on page 77 of Oshel's Book I. The necklace/belt was a combination of chain and white beads. B; $10-20. *Courtesy of Arcadia Historical Society.*

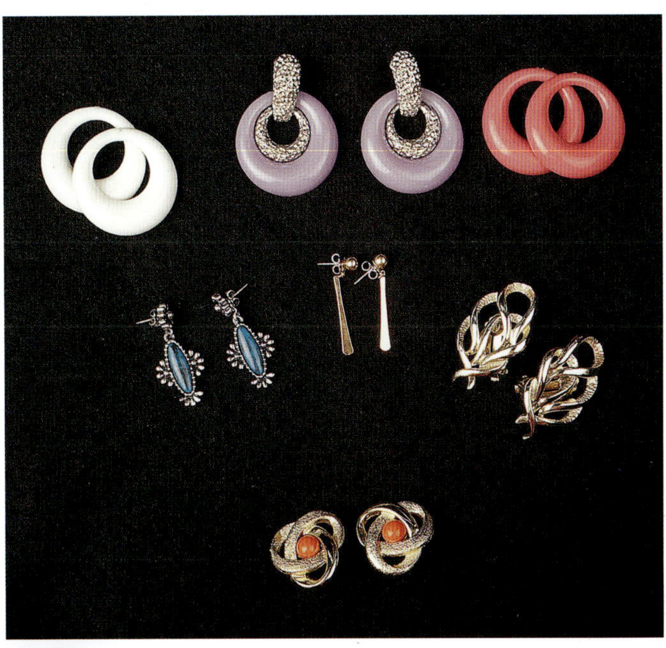

Top row: Pastel Parfait earrings (7581) are from 1973 in white, lavender, and hot pink. The center circle and silvertone clasp can be interchanged with the other colors, creating new jewelry to match any costume. Matching beads on pages 54 and 55. B; $10-20. **Middle row, left to right: Blue Cloud** earrings (7629) are from 1977. The dynamic contrast of the turquoise cabochons in antiqued silvertone make for rich looking fashion jewelry. C; $15-25. **Cleopatra** earrings (7025) are from 1980 in a dangling goldentone simple design. B; $8-15. **Town and Country** earrings (7757) are from the late 1950s or early 1960s. "...designed for the woman who loves distinctive jewelry." There was also a bracelet with the same design as these earrings. SarahSheen goldentone. A; $10-20. **Bottom: Orbit** earrings (7347) from 1971 combine gleaming and textured goldentone with a red cabochon center. There was also a set in silvertone with a green center. Matching pin on page 101 of Oshel's Book I. B; $10-20. *Courtesy of Arcadia Historical Society.*

Top row, left to right: Unidentified earrings are yellow enameled raindrop shaped with goldentone. No doubt from the early years. $10-20. **Accent** earrings (7640) are from before 1966. "The unusual abstract design makes it the ideal 'accent'...Run ribbon through the earrings for that go together look." A; $10-20. **Unidentified** earrings are gleaming goldentone clip earrings, no doubt from the early 1960s. $10-20. **Bottom row: Indian Maiden** earrings (7823) are from 1973. Turquoise colored cabochon sets in an antiqued silvertone mounting are eye-catching when worn with the matching pendant and ring on pages 28 and 69 or matching bracelet on page 127 of Oshel's Book I. There were also smaller pierced earrings. B; $15-30. *Courtesy of Pat Wyatt*

Top right: Azure Skies earrings (7524) are from 1973. Gold flecked turquoise cabochon stones set in goldentone are accented with tiny pearl beads. Matching pendant on page 112 and ring on page 131 of Oshel's Book I. B; $10-20. **Middle row, left to right: Crystal Snowflakes** earrings are six pointed star shapes in silvertone covered with faceted clear rhinestones. Matching pin on page 83 of Oshel's Book I. $15-30. **Angel Pink** earrings (7563) are from 1973 in a delicate goldentone design with pink cabochon surrounded by tiny pearl beads. There was also a matching ring and pendant. B; $10-20. **Daisy Time** earrings (7385) are from 1971. A striking contrast of turquoise and yellow cabochon sets on silvertone. B; $10-20. **Bottom: White Velvet** (7430) earrings from 1971 are white enameled goldentone leaf shapes giving the illusion of velvet. Matching pin on page 98 of Oshel's Book I. B; $15-30. *Courtesy of Arlena Jordan.*

Left to right: *Autumn Trio* earrings (7247) are from 1976. "The colorful pendants may be worn separately or inside the filigree frame." There were two other colors available. Matching pendant on page 61. B; $15-30. *Confetti* earrings (7710) are from the early 1960s. "Sparkling, twinkling, colored lights glistening in a shiny silvery sky give a look of gayety, happiness, and good times…makes you feel every day is a holiday." They are electro-plated gold and there was a matching ring as well. A; $15-30. *Royal Crown* earrings (7381) are goldentone peek-a-boo earrings with ruby center and a rhinestone cap from 1971. This crown shape also came in a matching pendant and ring. The ring is shown on page 69. B; $15-30. *Courtesy of Dawn Michael.*

Top row, left to right: *Pastel Parfait* pierced earrings (7593) are from 1973. These planet shaped colors were interchangeable on the stainless steel pierced wires. Matching beads on pages 54 and 55. B; $10-20. *Easy Going* earrings (7520) from 1978 are simple textured goldentone and also came in silvertone. B; $10-20. **Bottom row, left to right:** *Over the Rainbow* earrings (7427) from 1971 have aurora borealis prong set glass stone in silvertone setting. Matching pendant on page 118 of Oshel's Book I. B; $15-30. *Evening Snowflake* earrings (7926) are from early 1960s. "…fascinating and sparkling as a falling snowflake on a bright and moonlit night. A man-designed snowflake paved with tiny twinkling rhinestones swirling around a large black diamond (simulated)." SarahSheen silvertone. Matching brooch on page 27 of Oshel's Book I. A replica with a pearl center has also been added to the jewelry collection from the New Sarah Coventry company started in 2003. B; $15-30.

Top row, left to right: *Unidentified* earrings are delicate yet bold in a filigree goldentone geometric design dangle. Black jet cabochon sets highlight each section of the earring. $10-20. *Unidentified* earrings, no doubt from the early years, have a four leaf clover design highlighted by aurora borealis glass stones. $10-20. *Holiday Circles* earrings (7803) also came in goldentone. The set came with six circles in a variety of colors to be interchanged with the frame. They match the necklaces, one of which is pictured on page 111 of Oshel's Book I. C; $10-20. **Bottom row, left to right:** *Sea Urchin* earrings (7316) are from 1970. The unique goldentone design truly looks like a creature from the sea. Matching pin on page 25. A; $8-15. *Papillion* earrings (7907) are from 1975. Matching necklace on page 112 of Oshel's Book I. B; $10-20. *Unidentified* earrings are black enameled half swirls coming from a single base. The fan effect makes for a very simple design when worn, giving a lot of class. $10-20. *Courtesy of Pat Wyatt.*

Top row, left to right: *Anniversary* earrings (7840) are from 1974. Blue lapis stones are attractively set in the rhinestone paved silvertone star shape. Matching pin on page 36. B; $20-35. *Classic Partners Going Steady* earrings (7090) are from 1980 and also came in goldentone. They were available in pierced or clip style. B; $10-20. *Unidentified* earrings are silvertone dangles with texturing that gives the impression of depth. $10-20. **Bottom row, left to right:** *Springtime* earrings (7493) are from 1973. The variety of faceted crystal rhinestones make them sparkle like spring. Matching pin on page 98 of Oshel's Book I. B; $15-30. *Unidentified* earrings are elegant goldentone open ovals with attached dangling jet beads. $15-30. *Reflector* earrings (7016) from 1979 also came in goldentone. B; $10-20. *Dancing Jet* earrings (7604) are from 1968. "Milady's ears have never been so exciting or so important. Swingers for every occasion for that up-to-the-minute fashion feeling." A; $10-20. *Courtesy of Dawn Michael.*

Top row, left to right: *Pyramid Treasure* earrings (7451) from 1971 are unique silvertone gleaming and textured finish dangle. There was also a pierced set with surgical steel posts. Matching necklace on page 121 of Oshel's Book I. B; $8-15. *Unidentified* earrings are a triangle shape of open-weave silvertone. There is a slight curve to the shape. $10-20. *Scandia* earrings (7944) from 1977 feature hammered effect silvertone. There were other matching pieces. B; $10-20. **Bottom row, left to right:** *Swingalong* earrings (7494) are from 1972. Matching necklace on page 77 of Oshel's Book I. B; $10-20. *Roman Coins* earrings (7399) are from 1971 in goldentone. They also came in silvertone. Matching scarf keeper on page 169 of Oshel's Book I. B; $10-20. *Angel Pink* earrings (7563) are from 1973. There was a matching pendant and ring. B; $10-20. *Teahouse* earrings (7657) from 1977 have a unique oriental design. Matching pendant on page 48. B; $15-30. *Courtesy of Dawn Michael.*

Left to right: *Unidentified* earrings are very similar to several other kinds. However, these are unique in their elongated silvertone open design artfully decorated with large and smaller clear crystal rhinestones. My guess is that these were from the 1960s. $20-35. *Atlantis* earrings (7369) are from 1976. There was a similar set in 1968 called Wedding Band. Matching bracelet on pages 73 and 74. B; $10-20. *Courtesy of Brenda Bruzee and Marjory Ritter.*

Top: *Flair* earrings (7622) from 1976 are bell shaped sections of surgical steel wire. These won't have any indication of being Sarah Coventry, so may be hard to spot. B; $10-20. **Bottom:** *Showtime* earrings (7424) are classic hoop shapes that came in goldentone as well as silvertone in 1978. B; $10-20. *Courtesy of Marlene McIlwain.*

Left to right: *Silvery Fern* earrings (7338) are from the 1980s. The silvertone design of fern leaves is antiqued to give these hoops an old look, yet very modern fashion statement. They were available in clip or pierced. B; $10-20. *Unidentified* goldentone hoop earrings could be named "exquisite" as that is what they are. The beveled and ridged shape is adorned with crystal rhinestones, making a dynamic fashion statement in any era, for any age person. $15-30. *Courtesy of Bill Scheetz.*

Left to right: *Basic Hoop* earrings (7021) from 1979 also came in silvertone. B; $10-20. *Unidentified* earrings are no doubt from the early 1960s. The circle of twisted silvertone has simulated pearls and tiny crystal rhinestones nestled within its frame. $15-30. *Easy Going* earrings (7520) are from 1978 and came in silvertone as well. B; $10-20. *Show-stopper* earrings (7009) were from 1980. They also came in silvertone. Very classic and simple, yet unique. B; $10-20. *Courtesy of Arcadia Historical Society.*

Left to right: *Crystal Fire* necklace (8530) is from before 1966. "For the woman who doesn't mind stopping the show, Sarah has designed an exciting necklace…for evening wear. Crystal aurora stones twist and sparkle from a golden chain." SarahGlo goldentone. There were matching earrings that completed the "picture of 'sparkle on the rocks.'" B; $15-30. *Misty* necklace (8032) is a simulated opal in goldentone on a 16-18" adjustable chain. There was also a matching ring. D; $15-30. *Courtesy of Arlena Jordan.*

Golden Mum earrings (7219) are from 1969. The prong set centers of the earrings are "sparkling Austrian Rhinestones" in an amber color. The spiny goldentone design truly gives these earrings a mum look. Matching pin on page 67 of Oshel's Book I. B; $15-30. *Sarah Coventry patch* was often placed on jackets, blazers, caps, and shirts, as well as on this red velvet cloth used in wrapping jewelry to be placed in the suitcase carried from party to party. *Courtesy of Arcadia Historical Society.*

Left to right: *First Love* necklace (8399) is a dainty chain link with pearl beads and blade sections stationed throughout. $8-15. *Unidentified* necklace with Christmas charm of an enameled tree is no doubt from the children's section during the holiday season. $10-20. *Frolic* pendant (8119) is from 1978 "For Little Sarah…and Her Teen Years." The silvertone chain is approximately 15" and attached to a delicate blue enamel butterfly for the younger wearer. B; $10-20. *Pink Parfait* necklace (8057) is one chain of a two chain set. This 33" chain has pink glass beads encircled with goldentone and stationed throughout the chain. E; $10-20. *Summer Scheme* necklace (8770) from 1978 is this striking goldentone chain with stationed white spool beads. C; $15-25. *Holiday Beads* (8217) are off white plastic beads in 36" length. Other colors shown on page 55. B; $10-20. *Unidentified* necklace is a dainty goldentone chain of pearl beads and flattened oval swirls. The tag is oval, indicating that it is from the 1980s. $10-20. **Top Center:** *Puppy Love* poodle pendant in striking black and red enamel is from the late 1950s or early 1960s when poodle skirts were in vogue. The mark on the back is SAC. It no doubt was in the "young at heart" collection. This pendant is a real find as it is the first one I have seen and could be attached to a bracelet as well. $20-35. *Courtesy of Pat and Gary Wyatt.*

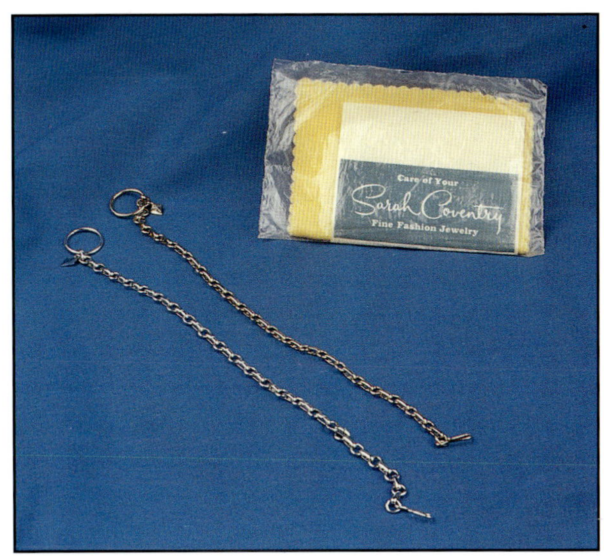

Left to right: *Necklace Extenders* (7522, SarahSheen; 7523, SarahGlo) from the 1960s. "Sarah is proud to add this wonderful service item to her already complete line of jewelry. These extenders allow those of us with more than ample charms to be as fashionable as our thinner sisters. They come in pairs so both your silver and gold jewelry, new or old, can be enlarged to fit more comfortably." In 1972, they were called *Choker Chain Set*; in Canada in 1974, they were called *Bracelet Converter Set.* B; $8-15. Also shown is a *Jewelry Cleaning Cloth,* no doubt a hostess item or gift item in the early years. I haven't located it in any of the catalogs as an item for sale. $8-15. *Courtesy of Marjory Ritter.*

Left to right: *Chan-Di-Lites* necklace (8644) is from 1966. "As sparkling as a lighted crystal chandelier and equally as beautiful with its dazzling rhinestones and loops of goldentone." There were matching earrings as well. SarahGlo goldentone. B; $25-40. *Silvery Sunset* necklace (8318) was identified from 1975. It also came in a Golden Sunset necklace and there were both golden and silvery earrings to match the circles in the necklace. D; $15-30. *Rendezvous* pendant (8176) is from 1979. Tiny glass beads are stationed throughout the dainty S chain. There was a detachable tassel not shown. E; $15-30. *Courtesy of Marjory Ritter.*

Top center: *Plain and Fancy* necklace (8673) is from the early 1960s or before. "Unusual and striking. A masterpiece of design and craftsmanship as different looking as it is daring and as striking as it is distinctive. This brilliance and use of two tones is a new and daring technique developed for your admiration and can be worn with either PLAIN or FANCY clothes." SarahSheen goldentone and silvertone finish. Matching earrings on page 39 of Oshel's Book I and bracelet on page 52. B; $20-35. **Bottom row, left to right:** *Hi-Lo Elegance* necklace (8478) is from 1972. This part of a two-part necklace set has a large "V" shape created from smaller diamond shaped open-weave sections. Three tassels are attached to each corner of the "V" shape. Single chain matching necklace on page 112 and earrings on page 105 of Oshel's Book I, *Sarah Coventry Jewelry.* D; $15-30. *Romanesque Cross* (8270) was from 1976. The stylized shape is enhanced by the gray enameled finish. It came with a 24" dark silvertone chain as well. D; $20-35. *Jet Set* necklace (8429) is from 1977. The imported Austrian glass hematite stone is offset in a gleaming silvertone mounting attached to a delicate 15-16" chain. There were both clip and pierced matching earrings, a bracelet, and a ring. Several other ensembles have the same name. C; $15-30. *Touch of Elegance* necklace (8326) is from 1971. It is created from an oval multi-faceted Austrian stone capped with mesh goldentone mounting. Matching pin on page 100 and earrings on page 105 of Oshel's Book I. B; $10-20.

Left to right: *Oriental Mood* choker (8726) is a 16" long golden chain with slightly curved sections separating forest green tear drop beads and smaller light blue barrel beads. It is truly an oriental look and had matching earrings and a bracelet in 1976. E; $15-30. *Golden Gypsy* necklace (8276) is from 1969 and features three slender, gleaming, concentric circles attached by a golden hoop to a delicate chain. There were also matching earrings the same size as the pendant. This was the second time this name was given to an ensemble. B; $10-20. *Spring Song* pendant (8553) from 1978 is enamel decorated with bird and leaves on a spectacular teal background with a silvertone mounting and 24" chain. A gift from my friend Reba that I will always treasure. D; $15-30. *Desert Scene* pendant (8543) is from 1978. The unique enameling on a goldentone oval shape truly depict a scene from the desert, as its name suggests. C; $10-20. *Concord* necklace (8665) from 1978 features 17-20" adjustable length in a striking contrast of purple beads and silvertone beads and tubes. Matching ring is Sugarplum on page 71. C; $10-20. *Lilac Time* choker (8208) is from 1976 and was part of a set including a 34" matching chain. The choker length of 16" was to lengthen the necklace, to be worn separately as a choker, or to be worn together with the 34" length for multiple strands. It could also be used as a bracelet. Matching necklace on page 114 of Oshel's Book I. There were also matching earrings. D; $8-15.

Left to right: *Love Knots* choker (8569) from 1977 is this "delightfully delicate" combination of pearlized beads and scrolled metal stationed to a dainty goldentone chain adjustable from 14-16". C; $8-15. *Angel Pink* pendant (8563) from 1973 is a dainty pendant of pink cabochon and tiny seed pearls situated in a filigree goldentone mounting. There was a matching ring and pair of earrings. B; $10-20. *First Love* pendant (8690) is from late 1950s and 1960s. "One of the newest and most popular fashion jewelry trends is the tiny heart or pendant hanging on a delicately fine chain. This was originally inspired by Queen Elizabeth's visit to America and since, has been adopted by many famous movie and TV personalities. The tiny heart symbolic of great and romantic love between man and woman and particularly your FIRST LOVE." It is electro-plated gold and paved with very small crystal rhinestones. A; $10-20. *Two-Tone Butterfly* pendant (8283) was created in the late 1970s and continued through 1980. The use of silvertone and goldentone together gives a 3-dimensional look and illusion of the butterfly in flight. C; $8-15. *Mirage* choker (8285) from 1975 has a faceted bead stationed on a striking hinged chain. Matching earrings on page 109 of Oshel's Book I. C; $10-20. *Hidden Pearl* (8903) has a simulated pearl in SarahGlo goldentone mounting. "The look of real jewelry is the design thought portrayed in this blossom-like pendant and earring combination – a lustrous imitation baroque pearl peeking out from under goldentone petals. Young and old alike will admire this classic design." A; $15-30. **Bottom:** Another view of the *Necklace Extenders* also shown on page 43.

Left to right: ***Three-Timer*** necklace (8246). This versatile necklace from the late 1970s has replaceable colors to accompany any color of costume. C; $15-30. ***Gabrielle Christmas Drop*** from 1977 could be worn as a necklace or used as a tree ornament. $8-15. ***Glamour*** necklace (8698) from 1978 has an adjustable hook of 16-18". The goldentone multiple chain creates a "Natural Beauty" to be worn with a variety of costumes. D; $12-20. *Courtesy of Arcadia Historical Society.*

Left to right: ***Tiara*** pendant (8451) from 1978 has a removable goldentone pendant. The pendant is made from both textured and smooth metal and smartly worn on this 24" rope chain. C; $10-25. ***Encore*** pendant (8639) is an inlaid painted drop stationed on the end of a 17" chain from 1978. C; $8-15. ***Morning Blossoms*** pin/pendant (8059) has a beautiful flower painted on a glass stone and can be worn as a pin or a necklace. The goldentone, antiqued look created in 1979 can tastefully and easily be worn today. C; $15-30. ***Spring Bouquet*** pendant is a reversible pendant from 1978. This side has a flower encased in an oval goldentone clear plastic case. The reverse side is in the next picture. D; $10-20. *Courtesy of Arcadia Historical Society.*

Left to right: *Cleopatra* bib-necklace (8025) is adjustable from 15-17". This 1978 necklace has matching earrings on page 39. D; $15-25. *Lites* pendant (8031) is a 25" necklace from 1974. C; $15-30. **Spring Bouquet** pendant (8651) shows the reverse side of the removable pendant also shown in previous picture. This side displays a leaf design created from solid goldentone with white inlay. D; $10-20. *Courtesy of Arcadia Historical Society.*

Left to right: *On The Move* necklace (8849) was featured in the late 1970s. "Beads are adjustable on cord," also adjustable from 17-21". D; $8-15. *Wire Wrap* pendant (8877) from 1979 is a 24" chain attached to a pendant with interchangeable black and cream colored plastic pieces. I have seen few of these pieces. D; $10-25. *Jet Ice* necklace (8832) is a 48" silver chain with a large crystal bead stationed between two black barrel shaped glass beads. "Parisian glamour in crystal and jet," from 1974. There were matching earrings as well. C; $15-25. *Courtesy of Arcadia Historical Society.*

Left to right: *Old Vienna* necklace shown here has the complete set of pin/pendant and smaller attached charm pendant. "Each glass stone has been hand painted with red, blue, black and 14K gold in West Germany…after each color is applied the stone is baked for additional luster and long wear." This set from 1976 is fairly easy to find. Matching ring on page 135 of Oshel's Book I. D; $15-30. **New Yorker** choker (8401) from 1976 is an attractive 15" black cord with a red and goldentone curved horn-shape stationed pendant. There were also matching earrings. C; $15-25. **Rosette** pendant (8514) from 1973 is a tiny goldentone pendant with red glass rhinestone center on a 16-18" adjustable chain. Matching ring on page 71. B; $10-18. *Evening Mist* (8067) is a 25" necklace of red glass and goldentone beads. Original price was $26. No doubt this will be difficult to find as it was from the New Sarah Coventry of 1982 and wouldn't have been available for more than a year. $15-20. **Autumn Beauty** pendant (8929) is an imported German red stone on a 22-24" adjustable chain from 1978. This is the only one I have seen, so may be difficult to find. C; $15-30. *Courtesy of Dawn Michael.*

Timeless pendant was originally unidentified in my first book on page 121. This pendant was also selected to be photographed at each step of the process and displayed in the corporate offices for visitors to understand the jewelry making process. Two of these pictures are on page 11 of this book. As the card states:
"Timeless…an exclusive Limited Edition creation, commemorating still another wondrous creation – the new C. H. Stuart complex.
"Timeless…sophisticated and chic, as polished Silvertone surrounds the German, simulated hematite stone, capped with a sparkling cluster of delicate rhinestones from the Tirolean Valley in Austria."
"Timeless…captured in a distinctive exhibition depicting its very creation…from design to assemblance, to the beautiful gift box."
"Timeless…exclusively C. H. Stuart…especially for you."
Courtesy of Arcadia Historical Society.

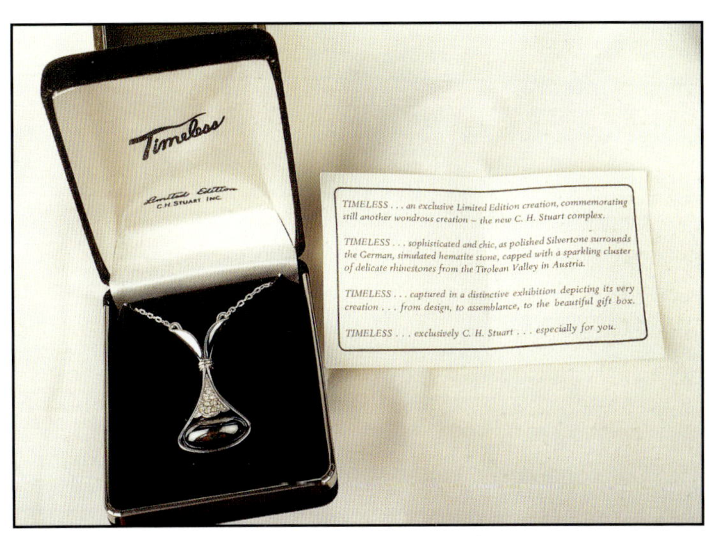

Left to right: *Golden Braids* choker (8953) from 1978 is 16-1/2" long and created from two solid goldentone twisted braids. C; $12-20. **Outer Space** pendant (8595) is a solid goldentone pendant giving an illusion of outer space on a 20-22" adjustable chain from 1976. B; $10-20. **Pink Lady** pendant (8830) from 1974 features pink glass with a tassel attached on a 24" chain. Matching ring on page 68. B; $10-25. **Unidentified** necklace has stationed sculptured pin beads on a silvertone chain of solid links. $10-20. *Rapture* necklace (2300) is from 1983. "Wrap yourself up in the beauty of Rapture goldentone necklace. A simulated pearl and crystal jeweled clasp hold the 3 lengths of twisted rope chain." The necklace is 19-1/2" long and can be worn with the clasp on the shoulder, in front, offset in the back, or the traditional back. The stones are imported crystal and the original price was $100. $45-60. *Courtesy of Dawn Michael.*

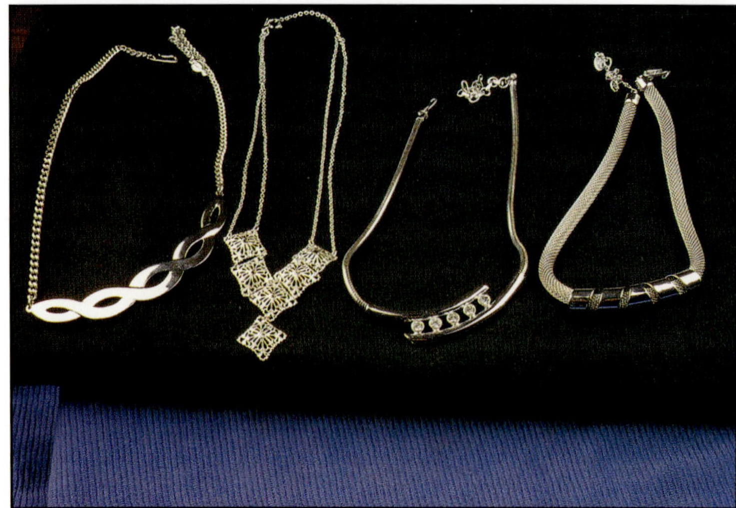

Left to right: *Fashion Braid* choker (8280) from 1976 had a matching barrette and bracelet. C; $10-20. *Royal Lace* bib-necklace (8776) from 1978 is a filigree design much like lace. D; $10-25. *Holiday Lites* choker (8456) is a sleek yet elegant necklace created from imported Austrian glass stones. There was also a matching bracelet from 1977. D; $15-30. *Fifth Avenue* choker (8833) is from 1978. The main 18" choker can be removed from the spiral silvertone. D; $10-20. *Courtesy of Dawn Michael.*

Left to right: *Duo Heart* choker (8702) on a 14-16" adjustable chain is from 1978. B; $8-15. *Change of Heart* choker (8534) from 1976 is an unusual heart designed necklace with sections of silvertone tubes alternating with beads on either side of a shiny silvertone heart. C; $15-30. *Party Hearts* necklace (8634) from 1978 combines these two chains, one 20" and one 33". Connected together, they form an overall length of 53". It also came in goldentone. C; $10-20. *Courtesy of Abby Bellamy.*

Left to right: *Bold and Beautiful* necklace (8726) "has the elegant feeling of very fine fashion jewelry. Every woman's jewelry wardrobe needs a black ensemble to make it complete. This white and silver set is softly designed and precisely tailored to give you flattery with style perfection." This was in the early 1960s and the similar black set is shown on page 45 of Oshel's Book I. B; $15-30. *Silhouette Perfume* pendant (8517) from 1978 is a dramatically designed pendant on a 24" goldentone chain. The pendant opens to provide a place for perfume. E; $15-30. *Essence* pendant (8562) is an intaglio rose of imported German glass stone from 1978. C; $15-30. *Courtesy of Dorothy DeMay.*

Left to right: *Sarah's Birthstone* pendant (8537) appears to be the aquamarine set for March. The glass stone is iridescent rather than a solid color, creating a dynamic pendant to be worn by the young and those who like small jewelry in 1967. B; $10-20. *Career Girl* necklace from the 1960s is a gathering of goldentone chains of varying sizes with a goldentone ridged cap. The tassel also features the cap and can be worn with the chains or the chains can be worn separately. The versatility of the tassel allows it be worn on other chains, beads, and with other necklaces. B; $10-20. *Teahouse* pendant (8657) from 1977 came on a 23-25" adjustable chain. I believe very few of these pendants were sold, so may be difficult to find. D; $15-30. **Two charms in center:** *Coventry Cameo* pendant (8427) from 1981 is a cameo flower of "delicate simplicity." C; $10-18. *Seashore* pendant (8171) originally came with a 30"chain in 1982-1984 and came only in goldentone. D; $10-25. *Courtesy of Arcadia Historical Society.*

Left to right: *Melissa* choker (8632) from 1978 has a 15-17" adjustable chain attached to this dainty oval shaped enameled pendant with purple flower. Matching ring on page 70. C; $8-15. *Mahogany* (8078) is a hoop necklace with a silvertone, textured and smooth, mahogany brown stone drop from 1976. C; $10-20. *Scandia* choker (8835) has an adjustable 18" necklace chain attached to this textured silvertone beauty. There is also a matching bracelet, earrings, and ring from 1977. C; $10-20. *Courtesy of Arcadia Historical Society.*

Left to right: Four 1978 necklaces: *New Design* choker (8700) is 14-16" adjustable. B; $8-15. *Copenhagen* pendant (8822) is on a 26" chain with a removable drop. D; $10-20. *Preview* choker (8512) is made from imported German glass hematite stones in an unusual design on a 15-16" adjustable chain. C; $15-30. *Park Avenue* choker (8783) is a classic design of blue and goldentone adjustable from 15-17". C; $10-20. *Courtesy of Dawn Michael.*

Mythology Cross (8506) is Sarah's 1978 Limited Edition cross. "Inspired by the ancient craft of hand painted porcelain, Sarah Coventry brings you this most distinctive cross. The Grecians were noted for perfecting the concept of showing jet black fields with painted or etched designs, and it is with this that Sarah's cross was designed in direct response to the early revolution of ceramics. Enhanced by the beauty and hand polished luster of the 18 kt. gold leaf pattern, this genuine porcelain cross uniquely combines the skill of this ancient craft with the art of modern jewelry design." The cross was available for purchase from the fall through Dec. 31, 1978, at which time the mold was destroyed. E; $15-30. *Courtesy of Dawn Michael.*

Left to right: *White 'N Bright* choker (8071) is a 15-17' adjustable necklace from 1980. B; $8-15. *Melon Accent* choker (8052) from 1979 is a 17" white bead choker with three melon colored barrel beads stationed in the front. C; $10-20. *Summer Scheme* necklace (8770) from 1978 has white beads stationed throughout the length of the 31" chain. C; $8-15. *White Elegance* necklace (8066) from 1979 has three white beads stationed throughout the 30" chain. C; $10-20. *White Magic* choker (8394) is a solid beaded 16" choker from 1980. C; $10-20. *Courtesy of Dawn Michael.*

Left to right: *Cameo Lady* pendant/pin (8833) on a 16-18" chain is from 1974. Matching ring on page 71. B; $10-20. ***Rose Cameo*** pendant (8653) is from early 1967. "The lady of the Cameo is an elegant representation of the 19th Century Cameos and will add a touch of yester-year to your wardrobe. The cameo is famous for its tradition and beauty." It was made from SarahGlo goldentone. A; $10-20. ***Fly Away*** necklace (8101) from 1976 is on a 14-16" chain and hand enameled. C; $10-20. ***Lovely Lady*** choker (8266) from 1978 is on a 15-17" adjustable chain and sports an imported German glass stone set in a spectacular goldentone mounting. C; $10-20. ***Sea Shell Lariat*** (8070) from 1980 is on a 47" chain to be used as a necklace or possibly a belt. Very versatile. C; $10-20. *Courtesy of Dawn Michael.*

Left to right: *Sensation* choker (8566) is a 17" necklace of white and golden beads stationed on this sectioned chain from 1977. C; $10-20. ***Glacier*** necklace (2294) from 1983 has "outspoken chips of white plastic creating this vivid necklace with a bold fashion look." G; $20-35. ***Caress*** necklace (2101) has 22 and 23" glass beads with a shell shaped clasp and was from the New Sarah Coventry collection in 1983. Original price was $125. Current value: $30-55. ***Teen Heart Locket*** (8993) from 1974 is a dainty goldentone locket with porcelain, hand-painted flower cover. The chain is 16-18" adjustable to be worn by younger and older customers and opens to carry a photo, priceless treasure, or perfume. B; $10-20. *Courtesy of Dawn Michael.*

Left to right: ***Reflections*** necklace (0814) is an imported Austrian glass stone with iridescent bright colors from 1978. It was worth 3400 points from the Hostess Bonus selections. $15-30. ***Silverspin*** choker (8630) is a 17" choker created from small silvertone beads in 1976. C; $10-20. ***Festival Beads*** (8832) from 1984 are "colorful glass shapes in goldentone to slide on a chain-a-bead chain." There was also a matching bracelet. C; $10-20. ***Austrian Crystal Lariat*** (8417) is a 37" lariat from 1981. "A flowing Lariat with the splendor of the Danube River as it journeys through the Austrian Alps and the Bohemian Forest. Here is the romance of Austria captured in beautifully faceted genuine crystal." F; $15-30. ***Unidentified*** goldentone necklace is a combination of square gleaming and textured sections hinged with large goldentone rings forming a flat necklace similar to the ***Young and Gay*** round set. $15-30. *Courtesy of Dawn Michael.*

Left to right: ***Chain Reaction*** necklace is a unique combination of two silvertone bold chains and two goldentone chains. There is also a matching bracelet allowing the length of the necklace to be lengthened or to accent the necklace. $15-30. ***Elegant Trio*** necklace (8077) is three chains of silvertone and goldentone in a length of 19" from 1980. Matching bracelet is shown here. C; $10-20. ***Paradise*** choker (8402) from 1978 is genuine porcelain with a painted blue bird. C; $10-20. ***Sweetheart Locket*** (8869) is attached to a 24" chain. The locket opened and could hold perfume or a picture and was "gift boxed for special occasions" in 1974. D; $10-20. *Courtesy of Dawn Michael.*

Left to right: *Unidentified* pendant on goldentone chain. The rounded corner triangle of thick amber plastic is embossed with a goldentone scroll design. $15-30. *Front Row* pendant (8578) is a goldentone square of geometric enamel black, orange, and yellow. "The earthy look of Sarah." It is attached to a 17" linked necklace and featured in 1977. C; $8-20. *Lotus Blossom* pendant (8030) is a brilliantly enamel floral pendant in goldentone on a 24" chain from 1980. D; $10-25. *Emberglo* necklace (8839) is a 37" chain with ember beads stationed along the entire length. Goldentone and ember combinations were a hit in 1978. C; $10-20. *Birthstone Heart* pendants (0836-0847) are imported Austrian glass stones in birthstones from garnet to blue zircon. The necklaces are dainty chains adjustable from 16-18". These were worth 900 Hostess Bonus points, rewarding hostesses having purchases and people becoming a hostess in 1979. $10-20. *Courtesy of Dawn Michael.*

Left to right: *Spring Fever* (8069) was originally featured on a 30" pink cord but could be worn on a gold chain. This is a "hand painted Cloisonne Heart" in goldentone from 1982. E; $10-25. *Festive* necklace (8460) is a lightweight goldentone 18" mesh chain exquisitely adorned with goldentone accents and a removable drop created from an ember glass stone. There is a matching ring. E; $15-35. *Imagination* necklace/belt (8522) is approximately 39" in length with an adjustable slide. It came in silvertone as well in 1978. C; $10-20. *Spring Beauty* pendant (8605) is a brightly enameled purple, red, and yellow flower attached to an adjustable 16-18" chain. The late 1970s brought about many of these colorful and delightful-to-wear pendants. C; $10-25. *Courtesy of Dawn Michael.*

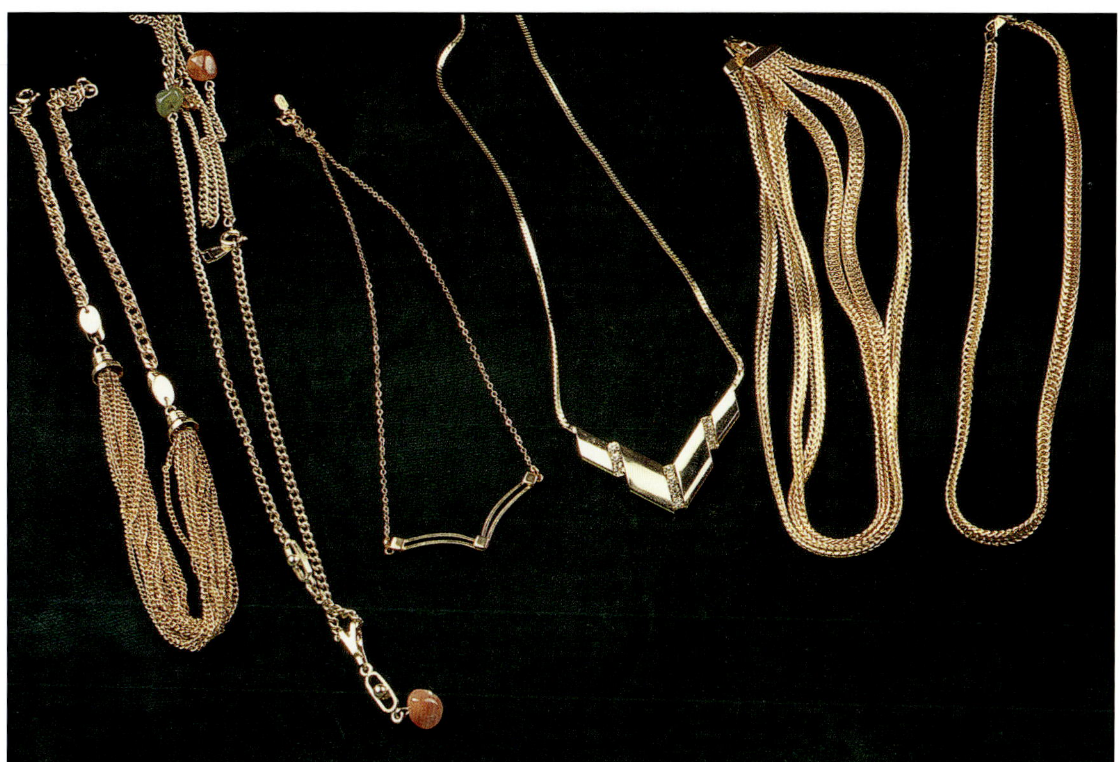

Left to right: *Glamour* necklace (8698) from 1978 is a 16-18" adjustable chain with a multi-strand front section. Very dramatic and especially glamorous. D; $10-20. *Nature's Treasure* necklace (8290) is a 19" and 34" chain combination. One has a drop while the other has stationed matching and contrasting colored beads. D; $12-25. *Gala* choker (8014) is a 16" chain attached to a 14K gold filled pendant. This necklace was part of the Lady Coventry collection in 1977. F; $10-20. *Unidentified* choker is very exquisite with a silvertone "V" shaped pendant and three slices of crystal rhinestones. A chain slides through the pendant so the length can be adapted to the costume. $20-35. *Daybreak* choker (8846) from 1984 is an exquisite trio of herringbone chains. It also came in silvertone. D; $20-35. *Dream Weaver* chain (2303) is elegant in design with a raised, smooth center. It came in 7" to 30" lengths in 1983. F; $15-30. *Courtesy of Dawn Michael.*

Left to right: *Lavender 'n Lace* necklace (8687) from 1976 is created from oval lavender crystal stones encircled with goldentone mounting and diamond shaped goldentone filigree spacers stationed on a 54" chain. "Round the clock with Sarah." C; $10-20. *Umber Tones* necklace (8042) is this multi-tone necklace of brown, umber, and gray beads spaced by chain links on 21" adjustable choker from 1975. Matching earrings on page 108 of Oshel's Book I. C; $10-20. *Monterey* necklace (8842) actually was a combination of two chains. The one pictured is 17" with three nests of pearls stationed in the center of the chain. The other chain had multiple nests of these pearls stationed throughout the 26" length chain. B; $10-20. *Pink Lady* pendant (8830) from 1974 is made of pink glass with a tassel attached to a 24" chain. Matching ring on page 68. B; $10-25. *Jet Set* versatile pendants (8312) are from 1971 and are actually tassels that can be clasped to the matching chain. Matching pieces in Oshel's Book I: bracelet on page 129, earrings page 105, ring page 131, and pin page 99. C; $10-20. *Outer Space* pendant (8595) is a solid goldentone pendant from 1976 that truly gives an illusion of outer space on a 20-22" adjustable chain. B; $10-20.

Left to right: *Sierra* choker in flame (8549) and blue (8548). The 18" length of variegated red/ peach or green/blue beads is from 1977. B; $8-20. *Pastel Parfait Beads* in yellow (8486) and pink (8485) are from 1973. These bead necklaces also came in lilac, white, kelly green, kelly green and yellow combined, and lilac and pink combined. The 37" length could be worn long or doubled, combined with other colors, or with chains. There were matching bracelets that could be worn separately or to extend the length of the necklace. Matching earrings on page 39. B; $8-15. *Courtesy of Dawn Michael.*

Top row, left to right: *Jewelfish* pendant (8434) from 1971 is a colorful enameled and silvertone pendant. B; $15-25. *Mushroom* pendant (8125) is a combined textured and gleaming goldentone charm from 1975. B;$20-35. *Magnolia Locket* pendant (8337) is an oval goldentone charm/locket with cream sculptured ivory magnolia flower center. C; $20-35. *Jug of Wisdom* drop (8805) is from 1976. B; $10-25. *Fantasia* pendant (8985) is from 1978. The imported Austrian glass stones in this goldentone design created an eye-catching jewelry item. C; $15-30. **Bottom row, left to right:** *Expressions* pendant (2285) is from 1984. "Combine the flash of goldentone with burgundy epoxy." Very elegant. There were also matching earrings. E; $20-35. *Creamy Shell* pendant drop (2127) is from 1981. D; $20-35. *In the Swim* (8666) is from 1977 and a unique pendant created from three levels of fish. A; $10-20. *Saturn* drop (8426) is from 1976. B; $15-30. *New Image* drop (8550) from 1977 features a red rectangular wavy center on silvertone mounting. B; $10-20. *Courtesy of Dawn Michael.*

Left to right: *Exquisite Lady* necklace (8612) from 1976 is a beautiful 36" strand of simulated pearls with an exquisite pearl studded silvertone clasp. There were both clip and pierced matching earrings. C; $20-35. *Timely* necklace (8341) is a 36" silvertone chain with cylinder sections making it a timely add-on to any other necklace or pendant in 1975. C; $10-20. *Trinity* necklace (8500) from 1973 is a delicate shiny finished silvertone cross with an engraved star design. B; $10-20. *Royal Flair* pendant (8116) from 1975 is an exquisite silvertone pendant with an amethyst faceted glass stone in the center. Worn on any plain colored costume, it would catch everyone's eye. D; $20-35. *Serenade* necklace (8826) is part of a two part necklace set from 1978. This is the 32" necklace with imported German glass stones stationed with long metal sections on a silvertone chain. Matching necklace on page 118 of Oshel's Book I. D; $15-30. *Fashion Basic* chain (8852) is from 1979. The silvertone chain in 30" length can be worn with pendants, doubled, or with other chains and pendants. Also came in goldentone. B; $10-20. *Amulet* pendant (8181) from 1980 is identified as "collectibles…" because of its ability to hold charms and drops. This was no doubt a great gift for mothers and grandmothers with birthstone charms of children and grandchildren added. D; $10-20.

Fashion Frost necklaces came in 36" length with matching earrings and a variety of colors in 1976. **Left to right:** Pink/Goldentone (8327) and earrings (7327); Blue/Silvertone (8325) and earrings (7325); Beige/Goldentone (8326) and earrings (7326). There was also a Black/Silvertone set. As shown, the beads could be twisted together in a thick choker, worn separately or in any combination a costume might require. Very versatile and could be coupled with chains and other pendants. C; $15-30. *Courtesy of Dawn Michael.*

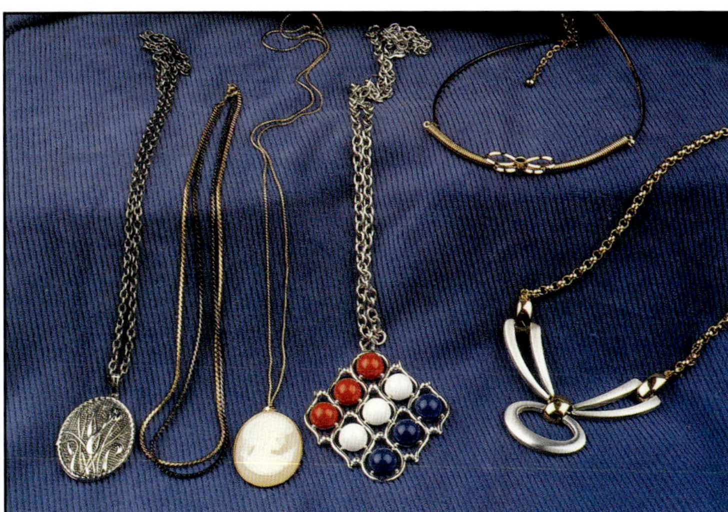

Holiday Beads are 36" strands that were coupled with silvertone or goldentone 36" chains in 1974. **Left to right:** Bermuda Blue (8896), Melon (8893), Jet Black, matching chain, Bright Blue (8895), Ice (8099), and Satin Sand (8930). B; $10-25. *Courtesy of Dawn Michael.*

Left to right: *New Summer Magic* necklace (8290) is this set of white beads in a squashed-look coupled with a goldentone chain in 1970. In the 1960s, this set was called Summer Magic and continued for nearly ten years by simply changing the name. I would guess it was very popular. This set also matched the pin and earrings on pages 30 and 34 of Oshel's Book I. B; $10-20. *Holiday Beads* from 1974 (also shown in previous picture) ranged from several colors in darker shades to many pastel shades, including this pink, blue, and lavender. B; $10-25. *Pastel Parfait Beads* (white, 8474; aqua; avocado, 8488; kelly green; pink, 8485; lilac, 8487) are from 1972. Other necklaces on page 54, matching earrings on page 39. B; $10-20. *Courtesy of Dawn Michael.*

Left to right: *Spangle-Bangles* pendants (8923 and 8105) are silvertone and goldentone examples of this versatile necklace. The 24" chain came with the plastic bangles that could be changed to coordinate with the costume color or taken off and worn as bracelets. Each necklace came with three bangles: red-white-blue, and brown-yellow-green. Very versatile and very popular in 1974. C; $10-20. *Rock Trio-hoop* necklace (8419) is from 1971 and came with the three inside pendants. As shown, any pendant, such as this *Danish Modern* pendant from 1976, could be worn on the silvertone hoop. This piece was identified for the younger customers, however, anyone could wear it. It also came with tiny pierced earrings to match each of the pendants. C; $15-30. *Courtesy of Dawn Michael.*

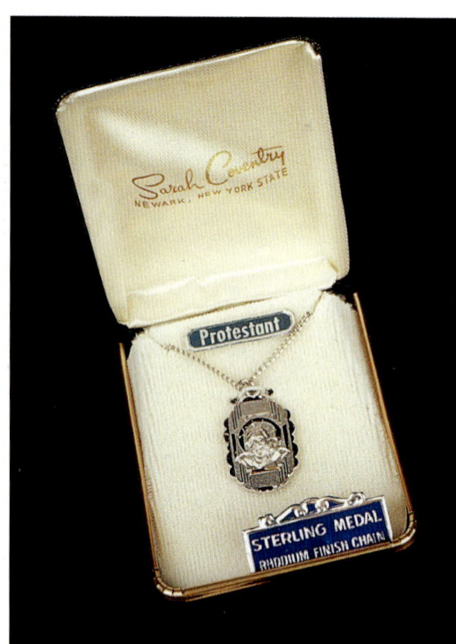

Protestant pendant was not located in any catalogs and wasn't remembered by any of the employees. It no doubt was a custom order for a conference or church group event. It is a sterling silver metal with a rhodium finish chain. The metal is engraved on the back with: "I AM A PROTESTANT." Since this is unusual, the current value may seem inflated at $35-50. *Courtesy of Marjory Ritter.*

Left to right: *Fashion Tie-up* (8549) is the tassel and was pictured in 1972 attached to an open lariat type chain. As with many of the versatile pieces of Sarah Coventry, the tassels, pendants, chains, pins, and earrings could be removed and added to another item. Here the chain is a *Silver Nugget* choker from 1977. D; $15-25. *First Star* pendant (8696) is from 1978. The 16-18" adjustable dainty silvertone chain holds the tooth shaped gleaming silvertone pendant which is centered with an imported Austrian glass stone. C; $20-35. *Zulu* choker (8334) from 1977 sports wooden beads in a variety of sizes, shapes, and colors in 16" length. "The earthy look of Sarah." D; $12-20. *Holiday Lites* choker (8456) from 1977 is a 14-16" adjustable bold silvertone chain attached to a unique pendant highlighted with imported Austrian glass stones. There was a matching bracelet. D; $20-35. *Courtesy of Marjory Ritter.*

Left to right: *Infinity Chain* (8357) is a goldentone chain combining tube links with flattened filigree circles. It came in silvertone as well. Attractive alone or coupled with a simple pendant. C; $10-20. *Pizzazz* choker (8278) from 1976 has a 14-16" adjustable silvertone chain attached to this unique variegated blue cylinder. B; $10-20. *Our Secret* pendant (8444) is a heart shaped combination of gleaming and textured goldentone on a 23" chain from 1977 "for the delicate look." C; $10-20. *Coronation* necklace from 1975 was silvertone with an amethyst stone; this is the goldentone version with the garnet prong set stone. Many times there was a change in the color of the stone and finish using the same name. D; $15-30. *Courtesy of Marjory Ritter.*

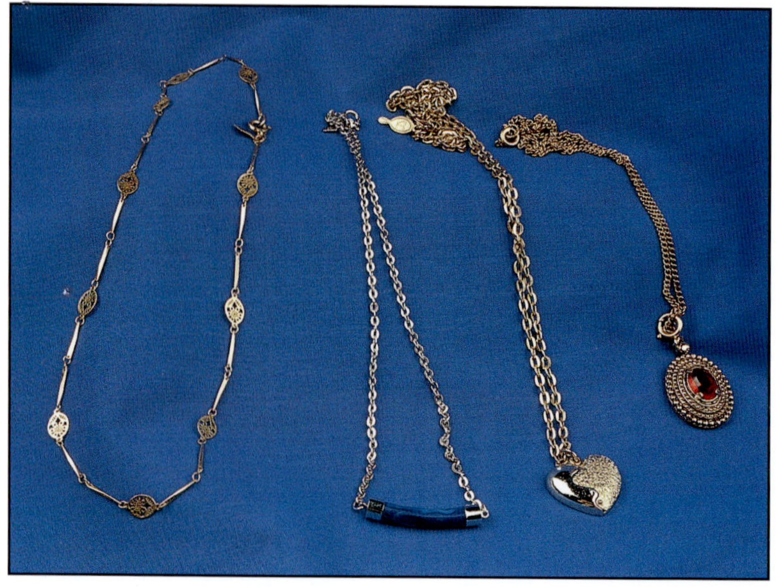

Left to right: *Rajah* drop (8405) is pictured here on a chain, however, it was sold on hand strung beads imported from Germany in 1976 (see Oshel's Book I, page 121). D; $15-30. *Nile Queen* pendant (8446) from the 1976 Holiday Jewelry Collection came in goldentone and silvertone. The link type chain is adjustable from 17-22" length. F; $15-30. *Courtesy of Allie and Jim Doyle.*

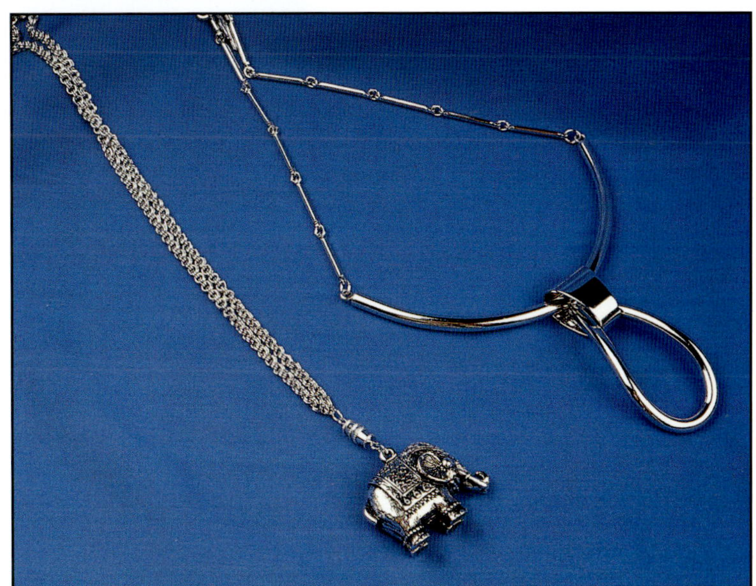

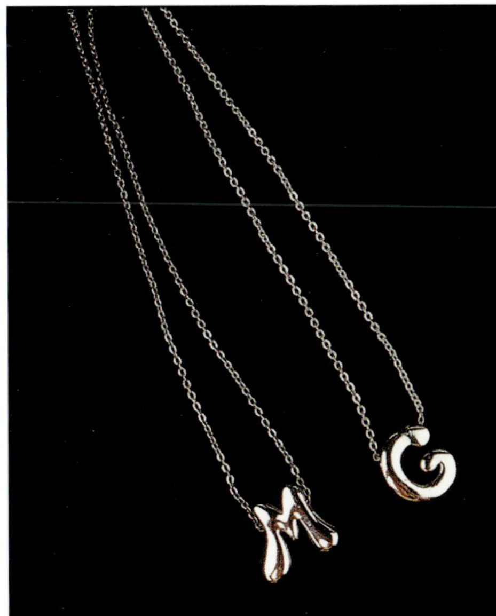

School Days Initial Pendants (0872 and 0866) were 1978 Hostess Gifts and customer items. The dainty chains were 16-18" adjustable and came in both silvertone and goldentone. B; $10-20. *Courtesy of Marlene McIlwain*

Left to right: *Samantha* choker (8955) from 1978 has a white pearlized bead in the center of a half circle of silvertone tube sections and beads attached to a linked 15-17" adjustable chain. It also came in goldentone. B; $15-30. *White Elegance* (8066) is from the late 1970s. The stationed white and goldentone beads on the chain truly create an elegance of fashion. D; $15-25. *Plum Lustre Triple Strand* necklace (8537) from 1982 is 36" long and features a simple yet elegant combination of plum colored beads separated by baroque white beads. There were also matching earrings. E; $20-35. *Raspberry Ice* necklace (8505) is from 1977. This dual chain necklace, 21" and 29" long, has raspberry beads stationed along with textured silvertone metal sections and beads, creating a striking fashion statement. D; $20-35. *Courtesy of Dawn Michael.*

Left to right: *Unidentified* necklace is a goldentone chain with stationed beads of tiger-eye shaped bells. Very unique yet simple. $10-20. *Frostfire* necklace (8943) is from 1984. "Coolly elegant frosted and faceted beads mingled with the warm glow of tiny goldentone beads." E; $15-30. *Sparkle Beauty* necklace came in 1980 with a 28" goldentone chain stationed with glass stones. There were several color choices of stones available. D; $15-25. *Unidentified* necklace of iridescent glass crystals is strikingly bold. The two strands decrease to one strand with a silvertone connection while the single strand creates the clasp section. A real collector's find. $20-35. *Oriental Mood* choker (8726) is from 1976. The 16" length is comprised of slightly curved goldentone metal sections with dark green and turquoise beads. D; $10-20. *Courtesy of Lanelle Peacock.*

Left to right: *Sterling Faith Cross* (8695) from 1977 is created from sterling and secured to a rhodium plated 16-18" adjustable chain. This was a part of the Lady Coventry collection. D; $15-25. *Jealous Heart* (8262) is a solid goldentone heart from the 1960s. Through the years, Sarah created a wide variety of hearts with a variety of names. A; $10-20. *Coventry Cameo* pendant (8427) is a 16" chain with "cameo-delicate simplicity" of white rose on blue stone. From 1980, a very delicate and artfully designed piece. C; $15-30. *Courtesy of Pat and Gary Wyatt.*

Left to right: ***Safari Necklace Beads*** (8984) from 1978 are 17" long. The rest of this necklace is on page 115 of Oshel's Book I. C; $10-20. ***Fashion Braid*** choker (8281) has a solid braid like section secured to a matching chain 18" long. It also came in silvertone in 1976. There was also a matching bracelet, barrette, and ring. C; $10-20. **On the Move** necklace (8849) was from 1977 and created from wooden and goldentone beads "adjustable on the cord." The length was 17-21" adjustable and could be worn with the beads spaced out as a long necklace or close together for a choker effect. D; $8-15. **Deep Burgundy** (8613) was from 1967. "Deep burgundy glass stones securely held by goldentone prongs will accent your costume day or night." Matching earrings on page 71, pin on page 66, and ring on page 81 of Oshel's Book I. A; $15-30. *Courtesy of Dawn Michael.*

Left to right: ***Moon Cloud*** pendant (8901) is this unique silvertone design from 1974. Matching ring on page 70. B; $10-20. ***Queen of Hearts*** choker (8567) is a genuine pewter drop stationed on a silvertone chain from 1978. C; $10-20. ***Indian Pride*** necklace (8041) is created by alternating single and multiple turquoise beads with silvertone beads to an adjustable length of 17-19". A striking necklace in 1982. G; $15-30. ***Unidentified*** necklace is this magnificent pendant with an oval multi-faceted teal glass stone mounted in a gleaming and textured dainty frame. $20-35. ***Lucky Lady*** necklace (8335) from 1976 has blue beads and glass beads stationed on a linked textured chain, 36" in length. D; $15-30. *Courtesy of Dawn Michael.*

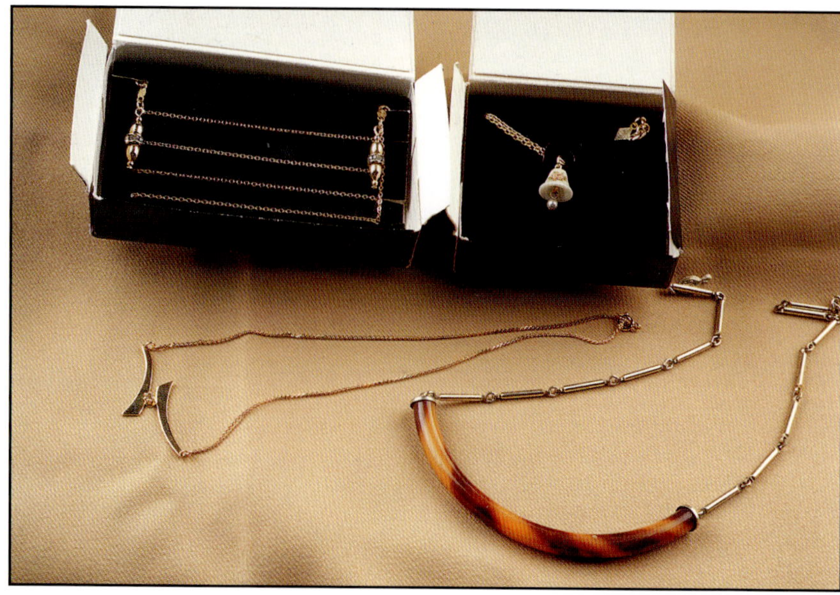

Top row, left to right: *Going My Way* necklace (8681) is from 1979. The 36" lariat has lantern shaped ends with glass stones in the center. Very attractive, yet simple. C; $15-30. *Tinkerbell* necklace (8895) is from 1984. "Strike up some fun with Tinkerbell necklace. The porcelain bell with a pink rose rings true with a simulated pearl, and swings from a goldentone cable chain." The chain was 14-16" adjustable. B; $15-25. **Bottom row, left to right:** *Starlite* choker (8850) is from 1979. The length of 15" is attached to the goldentone blades that unite in the center, focusing on the clear glass stone. There was also a matching ring. C; $10-20. *Carmel Twist* choker (8523) is from 1978. This "smiley face" curve in variegated brown plastic attached to a goldentone link chain makes a fashion statement for casual or work attire. C; $15-25. *Courtesy of Pat Wyatt.*

Left to right: *New Polonaise* choker (8956) from 1976 is shown with the matching earrings (7956). "Sarah after sundown." This choker is 14-15" in length and identical in style to the *Polonaise* pendant/pin on page 98 and dangling earring on page 105 of Oshel's Book I. F; $20-35. *Oriental Lanterns* necklace (8411) from 1979 is a 27" chain with barrel embertone and barrel lace beads stationed throughout the goldentone chain. There is a green version on page 112 of Oshel's Book I. D; $15-25.

Left to right: *Cord Belt or Necklace* (8152) from 1980 is a 43" length cord that can be worn as a belt or multiple wraps for a necklace. D; $15-30. *Hawaiian Fantasy* pendant (8450) from 1971 has a unique design created from three fish artistically shaped and attached to a heavy goldentone chain. The bronzed effect with red rhinestone eyes makes this a collector's must; however, it may be hard to find. C; $15-35. *Courtesy of Dawn Michael.*

Left to right: *Surfside* necklace is a 30" gold and white cord attached to a goldentone shell with other seashore related charms stationed on the cord. This necklace was originally $100 from 1982 and is the only one I have seen. There were earrings that matched the shell and a matching belt is shown on page 79. Today's value is difficult to estimate, especially if the owner understands the original pricing and quality of the necklace. $35-50, since it is very rare. *Rendezvous* pendant (8176) has glass beads stationed on a 32" chain with a removable tassel of chain and the same glass beads on the end. This is from the late 1970s. E; $15-25. *Autumn Trio* pendant (8247) has a goldentone filigree frame to be worn alone or with the plastic orange or brown inside. From the 1975 collection. Matching earrings on page 40. C; $15-30. *Sand Dune* choker (8513) from 1977 is a white sculptured glass stone mounted in gleaming goldentone on a 15-16" adjustable chain. C; $15-25. *Image* pendant (8028) from 1979 is attached to a 24" chain and has two interchangeable colors, cream and black, with a golden bead center or a flower shaped center which secures the necklace together. D; $15-30. *Courtesy of Dawn Michael.*

Left to right: *Heiress* lariat (8355) is 15-17" adjustable. "A regal understatement…"C; $8-15. *Starlite* choker (8850). also shown on previous page, is a 15" choker necklace with an imported Austrian glass stone from 1978-1980. C; $10-20. *Field Flower* (8039) is a 16-18" adjustable necklace from 1974. B; $10-20. *Bird of Paradise* pendant (8898) on a 24" chain is an imported German glass stone in a unique edged design. This piece from the late 70s may be difficult to locate and this is the second piece given this name. D; $15-30. *Splendor* 18" necklace (8081) came only in goldentone and was a smooth leaf shaped pendant; however, the exquisite shine gives it a textured look. The stone is imported crystal. There were fish hook pierced earrings to match. From the early 1980s. D; $15-25. *Courtesy of Dawn Michael.*

Headliner (8366) choker and necklace from the 1980s. The solid goldentone beads are bold and striking and could be worn together or separately. The choker could also double as a bracelet. G; $15-30. *Courtesy of Dawn Michael.*

Left to right: *Black Beauty* pendant (2223) from 1982 is a 24" chain with a simplistic goldentone and black inlaid pendant. E; $15-30. *Intrigue* necklace (8983) from 1984 is 30" long. "Goldentone bars accented with black epoxy and crystal baguettes merge with polished cable chain for great fashion." G; $20-45. *Instant Fashion* necklace (8204) is from 1969 and came in silvertone as well as goldentone. "Versatile chains in goldentone and silvertone combined with simulated pearls for instant fashion changes," from wearing long to doubled for evening wear fashion. B; $20-35. *Morning Blossoms* pin/pendant (8059) from 1979 is created from an imported German glass stone and attached to this 24" chain. Could also be worn as a pin. C; $15-30. *Courtesy of Dawn Michael.*

Left to right: *Unidentified* chain necklace has stationed cream colored, opaque jelly bean shaped beads secured between clear amber glass beads. I cannot determine the time frame for this necklace as this style was repeated frequently throughout the thirty-five years of Sarah's existence. $15-30. *Indian Summer* necklace (8045) is from 1979. Stationed multi-colored cylinders of varying colors on a 36" length silvertone chain reflect the first changes of color in the fall. C; $15-25. *Unidentified* pendant is a simple jet crystal stone nestled in a filigree cone attached to a silvertone chain. $15-25. *Sierra* (2243) is a 16-20" adjustable necklace created from eight strands of contrasting and coordinating beads. This 1982 necklace can be worn as shown or twisted into the look of one strand. Original price $48. I believe this necklace will be difficult to find so value is higher, $25-45. *Unidentified* chain is fashioned from cylinder links alternating with flattened circle links. Could be worn long or as a choker doubled. $10-20. *Sierra* pendant (8062) is from 1979 and not to be confused with the item above. The oval shape has cream and golden orange enameled sections attractively mounted in gleaming silvertone and secured to a silvertone 15-17" adjustable chain. C; $15-30. *Hi 'N Low Lariat* necklace (8151) is actually two necklaces: a 37" necklace and a 29" lariat. The brown glass stones are stationed on a uniquely fashioned goldentone chain from 1980. D; $15-30. *Courtesy of Dawn Michael.*

Left to right: **Cinnamon Swirl** necklace (8074) from 1980 has an adjustable chain on a 16-18" bead strand. D; $10-20. **Cinema** pendant (8406) is a 30" chain from 1980, with a removable and reversible drop. Tortoise-tone on one side and eggshell on the other. This is a dynamic pendant with the goldentone casing on the drop matching the links in the chain. D; $15-25. **Cosmopolitan** pendant (8137) on a delicate 16-18" chain is from 1980. The drop is a glass stone set in a gleaming goldentone mounting which could be removed from the chain. D; $15-25. **Lucky Lady** necklace (8373) is a 30" chain with stationed "Shamrock-green stones, for a lucky lady" from 1981. C; $10-20. **Dew Drop** pendant (0820) is from 1978 and fastened on a 17" nylon cord. This was an item on the Hostess Bonus list for 1350 points and identified as for men or women. $10-20. **Mint Delight** lariat (8241) is from 1980 and is 24" in length with the set able to slide where desired. E; $10-20. *Courtesy of Dawn Michael.*

Left to right: **Gentle Moods** choker (8053) from 1980 is created from simulated pearls and half-moon goldentone stationed on a dainty goldentone chain. B; $10-20. **Promenade** necklace (8056) was actually two necklaces. This one from 1979 has a nest of three pearl-like beads stationed in the center of a 17" chain. The other chain was 26" with the same beads stationed throughout the entire length. C; $10-20. **Victorian Bouquet** pendant (8111) is on a 16-18" adjustable chain and from 1975-76. A very dainty pendant in contrast to the other necklaces pictured here. Rest of the set on page 30. B; $8-15. **Bernie the Frog** pendant (8200) from 1975 is on a 29" chain and identified as "nature's friends." C; $10-20. **Golden Coin** pendant (8237) from 1975 is a unique coin design also duplicated in matching earrings. C; $10-20. **Tapestry** (5391) from 1973 is a hand painted design unique to Sarah and doesn't have any other pieces to match. B; $10-18.

Left to right: *Krackle Beads* (8338) from 1980 came in several colors. There was also a yellow set. The 36" length allowed for versatility. B; $15-30. **Sara-Zade** necklace (8293) from 1970 is similar to the Sultana design but with a detached frame of gleaming goldentone. The shiny geometric embedded pieces and tiny chaton cut rhinestones of varying pastel colors give this piece a look of elegance. Matching earrings on page 42 of Oshel's Book I. B; $15-30. **Devotion** pendant (8577) in goldentone is from 1978. It also came in silvertone in the men's collection. Engraved on the back: "God grant me the serenity to accept the things I cannot change, the courage to change the things I can, and the wisdom to know the difference." B; $10-20. *Courtesy of Dorothy DeMay.*

Left to right: *Unidentified* necklace is marked "SC". It is unique in its slightly curved, opaque white slender sets mounted on a silvertone chain. $10-20. **Pink Parfait** necklace (8057) from 1980 is a 33" chain with pink circular glass stones stationed throughout. There was a second chain of 36" in the set. "Pretty pink, hugged by Goldentone…" E; $15-30. **Desert Scene** pendant (8543) is from 1978. The unique enameling on the goldentone oval shape depicts a scene from the desert, as its name suggests. Very popular. C; $10-20. **Unidentified** pendant/pins pictured here are designed like a coat-of-arms chevron. One has a goldentone finish and the other an antiqued look, otherwise they are the same. The red rhinestones for the eyes are glass stones. They are marked "SC" and my guess is that they were created for a custom event locally, since they were found in the Newark, New York area. $20-35. *Courtesy of Marjory Ritter.*

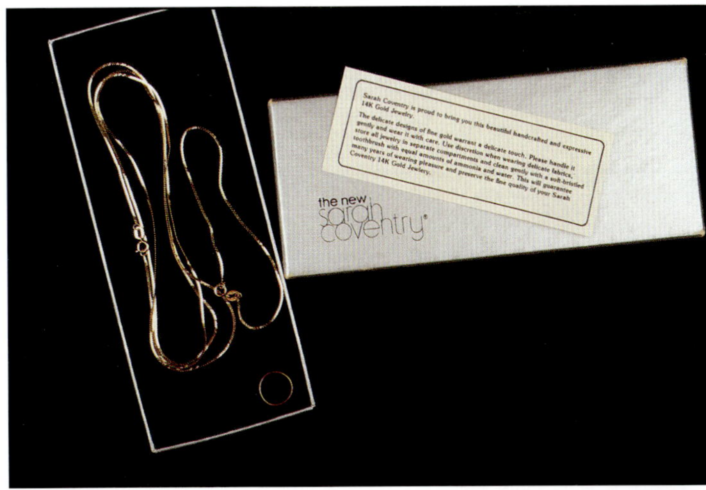

Fine "C" Chain (3359) is a 20" 14K gold chain from 1984. The bracelet is a 7" matching chain (3362). This was part of the New Sarah Coventry's effort to introduce expensive fashion and "real" jewelry to the line. These 14K gold chains were $80 for the necklace and $30 for the bracelet. There is no signature tag or mark to indicate Sarah Coventry, so unless in a box like this one, you will not know its authenticity. $20-35. *Courtesy of Marjory Ritter.*

Five examples from the New Sarah Coventry collection. This "14K gold-filled jewelry, also known as overlay…merges a layer of 14K gold with a layer of base metal to produce the look and feel of gold, at very affordable prices." **Left to right:** *Genuine Jade apple charm*; *Snowflake* (8733) "nature's most unique design in goldentone, accented by sparkling crystal chatons." This necklace pendant, along with a few other pieces, was from the Holiday Edition Christmas flyer for 1984, which in effect was perhaps the last catalog for Sarah Coventry as the doors closed at the end of 1984; *Genuine tiger eye heart*; *Flight* (8816) from 1984. "Fashion takes flight on the crystal wings of this delicate goldentone pendant"; and *blue lapis stone butterfly shape*. Original prices $15-35. Current value: $15-30. There were no marks on the charms, so unless found in an original box, they will be difficult to identify. *Courtesy of Pat Wyatt.*

Left to right: *Primrose* pendant (8073) and necklace (8075) are from 1980. The pendant with its removable drop is on a 24-30" adjustable chain. The necklace has the same kind of scored red beads in smaller proportions and various designs, as well as goldentone spiral beads stationed on a heavier chain. Matching earrings on page 37. Each was priced separately originally: D; $10-20 separately. *Egyptian Goddess* necklace (8139) is also from 1980. It has stationed reversible red leaves with solid goldentone on the back. The linked style chain gives a truly Egyptian flavor. D; $15-30. *Unidentified* pendant is a 3-dimensional red glass apple with goldentone stem and leaf. $10-25. *Trade Winds* necklace is 30" long and from 1982. It was created with a large red hand-painted cloisonné bead stationed on a fine chain, plus smaller red beads attached as a tassel and stationed along the chain near the clasp. "Whenever the trade winds blow, you can wear this colorful necklace fashioned from goldentone Boston links." E; $15-30. *Courtesy of Dawn Michael.*

Four rings, none marked, from a former employee. The first is **Dainty Combo** (5056-5060), sized from 5-9 with a genuine aventurine set and two glass stones on either side. E; $15-25. **Unidentified** second ring was a test ring given to office staff and employees to wear and abuse to determine durability. **Birthstone Duet** ring (5085) from 1980 was very short-lived because of problems in verifying the stones and the sheer number of glass stones involved. "Create your exclusive design with two stones from Sarah Coventry's elegant collection of glass birthstones. A special order form is required." C; $15-25. The fourth ring is **Autumn Haze** (5507) from 1975. C; $10-20. All of these rings were very special remembrances of the employee, who also received this 5-year pin containing an actual ruby stone. The 20-year pins held diamond stones. *Courtesy of Marlene McIlwain.*

Back row, left to right: *First Lady* ring was marked as SAC and is from the early years. Matching bracelet on page 72. $10-20. **Genuine Opal** ring (5880) has an opal set in a goldentone prong mounting. This was one of the Lady Coventry pieces from the 1970s. F; $10-25. **Garland** (2280-2282) from 1984 is identified as epoxy. D; $10-25. **Locket** ring (5510) from 1974. B; $8-15. **Front row, left to right:** *Victoria Blue* ring is from the early 1970s. B; $15-25. **Blue Lady** (5393) from 1974. B; $8-15. **Kathleen** is from the early 1960s. "Sparkling, fiery rhinestones paved in a sunburst design and centered around a brilliant emerald-type stone make a truly glamorous evening piece." The ring was not sized. Matching pin on page 27 and earrings on page 84 of Oshel's Book I, *Sarah Coventry Jewelry*. A; $20-35. **Jade 'n Pearl** ring (5610) is a cultured pearl and jade adjustable goldentone ring from 1976 in the Lady Coventry collection. E; $15-25. *Courtesy of Dawn Michael.*

Left to right: *Trulove* (5174-5180) is a sterling ring sized 4-10 with a glass stone from 1968. C; $15-30. *Cleopatra Perfumed* ring (5217) in goldentone from 1969. " A beautiful combination of fine fashion jewelry and a hauntingly beautiful fragrance that lingers long after you've left. The perfect gift to give or to receive." B; $10-20. *Yesterday* (5394) from 1974. B; $8-15.*Elegant* (5172) is an appropriate name for this large goldentone ring covered with tiny rhinestones in sectioned diamond crevices. From the mid-70s. C; $15-25. *Courtesy of Dawn Michael.*

Back row, left to right: *First Choice* ring (5601-5605) was sized from 5-9 in 1984. D; $10-25. *2 Ct. Cubic Zirconium* in 14K gold-filled settings. Sized from 5-7 in 1983. Original price $30. Current value $20-40 since few were made and they will be difficult to find. *Michelle* (5744) is a dainty heart shape with minute rhinestones in goldentone from 1977. B; $10-18. *Sterling Pearl* (5297-5309) from 1972 is a sized sterling ring with simulated pearl prong set. "Ring your fingers in glamour." C; $10-20. **Front row, left to right:** *Danish Modern* ring is a bold silvertone circle with turquoise enameled sections. B; $15-30. *Indian Princess* (5737) from 1977 has blue and red glass oval stones in a wide silvertone mounting. B; $10-20. *Genie* (5164) is an adjustable goldentone band with interchangeable stones easily removed to match any color of costume. In Sarah's early years, versatility was part of its uniqueness. This ring was from 1968. B; $10-18. *Courtesy of Dawn Michael.*

Left to right: *Coraline* (5495) ring has matching earrings and a pin/pendant on page 29 and is from 1974. A very striking coral stone attractively mounted in goldentone. B; $10-20. *Jonquil* (5518) is a handsome, wide, adjustable goldentone band with an ember colored glass stone encircled by tiny crystal rhinestones. B; $10-20. *Contessa* (5608) from 1976 is part of the matching set on page 26. The stone is very similar to what in Mexico is called the fire opal, however, no mention of this is given with the description from the catalogs. C; $15-30. *Courtesy of Marlene McIlwain.*

Back row, left to right: *Unidentified* ring may be one of the rings created after the sale of the name in 1984. $8-15. *Natasha* ring (0210) from 1979 is very similar to several open designs with glass crystal rhinestones. B: $15-30. *Moon Glo* ring (5850) is a mother-of-pearl shell stone in goldentone setting from 1980. B; $10-20. *Unidentified* ring is a spectacular long oval goldentone shape with a mauve colored glistening stone in the center. $15-30. **Front row, left to right:** *Sultana* is a solid goldentone ring with raised geometric goldentone shapes and pastel rhinestones recessed. Matching necklace on page 46 and earrings on page 73 of Oshel's Book I. The set began in the late 1960s and was carried through the 70s as a Hostess Bonus gift. This ring may be difficult to locate. B; $10-20. *Starstruck* (2186) is a sized ring from 1984. D; $15-25. *Sea Treasure* (5328) from 1973. B; $10-20. *Cameo Lady* (5462) from 1974 is pictured upside down. B; $10-20. *Courtesy of Dawn Michael.*

Back: *Golden Nugget* is a large goldentone nugget shape mounted on a SarahGlo goldentone adjustable ring from late 1960s. B; $10-25. **Front row, left to right:** *Unidentified* ring is a silvertone oval mint green framed in scallops. $10-20. *Unidentified* ring has bold goldentone ribbed mounting with a large robin's egg blue cabochon set. $10-20. *Two-Tone Stackable Rings* (22174-2179) are a set of three rings in either goldentone or silvertone, sized 5-7 in 1981. Matching bracelet on page 75. C; $10-20. *Night Lights* (2158-2160) from 1982 came in sizes 6-8. This was considered part of the New Sarah. E; $20-45. *Courtesy of Dawn Michael.*

Left to right: *Roxanne* was found only in the 1979 catalog as a Hostess Bonus ring worth 2450 points. Points were acquired by the hostess for customers present, purchases made, and parties booked. This is an elegant yet simple genuine jade stone surrounded by a goldentone frame. It is a non-adjustable ring. $15-30. *Jet Set* (5723) has an imported Austrian glass hematite stone and matches a bracelet and small pendant from 1978. There is another set with the same name. B; $8-18. *Camelot* (5224) was from 1969 and also came in silvertone. This exquisite ring has three rows of tiny glass crystal rhinestones. B; $10-18. *Jonquil* (5518) is a wide adjustable goldentone band with an ember colored glass stone encircled by tiny crystal rhinestones from 1978. B; $10-20. *Courtesy of Dawn Michael.*

Back row, left to right: *Dazzler* (5520) from 1974. C; $10-20. *Unidentified* ring is similar to some others, however, this one has a teardrop shaped pink cabochon set mounted in an open-weave metal accented with clear crystal rhinestones. $15-30. *Unidentified* ring is a silvertone mounting of a jet black faceted prong set stone. The clear rhinestones completely circling the black set create a magnificent contrast. $20-35. *Debutante* (5464) from 1973. "Gleaming pearls and sparkling rhinestones for that special occasion look." There was a set of matching earrings as well. B; $10-20. **Second row, left to right:** *Satin Elegance* (5513) from 1974. B; $10-20. *Princess* (5488) ring is an attractive "gleaming silvertone combined with pearls (simulated) and sparkling rhinestones." This ring is from the early 1970s. Matching earrings on page 110 and pendant on page 122 of Oshel's Book I. B; $10-20. *Stardust* (5461) is from 1974. C; $10-25. *Starlite* (5499) has a glass stone and is adjustable, from 1978. B; $10-20. **Third row, left to right:** *Jet Navette* (5378) from 1974 has an exquisite glass stone with smaller rhinestones on either side. B; $10-20. *Golden Ice* (5222) from 1969. B; $10-20. *Unidentified* ring is the same as second from left on top row with a more coral colored set. $15-30. *Hemisphere* (5312-5316) from 1981 is a sized ring from 5-9 with glass stones. E; $15-30. **Fourth row, left to right:** *Sea Treasure* (5328) is from 1972 with a simulated pearl and crystal rhinestone. B; $10-20. *Desire* (5463) from the mid-1970s. C; $10-20. *Lagoon* (5496) from 1974. C; $10-20. *Galaxy* (5750) from 1977. C; $10-20. **Front row, left to right:** *Unidentified* ring is an intaglio golden gladiator carved into black jet stone mounted on silvertone. $15-30. *Elite* (5747) from 1977. B; $8-15. *Courtesy of Allie and Jim Doyle.*

Back row, left to right: *Enchantment* (5502) from 1974. B; $10-20. *Coraline* (5495) from 1974. Matching pin and earrings on page 29. B; $10-20. *Pink Lady* (5500) from 1974. Matching pendant on page 47. B; $10-20. *Starry Nights* (5769) from 1978 has imported Austrian glass stones. C; $15-25. **Front row, left to right:** *Unidentified* ring is bold silvertone covered with clear rhinestones. Very dazzling. $15-30. *Illusive* (5530) ring from 1975 is antiqued silvertone with pearl and clear rhinestones. B; $10-20. *Yesterday* (5394) from 1974. B; $8-15. *Coronation* (5566) is a spectacular bright red glass rhinestone prong set in antiqued goldentone setting. Matching bracelet and pendant on page 29. *Courtesy of Dawn Michael.*

Back row, left to right: *Dazzler* (5520) from 1974. C; $8-15. *Gleaner* was a Hostess Bonus gift worth 3100 points and was created from Austrian glass stones in 1978. $10-20. *Capri* (5505) from 1974. B; $10-20. *Cameo Lady* (5462) from 1974 is upside down and had a matching pendant. B; $10-20. **Front row, left to right**: *Unidentified* ring has a simulated pearl offset by two crystal rhinestones. $15-30. A ring from the *Royal Crown* set. The underlying ruby colored stone peeks through the swirling goldentone. C: $15-30. *Vintage* (5467) from 1974. B; $8-15. *Unidentified* ring is a bold goldentone open-weave ring. Matching necklace on page 23. $15-30. *Courtesy of Dawn Michael.*

Back row, left to right: *Star Shine* (0944-0949) was a sized Hostess Bonus gift worth 1600 points. It has a genuine opal and imported Austrian glass stones from 1978. $15-30. *Mother of Pearl Cameo* (5229-5241) is from 1973 Lady Coventry collection. The ring is sterling silver and the cameo is carved from mother-of-pearl stone. Matching necklace and earrings on page 88 of Oshel's Book I. D; $10-20. *Tapestry* (5391) from 1973 is a hand painted design unique to Sarah and doesn't have any other pieces to match. B; $10-18. *Over the Rainbow* (5265) is from 1971 and created from an iridescent, aurora borealis stone. Matching earrings on page 40. B; $10-18. *Caress* (5534) is from 1978 and came in silvertone (shown here) and goldentone (shown on page 70). A; $5-10. **Front row, left to right**: *Carnelian Cameo* ring (5430-5442) was a sized ring from 4-7, 12K gold filled and a part of the Golden Collection created in 1974. There was also a matching pendant. Original price $22. Because of its rarity, current value is $20-40. *Indian Maiden* (5481) is from 1974. Matching pieces on page 28. B; $10-18. *Love Story* (5477) from 1973-1976 has imported Austrian glass stones. Matching pendant and earrings on page 124 of Oshel's Book I. B; $8-15. *Spanish Lites* (5665) is from 1976 and features a red oval cabochon stone nestled in a unique scroll design on a wide silvertone band. B; $10-20. *Courtesy of Pat Wyatt and Amanda Wyatt's hand.*

Left to right: *Vogue* (2277-2279) from 1984 was identified as epoxy, meaning painted like enamel. C;$10-25. *Crimson* (5322-5324) is a sized 6-8 ring from 1981. The bright glass stone is prong set in goldentone and very striking. D; $15-30. *Marie* (5675) is from 1976 with a red cabochon and tiny pearls. B; $8-15. *Unidentified* jade ring is offset in the goldentone slim mounting. $10-20. *Festive* (5798) is a stunning ember glass stone set in an exquisite goldentone mounting from 1979. Matching necklace on page 52. C; $15-30. *Courtesy of Dawn Michael.*

Left to right: *Wildflower* (5766) is from 1978. B; $10-20. *Vintage* (5467) is a unique grapes and leaves ring from 1974. B; $10-20. *Regina* (5858) is from 1979 and came in silvertone and goldentone. B; $8-15. *Blue Moonlet* (5330) is from 1973 and was identified with others as "Ring your fingers in glamour." B; $10-20. *Sport* (5615) is an adjustable ring in sizes 4-6 sporting a tennis racket for the avid tennis player. These rings were promoted in 1976. B; $10-20. *Courtesy of Arcadia Historical Society*

Back row, left to right: *Scandia* (5764) from 1978. B; $8-15. *Cleopatra* (5329) from 1973 has matching bracelet and earrings on page 26. B; $10-25. *Images* (5468) from 1974. B; $8-15. *Heritage* (5727) from 1976. C; $10-20. *Locket* ring (5510) from 1974 does open for displaying pictures. B; $8-15. **Front row, left to right**: *Fieldflowers* (5795) from 1978. B; $5-10. *Jet Navette* (5378) from 1974 has an exquisite glass stone with smaller rhinestones on either side. B; $10-20. *Ingrid* (5725) from 1976 may be hard to find. B; $10-25. *Moonmist* (5721) from 1976 B; $10-25. *Courtesy of Pat Wyatt and Amanda Wyatt's hand.*

Back row, left to right: *Citation* (5486) from 1974. B; $8-15. *Camelot* was a Hostess Bonus gift for 1900 points in 1978. It was sized 5-10 with imported Austrian glass stones. $12-25. *Caress* (5534) came in silvertone (see page 69) as well as goldentone in 1976. A; $5-10. *Cameo Lady* (5462) is from 1974 and had a matching pendant. B; $10-25. *Moon Cloud* (5492) is from 1974. Matching pendant on page 59. B; $10-25. **Front row, left to right:** *Blue Feather* (5664) from 1980. B; $10-20. *Buckle* (5063) shown here in silvertone also came in goldentone in 1980. B; $5-10. *Sugarplum* (5746) from 1977. B; $8-15. *Ember Beauty* (5768) has an imported German glass stone and is from 1978. B; $10-20. *Courtesy of Pat Wyatt and Amanda Wyatt's hand.*

Left to right: *Moon River* (0985) was a Hostess Bonus dinner ring of imported Austrian glass stones requiring 2600 points in 1978. $15-30. *Alexandria* (5643) in goldentone from 1976. C; $8-15. *Sarah's Traditional Birthstone* ring (5323) is peridot for August. The mounting was sterling silver, with imported glass stones in adjustable style. C; $8-15. *Aztec Treasure* (5762) has turquoise-like diamond shaped stones mounted on a wider silvertone band. B; $10-20. *Blue Moonlet* (5330) from 1973. B; $8-15. *Oriental Melody* (5791) from 1978 with unique jade-like set on goldentone mounting. B; $8-15. *Courtesy of Pat and Gary Wy*

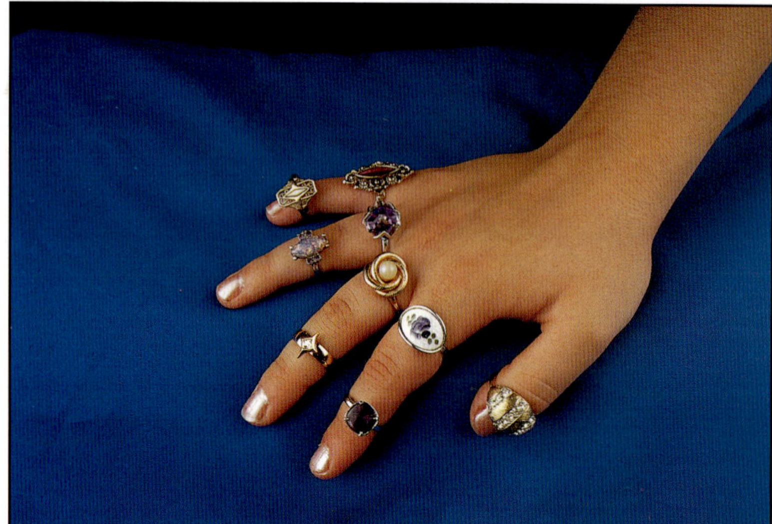

Left side, top to bottom: *Regina* (5858) from 1979 has a unique setting in goldentone in an adjustable ring. B; $8-15. *Contessa* is a stone similar to a fire opal and matches the pin, bracelet, and earrings on page 26. B; $10-20. *Morning Star* (5761) is an imported Austrian glass stone found in 1978. B; $8-15. *Deep Purple* (5672) from 1976. B; $8-15. **Right side, top to bottom:** *Yesterday* (5392) is from 1974. B; $8-15. *Sarah's Birthstone Ring* (5317) for February from early 1973. Many of these birthstone items were carried over three to four years. C; $10-20. *Lover's Knot* (5221) in goldentone is from 1969. B; $8-15. *Melissa* (5781) is from 1978. Matching necklace on page 49. C; $8-15. *Camelot* (5224) from 1969 with its unique rows of glass crystal stones also came in silvertone. B; $10-20. *Courtesy of Pat Wyatt and Amanda Wyatt's hand.*

Top row, left to right: *Sarah's Birthstone Ring* (5145) from 1971 is for August in peridot. "For centuries, birthstone rings have been a symbol of happiness and good fortune for the wearer. We present Sarah's sterling silver birthstone rings with imported glass stones." B; $8-15. *Unidentified* ring sports a rather large faceted clear rhinestone with a checked effect. $10-20. *Ballerina* ring (5159) was found in 1969 catalog. B; $10-20. *Shell* ring (5377-5379) is a sized 5-7 ring from 1981. C; $8-15. **Middle row, left to right:** *Misty* (5653) from 1977. C; $10-20. *Curved Arrow* (5681) from 1977. B; $5-10. *Fire Lite* (5676) from 1976. Matching necklace on page 112 of Oshel's Book I. C; $10-18. *Genuine Sodalite* (5714) adjustable ring. The blue sodalite set is missing. C; $8-15. **Bottom row, left to right:** *Charity* (5565) from 1977. A; $5-10. *Jade 'n Pearl* ring (5610) is a cultured pearl and jade adjustable goldentone ring from the 1976 Lady Coventry collection. B; $15-25. *Odyssey* (5038) from 1980 has a center glass stone. B; $8-15. *Mother of Pearl Cameo* (5229-5241) is a sterling silver ring from the Lady Coventry collection from 1973-1976. Matching pendant and earrings on page 88 of Oshel's Book I. D; $10-20. *Courtesy of Pat and Gary Wyatt.*

Back row, left to right: *Gay Pretenders* (5122) "A delicate ring in a captivating design with stones so real looking it's hard to believe they're jade pretenders. So much sheer fashion for so little…From Morn' til Night they're fashion right." This ring is from before 1966 and of SarahGlo goldentone. A; $10-20. *Pink Lady* (5500) from 1974. B; $10-20. **Front row, left to right:** *Sweet Briar* (5535) from 1976. B; $8-15. *Suzette* is a fire opal set in a striking goldentone mounting. B; $10-20. *Misty* (5653) from 1976. C; $10-20. *Unidentified* ring is an oval goldentone with exquisite mauve colored gleaming stone. $15-30. *Unidentified* ring is a jet black oval with golden maiden in cameo relief fashion. $20-35. *Starlite* (5799) is an adjustable glass stone ring from 1981. B; $8-15. *Indian Princess* is a silvertone band with red and turquoise-looking cabochon sets. B; $10-20. *Confetti* (5111) is from before 1966 . "Sparkling, twinkling colored lights glistening in a shiny silvery sky give a look of gayety, happiness, and good times." Matching earrings on page 41 of Oshel's Book I. B; $10-20. *Courtesy of Pat Wyatt and Amanda Wyatt's hand.*

Left to right: *Mediterranean* (5770) from 1978 is an imported German glass stone. B; $10-20. *Ambrosia* (5728) from 1976 may be difficult to find. C; $10 20. *Continental* (0981) with black set was a Hostess Bonus worth 600 points in 1978. $10-20. *Love Story* (5469-5480) (three birthstone rings) are from 1973 through the late 1970s. These were popular adjustable rings created from imported Austrian glass stones mounted in sparkling silvertone settings. There were also ensembles including matching pendants and pierced earrings. Matching pendant and earrings on page 124 of Oshel's Book I. B; $8-15. **Thumb:** *Sarah Coventry's Family Bouquet* ring (5570-5582). "This fashionable and unique ring is custom set with your personally selected birthstones, each representing someone close to you. Create your exclusive design with 7 stones…if you desire fewer than 7 birthstones, a crystal clear stone is available to complete your selection." The goldentone setting was mounted on a 14K gold-filled shank. This ring originally was $50 in the mid to late 70s. The rings I have found were not in very good condition, which tells me that the mothers who had them wore them a lot. $5-20. **Back row, right:** *Antique Bouquet* (5379) from 1973. B; $8-15. *Age of Aquarius* ring (5360) is from 1970 and part of a pin and earrings set shown on page 24. B; $10-20. *Zuni* (5636) from 1976. B; $8-15. *Julia* was a sized ring from 1979 given as a Hostess Bonus worth 3300 points. It had genuine opals and imported Austrian glass stones. It no doubt will be difficult to find. $15-30. *Courtesy of Pat Wyatt and Amanda Wyatt's hand.*

Clockwise, from top left: *Duo Fashion* ring (5773) from 1978 is a simple white ring of two oval sets, hence its name. B; $10-20. *Golden Embers* (5161) is from 1967. "Designed to match the necklace or to wear alone. Adds a finishing look of fashion to your costume before or after 5." This ring is goldentone with a large amber glass stone. B; $10-25. *Sugarplum* (5746) is from 1978 and has a purple stone offset in an oval silvertone setting. B; $10-20.

These three rings are identified with the Sarah Coventry name inside the rings, however, they do not have the quality of the 1980s rings. I believe they were part of the interim company utilizing the Sarah Coventry name from 1984 to 2003. Be careful in purchasing items with the Sarah Coventry mark or other identification. *Courtesy of Pat and Gary Wyatt.*

Back row, left to right: *Cameo Lady* (5462) is from 1974 and had a matching pendant. B; $10-25. *Spring Fever* (5734) is from 1978 and matched the Summer Scheme necklace on pages 42 and 49. B; $8-15. *Serenity* (5611-5612) came in goldentone and silvertone. Matching necklace on page 138 of Oshel's Book I. B; $8-15. *Dusk* (5514) is a unique ring with dark gray and lighter gray pearl (simulated) sets separated by crystal rhinestones. A dynamic ring set in silvertone to be worn day or night but for sure at dusk in 1975. B; $10-20. *Wings of Fashion* ring is from the mid-1970s. B; $15-30. *Taffy* (5400) is a large cream colored stone encased in a cage of goldentone mounting from 1973. B; $10-20. **Front row, left to right:** *Locket* ring (5510) from 1974. B; $8-15. *Elite* (5747) modestly sports two gray oval cabochon sets in an elongated silvertone design from 1978. B; $10-20. *Misty* (5653) from 1977. C; $10-20. *Blue Night* (5673) is a blue set in silvertone with unique mounting on either side of the Austrian glass stone. I found this ring in only 1976 catalogs. B; $10-20. *Rosette* (5341) is from 1972 and had a matching pendant and earrings. B; $10-20.

Left to right: *Evening Sands* bracelet is from the early 1960s. The floral links are textured goldentone with a center stripe of clear glass rhinestones. There was a matching necklace and earrings. A; $20-35. *Fashion Rope* bracelet (9640) is goldentone. It also came in silvertone in 1977 in 7-3/4" length. B; $10-20. *Daybreak* bracelet (2004) is a 7" bracelet in goldentone from 1982. There was a matching necklace and earrings set. E; $15-25. *Tempo* bracelet (9291) is a combination of goldentone oval shaped links and three simulated pearls. Very classic and simple in 1976. B; $10-20. *Unidentified* bracelet is a very dainty goldentone chain with clear faceted glass crystals stationed throughout. $15-30. *Courtesy of Dawn Michael.*

Far left: *First Lady* bracelet is from before 1966. The exquisite three strands of simulated pearls are attached to a silvertone circle with a large glass crystal in the center surrounded by smaller crystals. The look of "real" jewelry good enough for any First Lady. There was also a matching necklace. **Top:** *Highlight* hinged cuff bracelet (2028) from 1982 is an exquisite goldentone overlapping bracelet. There were matching earrings. E; $20-35. **Bottom:** *Little Love* bracelet from 1970 with a different charm attached. Many charms were available to be mixed and matched on young girls' bracelets. A; $10-20. **Next to far right:** *Sultana* bracelet (9768) is from the early 1960s. "The royal jewels of the Sultan were sprinkled lavishly on this colorful and romantic bracelet. Designed to enhance…and add fashion color to any costume." Electroplated gold with glass crystal rhinestones. Matching necklace on page 46 and earrings on page 73 of Oshel's Book I, *Sarah Coventry Jewelry.* A; $20-35. **Far right:** *Victorian Blue* bracelet (9197) is from 1975. This exquisitely designed goldentone bracelet sports dark blue cabochon oval stones separated by sections of two simulated pearls. Matching pendant on page 116, necklace on page 112, and ring on page 134 of Oshel's Book I. There were also matching earrings. C; $20-35.

Left to right: *Egyptian Temptress* bracelet has vertical teardrop shapes of goldentone cut from a solid piece of metal utilizing both textured and gleaming finish. Small gold balls dot the inside of each shape and accent the ends of each of the connection pieces. This is from the early 1960s. Matching earrings on page 41 of Oshel's Book I. A; $25-35. *Fancy Free* bracelet (9398) is from the early 1960s. "Gleaming, shining SarahSheen silvertone sparkling at your wrist." Matching earrings on page 40 of Oshel's Book I. There is also a matching necklace (see page 22) and several other sets with the same name. A; $20-35. *Dazzling Aurora* bracelet is from the early 1960s, identified from a cardex. The silvertone gleaming finish of the flowers encases five glass red aurora borealis stones hinged together to create an amazing fashion statement. Matching pin and earrings on page 17 of Oshel's Book I. A; $30-50. *Sabrina Fair* bracelet is a "rare collection of Sabrina stones assembled" to create this "appealing and feminine" piece of jewelry, with "each Sabrina stone tenderly guarded by sparkling chatons." Matching necklace on page 47 and ring on page 53 of Oshel's Book I. Matching earrings on page 37 of this book. A; $35-50.

Left to right: *Town and Country* bracelet (9757) is from the early 1960s. "…for the woman who loves distinctive jewelry. The wide bracelet, so much in demand, beautifully and tastefully designed to wrap your wrist in fashion." SarahSheen goldentone. Matching earrings on page 39. B; $20-35. *Butterfly Lace* bracelet (9913) is an early piece too. "The wide contour cuff bracelet designed in gleaming goldentone butterfly lace design. Wide in appearance and yet feather-light to wear because of its lacy design." SarahSheen goldentone. Matching earrings on page 41 of Oshel's Book I. B; $25-35. *Coffee and Cream* bracelet (9714) from 1973 is an exquisitely carved ivory and brown solid bracelet. Matching cream bracelet on pages 75 and 76. B; $25-40. **Lower right:** *Betsy* bracelet (9041) is from 1980. This 6-1/4" delicate silvertone chain with a tiny turquoise bead in silvertone circle was listed as "kid stuff." There was also a matching ring. B; $8-15. *Courtesy of Pat Wyatt.*

Left to right: *Bird of Happiness* (9345) is a little girl's bracelet from 1973. There was a matching necklace that carried over to the 1980s. A; $10-20. *Tailored Accent* bracelet (9590) is from 1976. There was a matching necklace/belt. B; $10-20. *Unidentified* bracelet is created from links of silvertone with blue oval lapis stones. This bracelet is no doubt from the early years. $25-40. *Frosted Leaves* bracelet (9516) is from the early 1960s. "Lacy design in brilliant silver tone gives a look of early morning frost to the beautiful and graceful stylized leaves." Matching pin on page 27 of Oshel's Book I. B; $25-40. *Fiesta* bracelet (9596) and earrings (7647) are from the early 1960s. "Bright, dashing color, and a suggestion of romance in this gay combination of sea-blue, strawberry-red, emerald-green, and stone-grey. The settings are reminiscent of the handcrafted art found in Latin Countries, and will bring a festive touch to any costume…blends with both Summer and Winter wear…goes anywhere you'll take it and always has a wonderful time!" There was a sea-blue earrings set also. C; $45-60. *Courtesy of Pat and Gary Wyatt.*

Left to right: *Little Love* bracelet (9704) is from the late 1960s and carried on through the early 1970s. This was "jewelry designed especially for the young in heart." A; $10-20. *Goldenrod* bracelet (9997) from 1976 has an intricate goldentone design of leaves and tiny gold balls as the flower center. Matching earrings on page 106 of Oshel's Book I. D; $15-25. *Unidentified* silvertone bracelet is created of a textured finish reminiscent of the paper circle links used for Christmas trim. $10-20. *Unidentified* silvertone bracelet is made from elongated twisted links with alternating textured and gleaming finish. No doubt created for adding charms. $10-20. *Panda Bear* charm (9009) from 1980 is created from solid silvertone gleaming and textured finish. It can be attached to a bracelet, necklace, or ankle bracelet. B; $10-20. *Courtesy of Marjory Ritter.*

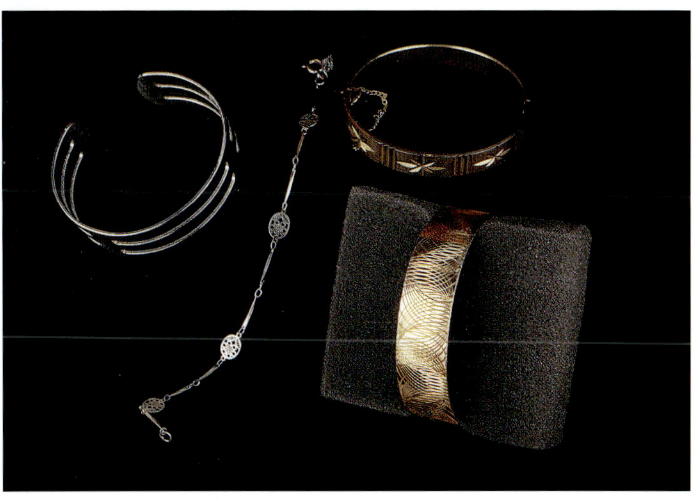

Top row, left to right: *Atlantis* bracelet (9369) is an adjustable silvertone band from 1977. Matching earrings on page 41. C; $10-20. *Infinite* bracelet (9059) is made of silvertone links and flat coins. It also came in goldentone. B; $10-20. *Star Attraction* bracelet is sparkling goldentone from 1975, hinged with a snap clasp and a safety chain for security. C; $15-30. **Bottom right:** *Golden Swirls* bracelet (9459) is from 1976. There was a matching ring and set of earrings. B; $10-20. *Courtesy of Marlene McIlwain.*

Left to right: *Swingalong* bracelet (8494) from 1972 actually doubled as a necklace made from a pin and chain with this section hanging down. Matching earrings on page 41. D; $10-20. *Unidentified* bracelet is created from goldentone rosette mountings cradling simulated cultured pearls. Very dainty yet bold. $20-35. *Inca* bracelet (9878) is from 1974. Matching pin on page 102 and earrings on page 107 of Oshel's Book I. C; $20-35. *Four Dimensions* bracelet (8660) is from 1977. It is also a part of a matching necklace that could be extended for added length. C; $10-20. *Milky Way* bracelet (9577) is from 1977. This solid bangle is goldentone with a white enamel center. C; $10-20. *Courtesy of Arcadia Historical Society.*

Top row, left to right: *Wrist-O-Crat* bracelet (0818) is a man's bracelet found in the Hostess Bonus credit section in 1978. It was worth 1050 points. $20-35. *All Around* bracelet (9121) is from 1978. The circular bracelet is 8", allowing it to be slipped over a hand. B; $10-20. *Autumn Leaves* bracelet (2246) is from 1982 as a part of the new Sarah Coventry. There was a matching necklace and earrings. F; $20-35. *Roundabout* bracelet (9102) is from 1977 in a wide alternating gleaming and textured silvertone finish. D; $15-30. *Turn-a-bout* bracelet is another wide design of both textured and gleaming goldentone sections. It is from the early 1960s and was capable of being worn with either side out. Matching necklace and earrings on page 21. A; $15-25. *Cossack* bracelet (9705) was listed in 1976 as a man's bracelet, however, many times these pieces were unisex. B; $10-20. **Bottom row, far left:** *Mural* bracelet (9727) was continued from 1976 through 1982. D; $20-35. *Courtesy of Dawn Michael.*

Left to right: *Jet Set* bracelet (9267) from 1976 has an imported Austrian glass hematite stone. There was a matching ring. C; $20-35. *Congo* bracelet (9029) is a hinged goldentone cuff with wider ends from 1978. D; $20-35. *Scandia* bracelet (9244) is from 1978. Matching ring on page 69, necklace on page 49, and earrings on page 41. B; $10-20. *Tailored Cuff* bracelet from 1971 has a gleaming and textured silvertone finish. The top side of the gleaming finish overlaps the bottom of the bracelet, giving a close fit. Matching goldentone bracelet on page 75. B; $15-25. *Atlantis* bracelet (9369) is from 1977. It is adjustable as a clip type bracelet. C; $10-20. *Courtesy of Dawn Michael.*

Top row, left to right: *Golden Bangle* bracelet (9568) is from 1966 or earlier. "The popular wedding band which is now the height of fashion and so flattering to everyone." Matching earrings on page 71 of Oshel's Book I. B; $15-30. *Unidentified* bracelet is a solid gleaming goldentone with an overlapping clasp. Very simple, very classic. $10-20. *Wisp* bracelet (9515) is from 1977 and, as its name suggests, "is a wisp of a little thing." B; $10-20. *Buckle Cuff* bracelet (9853) is from 1974. "Tailored Silvertone in Classic Designs." C; $15-30. *The Skimp* bracelet (9350) from 1979 has a unique goldentone design giving a lace effect in the center. A; $10-20. *Spangle-Bangles* (8106 or 8923) are from 1974 and were a part of the necklace shown on page 56. Taken off the silvertone or goldentone necklace, they could be worn as bracelets. A; $8-15. **Bottom row, left to right:** *Empress* bracelet (9539) from 1978 makes a wide gleaming adjustable fashion statement. C; $15-30. *Florentine* bracelet (9465) is from late 1972. It came in both goldentone and silvertone and there were matching earrings. B; $15-30. *Courtesy of Dawn Michael.*

Top left: *Gentle Trio* bracelet (9005) from 1980 is a 7-1/8" combination of three chains. C; $10-20. **Bottom left:** *Tourister* bracelets (9215, goldentone; 9214, silvertone) are from 1970. The plain charm can be engraved with names or other information. A; $10-20. **Left to right:** *Festoon* bracelet (9929) from 1974 is silvertone with a variety of stones. C; $20-35. *Fascination* bracelet (9057) is from 1976. Of the six stone links, four are imported Austrian glass stones in this silvertone gleaming and textured finish. D; $20-35. *Unidentified* gleaming bracelet has feather-like close links. $15-30. *Fashion Flirt* bracelet is from 1967. The baroque pearl tassel gives focus to the baroque pearls stationed along the goldentone chain. A; $10-20. *Courtesy of Dawn Michael.*

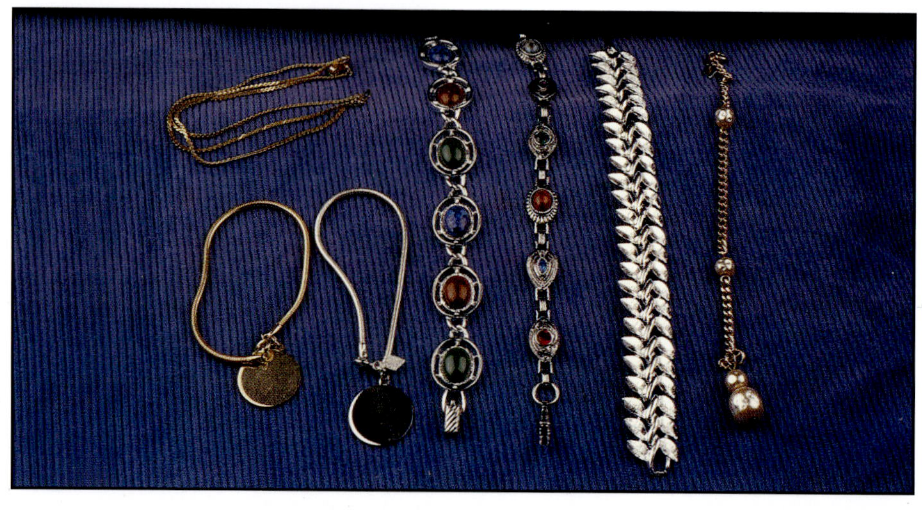

Top to bottom: **Designer's Choice** (9574) from 1973 also came in silvertone. C; $10-20. **Unidentified** combination of gleaming and textured bangles in silvertone. $10-20. **Dolphin** bracelet (9537) from 1978. C; $8-20. **Two-Tone** bangle bracelets (2170-2171) came in silvertone and goldentone with black enameled center stripe. Could be worn singly or two or three together. Matching rings on page 68. C; $8-20. **Classic Cuff** bracelet (9358) from 1977. B; $10-20. *Courtesy of Dawn Michael.*

Left to right: **Blue Lady** bracelet (9636) is from 1974. Matching ring on page 133 of Oshel's Book I. B; $20-35. **Snow Princess** bracelet is from the early 1960s. It is very bold with textured and gleaming goldentone and large white cabochon stones highlighted with clear rhinestones giving a crown effect. Matching earrings on page 39 of Oshel's Book I. B; $30-45. **Avenue** bracelet (9222) from 1979 also came in silvertone. Very sleek and yet classic in design. B; $10-20. **Unidentified** bracelet is a chain with a strikingly attractive circle bauble centered with a pearlized cabochon set. $10-20. **Classic Elegance** bracelet (9531) with a combination of mesh and chain is from 1978. C; $20-35. *Courtesy of Dawn Michael.*

Anniversary Charm Bracelets were prized by one of the management personnel who spent more than twenty-five years with the company – such charms and bracelets were given to company employees in remembrance of special events. Charms on the bottom bracelet honor the new building as well as the 25th year anniversary of the company. Finding one of these bracelets would be a wonderful addition to any collection. $25-40. *Courtesy of Dawn Michael.*

Left to right: **Cosmopolitan** bracelet of mesh hinged goldentone from the early 1960s. B; $20-35. **Coffee and Cream** bracelet (9714) is from 1973. This ivory and brown bracelet has carved designs in each section. There was an ivory only bracelet as well with similar carved designs. B; $30-45. **Golden Nile** bracelet (9452) is from 1971. This scroll work goldentone cuff matches a necklace on page 120 of Oshel's Book I. B; $20-35. **Tailored Cuff** bracelet from 1971 is in a gleaming and textured goldentone finish. The top side of the gleaming finish overlaps the bottom of the bracelet, giving a close fit. B; $15-25. **Boulevard** bracelet (9631) from 1978 is a combination of gleaming and textured goldentone. C; $20-35. *Courtesy of Dawn Michael.*

Left to right: *Embraceable Hinge* cuff bracelet (3943) from 1984 is sterling silver. There was also a matching baby bracelet. Original price $50. Current value $25-45. *Tri Twist* bracelet (9570) is from 1978. It is a combination of silvertone, goldentone, and coppertone. B; $10-20. *Double Twist* bangle bracelets (9034) are only in silvertone. B; $10-20. *Unidentified* bangle bracelets are goldentone with a center of white enamel. $15-30. *Posie* hand painted cloisonné bangle bracelet (9115) is from 1982. G; $25-35. *Unidentified* silvertone bangle bracelets are similar to the Scandia bracelet design. $15-30. *Courtesy of Dawn Michael.*

Left to right: *Golden Ice* bracelet (9728) from 1976 is a crystal and goldentone chain combination that can be worn as a bracelet or attached to the necklace shown on page 114 of Oshel's Book I. C; $10-20. *Golden Leaf* bracelet (9076) is from 1981. "No matter what your career is, you are always a woman first. Express your femininity with Golden Leaf. Or, if you're looking for a timeless, tailored piece for office wear, it's a sophisticated approach to professionalism." D; $10-20. *Evening Sands* bracelet is a beautiful goldentone and crystal rhinestone bracelet from the early 1960s. There was a matching necklace and earrings. A; $20-35.

Left to right: *Coffee and Cream* bracelet (9713) is carved from ivory colored solid plastic and featured in 1973. Variation bracelet on page 72. B; $25-40. *Cosmopolitan* bracelet (9257) is from 1969. This basic yet attractive design is a mesh hinged bracelet adding to any costume. It also came in silvertone. B; $20-35. *Courtesy of Dawn Michael.*

Lady Coventry and New Sarah

Lord and Lady Coventry was a unique collection of jewelry that started around 1967 and continued into the early 1980s. The items in this collection were made of high quality materials and genuine semi-precious stones or Austrian crystals. They were presented in black and gold cases with a soft white velour lining, making them very appropriate for special gift items. A selection of the Lord and Lady Coventry pieces is shown in the next three pictures. More detailed information about the semi-precious stones can be found on pages 85-89 of my first book, *Sarah Coventry Jewelry*.

Top row, left to right: *Genuine Tiger Eye* choker (8843) from 1977. Genuine tiger eye squares are stationed on this dainty goldentone chain of 15". There was a set of matching pierced earrings. F; $20-35. *Sterling Locket* pendant (8247) is a hand engraved, book shaped locket from 1970. D; $20-35. *Sterling Locket* pendant (8708) is from 1968 and has a hand engraved floral design. "A classic design for any age." C; $15-30. *Tiger Eye Cross* (8694) is from the early 1970s and features a solid tiger-eye cross shape with a chain through the top arm. D; $15-30. **Front row, left to right:** *Star Bright* necklace (8554) was also from 1968. It is a Dentelle stone with sterling silver star and chain. Very petite and exquisite. B; $15-30. *Solitude* (8555) necklace is from 1967. "The single pearl on a chain is in demand by women of all ages, and is never limited as to season or occasion." The cultured pearl in lustrous finish is capped with a sterling silver ornament. B; $15-30. *Courtesy of Dawn Michael.*

Top row, left to right: *Unidentified* ring on top edge of box is a jet black set in goldentone mounting. The sleek sized ring no doubt was from the later years. $20-35. *Jade Oval* bracelet (9242), pierced earrings (7243), and pin (6328) are from the early 1970s. The semi-precious genuine jade sets are mounted in goldentone settings with 12K gold filled posts on the earrings. F; $35-50. *Flowered Circle* pin and earrings set (5091) is from 1967. "The classic circle design is made more beautiful with the artistic use of semi-precious stones nestled among the leaves. This lovely set has the added beauty of genuine rose quartz (pink), Wyoming jade (green), sodalite (blue) and cultured pearl." C; $30-45. *Genuine Crystal Heart* pendant (8096) is from 1979. The lead crystal was imported from Germany where it was gem cut to produce the rainbow of delicate colors exhibited. The chain is sterling silver. E; $25-35. **Bottom row, left to right:** *Genuine Jade* pendant (8676) is from 1974. The goldentone pendant is 16-18" adjustable. C; $15-25. *Roxanne* ring was found only in the 1979 catalog listed under Hostess Bonus items for 2450 points. The genuine jade stone is mounted in a striking goldentone frame. $15-30. *Heather* pendant (8514) is from 1979. The stone is an imported German glass stone. C; $15-25. *Unidentified* ring is a unique goldentone mounting of one size fits all. The center of the design features a cultured pearl. $20-35. *Wedding Band* ring (5695-5713) was made for "His and Hers" ring sizes with this name in 1976. In the same year, it became known as the *Lord and Lady* ring. It is sterling with a black inlay under the ripple sterling design. E; $20-35. *Courtesy of Dawn Michael.*

Top row, left to right: *Filigree Onyx* set of earrings (7674), pendant (8674), and bracelet (9674) from 1974. In 1976, the same set was identified as *Filigree Jet*. G; $30-45. *Opal Treasure* bracelet (9698) is from 1973. It was part of the "Silvery Collection," with its semi-precious opal sets surrounded by garnet rhinestone sets. It was called *Antique Treasure* several years later. E; $25-40. *Golden Scarab* bracelet (9241) from 1970 has a variety of semi-precious stones from tiger-eye to rose quartz to jade. F; $20-35. **Bottom row, left to right:** *Onyx Tears* pin (6329) and bracelet (9329) are from 1970. Matching earrings on page 86 of Oshel's Book I, *Sarah Coventry Jewelry*. E; $25-40. *Togetherness* ring (woman's 5342-5354) is from 1972. "Togetherness…the ring that says we belong together. Each ring is beautifully crafted in sterling silver expertly antiqued to bring out the fine design. The genuine onyx stone is symbolic of your genuine love." The man's ring on page 82 was the same, only bolder and sized larger. F; $30-45. *Aqua Treasure* ring (5279-5291) was a sized sterling ring with this semi-precious stone. Rest of the set on page 86 of Oshel's Book I. This was only in one 1971 catalog. D; $20-35. *Silvery Moonstone* pendant (8698) and earrings (7698) set from 1974. The set is silvertone and also part of the Lord and Lady Coventry "Silvery Collection." G; $25-40. *Courtesy of Dawn Michael.*

The New Sarah Coventry line started in late 1981/early 1982 and was continued only a short time – less than two years. This new line featured 14 kt. gold and diamond jewelry including chains, pendants, drops, rings, earrings, initials, add-a-bead of 14 kt. gold, and cultured pearl beads. The stones were genuine opals, rubies, emeralds, amethyst, coral, sapphire, cultured pearl, and diamonds. These items were in line with real jewelry sold in stores, with special pricing available when ordering several items. As shown in the pictures, these items again utilized black cases, providing an elegant presence for the purchaser or gift recipient.

During this same time, several other catalogs and items were added to the line. These included luggage, sunglasses, and clothing.

From the catalogs it appears that the **New Sarah Coventry** line began in 1982. The items pictured here are called **10 Karat Plumb Gold**. This means that it is 10/24 pure gold sealed or mixed with tin, lead, and other alloys. It is the same as overlay. These delicate pieces were quite reasonable in price but can be hard to identify as there may be no signature. $10-20 each piece. *Courtesy of Dawn Michael.*

The New Sarah Coventry line also included **14 Karat Gold** jewelry. This example is very sleek yet elegant in design. Directions for care and wearing came with the jewelry. Because pure gold is very soft, it is rarely used in jewelry making. Combined with metal alloys such as copper, silver, and zinc, however, the gold's hardness is increased. $35-50. *Courtesy of Dawn Michael.*

Miscellaneous – Watches, Accessories, Men's Items, Christmas Items

Shown here is a selection of items representing some of the unique accessories designed throughout the 30+ years Sarah Coventry was in production. These include watches, which may or may not be from the original company, since companies that secured the name after 1984 also produced watches that were sold in department stores. Only a small amount of documentation on watches was found during this author's research and it is shown in the catalog section on page 84.

Besides creating wonderful jewelry, Sarah Coventry saw a need throughout the years for such other items as belts, charms, barrettes, key rings, and scarf rings. Men's jewelry was also a large part of the collection in the 1960s and 70s. The trend from men wearing cuff links, tie tacs, and dress jewelry to more casual wear can be easily seen through the catalogs. The following pictures depict this shift as well as the examples in my first book, *Sarah Coventry Jewelry*, on pages 164-168.

Limited Edition jewelry and other items were common in the 1970s. Each year, a cross was designed and sold with the mold destroyed at the end of the year. (For more in depth coverage of these crosses, see pages 87, 114, 138-139, and 167 of my first book.) Christmas decorations were also included in the Limited Edition concept. An example showing a bracelet of Christmas charms is on page 96 of my first book. Finding these non-jewelry items greatly adds to a collection, so keep your eyes open.

During the collecting process, watches keep popping up. Watches were given for awards throughout the years, and the top two might be examples of this as they have diamond chips near the top on the front. The bottom watch is unique in that it is a bug design pendant. Opening the case (the bug back) is done by squeezing the antennae. Very special and unique – a real find. All of the watches say "Sarah Coventry" on the back. As the company progressed from 1982-1984, many other items were added to the inventory and watches were one of these. This last watch might have been a part of that era. $15-30 each. *Courtesy of Marjory Ritter.*

Charms were very popular through the Sarah Coventry years. These are just a few of the examples that were available. They usually came with chains, however, many are found loose like these. **Top row, left to right:** *Unidentified* pineapple charm no doubt was available for a bracelet add on. $15-30. *Young Sailor* drop (8138) from 1980 came with a 15" chain under the heading of "kid stuff." B; $8-10. *#1 Drop* (8382) is also from 1980 as "young at heart." A; $8-10. *Owl* drop (8375) is also from 1980 as "young at heart." A; $8-10. *Little Love* charm (8704) from 1970 was a pendant that came with a bracelet or a necklace chain. A; $10-20. *Sailing* drop (9689) is from 1982 and was in the New Sarah Coventry line. A; $10-20. *Puffed Heart* drops (8239) are from 1980 and could be purchased to add to the Amulet Pendant on page 54. B; $10-15. **Bottom row, left to right:** Charms for Christmas were made as Limited Edition items. *Cherub Christmas* charm (9058) from 1980 is a crystal charm to be worn on a bracelet or chain and was sold until December 31, 1980. B; $10-20. *Three Wise Men* charm (9506) from 1978 was available "through December 31, 1978 only, at which time the mold will be destroyed." B; $12-25. *1979 Limited Edition* charm has a Christmas tree design. The mold was also broken at the end of the year, making these charms a great part of any collection. B; $12-25. *Courtesy of Dawn Michael.*

Left to right: *Snow Blossom* belt (8110, 25-28"; 8112, 29-32") only came in goldentone with an enameled white blossom attached to the metal stretch belt. There were matching earrings in 1982. F; $15-30. *Unidentified* belt is a long bold goldentone chain with an attached tassel for added accent. $10-20. *Courtesy of Dawn Michael.*

Left to right: *Surfside* belt (2234, 25-28"; 2235, 29-32") from 1982 was part of the New Sarah Coventry line with bolder and more expensive designs. It matches the necklace on page 61 and was originally $65. There also were matching earrings as well. $25-35. *Mood Mate* necklace/belt (8477) from 1973 has an attached 4-leaf clover. Looking at this brought back my memories of 4-H and how I wished I could have had a belt to compliment my 4-H uniforms during the years I was a member. C; $20-35. *Unidentified* belt/necklace is goldentone with coins stationed throughout the length. Very classic fashion accessory for any costume. $15-25. *Fashion Fortune* necklace/belt (8252) is from 1969. The goldentone chain with coins attached to the tassel gives it the name. The matching coin earrings were featured in only one catalog. B; $10-20. *Courtesy of Dawn Michael.*

Left to right: *Military Brass* belt (8754) is from 1968. "The latest look in fashion is the military look. Sarah's designers created this high fashion belt and you don't have to be a general to wear stars wherever you want. Finished in glamorous Goldentone." C; $30-45. *French Rope* chain (8720) is a 32" length for a belt from 1982. Other lengths of chain could also be purchased. G; $15-30. *Unidentified* stretch belt has a goldentone rosette clasp. I am guessing this is from the early 1980s. $20-35. *Unidentified* belt of heavy goldentone chain has a cut-out medallion for the clasp. Very unique and unusual. $20-35. *Courtesy of Dawn Michael*

Left to right: *Disco-Tek* belt (8875) from 1974 came in a 35" length. "Wear Disco-Tek as a belt or a necklace. Combine with the bracelet for additional versatility and fashion." It also came in goldentone. There were matching earrings and a matching bracelet is on page 128 of Oshel's Book I, *Sarah Coventry Jewelry.* D; $20-35. *Fashion Rope* necklace/belt (8909) is a 37" length to be worn as a belt or necklace. It also came in silvertone in 1974. C; $10-20. *Fashion Flair* chain (8051) is from a part of a set that could be taken apart in the mid-1970s and worn separately as belts or necklaces, in combination or separately. B; $10-20. *Tailored Accent* necklace/belt (8590) is from 1976. This was shown as a necklace worn long, looped several times around the neck, or as a belt. Matching bracelet on page 73. D; $10-20. *Camelot* belt (8447) has an antiqued bronze effect. It also came in an antique pewter in 1972. It could be worn as a necklace looping several times around the neck with about three to four links and either end hanging down. This gave an Egyptian look. D; $20-35. *Courtesy of Dawn Michael.*

Trio belt (8034) is from 1974. "Three belt lengths and one buckle in a trio of fashion colors. Black, Brown and White for all Seasons." F; $20-35. *Courtesy of Dawn Michael.*

Mood Mate belt/necklace and corresponding 1972 catalog page. The various ways of wearing this item are shown – as a necklace in three different lengths or as a belt. This page shows that it was priced at $8 while the 1973 catalog shows $10. Finding this item is a major coup for a collector as I haven't seen many in my travels. B; $20-35.

Sarah Coventry produced a variety of items beyond fashion jewelry – a selection of these items is pictured here. **Clockwise, from top right:** *Fashion-Hold* barrette (6545) from 1972 is pewter. There was also a bronze one. "Wear it in the hair or as a scarf holder." B; $10-20. *Shindig* pin/barrette (6549) is from 1966. "A brand-new young idea is this pin barrette with its modern lines and textured and polished goldentone finish. A 'first' in the fashion world and designed by Sarah for those who like to wear the latest in fashion." A; $12-25. *Key-Ringer* (5940) from 1972 was an accessory designed to be engraved. A; $10-20. *Key Note* key ring (5921) is from 1970. This unique key ring made putting keys together very easy by removing the ball end. A; $10-20. *White Charmer* holder (8248) was used to create a lariat from the white beads included with this set or by making it into a belt. B; $15-30. *Classic Beauty* scarf holder (5189) from 1975 was a very simple and classic accessory. There were also matching earrings. B; $10-20.

Left to right: *Goldenwood* necklace (8656) is a part of a necklace set designed for women, however this bold golden chain could be worn by men as well in the 1970s. Many of the items featured for men were also created for women. C; $10-20. *Devotion* pendant (8577) came in goldentone and silvertone pendants on an 18" chain in the late 1970s and early 80s. Engraved on the back is "God grant me the serenity to accept the things I cannot change, the courage to change the things I can, and the wisdom to know the difference. Amen." C; $8-15. *On the Square* tie tac (5957) is from the early 1960s. "The most popular piece of jewelry in a man's jewelry wardrobe is the tie tac – even the man who generally wears a tie bar likes to have at least one tie tac in his jewel case." SarahGlo Goldentone. A; $10-20. The Sarah Coventry patch could be attached to a jacket, suit coat, purse, or used in some other advertising manner. $5-10. *Courtesy of Arcadia Historical Society.*

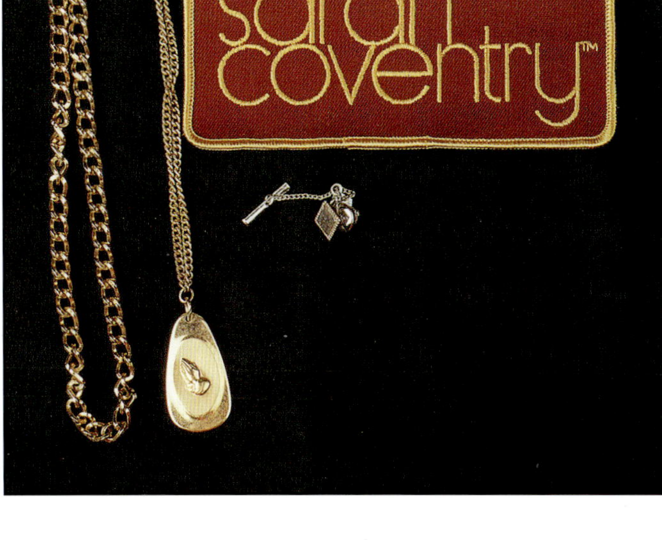

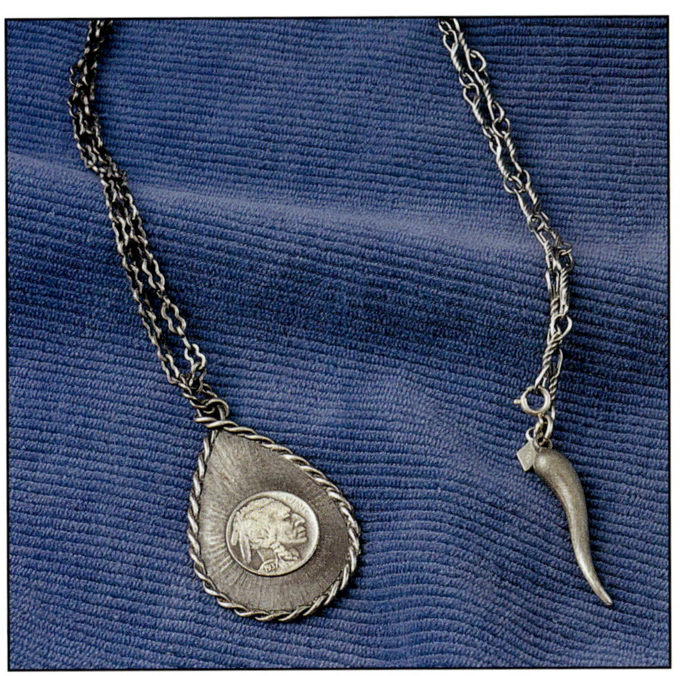

Left to right: *Indian Head* pendant (8438) is from 1978 in the men's collection. The stainless steel chain is 26" in length with a genuine pewter drop. The "reverse side of coin inscribed 'copy of U.S. Indian Head Coin Issued 1937.'" D; $20-30. *Italian Horn* pendant (8664) is also from 1978 for men. The 24" stainless steel chain features a genuine pewter drop in the shape of a horn. C; $15-25. *Courtesy of Pat and Gary Wyatt.*

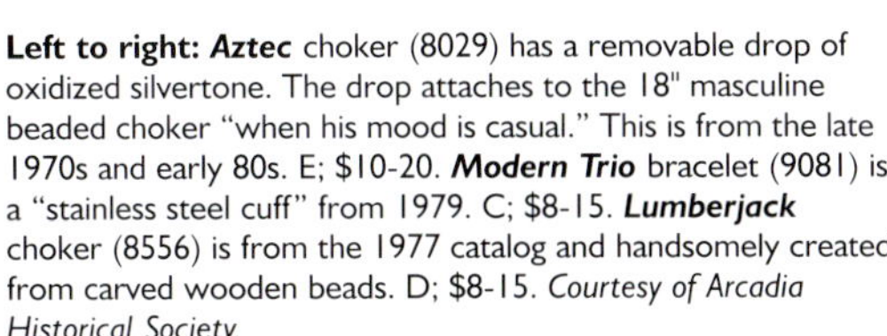

Left to right: *Aztec* choker (8029) has a removable drop of oxidized silvertone. The drop attaches to the 18" masculine beaded choker "when his mood is casual." This is from the late 1970s and early 80s. E; $10-20. *Modern Trio* bracelet (9081) is a "stainless steel cuff" from 1979. C; $8-15. *Lumberjack* choker (8556) is from the 1977 catalog and handsomely created from carved wooden beads. D; $8-15. *Courtesy of Arcadia Historical Society.*

Men's necklaces, left to right: *Gaucho* choker (8555) from 1978 is 18" in length with silvertone spacers separated by rust and black beads. C; $10-20. *Daytona* choker (8433) from 1978 is approximately 18" of masculine wooden beads with a removable antiqued silvertone sand dollar. E; $10-20. *Goldenwood* necklace (8656) from 1977 is an 18" wooden bead and golden beads section. This could be worn by men or women, coupled with a 36" chain. C; $10-20. **Men's bracelets, left to right:** *Dare Devil* bracelet (9995) is an oxidized bracelet with a unique and manly design from the mid 1970s. D; $10-20. **Men's I.D. Bracelet** (5945) from 1974 was created for engraving on the hinged center section. C; $10-20. *Explorer* bracelet (9293) from 1976 is an oxidized silvertone also. Many of these bracelets were held over for two to four years. B; $8-15. *Courtesy of Dawn Michael.*

Top row, left to right: *Unidentified* button covers are plain goldentone circles. As part of the Lord Coventry set, they came in this very attractive flat goldentone box. $10-20. *Tiger Eye* ring (5242-5254) was part of the Lord Coventry collection in the early 1970s. This genuine tiger eye stone is set in 12 kt. gold filled mounting and may be difficult to locate, so will be a great find if you do. G; $15-30. **Bottom row, left to right:** *Togetherness* ring (5355-5367) is a man's ring. There was also a woman's version, shown on page 77. "Togetherness…the ring that says we belong together. Each ring is beautifully crafted in sterling silver expertly antiqued to bring out the fine design. The genuine onyx stone symbolic of your genuine love." Original price was $30 in 1972 with a special offer for purchasing two other pieces. Current value: $20-35. *Eric* ring (5682-5694) is from 1977. "The bold man's ring made of the finest stainless steel in the Swedish tradition. Clean cut and simple in design, its beauty is enhanced by the elegant Sterling Silver insert. This sized ring will give him many years of handsome wear." Original price was $50 but could be purchased as a third item for half price. Current value: $15-30. *Courtesy of Dawn Michael.*

Christmas ornaments were a part of each catalog at Christmas time and, as they were dated, they became limited edition items for holiday collectors. The lower row displays some of the crystal drops from 1976-1980. These could be worn as necklaces or used as tree ornaments. "Impressions from designer selections. This lustrous disc of crystal clear acrylic shimmers and sparkles, reflecting every beam of light. In creating the design, skilled craftsmen employed numerous techniques to cut, carve, engrave, polish and develop texture in the acrylic. The deeply incised, delicately frosted design was made from a costly hand engraved die." Original pricing was from $15-20. Values now range from $8-15. *Courtesy of Dawn Michael.*

Advertising and Catalogs

Through the years, Sarah Coventry used a multitude of advertising strategies including advertising in major magazines such as *McCall's* and *Harper's Bazaar* as well as sponsorship of the TV show *Queen for a Day.*

A selection of Sarah Coventry advertising. *Courtesy of Arcadia Historical Society.* (Continued on following page)

The catalog shown next is from Christmas of 1984 and is most likely the last catalog printed since the company went out of business at the end of that year.

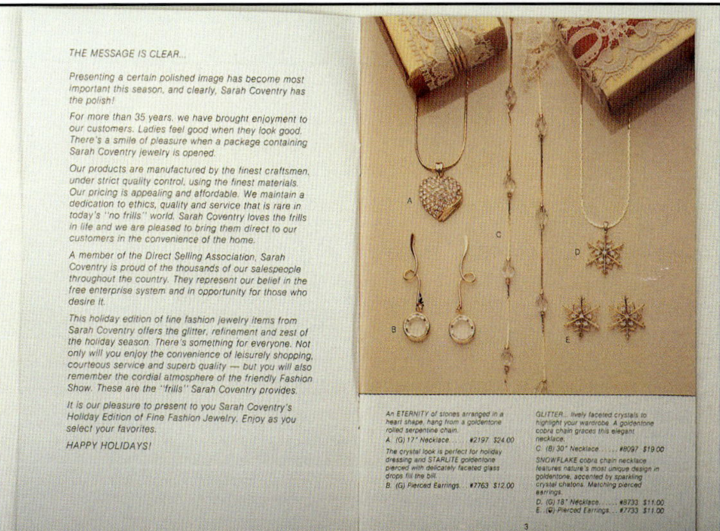

This Holiday Edition catalog dated 1984 may have been the last catalog published before the doors closed at the end of 1984. *Courtesy of Arcadia Historical Society.* (Continued on following page)

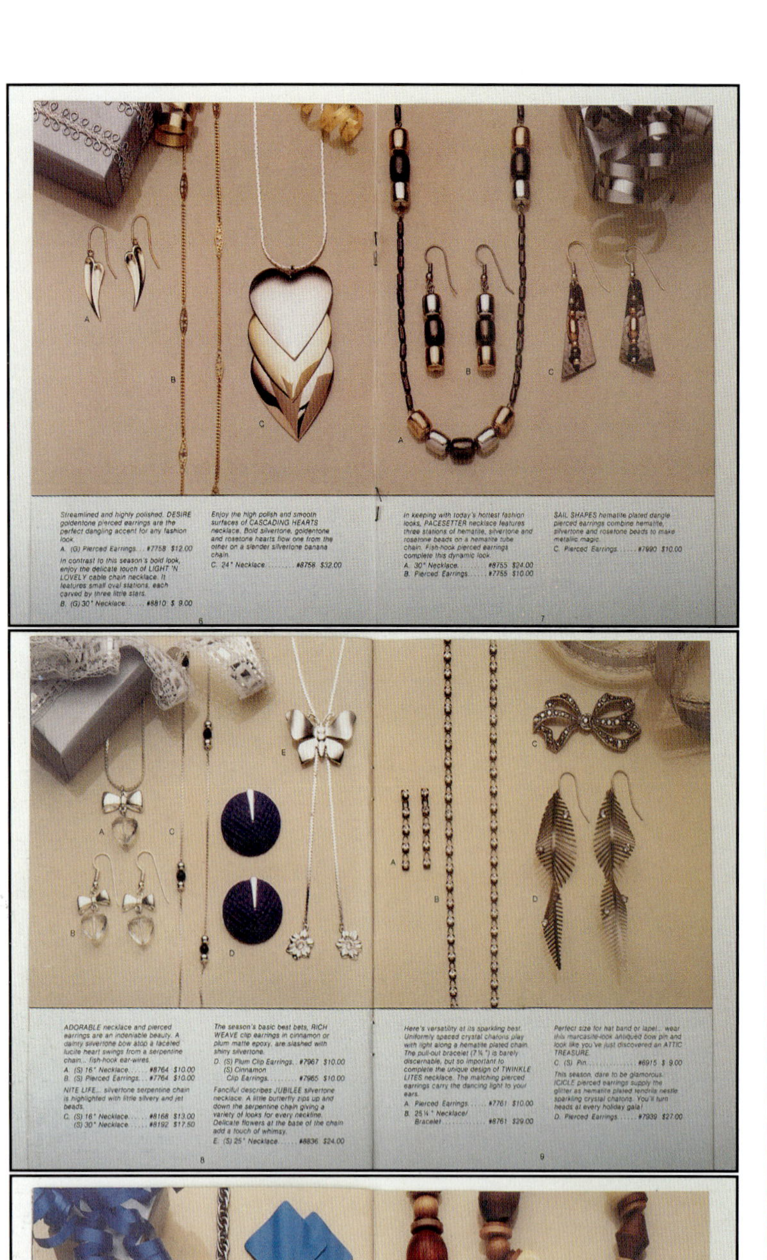

One consultant remembered that there were six catalogs she carried from party to party in the last years of the company. Shown here are the watches and sunglasses brochures. *Courtesy of Arcadia Historical Society.*

The final catalog pictures from Sarah Coventry include these pages from New Sarah Coventry brochures promoting watches and sunglasses. More catalog examples can be seen in my first book, which pictures catalogs from 1969, 1972, and 1982.

Chapter Three

Sarah Coventry International

While visiting Newark, New York in the summer of 2003, it was my pleasure to become acquainted with Jim and Allie Doyle. Jim became President of Sarah Coventry International in 1973. Sarah Coventry had begun international expansion in the early 1960s. The first subsidiary company to be organized was Sarah Coventry Limited in the United Kingdom. Their offices were in Glenrothes, Scotland, allowing expansion into England, Scotland, Wales, and Northern Ireland. At the same time, the Canadian subsidiary began operations near Toronto, spreading eventually to every Canadian Province. A third subsidiary was started a few years later with Sarah Coventry Pty., Ltd. in Australia. On the European continent, marketing of Sarah Coventry jewelry products began with the opening of a sales office in Belgium.

Allie Doyle mentioned that she enjoyed traveling with Jim on his trips to the other countries, which helped in developing a family feeling. She recalled that they traveled to Japan to test the suitability of opening a sales division there; however, they learned that the country's small homes and customs were not conducive to the party plan. They then checked out department stores for distribution of the jewelry, but that also wasn't feasible.

Jim discussed the process of selecting jewelry for the various countries. Each process consisted of nearly six thousand pieces of jewelry brought by the Sarah manufacturers and other design and manufacturing companies three times a year. The United States made their selection one week and International the next week. Once the jewelry selections were made, the other pieces were destroyed.

Of the all jewelry selected by the US and International, 50% were to become universal pieces, 25% could be a mixture of pieces, and 25% would be specific to the country. Regarding the universal pieces, I have noticed from the catalogs that each country could name these pieces specifically for their country or use the common name selected by the US. So, as you view the catalogs at the end of this section, you will notice some different designs that were specific to a country and not available in the US.

Prices from Scotland are indicated in pounds, with the pound sign £. It is not known exactly what the exchange rate was at that time, however, Jim mentioned that it would take $1.50 to $1.60 in US dollars to purchase a $1.00 item in the United Kingdom.

Again, I must stress the importance of making sure you check the back of items that look familiar or are already in your collection. They just might be marked Made in Canada or UK or Great Britain and are most worthy of being added to your collection. Take another look at the two bracelets on page 13.

A big thank you to Jim and Allie Doyle for contributing jewelry pieces and catalogs for this section. Without their assistance and kindness, this part of the book would not have been possible.

Sets - Sarah Coventry International

Left to right: *China Lady* necklace/collier (8342), earrings (7342), and bracelet (9342) are from Canada in 1975. Hand-painted cylinder black beads are stationed on a silvertone chain. The earrings are convertible and can be interchanged on various ear wires for pierced ears or illusion clips for non-pierced. A very creative way of allowing earrings to be utilized by every wearer. F; $30-45. *Light 'n Lovely* necklace (8375) and earrings (7351) were also from 1975 and marked Canada. Here there are two lengths, one 20" and the other 27". The stationed glass beads coupled with the black beads and double chain (both silvery and goldentone) create a dainty yet rich looking ensemble. F; $30-45. *Courtesy of Dawn Michael.*

Left to right: *Unidentified* pin and earrings set is marked Canada. This is a magnificent goldentone pin in a scalloped circle shape with fluted edges. The multi-colored gold flecked cabochon stones are highlighted by simulated pearls. The earrings are a smaller version. A very spectacular ensemble and no doubt very difficult to locate. $40-55. *Rainbow* pin (6126) and ring (5281) are from Canada, however, these were identified from a 1975 Scottish catalog. The glass stones have variegated colors that change from bright to pale shades when the stone is moved. The gleaming goldentone mounting sets off the rich colors. No original prices were given. $25-40. *Courtesy of Dawn Michael.*

Top to bottom: *Garland* bracelet (9321) and earrings (6321) are from Canada in 1975. The antiqued silvertone open-weave circles are hinged, creating the bracelet. Flowers are carved into each circle with an ellipse design of ridged metal below. There was a matching pendant with dangling chains and a marvelous pin containing four carved flowers and two ellipse designs. D; $30-55. **Blue Twilight** pin and bracelet were made in Canada. The goldentone, star shaped pin and bracelet of sapphire-blue colored rhinestones and pale blue round beads is accented with solid goldentone beads. Very delicate and strikingly beautiful. No original price was given. $30-55. *Courtesy of Dawn Michael.*

Unidentified bracelet and ring are marked Canada. They are similar in design to a 1975 amethyst set from the US called Mystique. The silvertone mounting sets off the pale blue rhinestones. $20-35. *Courtesy of Dorothy De May.*

Left to right: *Chateau* pendant (8212) and earrings (7212) are from Canada in 1975. As in the US, this set included a matching ring and bracelet. The unique stones in the center of the pendant and in the earrings are fire opals, highlighted by multi-colored crystal rhinestones set in antiqued goldentone mounting. G; $30-45. *Unidentified* button earrings are gleaming and twisted silvertone set with turquoise and white beads. The stenciled star shape in the center adds a striking contrast. $20-35. *Courtesy of Dawn Michael.*

Left to right: *Sunspray* pin (6056) and earrings (7056) are marked Canada, however, the name identification came from a 1973 Australian catalog. This set is very striking, with elongated brown glass stones and round orange stones mounted with a twisted goldentone design. D; $30-45. *Unidentified* pin and earrings marked Canada have a unique silvertone design of overlapping textured finish petals and gleaming ball center and stem. $30-45. *Courtesy of Dawn Michael.*

Norwegian Wood ring/bague (5552), pin/broche (6461) and earrings/boucles d'oreilles (7461) are marked GB for Great Britain but were identified from the Canadian catalog of 1976. This spectacular variegated brown glass stone is set in a bold antiqued goldentone mounting. There is a similar set with a black stone on page 90. F; $40-65. *Courtesy of Dawn Michael.*

Left to right: *Fashionaire* pin/broche (6181) and earrings (7181) are marked Canada from 1973. This dynamic goldentone 4-leaf clover shaped pin is highlighted with a square amber stone. The earrings are an open leaf dangling from a pierced amber stone post that can be removed and worn separately. E; $30-45. *Unidentified* pin and earrings are a sunburst shaped flower of gleaming and textured silvertone. The cluster of aurora borealis crystal rhinestones in the center catches the light and reflects surrounding colors. The earrings are a smaller version, but equally striking. $40-55. *Courtesy of Dawn Michael.*

Clockwise, from lower left: *Petit Point* pin (6377) is marked GB from 1976. It was also marketed in Canada. C; $15-30. *8" Ball* pin/broche (6512) is from Canada in 1978. This one is goldentone/doree, and also came in silvertone/argentee. B; $10-20. *Heritage* pins in silvertone and goldentone (6634) are marked UK for United Kingdom and were also sold in Scotland in 1979. £2.90. $15-30. *Courtesy of Allie and Jim Doyle.*

Top row, left to right are all identified as Canadian: *Unidentified* pin is an antiqued goldentone circle with Victorian textured swirls as if moving to the center. Each swirl is accented with a red bead. $10-25. *Pitter Patter* (1328) are two shoe print pins from Canada very appropriately titled for the "pitter patter of little feet." $10-20. **Bottom row, left to right:** *Unidentified* pin has two fish shapes overlapping in silvertone. The large silvertone bead could be the eye, however without a name and information that is only speculation. $20-35. *Colonial* pin (6082) is an antiqued goldentone pin from Australia. The turquoise oval cabochon stone in the center is surrounded by four bright blue rhinestones and tiny pearlized beads. B; $15-30. *Unidentified* goldentone oval shape is accented with five orange beads in a straight line. Very simple yet unique. $10-20. *Courtesy of Dawn Michael.*

Left to right: *Warm Heart* pin (6001) is marked UK. It was in a Canadian catalog in 1977. B; $10-20. *Lady Coventry* mother-of-pearl pin/broche (6632) also marked UK was in a Canadian catalog in 1977. "Genuine Mother of Pearl Stone." D; $20-35. *Reefer* pin (1166) in silvertone also marked UK in Scotland in 1979. £3.50; $10-20. *Courtesy of Jim and Allie Doyle.*

Unidentified leaf pin is marked Canada. It is silvertone with a combination of textured and twisted rope-like edging on the leaves. Very striking with the silhouette cut out design. $20-35.

Unidentified circle pin is marked GB for Great Britain. This pin is an example of the many combinations of jewelry design, with gleaming, textured, open-weave rope, enamel, and engraved star. Very unique and no doubt difficult to locate. $25-40. *Courtesy of Dawn Michael.*

Left to right: *Beau-Tie* scarf pin (6049) marked Canada is from 1973. It came in both silvertone and goldentone. A; $10-20. It was sold in Scotland as *Whirlwind* scarf clip (6049) in 1975, shown in goldentone. No price was given. $15-25. *Golden Era* pin/broche (6030) from 1973 is marked "Made in Canada". In Australia, it was called the *Heritage* pin (6030) in 1973. It is similar to Catherine in the US, but with a tiger eye type cabochon set. B; $15-30. *Saffron* pin is marked "Made in Canada" but was found in an Australian catalog from 1973. It is goldentone with simulated pearls. B; $20-30. *Courtesy of Allie and Jim Doyle.*

Top row, left to right: *Sea Swirl* pin (6246) in goldentone is from 1975 and marked "Sarah Canada." B; $15-30. *Austrian Lites* pin/ broche (6633) is from 1973. There were earrings that matched as well. C; $20-35. *Silvery Sunburst* pin (6255) and earrings (7255) are from 1973. C; $15-30. **Bottom row, left to right:** *Gillian* pin (6187) was from 1974 and named for Gillian Regehr, who was Miss Canada 1973. There were matching earrings as well. B; $20-35. In Australia, this piece was called *Simulated Pearl* in 1973. C; $20-35. In Scotland it was called *Miranda* pin (6187) with no price given. $20-35. *Mandolin* pin (6582) is from 1977. B; $10-20. *Courtesy of Jim and Allie Doyle.*

Left to right: *Isabella* pin/broche (6063) from 1974 in Canada is a very exquisite marbleized turquoise cabochon on antiqued silvertone accented with simulated pearls. There was a matching bracelet, earrings, and ring. C; $20-35. *Regal* pin (6581) from 1977 is pictured upside down. B; $15-30. *Courtesy of Jim and Allie Doyle.*

Top row, left to right: *Mr. Sea Gull* pin (6431) is from 1976 in gleaming silvertone. C; $10-20. *Spring Bouquet* pin (6289) is from 1976. There was also a matching ring. B; $20-35. *Caprice* pin (6081) in goldentone is marked Canada and was also in Australia in 1973. There were matching earrings. B; $20-35. **Bottom row, left to right:** *Unidentified* tree pin with green and red enamel sectioned off by gleaming goldentone. $15-30. *Who's Who?* pin (6322) is from 1976. This stunning goldentone one-eyed owl is delightful to wear. B; $15-30. *Gillian* earrings (7187) from 1977 match the pin above. B; $10-20. *Courtesy of Allie and Jim Doyle.*

Unidentified pin from Canada is a remarkably designed starburst shape. An antiqued goldentone piece bursting with color from the red rhinestones, small blue beads, and larger simulated pearl beads. $25-45. *Courtesy of Marjory Ritter.*

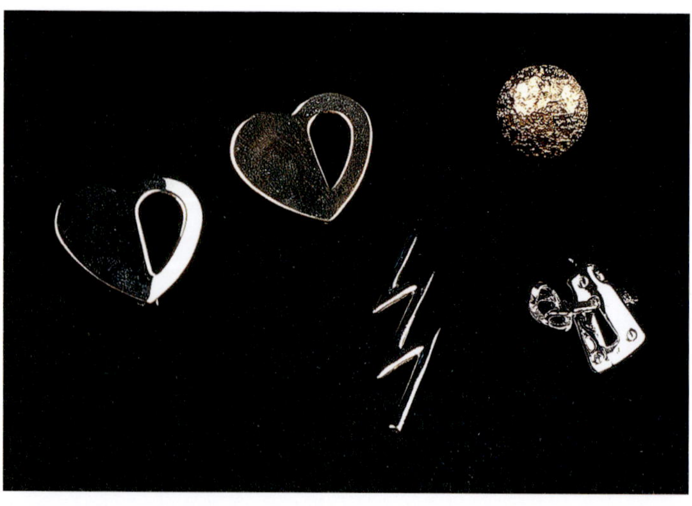

Top row, left to right: *Unidentified* silvertone and goldentone pins are gleaming hearts with a half heart section open. $10-20. *Unidentified* bolo slide is a solidly designed textured goldentone button with double slide on the back. $10-20. **Bottom row, left to right:** *Lightning* pendant (3307) is from 1980. D; $15-30. *Interlocking Love Accessory* (3412) is a pendant from 1980 that can be worn with or without the key. No mention was made, but each could probably be worn separately by a different person, indicating true love. C; $15-30. *Courtesy of Allie and Jim Doyle.*

Left to right: *Coraline* pin/pendant (8924) is from 1975 and marked Canada. There were matching earrings and a ring. D; $15-25. It was called *Florentina* (8924) in the 1975 Scottish catalog with no price given. $15-25. *Unidentified* pin in silvertone has an open scroll-like weave highlighted with a large, off center pearl. $15-30. *Courtesy of Pat and Gary Wyatt.*

Left to right: *Golden Snowflake* pin (6343) is from 1975 and marked Canada Coventry. It also came in *Silvery Snowflake* (6347). Both pins were antiqued and very striking. B; $20-35. *Sea Swirl* pins in goldentone (6246) and silvertone (6247) are from 1975 and marked Canada. B; $15-30. *Courtesy of Arcadia Museum.*

Left to right: *Unidentified* Christmas charm marked 1978. It is the "partridge in a pear tree" design in goldentone and accented with colored leaves. $15-30. *Blitzen* pin/broche (6026) is from 1973 and identified as part of "Sarah's Christmas Collection." This stylized deer in goldentone is a magnificent find. A; $15-25. *Courtesy of Arcadia Historical Society.*

Stick pins and bar pins were very popular in the 1970s and 1980s. **Top row, left to right:** *Unidentified* star shape stick pin. Each point of the star is accented with a clear rhinestone. B; $10-20. *Carousel* stick pin (1267) is from 1980. B; $10-20. *Cupid* stick pin (1320) is also from 1980. C; $15-25. *Changing Times* stick pin (6009) is from 1979. Each 2" stick pin included one heart, one initial (A is for Allie) and one flower to be arranged in any order on the stick pin. An imported Austrian glass stone serves as the center of the flower. C; $10-20. *Unidentified* flattened pearlized stick pin. $10-20. **Center:** *Heritage* tac pin has a goldentone fluted mounting with sparkling center. B; $10-20. **Top bar pin:** *Unidentified* bar pin is similar to Emily, however, this has one medium sized pearl in the center of paved rhinestone leaves. $15-30. *Reefer* pin (1166) is from Canada, however was identified in Scotland with this name in 1979. A; $10-20. *Courtesy of Allie and Jim Doyle.*

Back row, left to right: *Unidentified* pin or *Woodland Flight* as a necklace. In the US, this was a pin only, but this one marked Canada has a loop on the back for a necklace chain. $15-30. *Mr. Sea Gull* pin (6431) is from 1976 in gleaming silvertone. C; $10-20. *Silvery Sunburst* pin (6255) from 1973 is the same silvertone with gleaming and textured finish and a large simulated pearl center. Matching earrings on page 88. B; $10-25. **Center front:** *Candy Apple* pin/broche (6020) from 1973 has a transparent ruby red stone highlighted with silvertone stem and leaves. B; $15-30.

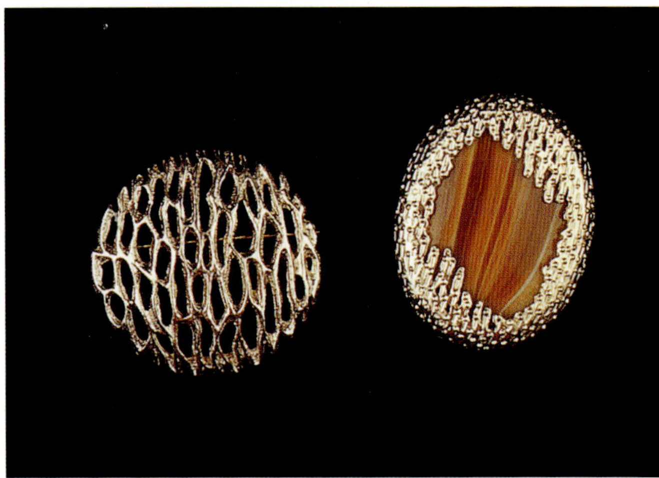

These two pins are marked GB for Great Britain. **Left to right: *Unidentified*** pin is a slightly oval shape of gleaming goldentone with an open-weave of criss-cross goldentone. Simple, yet strikingly beautiful. $15-30. ***Unidentified*** pin is also an oval shape, with tiger-eye stone. The goldentone mounting creates a shadow effect encasing the outer edges of the stone. $20-35. *Courtesy of Arcadia Historical Society.*

Top: *Unidentified* set marked Canada is designed like the Norwegian Wood pin except this set is black rather than brown. It is also in antiqued silvertone rather than the goldentone of the brown set. I wasn't able to locate this in a catalog, so it may have had a different name. $25-35. ***Unidentified*** leaf pin marked Canada is open-weave goldentone with a unique design as if blowing in the breeze. $20-35. *Courtesy of Arcadia Historical Society.*

Left to right: *Unidentified* necklace is a unique goldentone necklace of two different chains with stationed red, black, and goldentone caps creating a flower effect. $15-30. ***Avanti*** pendant/pendentif (8339) is from Canada in 1975. D; $20-35. *Courtesy of Dawn Michael.*

Left to right: *Madame Butterfly* pendant (8670) is from Canada in 1978. This uniquely designed silvertone pendant has a very exquisite design of a butterfly. C; $20-35. ***Unidentified*** goldentone chain has an amber crystal locking the two chains together with amber beads at the ends creating tassels. $15-30. ***Hocus Pocus*** necklace (8666) is from Canada in 1978. This 43" length lariat can be worn open or closed as pictured. Matching bracelet on page 94; there were matching earrings as well. E; $15-30. *Courtesy of Dawn Michael.*

Left to right: *Rajah Elephant* pendant (8560) on a chain is from Scotland. There was one in the United States attached to beads. $20-35. *Lion* charm holder (8603) is marked Scotland made in Britain. $20-35. *Unidentified* nut pendant is marked U.K. This solid goldentone pendant is bold and attractive. $25-35. *Courtesy of Dawn Michael.*

Magic Moods pendant goldentone (8052) is from Australia, even though the card says "Made in UK." It was featured in 1973. D; $15-30. *Courtesy of Dawn Michael.*

Left to right: *Blue Cloud* necklace/collier (3007) is 18" long with a combination of antiqued silvertone and oval shaped turquoise sets. There was a matching earrings set, a ring, and a bracelet. E; $30-45. *Malibu* pendant (8382) is from 1976. There was a matching ring, bracelet, and earrings. C; $20-35. *Two Timer* necklace (8710) is an 18" strand of pearls with this pendant that can be worn with the beads, separately as a pin, or matched together as a necklace and a pin on the shoulder. D; $20-35. *Courtesy of Dawn Michael.*

Left to right: *Imperial* pendant (8201) is from Canada in 1974. There was a matching ring. D; $20-35. *Unidentified* lariat is of beaded chain with a slide of forest green set and large goldentone balls on the end of each chain forming a tassel. $20-35. *Chain Reaction* necklace (8150) is from Canada in 1974. This combination of goldentone chain and a bolder silvertone chain also has a bracelet attached, thus adding to the length or allowing a complete ensemble of necklace and bracelet. There were also matching chain earrings. D; $20-35. *Courtesy of Dawn Michael.*

Left to right: *Charisma* necklace/collier (8069) is from Canada in 1973. There were matching earrings and it also came in goldentone. D; $15-30. *Polka* pendant (8238) is from Canada in 1976. There were earrings that matched this barrel-shaped bead with turquoise hand-painted design attached to a 4-leaf clover goldentone design. C; $15-25. *Jet Set* necklace (3244) is from 1980 in Canada. There was a 33" and a 26-1/2" chain, one with the stationed jet black sets. In Scotland, this was called *Black Beauty*. F; $25-35. *Fashion-Rite* necklace (8541) is from Canada in 1974 and features a combination of two strands of pearls with a clasp artfully designed to be worn in front as well as at the back of the neck. There were also matching earrings. C; $20-35.

Left to right: *Textured Links* pendant (8325) is from Canada in 1976. There were matching earrings and a matching bracelet. C; $15-30. *Night Owl* pendant (8871) is from Canada in 1975. The moveable body and tail make this a unique pendant. C; $15-30. *Rose-Marie* necklace (3170) of goldentone is from Scotland in 1979. The antiqued look gives the flower design an added focus. In 1980 in Canada, it was known as the *Floral Fantasy* pin and could be worn on a hoop necklace. This was a Design Award winner in August 1978. £9.90; $20-35.

Left to right: *Crusader* pendant (8403) is from Canada in 1973. It combines silvertone filigree mounting with white and amethyst colored cabochon sets. C; $15-30. *Heirloom* locket/medallion (8471) from 1974 is a locket of goldentone with a scroll design on the front. There is no mark of Sarah Coventry on the locket, only on the chain. D; $15-30. *Roman Holiday* pendant (8637) is from 1974. The pendant is removable and reversible. D; $20-35. *Talisman of Love* pendant (8500) is from 1973 in Canada. In Australia, it was called *Aztec Pendant*. C; $20-35.

Left to right: *Isabella* ring/bague (5270) is a 1974 Canadian multi-colored turquoise set in an antiqued silvertone mounting. Tiny pearl-like beads surround the center navette shaped stone. Matching pin on page 88. B; $20-35. *Butter Finger* ring (5278) is a striking butterfly in a gleaming goldentone mounting surrounding a navette emerald crystal stone with four lime green crystal stones accenting each wing of the butterfly. It is from 1974 in Canada. B; $15-30. *Courtesy of Dawn Michael.*

Left to right: *Unidentified* ring is marked GB. The ring is very bold with gleaming and textured goldentone. It might be a stylized "SC" for Sarah Coventry and therefore an award item. $15-30. *Rose Garden* ring (5588) is marked UK and identified in a Canadian catalog from 1977. There was a matching pendant. C; $20-35. *Courtesy of Dawn Michael.*

Left to right: *Jubilee* ring/bague (5285) is marked Sarah Canada from 1975. This elongated antiqued silvertone ring was also sold in Scotland in 1975, where it was called *Cretan* (5295). B; $15-30. *Unidentified* ring is marked UK and has a unique reddish color tiger eye. $20-35. *Courtesy of Arcadia Historical Society and Marjory Ritter.*

Top to bottom: *Textured Links* bracelet (9325) is from Canada in 1976. Matching necklace on page 92. C; $15-30. *Kismet* bracelet (9039) is from Canada in 1973. The variety of linked shapes and varying cabochon colored sets makes this an attractive and striking bracelet to be worn with any color of costume. C; $20-35. *Courtesy of Dawn Michael.*

Left to right: **Unidentified** bracelet is artfully designed in silvertone. The hinged cuff is overlaid with a silvertone leaf and a large black faceted crystal with an intaglio Victorian woman's head in silver. Very simply designed, yet very elaborate. Marked Great Britain. $30-45. **Hocus Pocus** bracelet is from Canada in 1978 and matches the necklace on page 90. B; $15-30. *Courtesy of Dawn Michael.*

Left to right: **Caprice** bracelet (9667) is from Canada in 1978. This solid goldentone bracelet with swirling design is unique, yet simple enough to be worn with any costume. C; $15-30. **Unidentified** buckle bracelet could actually have been named this. It was marked Canada and no doubt came in goldentone as well as silvertone. $20-35. **Chain Reaction** bracelet (9150) is from Canada in 1974. It came with a matching necklace and could be worn separately or attached to the necklace allowing the length to be extended. B; $10-20. *Courtesy of Dawn Michael.*

Romanesque Clasp (6545) was the name given to this item in Australia in 1972, while in Canada in 1973 they were called **Fashion-Hold** barrettes in silvertone (argentee) and goldentone (doree). B; $15-30. *Courtesy of Dawn Michael.*

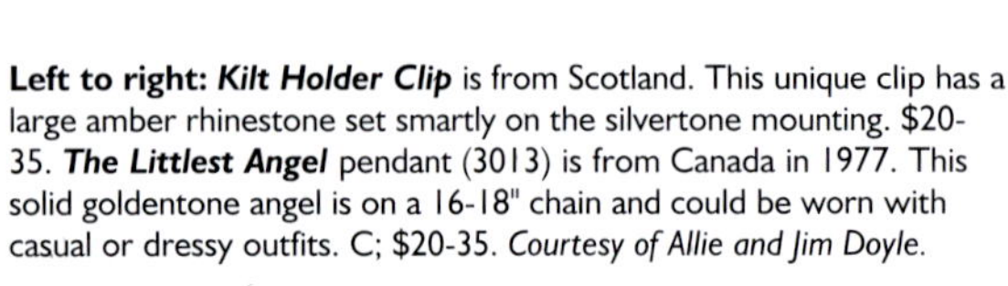

Left to right: **Kilt Holder Clip** is from Scotland. This unique clip has a large amber rhinestone set smartly on the silvertone mounting. $20-35. **The Littlest Angel** pendant (3013) is from Canada in 1977. This solid goldentone angel is on a 16-18" chain and could be worn with casual or dressy outfits. C; $20-35. *Courtesy of Allie and Jim Doyle.*

Early 1970s

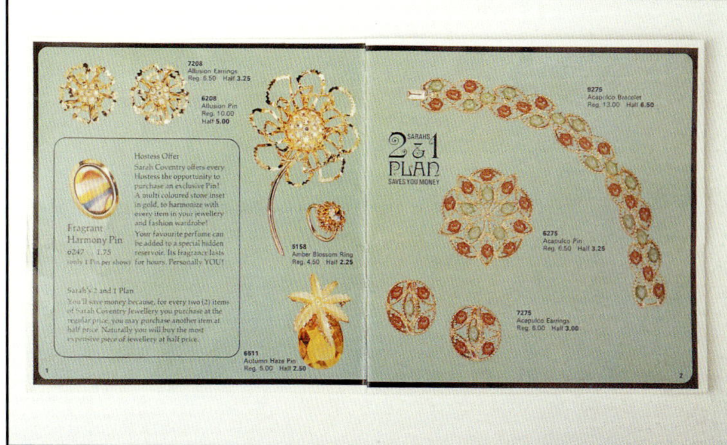

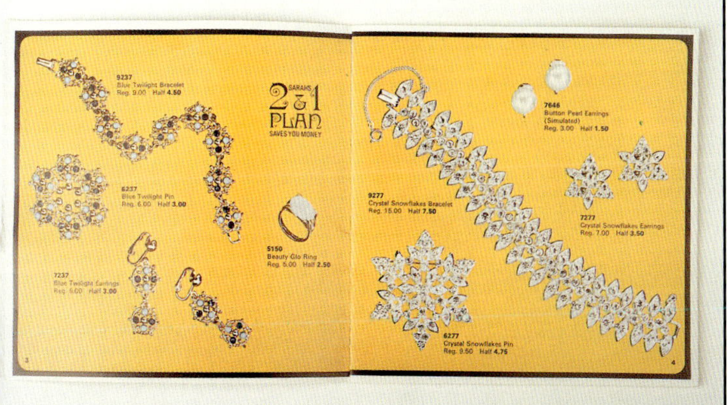

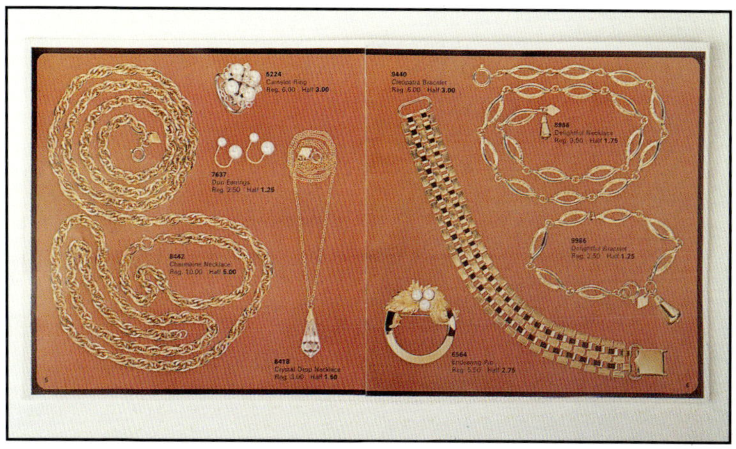

Continued on following page

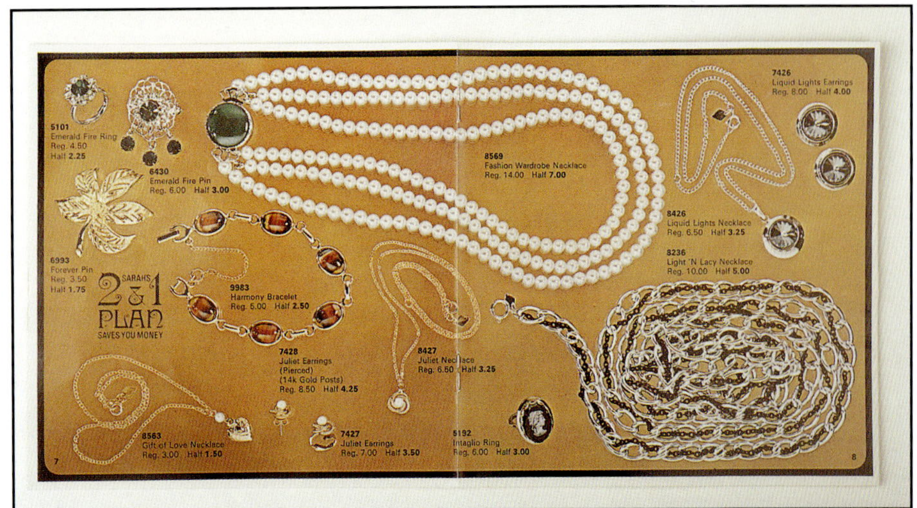

5101 Emerald Fire Ring Reg. 4.50 Half 2.25
6430 Emerald Fire Pin Reg. 6.00 Half 3.00
6993 Forever Pin Reg. 3.50 Half 1.75
SARAHS 2 & 1 PLAN SAVES YOU MONEY
9983 Harmony Bracelet Reg. 5.00 Half 2.50
8569 Fashion Wardrobe Necklace Reg. 14.00 Half 7.00
7428 Juliet Earrings (Pierced) (14k Gold Posts) Reg. 8.50 Half 4.25
8427 Juliet Necklace Reg. 6.50 Half 3.25
8563 Gift of Love Necklace Reg. 3.00 Half 1.50
7427 Juliet Earrings Reg. 7.00 Half 3.50
5192 Intaglio Ring Reg. 6.00 Half 3.00
7426 Liquid Lights Earrings Reg. 8.00 Half 4.00
8426 Liquid Lights Necklace Reg. 6.50 Half 3.25
8236 Light 'N Lacy Necklace Reg. 10.00 Half 5.00
7
8

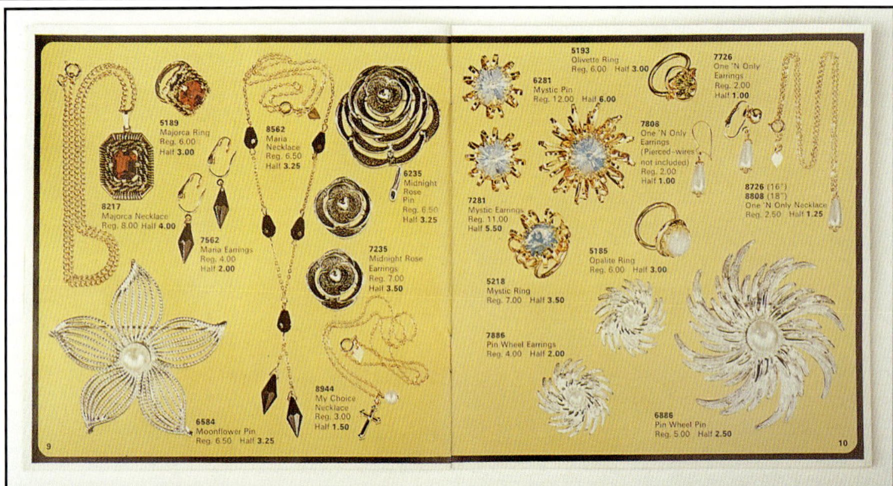

5189 Majorca Ring Reg. 6.00 Half 3.00
8217 Majorca Necklace Reg. 8.00 Half 4.00
7562 Maria Earrings Reg. 4.00 Half 2.00
8562 Maria Necklace Reg. 6.50 Half 3.25
6235 Midnight Rose Pin Reg. 6.50 Half 3.25
7235 Midnight Rose Earrings Reg. 7.00 Half 3.50
8944 My Choice Necklace Reg. 3.00 Half 1.50
6584 Moonflower Pin Reg. 6.50 Half 3.25
5193 Olivette Ring Reg. 6.00 Half 3.00
6281 Mystic Pin Reg. 12.00 Half 6.00
7281 Mystic Earrings Reg. 11.00 Half 5.50
5218 Mystic Ring Reg. 7.00 Half 3.50
7886 Pin Wheel Earrings Reg. 4.00 Half 2.00
7808 One 'N Only Earrings (Pierced—wires not included) Reg. 2.00 Half 1.00
5185 Opalite Ring Reg. 6.00 Half 3.00
7726 One 'N Only Earrings Reg. 2.00 Half 1.00
8726 (16") 8808 (18") One 'N Only Necklace Reg. 2.50 Half 1.25
6886 Pin Wheel Pin Reg. 5.00 Half 2.50
9
10

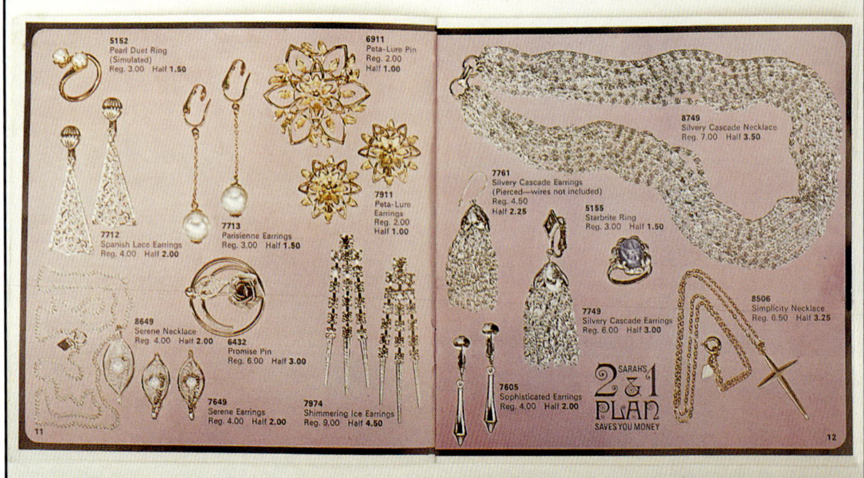

5152 Pearl Duet Ring (Simulated) Reg. 3.00 Half 1.50
7712 Spanish Lace Earrings Reg. 4.00 Half 2.00
7713 Parisienne Earrings Reg. 3.00 Half 1.50
6911 Peta-Lure Pin Reg. 2.00 Half 1.00
7911 Peta-Lure Earrings Reg. 2.00 Half 1.00
8649 Serene Necklace Reg. 4.00 Half 2.00
6432 Promise Pin Reg. 6.00 Half 3.00
7649 Serene Earrings Reg. 4.00 Half 2.00
7974 Shimmering Ice Earrings Reg. 9.00 Half 4.50
8749 Silvery Cascade Necklace Reg. 7.00 Half 3.50
7761 Silvery Cascade Earrings (Pierced—wires not included) Reg. 4.50 Half 2.25
5155 Starbrite Ring Reg. 3.00 Half 1.50
7749 Silvery Cascade Earrings Reg. 6.00 Half 3.00
8506 Simplicity Necklace Reg. 6.50 Half 3.25
7605 Sophisticated Earrings Reg. 4.00 Half 2.00
SARAHS 2 & 1 PLAN SAVES YOU MONEY
11
12

8279 Symphony Necklace Reg. 6.00 Half 3.00
7691 Venetian Earrings Reg. 5.00 Half 2.50
6691 Venetian Pin Reg. 5.50 Half 2.75
6587 Water Lily Pin Reg. 6.00 Half 3.00
9733 Young and Gay Bracelet Reg. 3.00 Half 1.50
7234 Wedding Band Earrings Reg. 3.50 Half 1.75
7291 Valencia Earrings Reg. 4.00 Half 2.00
8843 Beauty Chain (12KGF) 18" Reg. 3.00 Half 1.50
7441 Pierced Ear Wires (Sterling Silver) Reg. 2.00 Half 1.00
7440 Pierced Ear Wires (14k Solid Gold) Reg. 3.00 Half 1.50
5980 New Yorker Cuff Links Reg. 6.00 Half 3.00
5979 New Yorker Tie Tac Reg. 3.50 Half 1.75
6291 Valencia Pin Reg. 5.50 Half 2.75
SARAHS 2 & 1 PLAN SAVES YOU MONEY
8779 Silvertone 8780 Goldentone Versatility Chain Reg. 3.00 Half 1.50
5902 Aristocrat Cuff Links Reg. 4.00 Half 2.00
5901 Aristocrat Tie Tac Reg. 3.00 Half 1.50
13
14

1973

Continued on following page

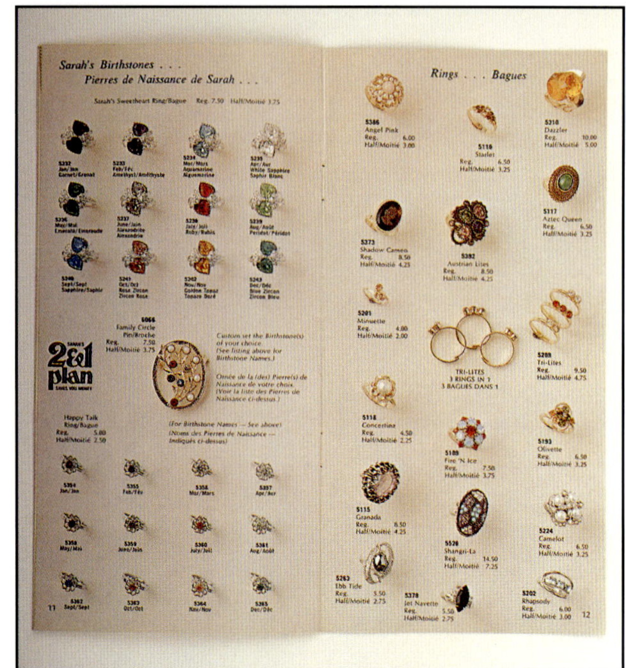

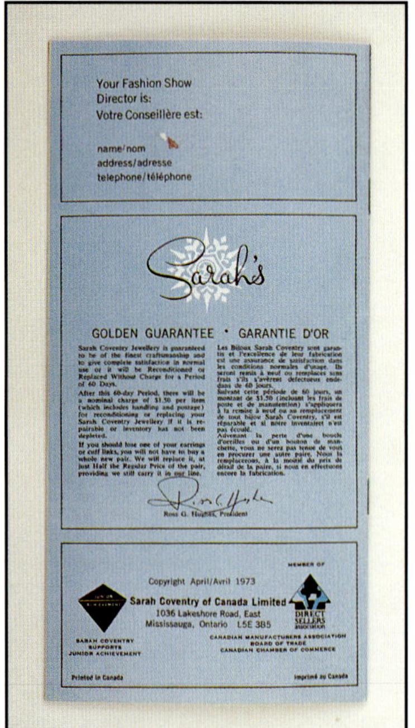

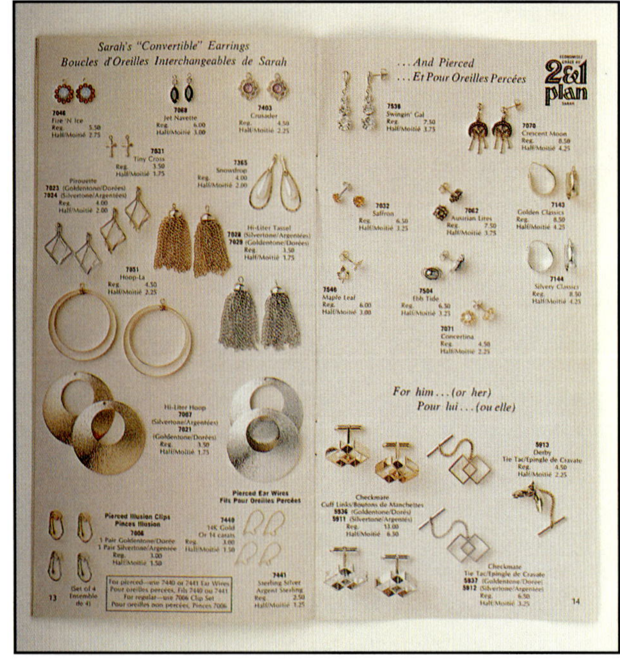

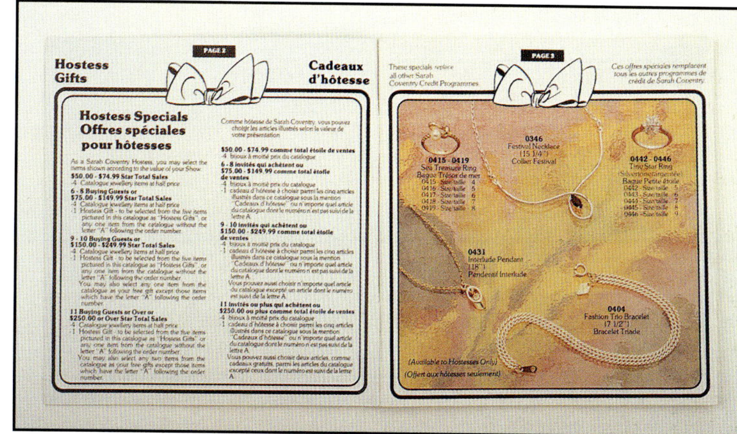

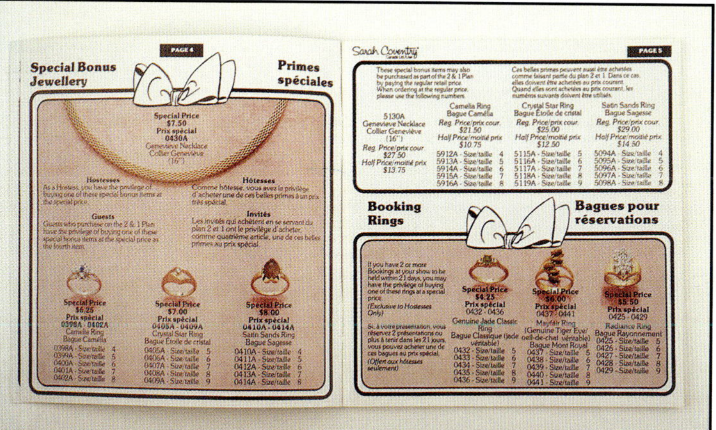

Continued on following pages

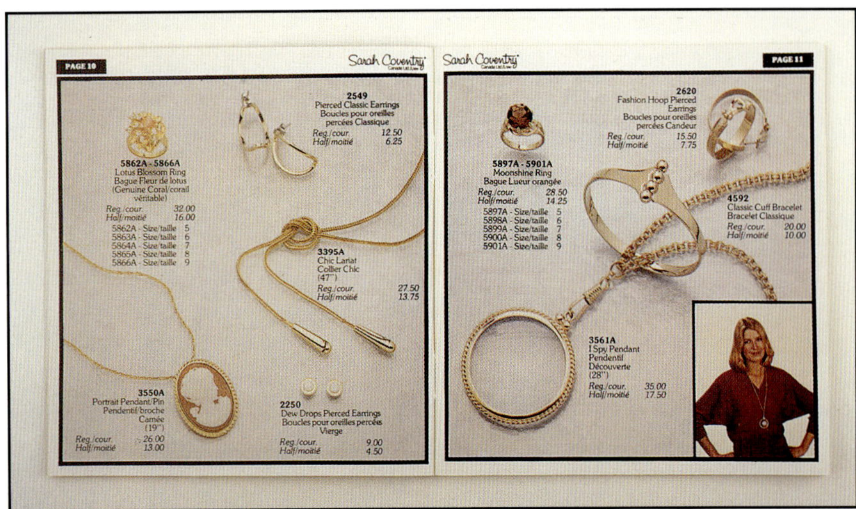

PAGE 10
Sarah Coventry
Canada Ltd./Ltee

5862A - 5866A
Lotus Blossom Ring
Bague Fleur de lotus
(Genuine Coral/corail véritable)
Reg./cour.   32.00
Half/moitié   16.00
5862A - Size/taille 5
5863A - Size/taille 6
5864A - Size/taille 7
5865A - Size/taille 8
5866A - Size/taille 9

2549
Pierced Classic Earrings
Boucles pour oreilles percées Classique
Reg./cour.   12.50
Half/moitié   6.25

3395A
Chic Lariat
Collier Chic
(47")
Reg./cour.   27.50
Half/moitié   13.75

3550A
Portrait Pendant/Pin
Pendentif/broche Camée
(19")
Reg./cour.   26.00
Half/moitié   13.00

2250
Dew Drops Pierced Earrings
Boucles pour oreilles percées Vierge
Reg./cour.   9.00
Half/moitié   4.50

PAGE 11
Sarah Coventry
Canada Ltd./Ltee

5897A - 5901A
Moonshine Ring
Bague Lueur orangée
Reg./cour.   28.50
Half/moitié   14.25
5897A - Size/taille 5
5898A - Size/taille 6
5899A - Size/taille 7
5900A - Size/taille 8
5901A - Size/taille 9

2620
Fashion Hoop Pierced Earrings
Boucles pour oreilles percées Candeur
Reg./cour.   15.50
Half/moitié   7.75

4592
Classic Cuff Bracelet
Bracelet Classique
Reg./cour.   20.00
Half/moitié   10.00

3561A
I Spy Pendant
Pendentif Découverte
(28")
Reg./cour.   35.00
Half/moitié   17.50

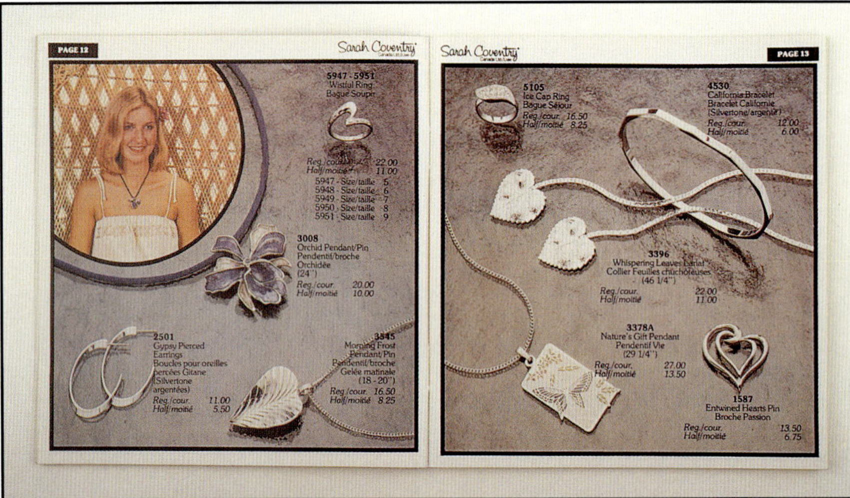

PAGE 12
Sarah Coventry
Canada Ltd./Ltee

5947 - 5951
Wistful Ring
Bague Soupir
Reg./cour.   22.00
Half/moitié   11.00
5947 - Size/taille 5
5948 - Size/taille 6
5949 - Size/taille 7
5950 - Size/taille 8
5951 - Size/taille 9

3008
Orchid Pendant/Pin
Pendentif/broche Orchidée
(24")
Reg./cour.   20.00
Half/moitié   10.00

2501
Gypsy Pierced Earrings
Boucles pour oreilles percées Gitane
(Silvertone/argentées)
Reg./cour.   11.00
Half/moitié   5.50

3545
Morning Frost Pendant/Pin
Pendentif/broche Gelée matinale
(18 - 20")
Reg./cour.   16.50
Half/moitié   8.25

PAGE 13
Sarah Coventry
Canada Ltd./Ltee

5105
Ice Cap Ring
Bague Séjour
Reg./cour.   16.50
Half/moitié   8.25

4530
California Bracelet
Bracelet Californie
(Silvertone/argenté)
Reg./cour.   12.00
Half/moitié   6.00

3396
Whispering Leaves Lariat
Collier Feuilles chuchoteuses
(46 1/4")
Reg./cour.   22.00
Half/moitié   11.00

3378A
Nature's Gift Pendant
Pendentif Vie
(29 1/4")
Reg./cour.   27.00
Half/moitié   13.50

1587
Entwined Hearts Pin
Broche Passion
Reg./cour.   13.50
Half/moitié   6.75

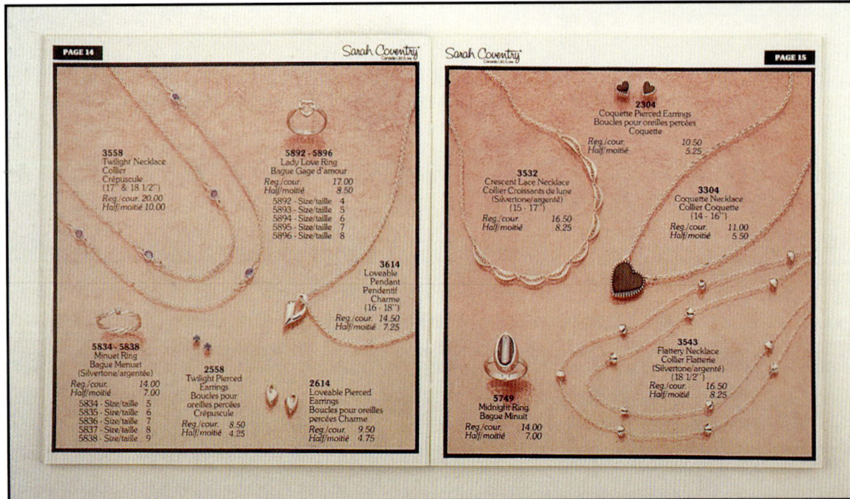

PAGE 14
Sarah Coventry
Canada Ltd./Ltee

3558
Twilight Necklace
Collier Crépuscule
(17" & 18 1/2")
Reg./cour.   20.00
Half/moitié   10.00

5892 - 5896
Lady Love Ring
Bague Gage d'amour
Reg./cour.   17.00
Half/moitié   8.50
5892 - Size/taille 4
5893 - Size/taille 5
5894 - Size/taille 6
5895 - Size/taille 7
5896 - Size/taille 8

3614
Loveable Pendant
Pendentif Charme
(16 - 18")
Reg./cour.   14.50
Half/moitié   7.25

5834 - 5838
Minuet Ring
Bague Menuet
(Silvertone/argenté)
Reg./cour.   14.00
Half/moitié   7.00
5834 - Size/taille 5
5835 - Size/taille 6
5836 - Size/taille 7
5837 - Size/taille 8
5838 - Size/taille 9

2558
Twilight Pierced Earrings
Boucles pour oreilles percées Crépuscule
Reg./cour.   8.50
Half/moitié   4.25

2614
Loveable Pierced Earrings
Boucles pour oreilles percées Charme
Reg./cour.   9.50
Half/moitié   4.75

PAGE 15
Sarah Coventry
Canada Ltd./Ltee

2304
Coquette Pierced Earrings
Boucles pour oreilles percées Coquette
Reg./cour.   10.50
Half/moitié   5.25

3532
Crescent Lace Necklace
Collier Croissants de lune
(Silvertone/argenté)
(15 - 17")
Reg./cour.   16.50
Half/moitié   8.25

3304
Coquette Necklace
Collier Coquette
(14 - 16")
Reg./cour.   11.00
Half/moitié   5.50

3543
Flattery Necklace
Collier Flatterie
(Silvertone/argenté)
(18 1/2")
Reg./cour.   16.50
Half/moitié   8.25

5749
Midnight Ring
Bague Minuit
Reg./cour.   14.00
Half/moitié   7.00

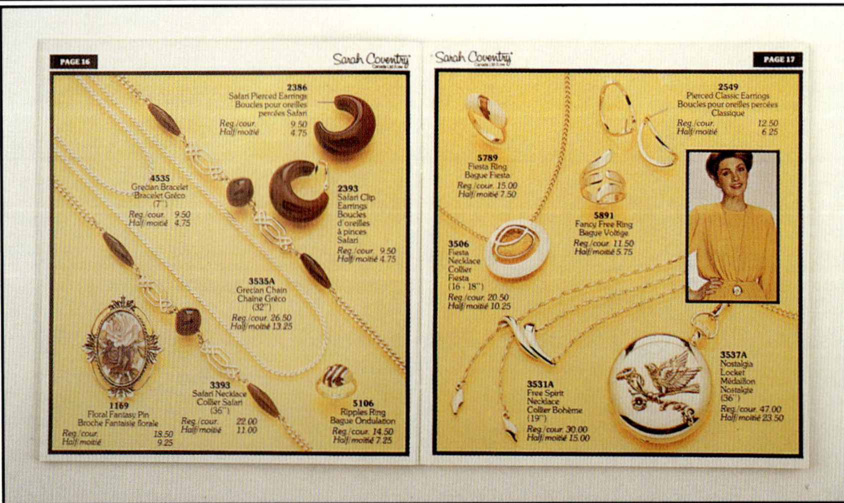

PAGE 16
Sarah Coventry
Canada Ltd./Ltee

2386
Safari Pierced Earrings
Boucles pour oreilles percées Safari
Reg./cour.   9.50
Half/moitié   4.75

4535
Grecian Bracelet
Bracelet Gréco
(7")
Reg./cour.   9.50
Half/moitié   4.75

2393
Safari Clip Earrings
Boucles d'oreilles à pinces Safari
Reg./cour.   9.50
Half/moitié   4.75

3535A
Grecian Chain
Chaîne Gréco
(32")
Reg./cour.   26.50
Half/moitié   13.25

1169
Floral Fantasy Pin
Broche Fantaisie florale
Reg./cour.   18.50
Half/moitié   9.25

3393
Safari Necklace
Collier Safari
(36")
Reg./cour.   22.00
Half/moitié   11.00

5106
Ripples Ring
Bague Ondulation
Reg./cour.   14.50
Half/moitié   7.25

PAGE 17
Sarah Coventry
Canada Ltd./Ltee

2549
Pierced Classic Earrings
Boucles pour oreilles percées Classique
Reg./cour.   12.50
Half/moitié   6.25

5789
Fiesta Ring
Bague Fiesta
Reg./cour.   15.00
Half/moitié   7.50

5891
Fancy Free Ring
Bague Voltige
Reg./cour.   11.50
Half/moitié   5.75

3506
Fiesta Necklace
Collier Fiesta
(16 - 18")
Reg./cour.   20.50
Half/moitié   10.25

3531A
Free Spirit Necklace
Collier Bohème
(19")
Reg./cour.   30.00
Half/moitié   15.00

3537A
Nostalgia Locket
Médaillon Nostalgie
(36")
Reg./cour.   47.00
Half/moitié   23.50

100

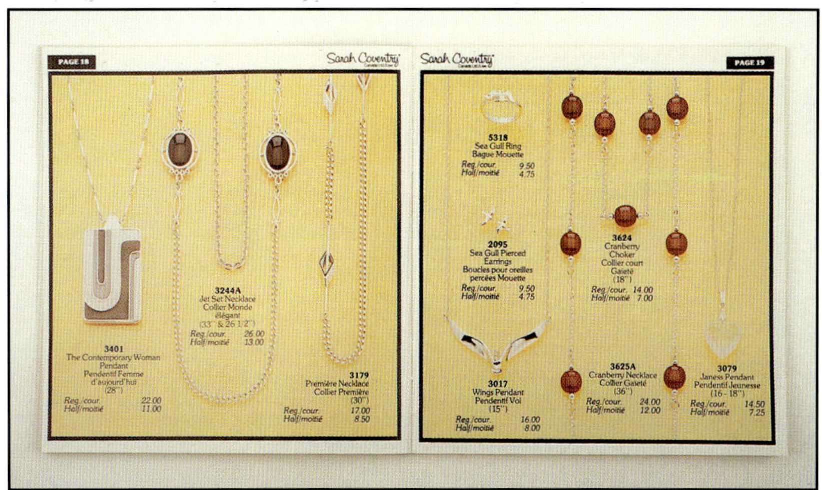

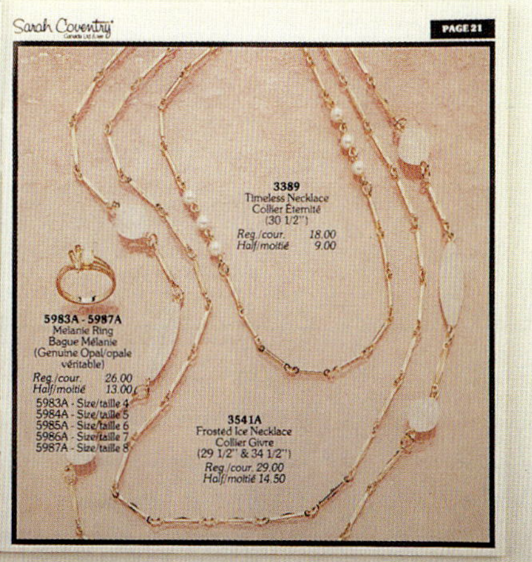

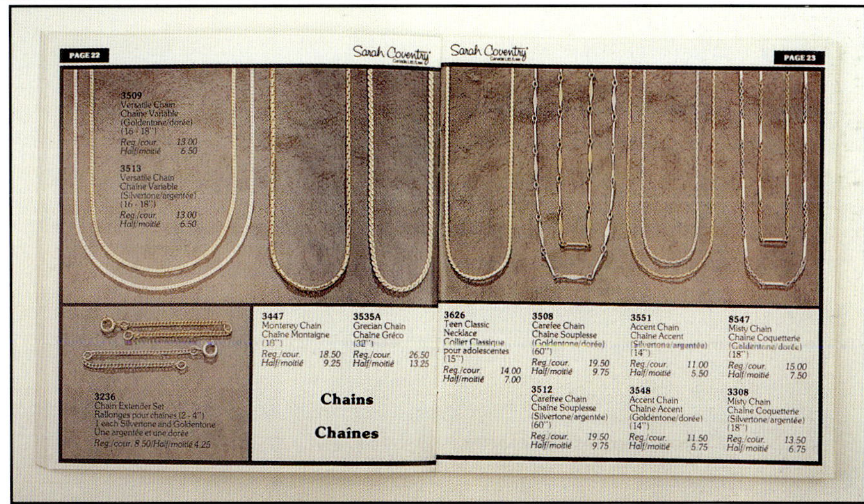

Continued on following pages

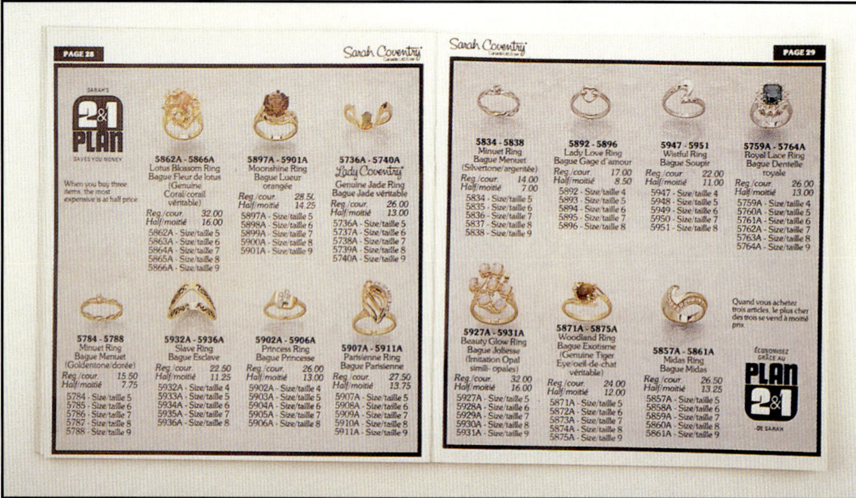

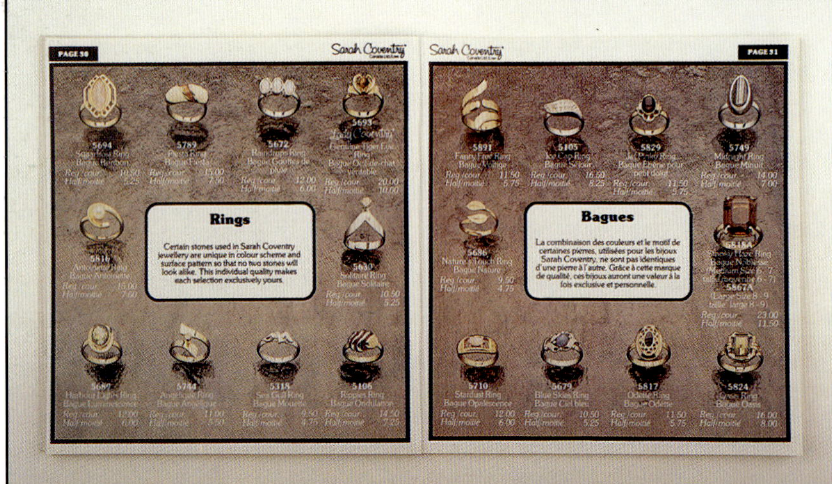

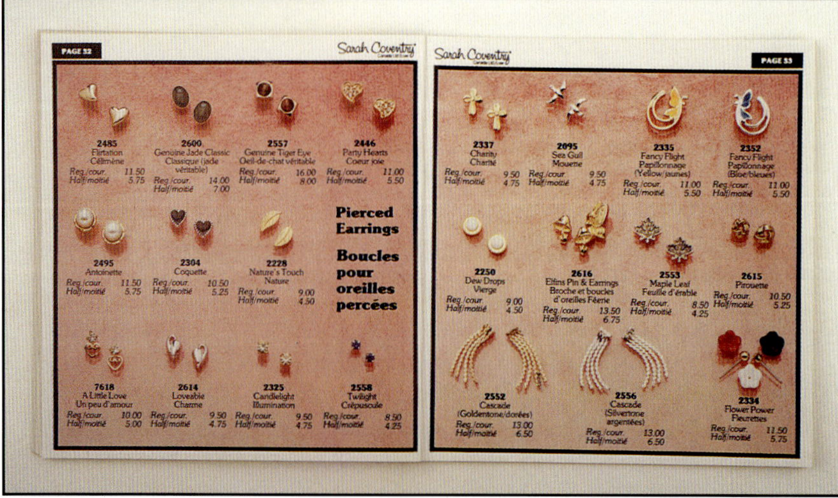

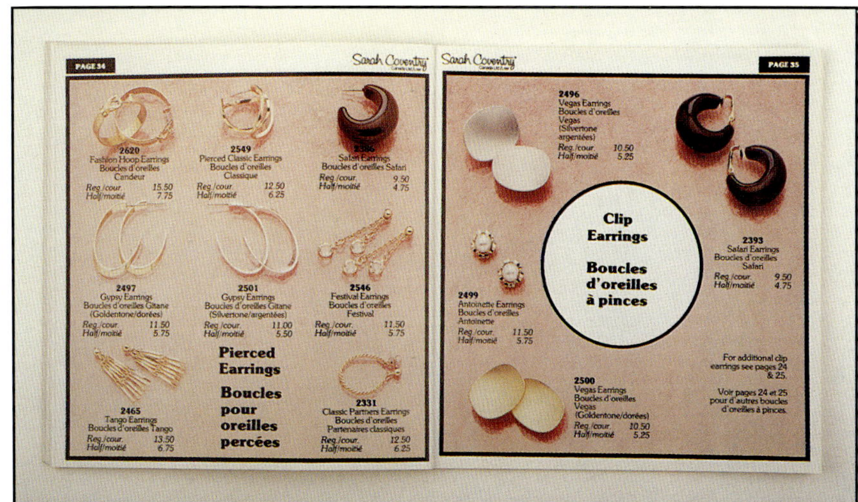

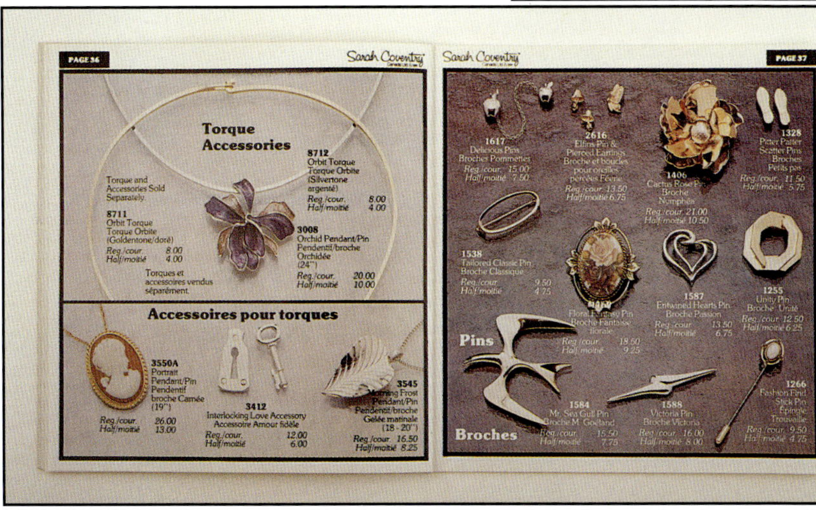

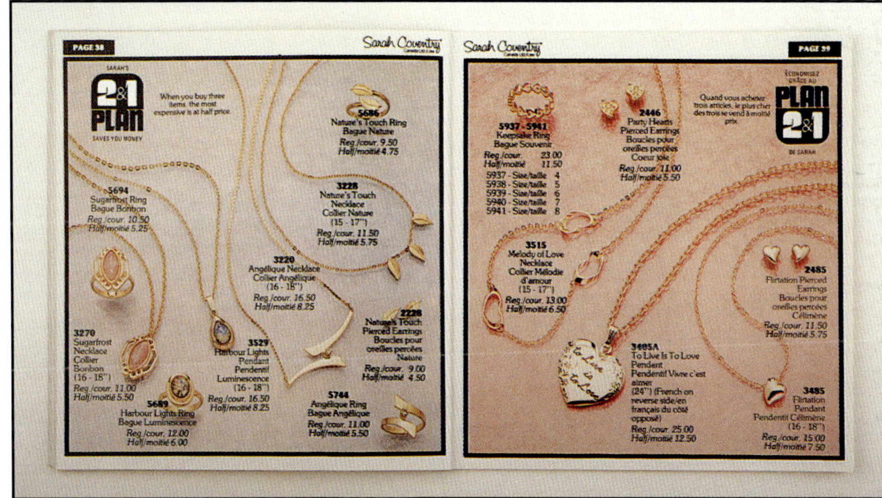

Continued on following pages

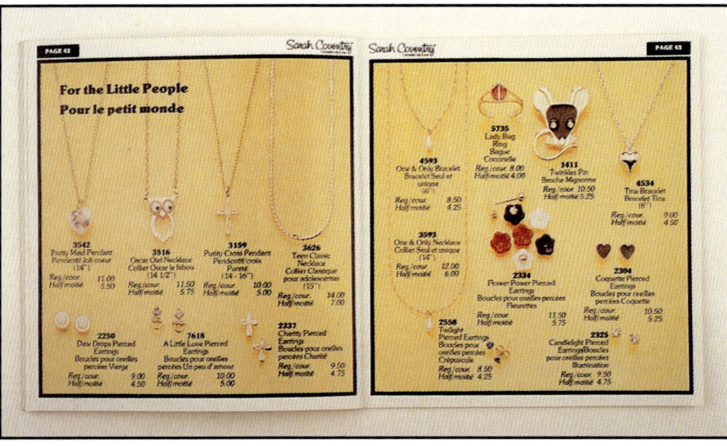
For the Little People
Pour le petit monde

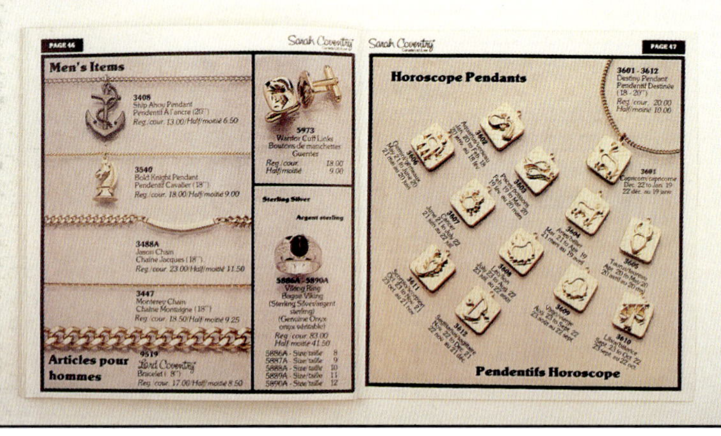
Bracelets

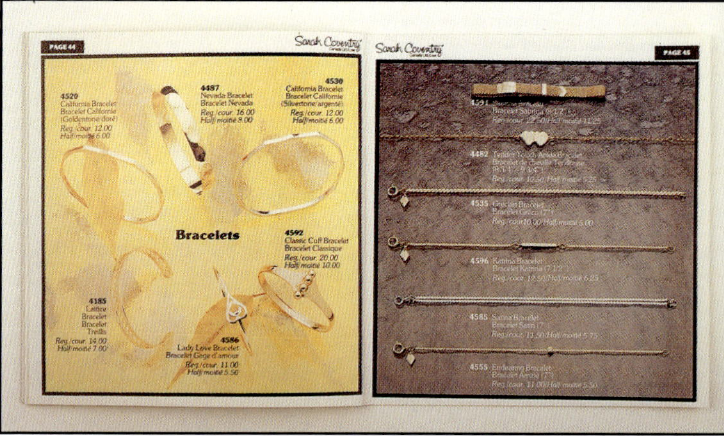

SARAH'S
2&1 PLAN
SAVES YOU MONEY
YOUR FASHION SHOW DIRECTOR
Votre conseillère
Telephone/Téléphone
ÉCONOMISEZ GRÂCE AU
PLAN 2&1
DE SARAH

Golden Guarantee
Sarah Coventry Jewellery is guaranteed for your complete satisfaction.
During the first ninety days: should your jewellery be unsatisfactory or should it become damaged due to normal use, it will be replaced or your purchase price will be refunded.

Additional Service
After ninety days: should your jewellery become damaged due to normal use, it will be repaired or replaced for $2.50 providing the item is still carried in stock. Should this item not be in stock, no substitutions will be made.

How to obtain Repairs, Replacements or Refunds
Mail • the jewellery item
• the Guest Receipt
• a note instructing the Company as to whether you wish a refund or replacement
• $2.50 per item (for repairs or replacements after 90 days)
Mail to: Sarah Coventry Canada Ltd., Cambridge, Ontario N3C 3H1
The Fashion Show Director is not authorized to accept returns.
All prices are subject to change without notice.

A part-time opportunity or a career in the lucrative, fun world of fashion could be yours. Ask your Fashion Show Director or write to the Sales Department at Sarah Coventry Canada Ltd.

Garantie d'or
Les bijoux Sarah Coventry sont garantis pour votre satisfaction complète.
Durant les 90 premiers jours: Si vous n'êtes pas satisfait(e) ou si votre bijou devient endommagé sous conditions normales d'usage, il sera remplacé ou le prix que vous avez payé vous sera remboursé.

Service additionnel
Après 90 jours: Si votre bijou devient endommagé sous conditions normales d'usage, il sera réparé ou remplacé au prix de $2.50 pourvu que l'article soit encore en stock. Si l'article n'est pas en stock, aucune substitution ne sera faite.

Comment obtenir une réparation, un remplacement ou un remboursement
Expédiez: • le bijou
• le reçu d'invité(e)
• une note informant la compagnie si vous désirez un remboursement ou un remplacement
• $2.50 par article (pour réparation ou remplacement après 90 jours)
Expédié à: Sarah Coventry Canada Ltée, Cambridge, Ontario N3C 3H1
La conseillère n'a pas le droit d'accepter les bijoux retournés.
Tous les prix peuvent varier sans avis préalable.
L'occasion d'un emploi à temps partiel ou d'une carrière dans le domaine amusant et lucratif de la mode est à votre portée. Adressez-vous à votre conseillère ou écrivez au Service des ventes à Sarah Coventry Canada Ltée.

Fashions Co-ordinated by
Dasha's Boutique
Cambridge, Ontario

Vêtements harmonisés par
Dasha's Boutique
Cambridge, Ontario

Member of Direct Sellers Association / Membre de l'association de ventes à domicile

Copyright September 1980

Droit d'auteur, septembre 1980

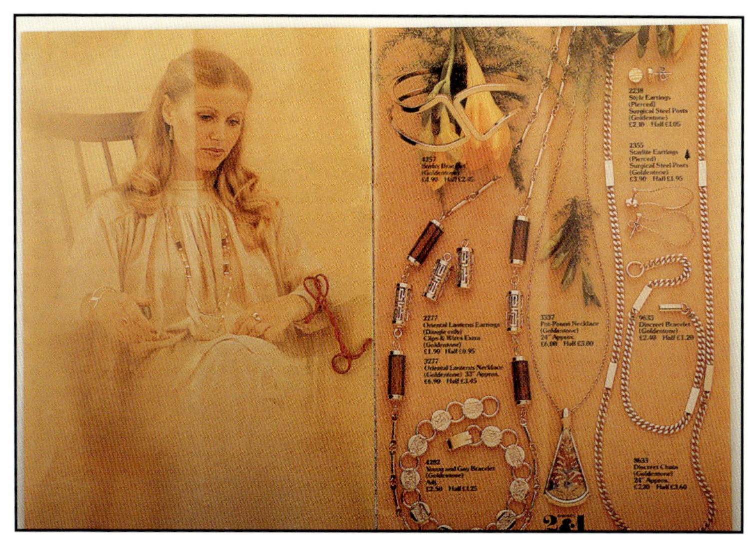

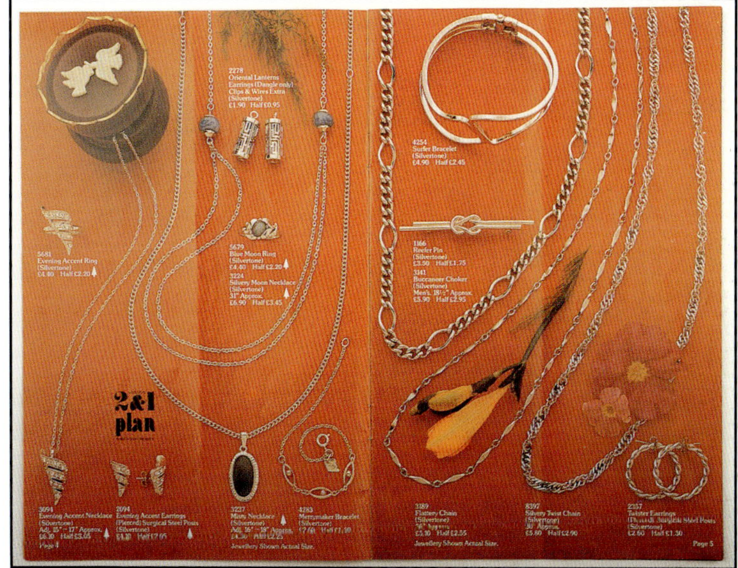

Continued on following pages

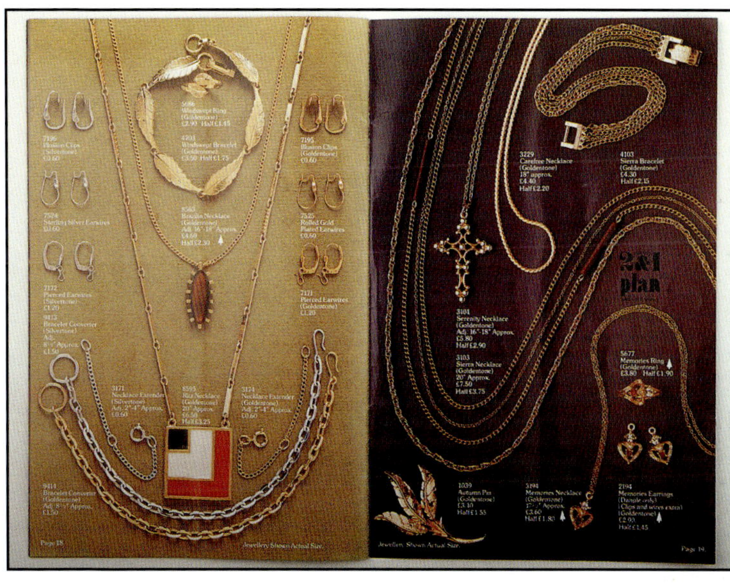

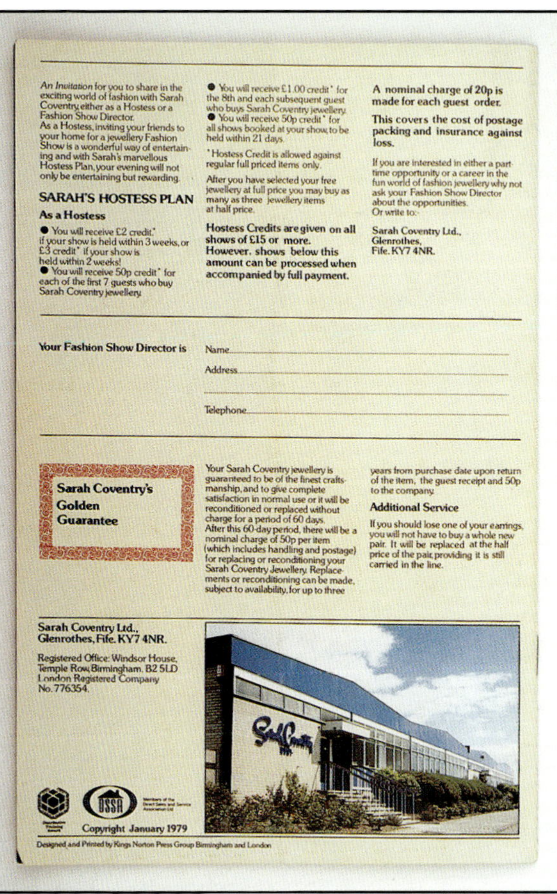

An Invitation for you to share in the exciting world of fashion with Sarah Coventry either as a Hostess or a Fashion Show Director.
As a Hostess, inviting your friends to your home for a jewellery Fashion Show is a wonderful way of entertaining and with Sarah's marvellous Hostess Plan, your evening will not only be entertaining but rewarding.

SARAH'S HOSTESS PLAN

As a Hostess

● You will receive £2 credit.*
if your show is held within 3 weeks, or £3 credit* if your show is held within 2 weeks!
● You will receive 50p credit* for each of the first 7 guests who buy Sarah Coventry jewellery.

● You will receive £1.00 credit* for the 8th and each subsequent guest who buys Sarah Coventry jewellery.
● You will receive 50p credit* for all shows booked at your show to be held within 21 days.

* Hostess Credit is allowed against regular full priced items only.

After you have selected your free jewellery at full price you may buy as many as three jewellery items at half price.

Hostess Credits are given on all shows of £15 or more. However, shows below this amount can be processed when accompanied by full payment.

A nominal charge of 20p is made for each guest order.

This covers the cost of postage packing and insurance against loss.

If you are interested in either a part-time opportunity or a career in the fun world of fashion jewellery why not ask your Fashion Show Director about the opportunities.
Or write to:

Sarah Coventry Ltd.,
Glenrothes,
Fife. KY7 4NR.

Your Fashion Show Director is

Name

Address

Telephone

Sarah Coventry's Golden Guarantee

Your Sarah Coventry jewellery is guaranteed to be of the finest craftsmanship, and to give complete satisfaction in normal use or it will be reconditioned or replaced without charge for a period of 60 days. After this 60-day period, there will be a nominal charge of 50p per item (which includes handling and postage) for replacing or reconditioning your Sarah Coventry Jewellery. Replacements or reconditioning can be made, subject to availability, for up to three years from purchase date upon return of the item, the guest receipt and 50p to the company.

Additional Service

If you should lose one of your earrings, you will not have to buy a whole new pair. It will be replaced at the half price of the pair, providing it is still carried in the line.

Sarah Coventry Ltd., Glenrothes, Fife. KY7 4NR.

Registered Office: Windsor House, Temple Row, Birmingham. B2 5LD
London Registered Company No. 776354.

Copyright January 1979

Designed and Printed by Kings Norton Press Group Birmingham and London

Sarah Coventry
PTY. LTD.
Jewellery Fashions
FOR SPRING & SUMMER

6063
Westminster Pin
Silvertone
Reg. Half
$16.00 $8.00

8403
Crusader Pendant
Silvertone
Reg. Half
$12.00 $6.00

8749
Silvery Cascade Necklace
Silvertone
Reg. Half
$9.50 $4.75

7255
Silvery Sunburst Earrings
Silvertone
Simulated Pearl
Reg. Half
$6.00 $3.00

9749
Silvery Cascade
Bracelet
Silvertone
Reg. Half
$8.00 $4.00

6255
Silvery Sunburst Pin
Silvertone
Simulated Pearl
Reg. Half
$7.00 $3.50

2&1 PLAN

7028
Satellite Earrings
Silvertone
Price does not include
Clips or Wires
Reg. Half
$5.00 $2.50

6007
Clair de Lune Pin
Silvertone
Reg. Half
$8.50 $4.25

7007
Apollo Earrings
Silvertone
Price does not include
Clips or Wires
Reg. Half
$4.50 2.25

5329
Infinity Ring
Silvertone
Reg. Half
$9.50 $4.75

9053
Barossa Bracelet
Silvertone
Reg. Half
$12.50 $6.25

EXCLUSIVE . . .
FOR Sarah's HOSTESSES

9344
Wood Nymph Bracelet
Goldentone
$8.00
in Hostess Credits

5127
Wood Nymph Ring
Goldentone
$6.00
in Hostess Credits

"Wood Nymph" — matching the lovely Wood Nymph Necklace
simulates the colour of natural Australian woods. No two stones
are alike in their unique shadings of rich golden browns.
Obtainable only by Sarah's Hostesses with "Hostess Credits".

105
Majorca Ring
Goldentone
$4.00

Something special for your
special friend — your Hostess.
Majorca Ring. It cannot be used
on the 2 & 1 Plan or on Hostess
Credit, and only one ring is
allowable per Hostess.

SARAH'S BIRTHSTONE RINGS
The Birthstone Ring — a symbol of happiness and good
fortune — with beautiful, imported glass stones in a magnificent
silvertone setting.

Each—Reg. $4.50 Half $2.25

5342
January
Garnet

5343
February
Amethyst

5344
March
Aquamarine

5345
April
White Sapphire

5346
May
Emerald

5347
June
Alexandrite

5348
July
Ruby

5349
August
Peridot

5350
September
Sapphire

5351
October
Zircon

5352
November
Golden Topaz

5353
December
Blue Zircon

8160
Wood Nymph Necklace
Goldentone
Reg. Half
$14.50 $7.25

7056
Sunspray Earrings
Goldentone
Reg. Half
$8.00 $4.00

6056
Sunspray Pin
Goldentone
Reg. Half
$9.50 $4.75

2&1 PLAN

8152
Golden Cross Pendant
Goldentone
Reg. Half
$11.00 $5.50

5396
Rhapsody Ring
Goldentone
Reg. Half
$8.00 $4.00

7234
Wedding Band Earrings
Goldentone
Reg. Half
$4.50 $2.25

7395
Golden Cross Earrings
Goldentone/Pierced
Reg. Half
$7.50 $3.75

6092
Colonial Pin
Goldentone
Reg. Half
$9.00 $4.50

8109
Versatility Chain
Goldentone 29"
Reg. Half
$7.00 $3.50

8052
Magic Moods Pendant
Goldentone
Reg. Half
$19.00 $9.50

6030
Heritage Pin
Goldentone
Reg. Half
$9.00 $4.50

5271
Heritage Ring
Goldentone
Reg. Half
$9.00 $4.50

7030
Heritage Earrings
Goldentone/Pierced
Reg. Half
$9.00 $4.50

7181
Wildwood Earrings
Goldentone
Price does not include
Clips or Wires
Reg. Half
$8.00 $4.00

6181
Wildwood Pin
Goldentone
Reg. Half
$20.00 $10.00

2&1 PLAN

Sarah Coventry

"EXCLUSIVE" HOSTESS PLAN

You receive $1.00* Credit for each guest who buys Sarah Coventry Jewellery.
You receive $1.00* Credit for each guest who books a Fashion Show of her own.
PLUS $2.00 EXTRA* Credit when YOUR Show is held within two weeks of contacting the Fashion Show Director.

A SPECIAL HOSTESS PRIVILEGE

After you have selected your FREE jewellery at full retail for the credits due, you may select three jewellery items of your choice at ½ the regular price.
* Hostess Credit applies to regular priced items.

PREFERRED HOSTESS PLAN

When you have held 3 Shows of $50.00 or more within one year you may select an additional 10% in jewellery on your three Shows. A fun and fashionable way to select your complete jewellery wardrobe.

SARAH'S 2 AND 1 PLAN

Saves you money because, for two items of Sarah Coventry Jewellery you purchase at regular price, you may purchase another item at ½ price. You'll naturally buy the most expensive piece of jewellery at ½ price.

Sarah's

GOLDEN GUARANTEE

Sarah Coventry Jewellery is guaranteed to be of the finest craftsmanship and to give complete satisfaction in normal use, or it will be reconditioned or replaced without charge for a period of 60 days. After this 60-day period there will be a nominal charge of $1.50 per item (which includes handling and postage) for replacing or reconditioning your Sarah Coventry Jewellery. Replacements or reconditioning cannot be made if over three years from purchase date.
If you should lose one of your earrings, you will not have to buy a whole new pair. We will replace it, at just half the retail price of the pair, providing we still carry it in our line.

For more information, contact me — your Fashion Show Director.

Name

Chapter Four

Emmons Jewelry

As I begin discussing Emmons Jewelry, I want to introduce to you Mary Beth Coffman, who has become a good friend and lives very close to me. Mary Beth joined the Emmons company as a Fashion Show Director in 1965 and continued through 1968 in the Kansas City, Missouri area. I met Mary Beth while promoting my first book, and that is when she challenged me to do another book, this time including Emmons, as she is partial to its beauty. She also indicated that she had a lot of jewelry I could include.

Mary Beth Coffman was employed with Emmons as a Fashion Show Director from 1965 to 1968 in the Kansas City, Missouri area. Although she was with Emmons for only a short time, she sings the their praises as a wonderful company with very high quality and beautiful jewelry.

Mary Beth provided me with lots of information about experiences she had with Emmons, and one was rather unique. On her way to a Republican meeting, her car was rear-ended. She shared this very distressing situation at an area gathering of Emmons consultants where Tom Healy, Vice President of Sales, was also in attendance presenting awards and jewelry to area achievers. Tom heard her talking about the accident as well as her interest in the Republican party and especially her passion for elephants. Mary Beth mentioned to him her idea of creating an elephant pin that might be of interest to other Republican women or elephant collectors. At a later event, Tom presented her with the elephant below, stating that it was a one-of-a-kind piece, since the mold had been broken. Mary Beth, to say the least, is very proud of this item.

During my visit to Newark, New York, I had the pleasure of being introduced to Bill and Carol Scheetz. Bill had been employed with C.H. Stuart in the Emmons Nursery division prior to 1949. When this nursery merged with another of Stuart's nursery companies, Bill – along with several others – was asked by Lyman Stuart to develop a jewelry company utilizing the home party plan and continuing the Emmons name through this company. Bill served as Executive Vice President from 1949 through 1960, at which time he became President of the division through 1969. Bill was not certain, but believes it was in late 1968 or early 1969 when the name "Caroline" was added to the company name. It was felt that this would add personality to the company, since Sarah Coventry was doing very well with a two-name title. The signature on the jewelry wasn't changed, but the promotional materials and catalogs added the name "Caroline." "Emmons" was the maiden name of C.H. Stuart's wife. Her first name was Caroline, so this was the reason for the jewelry name. (See more information on page 132 about a piece of jewelry specially designed for Caroline Emmons Stuart.)

Emmons did not enter the international market, although at one time the company was thinking of going to Japan. Because of cultural differences and customs, however, this turned out not to be feasible. Bill also mentioned that in the early years, Sarah Coventry would begin FSDs in one city in California, San Francisco, and Emmons would take Los Angeles so there wouldn't be any overlapping. However, it appears that eventually these division lines were removed and Fashion Show Directors could function wherever they wanted.

Bill was presented with a plaque during the 1977 building dedication for his long-time efforts with the company. In the picture to the right of the plaque, he is shown with his wife, Carol, and Aileen VanTyle, Publicity Director of Sarah Coventry. This was taken in 1973, a short time after Bill retired.

Bill Scheetz received this plaque at the C.H. Stuart building dedication in 1977. He is also pictured in the photo at far right. *Courtesy of Arcadia Historical Society.*

A one-of-a-kind pin owned by Mary Beth Coffman, given to her by Tom Healy, Vice President of Sales. She had suggested to him that Emmons might be interested in creating an elephant pin and not long after he presented her with this stylized red, white, and blue pin. She was told that this was the only one made before the mold was broken. What a truly marvelous gift and remembrance. *Courtesy of Mary Beth Coffman.*

These kinds of special awards and other promotional assistance and support from Emmons made Mary Beth and many of the other sales personnel feel very important and special. Following are some of the brochures that promoted opportunities with Emmons, One of the constantly mentioned phrases was "fashion magic," referring to the versatility of the jewelry and the many pieces that were created to be taken apart and worn separately or together. Notice these pieces throughout the pictures.

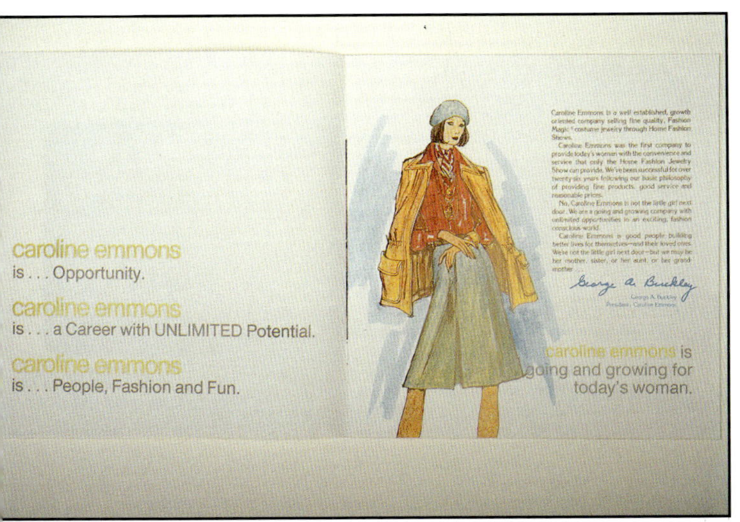

Promotional materials for Caroline Emmons, describing the advertising used, the great versatility of the jewelry, and the career opportunities available. *Courtesy of Arcadia Historical Society.*

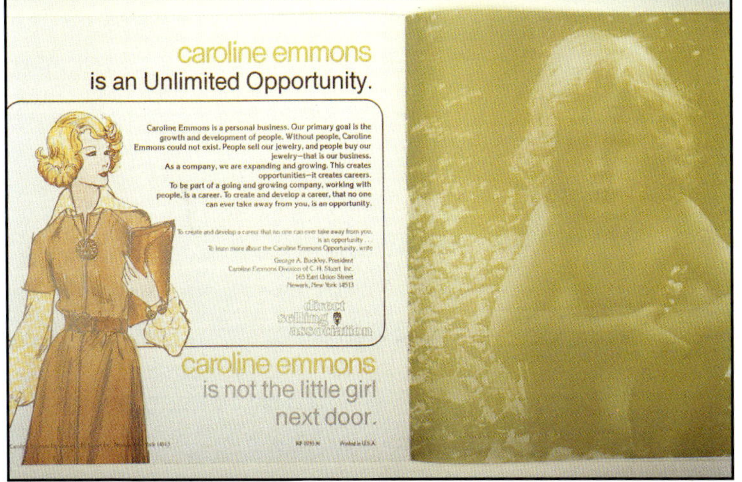

Through their cadre of Fashion Show Directors, Emmons was able to spread throughout the United States, presenting dynamic costume jewelry to many housewives and newly rising business women. One promotion designed to spur the Fashion Show Directors on was entitled "Magic Lantern." Parts of the literature describing this special are shown below.

The Magic Lantern or Magic Mirror campaign was held from November 5, 1960 through January 6, 1961. I am sure many members of the sales force became excited and were urged on by this promotion. *Courtesy of Arcadia Historical Society.*

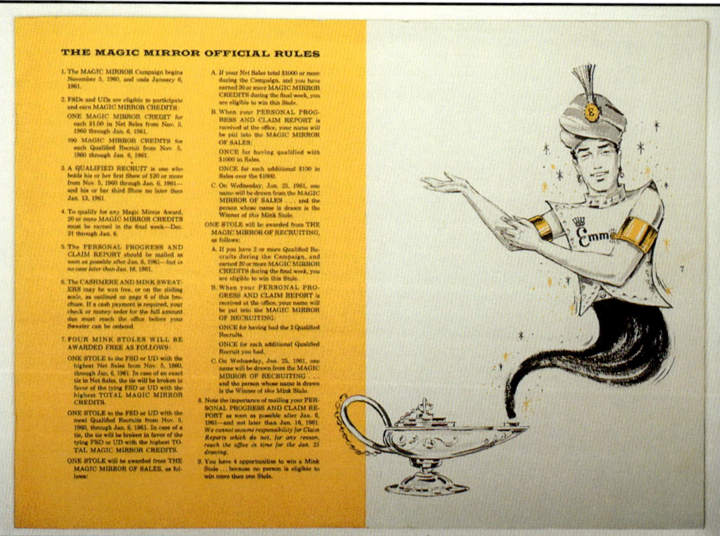

As with Sarah Coventry, the party plan concept depended on parties being set up at someone's house. Shown next is a flyer illustrating some of the benefits of being a hostess. At that time, the orders were sent to the hostess who would then finish collecting for the pieces and deliver to the guests. Hostesses felt the benefit of getting free jewelry outweighed the effort of getting the jewelry to their friends.

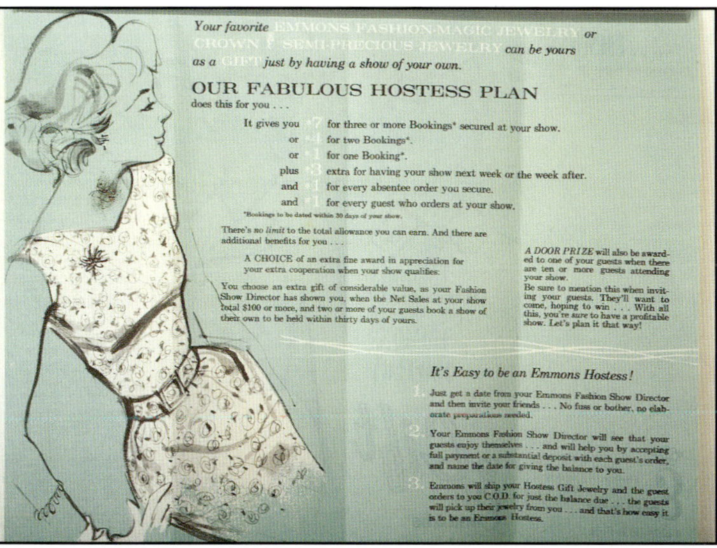

A flyer delineating the benefits of being a hostess for an Emmons party. Many hostesses were quite pleased with the jewelry benefits and gladly asked a few friends over to look at the jewelry and order items for themselves or as gifts. *Courtesy of Arcadia Historical Society.*

Ginny Williams sent me information about herself along with her prized catalog from 1976 signed by Miss America. *Courtesy of Ginny Williams.*

In talking with Fashion Show Directors, comments are always made about how the company cared for their employees. Voices become very emotional as the former FSDs recall some of their fond memories. One such employee I was not able to meet in person was Ginny Williams. She provided me with some of the catalogs and other promotional materials used in this chapter.

Ginny was with Caroline Emmons from 1971 through the very end in 1981, when the merger with Sarah Coventry took place. Ginny considered those ten years "the greatest ten years of my life." Going with Sarah Coventry seemed like an affront to her feelings of great loyalty to Caroline.

In 1976, Emmons helped with sponsorship of the Miss America Pageant and the winner that year was Tawny Godin, Miss New York State. The cover of the Spring and Summer catalog pictured here featured Miss Godin wearing an Emmons necklace. She also signed this catalog, which Ginny cherishes as one of her most memorable keepsakes. The company sponsored other events as well, including the Winter Olympics in 1980. The C.H. Stuart company and Emmons were very dedicated to supporting and donating not only to local events, but to national events as well that would keep their name in front of prospective customers.

Becoming a Fashion Show Director with Emmons was the first step in the company's recruitment process. From that point on, FSDs were encouraged to recruit others, thereby moving toward management positions themselves. The promotional information shown here speaks to this concept.

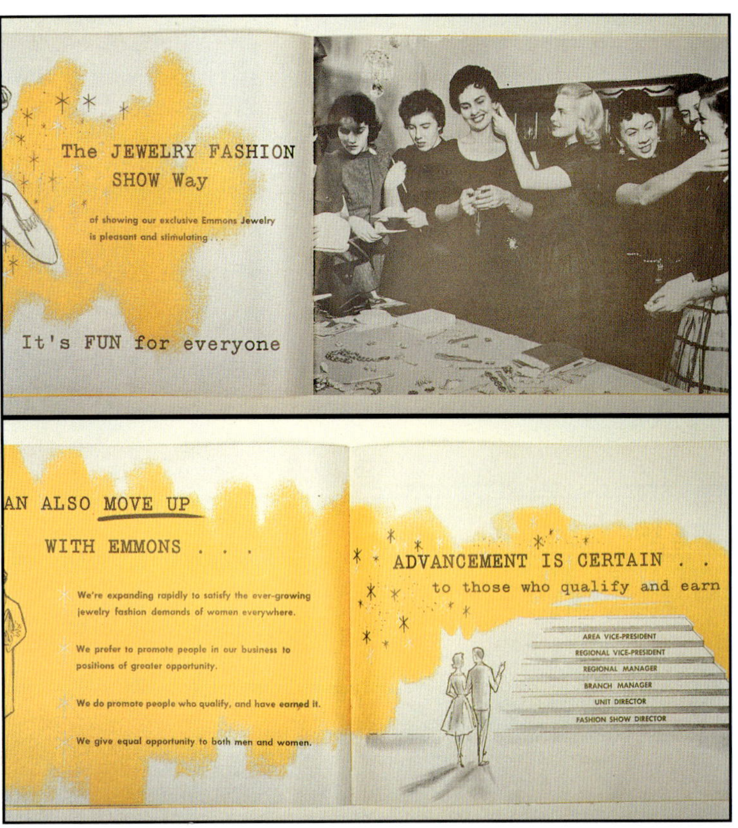

Promotional brochure designed to provide employees with the incentive to work hard and advance. *Courtesy of Arcadia Historical Society.*

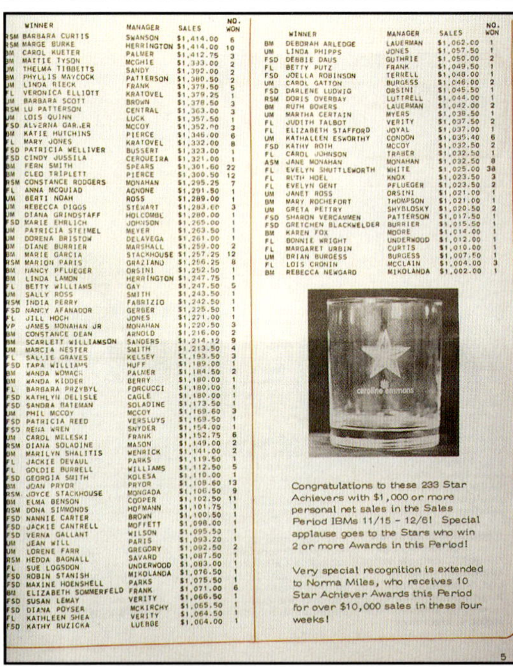

	WINNER	MANAGER	SALES	NO. WON
RSM	BARBARA CURTIS	SWANSON	$1,414.00	6
RSM	MARGE BURKE	HERRINGTON	$1,414.00	10
BM	CAROL KUETER	PALMER	$1,412.75	3
BM	MATTIE TYSON	MCGHIE	$1,393.00	2
UM	THELMA TIBBETTS	SANDY	$1,392.00	2
BM	PHYLLIS MAYCOCK	PATTERSON	$1,380.50	2
UM	LINDA RIECK	FRANK	$1,379.50	5
FL	VERONICA ELLIOTT	KRATOVEL	$1,379.25	1
UM	BARBARA SCOTT	BROWN	$1,378.50	3
RSM	LU PATTERSON	CENTRAL	$1,363.00	3
UM	LOIS QUINN	LUCK	$1,357.50	1
FSD	ALVERNA GAR..ER	MCCOY	$1,352.00	3
BM	KATIE HUTCHINS	PIERCE	$1,346.00	6
FL	MARY JONES	KRATOVEL	$1,332.00	8
FSD	PATRICIA WELLIVER	BUSSERT	$1,323.00	1
FSD	CINDY JUSSILA	CERQUEIRA	$1,321.00	1
BM	FERN SMITH	SPEARS	$1,301.60	22
BM	CLEO TRIPLETT	PIERCE	$1,300.50	12
RSM	CONSTANCE RODGERS	MONAHAN	$1,295.25	7
FL	ANNA MCQUIAD	AGNONE	$1,291.50	1
UM	BERTI NOAH	ROSS	$1,289.00	1
UM	REBECCA DIGGS	STEWART	$1,283.60	3
UM	DIANA GRINDSTAFF	HOLCOMBE	$1,280.00	1
FSD	MARIE EHRLICH	JOHNSON	$1,265.00	1
UM	PATRICIA STEIMEL	MEYER	$1,263.50	1
UM	DORENA BRISTOW	DELAVEGA	$1,261.00	1
BM	DIANE BURRIER	MARSHALL	$1,259.00	2
BM	MARIE GARCIA	STACKHOUSE	$1,257.25	12
RSM	MARION PARIS	GRAZIANO	$1,256.25	8
BM	NANCY PFLUEGER	ORSINI	$1,252.50	1
BM	LINDA LAMON	HERRINGTON	$1,247.75	1
FL	BETTY WILLIAMS	GAY	$1,247.50	5
UM	SALLY ROSS	SMITH	$1,243.50	1
RSM	INDIA PERRY	FABRIZIO	$1,242.50	1
FSD	NANCY AFANADOR	GERBER	$1,225.50	1
FL	JILL HOCH	JONES	$1,271.00	1
VP	JAMES MONAHAN JR	MONAHAN	$1,220.50	3
BM	CONSTANCE DEAN	ARNOLD	$1,216.00	2
BM	SCARLETT WILLIAMSON	SANDERS	$1,214.12	9
UM	MARCIA NESTER	SMITH	$1,213.50	4
FL	SALLIE GRAVES	KELSEY	$1,193.50	3
FSD	TAPA WILLIAMS	HUFF	$1,189.00	1
BM	WANDA WOMACK	PALMER	$1,184.50	2
UM	WANDA KIDDER	BERRY	$1,180.00	1
FL	BARBARA PRZYBYL	FORCUCCI	$1,180.00	1
FSD	KATHLYN DELISLE	CAGLE	$1,180.00	1
FSD	SANDRA BATEMAN	SOLADINE	$1,173.50	1
UM	PHIL MCCOY	MCCOY	$1,169.50	3
FSD	PATRICIA REED	VERSLUYS	$1,169.50	1
UM	REVA WREN	SNYDER	$1,154.00	1
UM	CAROL MILESKI	FRANK	$1,152.75	4
RSM	DIANA SOLAGINE	MASON	$1,149.00	2
UM	MAHILYN SHALTIS	WENRICK	$1,141.00	2
FL	JACKIE DEVAUL	PARKS	$1,135.50	1
FL	GOLDIE BURRELL	WILLIAMS	$1,112.50	5
FSD	GEORGIA SMITH	KOLESA	$1,110.00	1
BM	JOAN PRYOR	PRYOR	$1,109.60	13
RSM	JOYCE STACKHOUSE	MONGADA	$1,106.50	9
UM	ELMA BENSON	COOPER	$1,102.50	11
UM	DONA SIMMONDS	HOFMANN	$1,101.75	1
FSD	NANNIE CARTER	BROWN	$1,100.50	1
FSD	JACKIE CANTRELL	MOFFETT	$1,098.00	1
UM	VERNA GALLANT	WILSON	$1,095.53	1
UM	JEAN WILL	PARIS	$1,093.20	1
UM	LORENE FARR	GREGORY	$1,092.50	2
RSM	HEDDA MCDNALL	SAVARD	$1,087.50	1
BM	SUE LOGSDON	UNDERWOOD	$1,083.00	1
FSD	ROBIN STANISH	MIKOLANDA	$1,076.50	1
FSD	MAXINE HOENSFELL	PARKS	$1,075.50	1
BM	ELIZABETH SONNERFELD	FRANK	$1,071.00	6
FSD	SUSAN LERAY	VERITY	$1,066.90	1
FSD	DIANA POYSER	MCKIRCHY	$1,065.50	1
FL	KATHLEEN SHEA	VERITY	$1,064.50	1
FSD	KATHY RUZICKA	LUERBE	$1,064.00	1
BM	DEBORAH ARLEDGE	LAUERMAN	$1,062.00	1
UM	LINDA PHIPPS	JONES	$1,057.50	1
FSD	DEBBIE DAUS	GUTHRIE	$1,050.00	2
FSD	BETTY PUTZ	FRANK	$1,049.50	1
FSD	JOELLA ROBINSON	TERRELL	$1,048.00	1
UM	CAROL GATTON	BURGESS	$1,046.00	2
FSD	DARLENE LUDWIG	ORSINI	$1,045.50	1
RSM	DORIS OVERBAY	LUTTRELL	$1,044.00	1
BM	RUTH BOWERS	LAUERMAN	$1,042.00	2
UM	MARTHA CERTAIN	MYERS	$1,038.50	1
FL	JUDITH TALBOT	VERITY	$1,037.50	2
FL	ELIZABETH STAFFORD	JOYAL	$1,037.00	1
UM	KATHALEEN ESWORTHY	CONDON	$1,035.40	6
FSD	KATHY ROTH	MCCOY	$1,032.50	2
FL	CAROL JOHNSON	TRABER	$1,032.50	1
ASM	JANE MONAHAN	MONAHAN	$1,032.50	8
FL	EVELYN SHUTTLEWORTH	WHITE	$1,025.00	38
FL	RUTH HOEL	KNOX	$1,023.50	3
FL	EVELYN GENT	PFLUEGER	$1,023.50	2
UM	JANET ROSS	ORSINI	$1,021.00	1
BM	MARY ROCHEFORT	THOMPSON	$1,021.00	1
UM	GRETA PETTRY	SHYBLOSKY	$1,020.50	2
FSD	SHARON VERCAMMEN	PATTERSON	$1,017.50	1
FL	GRETCHEN BLACKWELDER	BURRIER	$1,015.50	1
BM	KAREN FOX	MOORE	$1,014.00	1
FL	BONNIE WRIGHT	UNDERWOOD	$1,012.00	1
UM	MARGARET URBIN	CURTIS	$1,010.00	1
UM	BRIAN BURGESS	BURGESS	$1,007.50	1
FL	LOIS CRONIN	MCCLAIN	$1,004.00	3
BM	REBECCA NEWGARD	MIKOLANDA	$1,002.00	1

Congratulations to these 233 Star Achievers with $1,000 or more personal net sales in the Sales Period IBMs 11/15 - 12/81! Special applause goes to the Stars who win 2 or more Awards in this Period!

Very special recognition is extended to Norma Miles, who receives 10 Star Achiever Awards this Period for over $10,000 sales in these four weeks!

The last person I would like to introduce here truly took this concept to heart. Norma Miles became a Fashion Show Director with Emmons in 1957 and continued through the closing hours of Emmons in 1981. Her continued pride in the company is evident in the awards and trophies prominently displayed some thirty to forty years later in her home. As with any company, Emmons' existence depended on their employees — the Fashion Show Directors — and they were careful to affirm and reward these individuals and their achievements.

This is Norma Miles, a very gracious lady who assisted me in gathering a majority of these pictured items. Thanks, Norma.

In the waning years of Caroline Emmons, Fashion Show Directors and higher management were given the chance to join with Sarah Coventry. Many did so, and continued with that company for several more years until Sarah closed its doors. Others that I spoke with made the initial transfer but chose to leave shortly after, while still others who were very committed to Caroline Emmons chose not to transfer at all and discontinued employment in 1981.

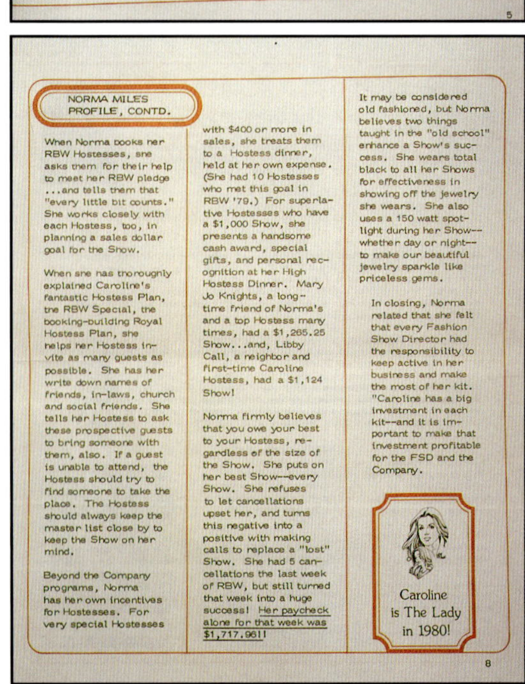

NORMA MILES PROFILE, CONTD.

When Norma books her RBW Hostesses, she asks them for their help to meet her RBW pledge ...and tells them that "every little bit counts." She works closely with each Hostess, too, in planning a sales dollar goal for the Show.

When she has thoroughly explained Caroline's fantastic Hostess Plan, the RBW Special, the booking-building Royal Hostess Plan, she helps her Hostess invite as many guests as possible. She has her write down names of friends, in-laws, church and social friends. She tells her Hostess to ask these prospective guests to bring someone with them, also. If a guest is unable to attend, the Hostess should try to find someone to take the place. The Hostess should always keep the master list close by to keep the Show on her mind.

Beyond the Company programs, Norma has her own incentives for Hostesses. For very special Hostesses with $400 or more in sales, she treats them to a Hostess dinner, held at her own expense. (She had 10 Hostesses who met this goal in RBW '79.) For superlative Hostesses who have a $1,000 Show, she presents a handsome cash award, special gifts, and personal recognition at her High Hostess Dinner. Mary Jo Knights, a long-time friend of Norma's and a top Hostess many times, had a $1,265.25 Show...and, Libby Call, a neighbor and first-time Caroline Hostess, had a $1,124 Show!

Norma firmly believes that you owe your best to your Hostess, regardless of the size of the Show. She puts on her best Show—every Show. She refuses to let cancellations upset her, and turns this negative into a positive with making calls to replace a "lost" Show. She had 5 cancellations the last week of RBW, but still turned that week into a huge success! Her paycheck alone for that week was $1,717.96!!

It may be considered old fashioned, but Norma believes two things taught in the "old school" enhance a Show's success. She wears total black to all her Shows for effectiveness in showing off the jewelry she wears. She also uses a 150 watt spotlight during her Show—whether day or night—to make our beautiful jewelry sparkle like priceless gems.

In closing, Norma related that she felt that every Fashion Show Director had the responsibility to keep active in her business and make the most of her kit. "Caroline has a big investment in each kit—and it is important to make that investment profitable for the FSD and the Company."

Jewelry cases were also created for Emmons Fashion Show Directors to carry their jewelry items and other materials to the parties. The two cases pictured here show a regular simulated leather case in natural finish compared to a gold case given to Norma Miles as an award. These cases will be more difficult to locate as there weren't as many FSDs in Emmons as there were in Sarah Coventry.

I believe acquiring Emmons jewelry will add greatly to the value of your collection, since not as many of the pieces were made as compared to Sarah Coventry. This is because the company was smaller and only produced two catalogs of jewelry each year while Sarah Coventry produced three. Look for boxes, promotional items, and the wonderful jewelry ranging from very simple designs to the magnificent pieces yet to be seen in this book.

Left and above:
During Norma's career with Caroline Emmons from 1957-1981, she gathered many awards and trophies and was featured in 1980 as top sales person. In the photograph with the trophies, you can see the company's old logo on the two left hand trophies, which are from 1967 and 1968. The new logo is displayed on the trophies at right, which are from 1975 and 1976. Such awards and trophies prominently displayed some thirty to forty years later in the homes of former employees such as Norma is evidence of their continued pride in the company. *Courtesy of Norma Miles.*

In looking for Emmons – Caroline Emmons Jewelry, be on the lookout for two hang tags, as shown in the photograph here. One is part of the Crown E collection, which was more upscale in the fashion line with semi-precious stones and more detailed fashion jewelry. The other tag, the rectangular one, will be the common one found on most pieces. In addition, you will also find the word EMMONS in raised metal or engraved letters under the piece – very similar to Sarah Coventry. Earrings can be identified with the word EMMONS, EmJ, or a crown/shell effect engraved on the clasp. I know I have missed some of these earrings not knowing of that signature mark, so look carefully.

Several hang tags were utilized by the Emmons designers throughout 1949 to 1981. The one on the left is an example of the Crown Collection of semi-precious jewelry, referred to as Crown E. "Distinctive…quiet good taste…for those who prefer real jewelry for themselves and for special gifts." The rectangular symbol on the right was used on regular pieces of Emmons jewelry with the Emmons name engraved on it. *Courtesy of Bill Scheetz*

The Emmons Fashion Show Directors were given carrying cases for transporting the jewelry samples from party to party. The example shown in the top photo is a brown imitation leather case with black trim. Also displayed are several examples of the boxes used when sending jewelry items to the customer. The box on the left is from the Crown Collection, as distinguished by the crown over the "E." The second case, shown in the bottom photo, is the property of Norma Miles and is gold with black trim. Fashion Show Directors who acquired upper management status were rewarded with this distinctive carrying case. Shown with this case is the ring sizer used for proper sizing of rings. *Courtesy of Norma Miles and Arcadia Historical Society.*

An Emmons collection can include many items, from giveaway pieces such as this mirrored case, to the Crown Emmons series as pictured by this box, to very simple items as illustrated by the **Fashion Flavor** necklace (3153 in chocolate) on a 20" nylon cord. It also came in a vanilla color in the late 1970s. *Courtesy of Arcadia Historical Society.*

So Mary Beth, Ginny, Norma, Bill, and I all invite you to enjoy the pieces of Caroline Emmons jewelry in the final chapter of this book. We hope you enjoy them and will begin looking and collecting yourself.

Sets - Emmons Jewelry

Unidentified necklace, pin, and earrings are a magnificent set of golden mounting highlighted with red crystal rhinestones offset with half moons of clear rhinestones. This has to be an early set, no doubt from the 1950s and isn't marked on any of the pieces. However, the bracelet is attached to a card identified as #1467 "Jewelry by Emmons." This set will be very difficult to find. $30-50. *Courtesy of Mary Elizabeth Snawder.*

Rainbow Star pin (1610), large earrings (2687), and regular earrings (2610) are from the 1960s and were continued for many years. "A joy to behold, a thrill to own, is our Rainbow Star. As happy and inspiring as a rainbow, you'll feel that you've found the Pot of Gold. Especially pleasing when doubled as a necklace (using Glamour Chain), nestling at your throat. Your choice of two earrings, large (same size as pin) or small." These were very popular as stated by the two employees I have featured here, so there will be many to locate. This set was also given as an award to Norma Miles (see page 114) and the pin is also shown on page 135. *Courtesy of Norma Miles.*

Unidentified set is no doubt from the early years, 1950-1960s. This is a magnificent set still in great shape and desirable for wearing today. The necklace features tear drop shaped crystal rhinestones surrounded by smaller crystal rhinestone in silvery mounting, linked together and attached to a rhinestone chain. The earrings are the same design on screw backs. $30-50. *Courtesy of Mary Elizabeth Snawder.*

Unidentified set of white plastic snowflake design is no doubt from the late 1950s and early 1960s. The silvery mounting and clear crystal rhinestones in the centers of the snowflakes give the illusion of glistening as snow does. These will be very difficult to find as this is the only set I have seen. $25-40. *Courtesy of Mary Elizabeth Snawder.*

Three sets from the 1950s. **Left to right:** *Unidentified* set is unmarked, but known to be Emmons. The multi-colored crystal rhinestones set in golden mounting are very bold, suggesting the 1950s, and sought after for today's wearer and collector. $30-50. *Unidentified* set is also unmarked also but very unique with its combination of oval shaped simulated pearls and small country blue rhinestones in a striking golden mounting. $20-35. *Unidentified* set belonged to Norma Miles' mother in the 1950s. These were quite exquisite, created from open-weave golden swirls and tiny clear and pale blue crystal rhinestones. $25-35. *Courtesy of Mary Elizabeth Snawder and Norma Miles.*

Unidentified necklace and earrings set is a silvery double lariat chain with pearlized shades of gray beads stationed throughout the chain and tassels attached on each side. The matching dangle earrings are the same pearlized beads. $15-30. *Courtesy of Arcadia Historical Society.*

Olympiad tac pin (1210) on the left and matching *Olympiad* pendant (3210) on the right are cleverly designed skis made from genuine pewter. Emmons sponsored the Winter Olympics in 1980 and these men's items were designed to commemorate this event. The tac pin is a reduced version of the pendant. E; $10-25. *Courtesy of Arcadia Historical Society.*

Regal Splendor pin (1221) and clip earrings (2222) are from 1970. This set is very dynamic with its combination of orange and various shades of green rhinestones in a cross effect shape, hence its name. It was described as "Classic style…Exciting color." D; $30-45. *Courtesy of Arcadia Historical Society.*

Chantilly necklace (3442), earrings (2442), and bracelet (4442) are from 1974. "Chantilly goes everywhere! Great for Sportswear; Elegant for After 5!" This set personifies the versatility of Emmons jewelry by creating the pieces from textured silvertone metal. It gave the purchaser a chance to exercise the 2 & 3 plan by buying two items at regular price and paying only $3.00 for the third item. D; $30-45. *Courtesy of Arcadia Historical Society.*

Cinnabar bracelet (4173) and earrings (2173) are from 1969. "Antique look is IN." The opalescent red stones against antiqued silvertone give this set an expensive look for very little money. C; $20-35. *Courtesy of Arlena Jordan.*

Cleopatra necklace, earrings, and bracelet set (0533) is from 1976 and a most exquisite set to locate. The combination of various colored rhinestones and the unique shaping of antiqued goldentone made it very attractive then and sought after now. G; $35-55. *Courtesy of Arlena Jordan.*

Milky Way pendant (3217) and clip earrings (2217) are from 1970. "Dainty Pendants…Important Fashion Brings Joy at Christmas." The earrings came in a pierced set with 14 kt. posts and there was a matching ring as well. There was a savings of $1 for buying the ensemble. C; $15-30. *Courtesy of Arlena Jordan.*

Golden Scroll pin (1431) and earrings (2431) are from the Christmas catalog of 1972. This goldentone open-weave oriental design is very striking when worn against a dark colored costume. C; $15-30. *Courtesy of Arle*

Left to right: *Unidentified* large silvery leaf pin and earrings set created from both textured and gleaming silvertone. This could be from the 1960s. A magnificent set very much in style even today. $15-30. *Unidentified* sun pin with center stone of flowers and confetti embedded in a clear plastic. $10-20. *Courtesy of Arlena Jordan and Brenda Bruzee.*

Capriccio necklace, earrings, and ring ensemble (0545) is Caroline's first Limited Edition in a design by Jens Von Edler. "The trapeze pendant suspends from a serpentine chain and the highly polished surfaces reflect light and images from the sparkling chatons in a raised triangular pattern. Ring and earrings follow the exciting motif to form an elegant ensemble for your finest occasion." This set was on sale from July 1, 1977 through July 1, 1978, at which time the mold was destroyed. It was also offered for $20 when buying two other items at the regular price. G; $40-60. *Courtesy of Bill Scheetz.*

Left to right: *Unidentified* white enameled flower pin and matching earrings. The center is a shiny cabochon set mounted in gleaming golden setting. $15-30. **Gay Marguerita** pin and earrings (699) are from the 1960s. "Scintillating Marguerita stones are the highlight of this jewelry bouquet. A very special stone, known for its quality and many-faceted color scope, Gay Marguerita captures light in every direction and sparkles back in varying hues its delicate, feminine colors. A bright bouquet to heighten your charms! Wear it in your hair with Emmons' Wonder Clips…nice for scarves, on your handbag, too! The Pin makes an excellent pendant necklace when you want a change of pace." Locating this set will be a wonderful find. $30-45. *Courtesy of Bill Scheetz.*

Left to right: *Unidentified* curved snail shaped pin and earrings set. This is a dynamic, yet simple example of Emmons jewelry. The white enameled metal piece has raised golden designs giving it a rich and textured surface. This no doubt is from the early years, in the 1960s. $20-35. *Unidentified* necklace and matching earrings have a mosaic effect in silvertone mounting. $20-35. *Courtesy of Bill Scheetz.*

Top to bottom: *Unidentified* large white pin and earrings set. This unique pin is a spiral of metal covered with tiny, daisy shaped flowers, stems, and seed pods painted/enameled white. This set is no doubt from the 1960s. $20-35. **Starlite** pin (1159) and earrings (2159) were continued from 1973 through 1978. The combination of pearl and rhinestones makes for "Starry Nights and Caroline." The faceted rhinestones capture the color of objects around them. D; $15-30. *Courtesy of Pat and Gary Wyatt.*

Magic Lantern bracelet (4690) and earrings (1690) are from the 1960s. "Looking ever-so-much like artistic lanterns, the dangles on Magic Lantern inspired its name. And the many things, or tricks, you can do with it, completes the magic idea…The lantern dangles are removable." There was a lariat as well that could be used as a necklace or a belt. The removable lanterns could be added to other pins or other chains, and the necklace chain or bracelet could be added to other pins as a sweater clip. Imagination along with this jewelry created wonderfully versatile additions. B; $25-35. *Courtesy of Pat and Gary Wyatt.*

Unidentified necklace, bracelet, and earrings set from the early years. The necklace and bracelet are hinged sections of small enameled white daisy flowers with centers of multi-colored crystal rhinestones. The earrings are a cluster of three flowers with rhinestones. A wonderful find for the avid collector. $25-40. *Courtesy of Pat and Gary Wyatt.*

African Queen pin/pendant (3548) and two bracelets (4548) fastened together to create a choker are from 1976. They feature the versatility of Emmons as the pendant can also be worn as a pin. A fabulous combination of orange, green and yellow rhinestones and cabochon sets in an antiqued goldentone mounting. There were matching earrings. D; $20-35. *Courtesy of Pat Wyatt.*

Fashion Tracery pins (1212, 1214, 1211) and earrings (2212, 2214, 2211) were advertised as "…refreshing as the gentle breezes" with their combination of plastic and metal swirls adapted to the goldentone and silvery coloring in pink, orange/red, or black. These flowers were complete with the addition of the opaque beads in the center. There was also a white set. C; $15-30. *Courtesy of Mary Elizabeth Snawder.*

Top to bottom: *Sea Beauty* pin (1174) and earrings (2174) are from 1969 and identified as "All-Season Favorites." The textured silvery metal is designed to give the impression of being paved with rhinestones. The black cabochon in the center is very striking and accented by silvery legs truly looks like a sea creature. B; $15-30.
Budding Romance pin (1200) and earrings (2200) from 1969 were described as "Highlights with Color and Sparkle." This fabulous golden filigree pin is stunningly accented with reddish/orange baguette stones and small amber, orange rhinestones. C; $20-45. *Courtesy of Mary Elizabeth Snawder.*

Left to right: *Bluebell* pin (1296) and earrings (2296) from 1971 are a spectacular work of art with textured and gleaming silvery flower, stem, and leaves. The flower is a large gleaming blue cabochon stone hence, the "bluebell" name. The earrings have the same blue cabochon in a smaller flower design. B; $20-35. *Fireworks* pin (1266) and earrings (2266) are also from 1969. The spiraling design of silvery metal is accented by clear crystal rhinestones outside the center cluster of rhinestones. These were truly "evening glamour!" C; $20-35. *Courtesy of Mary Elizabeth Snawder.*

Left to right: *Unidentified* pin and earrings are dynamically created from textured silvery and twisted metal, giving the illusion of being paved with rhinestones. The hot pink crystal rhinestone centers make these pieces very attractive and highly sought after. $20-45. *Sculpture* pin (1161) and earrings (2161) are from 1971. The silvery finish is engraved (sculptured) with flowers, leaves, and stems, hence its name. It also came in golden, shown on page 133. B; $15-30. *Courtesy of Mary Elizabeth Snawder.*

Left to right: *Americana* pin (1237) and earrings (2237) are from 1969 and created from enameled white, red, and dark blue spears that spiral over the top, displaying the silvery underside of the pin. B; $15-30. *Victoria* pin (1304) and drop earrings (2304) are striking golden rounded triangle shapes with forest green stones outlined with golden open circles. The earrings are merely golden drops of dark forest green stones dangling from look-like pierced earrings. B; $15-30. *Courtesy of Mary Elizabeth Snawder.*

Left to right: Three sets from 1971. ***Aztec Princess*** pin/pendant (2027) is a unique necklace/pin that can be worn with the tassel or without, as a pin or as a necklace. The light turquoise cabochon and beads against the striking silvery design makes for a "princess effect." It can be matched up with the ***Tie 'n Tassel*** earrings (2108) that match the silvery chain. D; $20-35. ***Midnight Lace*** pendant (3241) and earrings (2241) have an antique look with black enameled Victorian looking lace around the opaque oval cabochon cream stones. Crystal clear rhinestones spaced around the outer edge of the black mounting highlight the center stone. The pendant is attached to a black linked chain while the earrings are dainty black filigree with center crystal rhinestones. C; $20-35. ***Syncopation*** pin/pendant (3356) is a golden pendant attached to a matching chain, the interlocking encased golden balls on the chain matching those dangling from the pendant. Doubling as a pin makes this piece very striking and sought after. There were no earrings. B; $15-30. *Courtesy of Mary Elizabeth Snawder.*

Left to right: ***Zigzag Silvery*** pin (1298) and earrings (2298) and ***Zigzag Golden*** pin (1299) are from 1971. The name describes these pieces so appropriately. B; $10-20. ***Unidentified*** pin and earrings set sports a bold amber stone held securely by prongs sliced from the golden mounting. Very striking and unique, yet simple and elegant. $20-45. *Courtesy of Mary Elizabeth Snawder.*

Left to right: ***Crimson Glory*** pin (1537) and earrings (2537) are from the early 1960s. "The dazzling beauty of flashing stones heralds a season of exciting fashions! Heading the parade is the importance of color and Emmons has chosen this magnificent ensemble in a rich combination of deep cranberry and aurora to satisfy the demand for brilliant jewelry which takes the spotlight in fashion. Its sumptuous design with matching earrings will become a treasured favorite you'll delight in wearing." B; $30-50. ***Unidentified*** pin and earrings are enameled white petals forming an off-sided flower. In the center is a magnificent multi-colored faceted stone created in such a way as to reflect surrounding colors and sparkle glamorously. $20-35. *Courtesy of Mary Elizabeth Snawder.*

Left to right: ***Rhapsody in Blue*** pin (1669) and earrings (2669) are from the late 1960s. "This star doesn't just twinkle – it dazzles!!! Many faceted, brilliant blue stones sparkle and dance with the brilliance only the celestial aurora borealis itself can capture." The earrings are a smaller star version. D; $25-40. ***Ice Bouquet*** pin (1360) and button earrings (2360) are from 1971. The rhinestone flower on the earrings is surrounded by rhinestone leaves on the pin in a silvery mounting, saying "You're lovely night and day." C; $20-45. *Courtesy of Norma Miles and Mary Elizabeth Snawder.*

Queen of Fashion necklace, earrings, and bracelet set from the late 1960s. "Beautiful Fashion Jewelry brings out the loveliest you…makes you Queen of Fashion! Emmons fashion designers have achieved new dimensions in artistry with the creation of this lovely ensemble, combining simulated fresh water pearls and rhinestones in dramatic rhythm and refreshing contrast…created exclusively for Emmons QUEEN HOSTESSES. The fresh water pearl, which first found popular favor in high fashion circles of Paris, is gradually attaining real fashion stature in America. You will be in the forefront of fashion and will know that you look your loveliest when you wear it." When a hostess had sales of $100 or more and two parties were booked, the hostess could choose this wonderful set. Be on the lookout for this set, as it will be difficult to find. $50-75. *Courtesy of Mary Elizabeth Snawder and Mary Beth Coffman.*

Left to right: *Legacy* ring, bracelet, and earrings from the early 1970s have a geometric design with rectangles and circles mounting a rectangular purple cabochon hinged to golden circles housing smaller rectangular baguettes of purple and teal. The ring and earrings match the circles of the bracelet. $20-35. *Unidentified* earrings and bracelet are created from golden rippled circles encircling a cluster of salmon colored leaves to create a flower blossom. The resin flowers are magnificent and will be a wonderful addition to any collection. $20-40. *Courtesy of Mary Elizabeth Snawder.*

Left to right: *Daughter of the Nile* necklace and bracelet set (523) were featured in 1972 as a "Royal Hostess Gift." When a hostess had sales of over $100 and two shows booked, she could receive specific bonus items in addition to the regular hostess plan. This necklace was worn as a choker with the pendant looking like a tie. It was very much an eye-catcher in the 1970s, especially when worn with the matching bracelet. $20-35. *Midnight Magic* necklace (3662), bracelet, and earrings (2662) are from the early 1960s. "Jet always spells excitement and intrigue! …light and satiny-soft chain. When you first pick it up, you see a matinee length necklace. Thru the magic of interlocking jump rings, one section of the necklace can be removed and you have a lovely matching bracelet. Glinting strands of silvery brilliance combine with lustrous jet for a beautiful ensemble, complete with glamorous dangle earrings for your most stunning gown or simple sheath. A must for every wardrobe for those many occasions when you want an unusual necklace and earrings to set off your costume." B; $25-40. *Courtesy of Mary Elizabeth Snawder.*

Left to right: *Love Story* necklace (3367) and earrings (2368) from 1972 have amethyst crystal stones. The earrings were also on surgical steel posts. C; $15-30. **Unidentified** necklace and earrings feature abalone shell leaves with inscribed veins, creating a unique pendant. There was a matching ring covered with a concave oval golden shape with golden ball in the center. A unique contrast for the white shell. $20-45. **Unidentified** necklace and earrings are created from large white translucent beads. The pendant has a snap-on ring with a tassel of chain and smaller beads secured through the bead on silvery filigree. The earrings are the same size with shorter tassel chains. $15-30. *Courtesy of Mary Elizabeth Snawder.*

Left to right: *Unidentified* necklace/lariat/belt and bracelet set is shaped like a lantern or purse of open-weave goldentone, attached to bold golden chains. The lariat is very long and open on the ends to also be used as a belt. $20-45. **Coco** necklace and earrings (894) from 1971 have amber colored barrel beads stationed on a three strand necklace of varying sizes and shapes of chain. The earrings are matching beads with tassels. A popular necklace then and sought after now. D; $15-30. **Blossom Time** necklace and earrings (832) are from 1969. "Dainty Pendants…Important Fashion." The golden blossom and filigree gently caress a tiny simulated pearl, providing wearable fashion for many years. There was also a matching ring. B; $15-30. *Courtesy of Mary Elizabeth Snawder.*

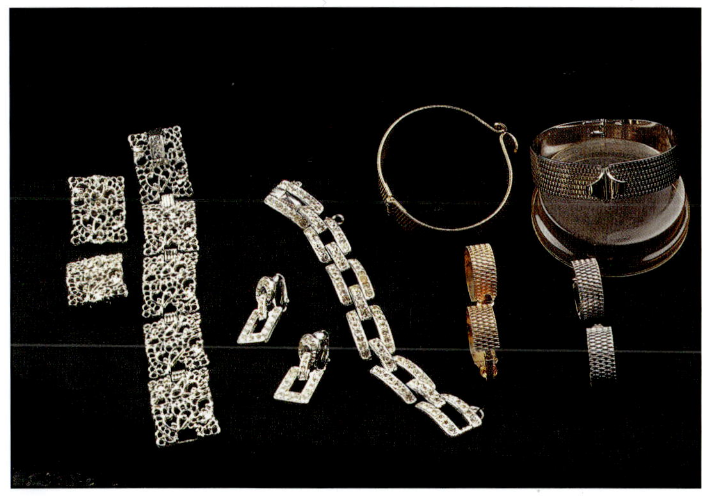

Left to right: *Unidentified* bracelet and earrings have a silvery lace effect. The rectangular lace of the bracelet is duplicated in the bold earrings. $20-35. **Royal Princess** bracelet and earrings (516) are from 1971 and were featured as a "Gift for a Royal Princess Hostess," thus the special name. The open links of silvery mounting paved with crystal rhinestones were for the hostess who had sales of $75-$125 and two shows booked and held. $20-35. **Roundabout** bracelet and earrings in Golden (866) and Silvery (867) are from 1970. These textured metal bracelets are closed with a reverse display of gleaming metal for the name of "roundabout." Matching hoop earrings provide "the complete look." B; $15-30. *Courtesy of Mary Elizabeth Snawder.*

Left to right: *Unidentified* necklace**,** bracelet, and earrings are from the earlier years. This beautifully designed white rose set on a gleaming golden mounting offset with clear crystal rhinestones is dynamically beautiful. $30-45. **Lady Love** pendant (3267), earrings (2267), and ring (1093) from 1971 feature glamorous smoky gray navette shaped crystal rhinestones. The intricate filigree silvery mounting makes this set "real looking." C; $20-35. *Courtesy of Mary Elizabeth Snawder.*

Left to right: *Heart Throb Take-apart Heart* pendant (3629) and pierced earrings (2629) are from 1976. The white heart pendant can be easily unclasped from the golden necklace to be worn alone. Very simple, very classy, "All Season Favorites!" D; $20-35. *Czarina* pendant (3275) and earrings (2275) are from 1971. "Antique Look is IN" describes this set of pendant and bold earrings highlighted with smoky gray crystal rhinestones. There was a matching ring and the earrings could also be pierced style. C; $20-35. *Courtesy of Mary Elizabeth Snawder and Norma Miles.*

Left to right: *Delicate Spiral* necklace (3663) and earrings (2663) are from 1975. The necklace is comprised of three spiral circles of gleaming silvery metal linked together. The earrings are matching spirals. There was a matching bracelet also. C; $20-35. *Crimson Beauty* choker (3940) from 1978 is 16-1/2" with red sculptured beads stationed throughout the length of silvery chain. C; $15-25. *Crystal Lights Rhinestone Chain* necklace (0531) is from 1976. The large crystal rhinestone surrounded by smaller rhinestones and attached to the rhinestone chain against a silvery mounting makes for a truly exquisite necklace. Matching earrings on page 138. D; $20-35. *Courtesy of Mary Elizabeth Snawder and Norma Miles.*

Left to right: *Ducks in Flight* pendant/pin, bracelet, and earrings are thought to be from the early 1960s. This set is very much like a circular set from Sarah Coventry made during the same time frame. $20-35. *Unidentified* necklace and bracelet are uniquely shaped from silvery metal 3-dimensional open-weave leaves hinged together. I am guessing this is from the 1960s also. $20-35. *Courtesy of Norma Miles and Mary Elizabeth Snawder.*

Left to right: *Champagne* necklace (3505) and earrings (2505) are from the 1960s. "To look your very sweetest, dress for romance with Emmons' sparkling Champagne! His eyes will stray from yours, that's true, but you won't mind when he tells you what a beautiful necklace you have – and earrings, too. You will look your loveliest, you know, when you rely upon dainty champagne to add the sparkle of rhinestones to your evening out." This set is forty years old and as wearable today as then – that's the marvel of Emmons' manufacturers. B; $20-35. *Bewitching* pendant (3712) and earrings (2712) have fantastic teal multi-faceted tear drop crystals with silvery hooks attached to a dainty silvery chain and to pierced look earrings. They were featured in 1969. B; $20-35. *Festival* pendant (3386) and earring (2386) are from 1975. The bold pendant and earring are created from a large white plastic cabochon dangling from a gleaming golden swing with attached white dangle beads. C; $20-35. *Courtesy of Mary Elizabeth Snawder.*

Left to right: *City Slicker* chain (3868) and pierced earrings (2743) are from 1980. The length of this chain is 18" but it also came in 15" and 24" and in goldentone as well as silvery. F; $15-30. *Cobra* chain (3316) and pierced earrings are from 1980 with an initial added. This 18" chain also came in 15", 24", and 30" lengths in goldentone and silvery. There was a matching bracelet and ankle bracelets to mix and match with pendants or to be worn alone. F; $15-30. *Courtesy of Norma Miles.*

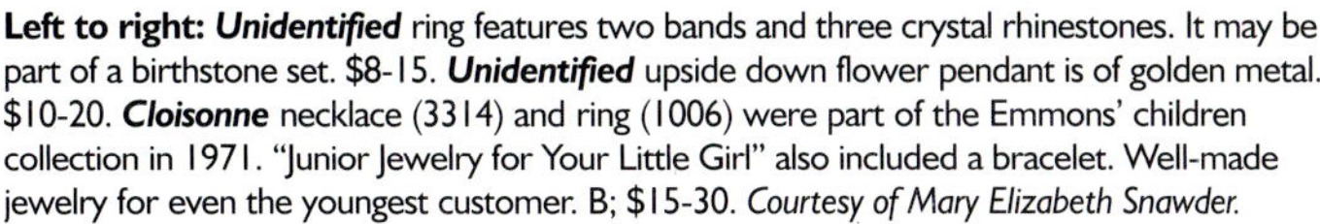

Left to right: *Unidentified* ring features two bands and three crystal rhinestones. It may be part of a birthstone set. $8-15. *Unidentified* upside down flower pendant is of golden metal. $10-20. *Cloisonne* necklace (3314) and ring (1006) were part of the Emmons' children collection in 1971. "Junior Jewelry for Your Little Girl" also included a bracelet. Well-made jewelry for even the youngest customer. B; $15-30. *Courtesy of Mary Elizabeth Snawder.*

As noted earlier, Caroline Emmons had a Crown Collection featuring semi-precious jewelry. These pieces are from 1971. "Distinctive…quiet good taste…for those who prefer real jewelry for themselves and for special gifts…attractively boxed for your gift-giving convenience." **Left to right:** *Genuine Carved Ivory* pierced earrings (2349) had 14 kt. gold-filled posts. There was a matching pendant (next photo) and bracelet. C; $15-25. *Jade* pendant (genuine jade and 12 kt. gold-filled) (3253) and earrings (2253) with prong set genuine jade stones also had a matching ring. E; $20-45. *Cultured Pearl* pendant (3249) and regular earrings (2249) are also 12 kt. Gold-filled. All pierced earrings have 14 kt. posts. E; $15-30. *Courtesy of Mary Elizabeth Snawder.*

More from the Crown Collection, with semi-precious jewelry from the early 1970s. **Top row, left to right:** *Genuine Carved Ivory* pendant (3348) matches the earrings above. The mounting was 12 kt. gold-filled. C; $15-30. *Unidentified* pendant of opalescent stone in golden mounting. $10-18. **Bottom row, left to right:** *Opal* pendant (3346) and pierced earrings (2347) are captive opal and 12 kt. gold-filled while posts are 14 kt. gold-filled. F; $20-35. *Cameo* regular earrings (2251) are created from Sardonyx cameo and are 12 kt. gold-filled. There was a matching pendant and ring. C; $10-20. *Jade* ring (3053) is the matching ring for the jade pendant and earrings shown in previous photo. The jade is genuine and 12 kt. gold-filled. E; $20-35. *Courtesy of Mary Elizabeth Snawder.*

Portrait in Black (514) bracelet and earrings set from 1969 was a part of the "Gift for a Royal Queen Hostess" set. This magnificent set of black square jet stones set off with a textured and gleaming golden mounting gives the feel of brocade. By featuring such beautiful jewelry for free, the company encouraged hostesses to "build lavish jewelry wardrobes without opening their purses." These gifts were in addition to the money bonuses given. Locating this set would make any collection complete. $30-45. *Courtesy of Norma Miles.*

Unidentified pins and earrings are from the late 1960s. The metal enameled petals overlap, creating very realistic flowers with contrasting colored centers of white or black. There were mint green, white, yellow, and salmon colored sets including matching smaller earrings. $15-30. *Courtesy of Mary Beth Coffman.*

Unidentified pin, necklace, earrings, and bracelet set is in the original box from the 1960s. It is a delicate goldentone mounting with a Victorian look of simulated pearls and rhinestones. A marvelous find for any collector. $50-75. *Courtesy of Mary Beth Coffman.*

An advertisement for **Her Majesty Ensemble**.
Courtesy of Arcadia Historical Society.

Her Majesty Ensemble was part of the Emmons Queen Hostess selection. "This Queenly ensemble is the height of fashion in style and color. The beautiful hues of smoked topaz, enriched with accents of shimmering green, lend an aristocratic air to its exquisite antique finish. The solitaire Pendant on a fine snake chain is also a brooch to wear separately on suits, dresses, or coats…lovely Bracelet and Earrings to match offer many exciting combinations for your delight and pleasure." Good luck in your search for this wonderful set – it is magnificent. $50-75. *Courtesy of Mary Beth Coffman.*

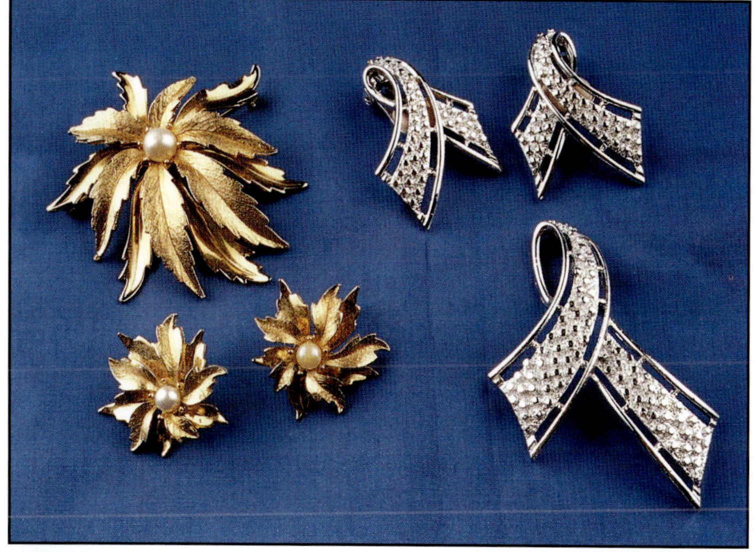

Left to right: *Classic Beauty* pin (1523) and earrings (2533) are from the 1960s. "Truly a beauty! This costume jewelry design is a touch of Nature's own glory in a beautiful double leaf pattern. It seems to echo a prelude to the happiness ahead while lending a precious, brief glance at Nature's beauty of the moment…will give everlasting pleasure and a feeling of nostalgia every time you wear it. Lovely diminutive earrings form an ensemble to be worn any time…anywhere with pride!" And here it is over forty years later as great as any piece of jewelry made today. B; $20-40. *Spectator* pin (1167) and earrings (1267) are from the 1960s. "Here is an ensemble that is always 'just right.' At home or away, it is perfect to accessorize everything you wear! You'll love its sleek bow-knot design that sparks attention and bright, silvery lustre that makes it a star attraction!" B; $18-30. *Courtesy of Mary Beth Coffman and Pat Wyatt.*

Left to right: *Shimmering Lace* pin (1538) and earrings (2538) are from the 1960s. "The 'Gentle woman Look' is personified in this feminine, lacy, absolute confection of an ensemble. Its delicate tracery of leaves, all sparkling with the beauty of subdued color tones, picks up every reflection. A stunning Pin and Earrings to shimmer and shine your way through an exciting evening. Luscious on deep tones and solid colors that will enhance its beauty and make even the most simple gown a vision of beauty." B; $30-45. *Unidentified* pin and earrings are no doubt from the 1960s as well. This flower of silvery finish combines both textured and gleaming metal coupled with small clear crystal rhinestones. This set is truly dramatic and would add greatly to a collection. $30-45. *Courtesy of Mary Beth Coffman.*

Left to right: *White Camellia* pin (1638) and earrings (2638) are from early 1960s. "This is a beautiful ensemble – reminiscent of warm, fragrant evenings and romance. The delicate molding of white petals outlined in golden shadows is most striking! It's bold enough to be worn on suits, yet delicate enough for light dresses. White is so versatile – worn with so many things – a truly all season favorite!" B; $15-30. *Unidentified* pin and earrings are striking and different. The beautiful large amber crystal multi-faceted stone is prong set with veined golden leaves. The earrings are faceted and pointed drops of amber attached to clips that look like pierced. $25-40. *Courtesy of Mary Beth Coffman.*

Left to right: *Unidentified* pin and earrings are enameled green leaves on golden mounting. The simulated pearl centers set off the piece. $15-30. *Unidentified* pin with matching earring has salmon colored beads set in mountings of smaller golden balls, all surrounding the center of simulated pearl. A very unique piece with very simple earrings made of the dangling salmon beads. $15-30. *Courtesy of Mary Beth Coffman*

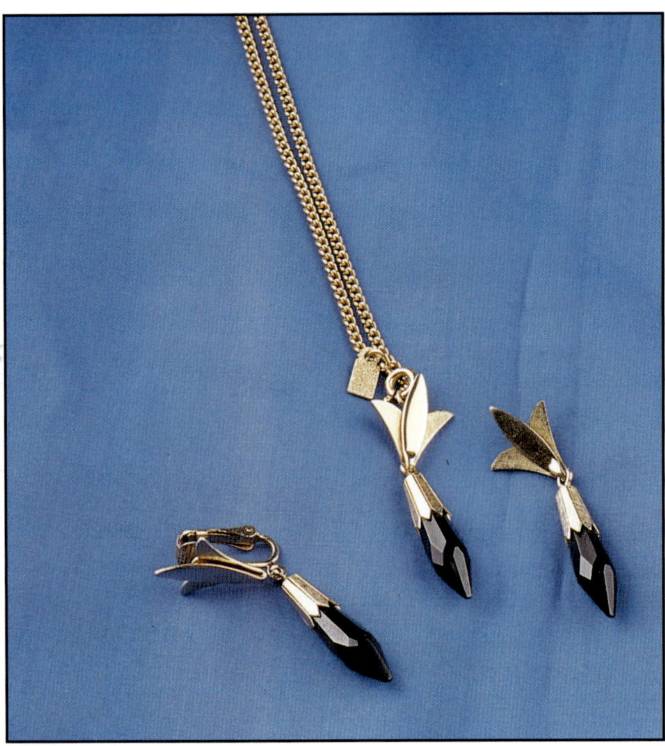

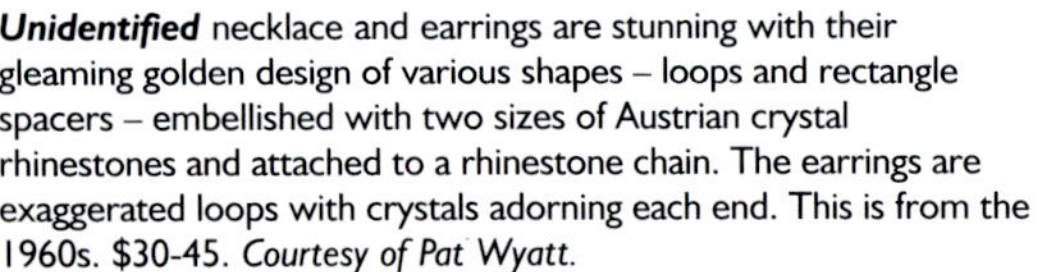

Interlude necklace (3796) and earrings (2796) are from the 1960s. "Twilight discloses the most beautiful time of day. So, too, it's a time when milady becomes her most radiant self...ready for a dreamy evening and looking her best. To complete her beauty...just made to be worn for an evening out. Subtle charm is yours." B; $20-35. *Courtesy of Mary Beth Coffman.*

Unidentified necklace and earrings are stunning with their gleaming golden design of various shapes – loops and rectangle spacers – embellished with two sizes of Austrian crystal rhinestones and attached to a rhinestone chain. The earrings are exaggerated loops with crystals adorning each end. This is from the 1960s. $30-45. *Courtesy of Pat Wyatt.*

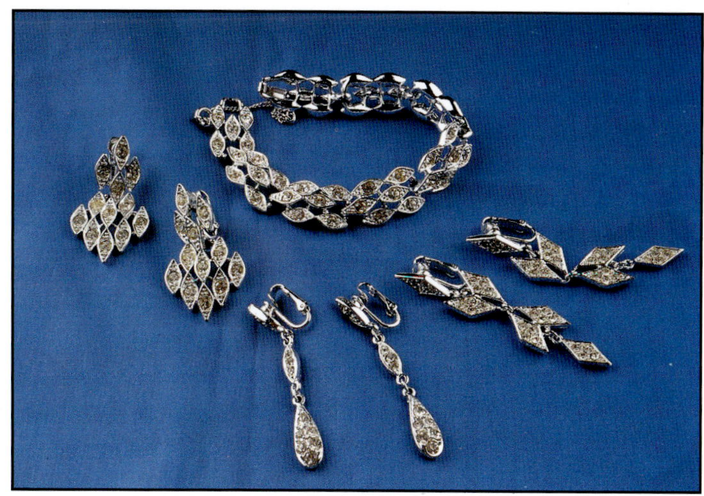

Left to right: **Unidentified** pin and earrings are the same size as many others designed in the 1960s. The flowers are white enameled petals surrounding a textured golden center encased in fluted edges. $20-35. **Unidentified** pin and earrings set was created with a pinwheel shape. This wonderful design has multi-colored stones centered on the open-weave of each pinwheel section. The earrings are the same version of each section. These are truly beautiful and very unique. $20-35. **Unidentified** pin and earrings of maple leaf shape have a gleaming silvery finish inlaid with a rough white texture. Very simple yet attractive. $20-35.

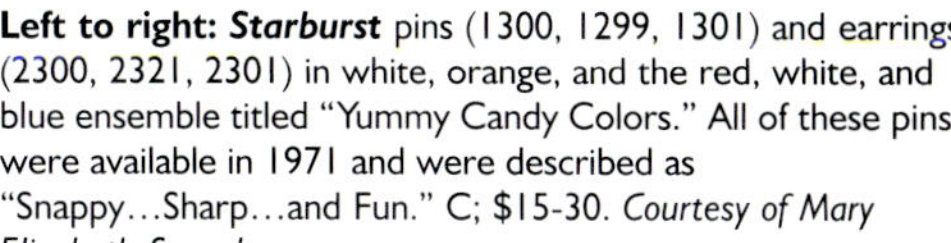

Left to right: **Starburst** pins (1300, 1299, 1301) and earrings (2300, 2321, 2301) in white, orange, and the red, white, and blue ensemble titled "Yummy Candy Colors." All of these pins were available in 1971 and were described as "Snappy…Sharp…and Fun." C; $15-30. *Courtesy of Mary Elizabeth Snawder.*

Left to right: **Jet Splendor** bracelet (1429) and earrings (1229) are from the early 1960s. "Bold and beautiful is this stunning creation! Prominent black stones, buffed to velvety sheen, nestle in a regal setting with lacy, silver-like finish which richly highlights this imperial ensemble. Prestige and dignity are yours when you don 'Jet Splendor' for that special occasion. Two bracelets make a heavenly choker and the earrings become gorgeous clips for your dress and all your lovely accessories." This is a fabulous set. B; $30-45. **Nostalgia** necklace (3747), bracelet (4635), and ring (1975) are from 1976 and identified as "The Beautiful Classics." The center set in each piece is a black enameled metal with intricately painted flowers. The antiqued silvery finished mounting give a Victorian impression. The wide hinged bracelet is delicately engraved with flower, leaves, and stems to further enhance the painted center. This set is one of my favorite finds. H; $40-65.

Left to right: ***Unidentified*** bracelet and earrings are from the early 1960s. This set is a unique combination of speckled colored glass stones in turquoise, blue, black, and orange/red with an exquisite golden leaf mounting. The earrings copy the leaf mounting in an offset fashion and utilize the orange to accent the two identical stones in the bracelet. This set is a joy to wear and gets many compliments. $40-50. ***Pearly Pinwheel*** pin (1665) and earrings (2688) are also from the 1960s. "A pinwheel of simulated pearls swirling gracefully to add charm to any outfit. Worn in pairs or sets of three they are especially lovely. For something different and original, pin them on your favorite hat or handbag." B; $20-35.

Clockwise, from top left: ***Starburst*** pin (white, 1300) is from 1971. B; $10-20. ***Camellia*** (white) pin has beautifully enameled 3-dimensional petals secured to leaf shapes outlined in metal with the repeat design in the center. $10-20. ***Autumn Echoes*** pin (1108) is from the 1960s. "The glint of sunlight on autumn's golden leaves is a never-forgotten sight. Emmons Autumn Echoes, richly veined…to conjure such memories. It will enrich any costume and you will wear it often – keep it forever!" A; $10-20. ***Mother's Pin*** (0101-0108) was featured from 1971 through the early 1980s. It was created in a double heart shape with the solid heart sparkling from the custom stones set to represent the birth months of the wearer's children. The finished product depended on the number of children's stones, as the positioning was determined by a "birthstone sequence setting chart" for eight birthstones with fewer stones completed with simulated seed pearls. There was also a father's tie tac composed of similar stones. C; $10-20. *Courtesy of Arcadia Historical Society.*

Clockwise, from top left: ***Starburst*** pin (1711) and earrings (2711) are from the early years. The pin is shaped from golden cone shaped, textured, and fluted metal set strikingly together and adorned with stems of clear crystal rhinestones. The earrings are half of the pin design, giving an offset effect. Very rich and extravagant looking. B; $25-45. ***Unidentified*** pin and earrings have the look of golden lace. The folded filigree, overlapping scallops, and gleaming bead center add a glamorous look to any simple outfit. $20-45. ***Gleaming Bows*** bracelet (1480) and earrings (1280) in goldentone are from the early 1960s. "Try to picture a feminine Rumplelstiltskin spinning golden threads and using her magic touch to weave them into delicate bows. Then she carefully ties them together and polishes them to gleaming perfection! And here you see it all…ready to add a bright golden gleam to your smartest day-into-evening dresses." There was a silvertone set as well. B; $30-45. Luckily these are all my treasures.

Top to bottom: ***Fireworks*** pin (1266) from 1970 is a spiraling array of silvertone and crystal rhinestones designed for "evening glamour." There were matching earrings as well. B; $15-30. ***Caroline Stuart*** signed pin is a replica of a piece of jewelry C.W. Stuart had made for his wife, Caroline Emmons Stuart, when he owned a jewelry store in Syracuse, New York before moving to Newark and beginning the multiple Stuart companies known around the U.S. and the world. This would truly be a find for any collector and will be extremely difficult to locate. There was no documentation as to the original price but because of its rarity it could bring $35-70 today. The back is pictured in the bracelet section on page 153. *Courtesy of Arcadia Historical Society.*

Twinkling Butterfly pin (1132) is from the 1960s. "With colors that dance before your eyes in a constantly changing vista of sunlight or moonglow reflections, 'Twinkling Butterfly' was made to attract! In your hair, pinned to your waist, on the back of your low cut gown, or high on your shoulder, the subtle flashing tints will charm your admirers." A; $15-30. *Courtesy of Arlena Jordan.*

Misty Blue pin (1192) is this sparkling blue cabochon and pearl set in an antiqued silvery four-petal flowery pin created in 1969. "Highlights with color and sparkle." There were matching earrings. B; $15-30. *Courtesy of Marjory Ritter.*

Clockwise, from top: ***Starfish*** pin (1657) is from the early 1960s. "From the depths of the sea, man has found treasures of incredible beauty. One of these is the Starfish – the inspiration for this lovely ensemble. A glowing, sparkling replica of the Starfish is available in your choice of shimmering silvery finish or gleaming golden color…with the tailored prettiness of artistry in jewelry." There were matching smaller earrings. A; $10-25. ***Victorian Lace*** pin/pendant (3498) from 1974 was described as "Lovely Fashion Treasures," truly accurate for this black onyx stone artfully set in an antiqued silvery mounting. C; $15-30. ***Sculptura Silvery*** pin (1161) from 1969 had matching earrings and also came in goldentone. B; $10-20. ***Love Knot*** pin (1510) from 1974 could also be used as a pendant and worn on multiple chains. It also came in golden. B; $10-20. *Courtesy of Marjory Ritter.*

Top row, left to right: ***Unidentified*** yellow flower with textured goldentone center is an artfully enameled pin from the 1960s. $10-20. ***African Queen*** pin/pendant (3548) was from the mid-1970s. A fabulous combination of orange, green, and yellow rhinestones and cabochon sets in an antiqued goldentone mounting. Matching bracelets, shown on page 121, could be connected together to create a choker necklace. D; $20-35. **Bottom row, left to right:** ***Jelly Bean*** pin (1240) from 1970 has "Colors Bright and Gay" with bright yellow and mint green plastic cabochon sets in an open goldentone mounting. There were matching earrings also. B; $10-25. ***Highlights*** pin (1644) in golden came also in silvery and had matching earrings for a quite simplistic and yet rich looking design. B; $10-20. *Courtesy of Marjory Ritter.*

Top row, left to right: ***Unidentified*** flower pin and matching earrings are white enamel with gleaming golden centers. $15-30. ***Unidentified*** multi-petal flower pin is white enamel with a highly textured golden center with delicate golden mounting. $10-20. **Bottom row, left to right:** ***Unidentified*** leaf pin with turquoise enameled open spines is a most unusual pin and no doubt from the early 1960s. $20-30. ***Unidentified*** pin with a shooting star effect is created from both gleaming and textured golden metal. Very simplistic in design yet bold in size, reminiscent of the 1950s and 1960s. $15-30. *Courtesy of Bill Scheetz.*

Top row, left to right: *White Olive* pin (1512) is from the early 1960s. "…for your dark wools – dress, suit or coat – try Emmons' White Olive when you want your accessories subdued." This is a unique combination of silvery gleaming and textured mixed with simulated pearls, giving a very soft and yet bold pin. There were matching earrings. $15-30. *Unidentified* pin of silvery gleaming and textured mix has a simple and yet artfully designed leaf motif. $15-30. **Bottom row, left to right:** *Unidentified* pin is very similar to a set in the 1960s called Calypso created from goldentone and stones in this unique setting. This pin, however, utilizes a combination of gleaming and textured goldentone. $15-30. *Unidentified* crown pin is created from simulated pearls adorning a solid goldentone crown shape. $10-20. *Courtesy of Bill Scheetz.*

Left to right: *Unidentified* pin is like a lily of the valley with golden mounting and simulated pearls accenting the center of the flowers. A truly dynamic and realistic piece of jewelry. $15-30. *Calypso* pin (1518) is from the early 1960s. "Need a lift? Here's a pin in a young, gay mood that will send your spirits soaring! The tempo is fast; the beat is Calypso! Just the bright note for your suit or dress." The earrings were the same size as the pin to "make beautiful clips on accessories like shoes, hats, bags and gloves. Put new life into your jewelry wardrobe with CALYPSO!" A; $15-30. *Courtesy of Mary Elizabeth Snawder.* *Starry Night* pin (1419) was featured in the early 1970s. The jet cabochon sets in a star design with Austrian crystals twinkle like a starry night on this silvertone mounting. There were matching earrings as well. B; $15-30. *Sorcery Lavalliere* pin (520) doubles as a necklace by attaching a chain to the back of the pin. This unique pin from 1971 was featured as a "Gift for a Royal Princess Hostess." $15-30. *Courtesy of Nina Mooney.*

Emmons jewelry featured a wide variety of pins, as shown by this display. **Top row, left to right:** *Locket/pin* (1046) is from 1980 and has a removable locket leaving just the golden bow pin. The engraving allows up to three letters. E; $15-30. *Unidentified* initial pins and tacs were very popular in a variety of styles and sizes. $8-20. *Unidentified* devil pin may have been a custom item or used as an award, as I couldn't locate it in my materials. *Courtesy of Norma Miller.* **Bottom row, left to right:** *Tie 'n Tassel* pins (Silvery, 1205; Golden, 1109) are from 1973. Matching earrings on page 123. B; $10-20. *Courtesy of Mary Elizabeth Snawder*

Left to right: *Gibson Girl* pin (1760) is from the early 1960s. "Some like to wear it just below the collar of a tailored blouse…others, on hats or bags…or pocket. Whichever way you choose, Gibson Girl will gain many compliments for you. Sweet femininity personified…a perennial favorite of so many." A; $15-30. *Beauty Vine* pin (1559) is from 1969 and described "Pearl and Gold…Basic and Classic." A marvelous piece that has withstood the test of time for thirty-five years. Spectacular jewelry. A; $20-35. *Double-Take* pin (1302) also came in silvery at Christmas time in 1971. A very simple yet stunning combination of gleaming and textured finish. A; $10-20. *Courtesy of Mary Elizabeth Snawder.*

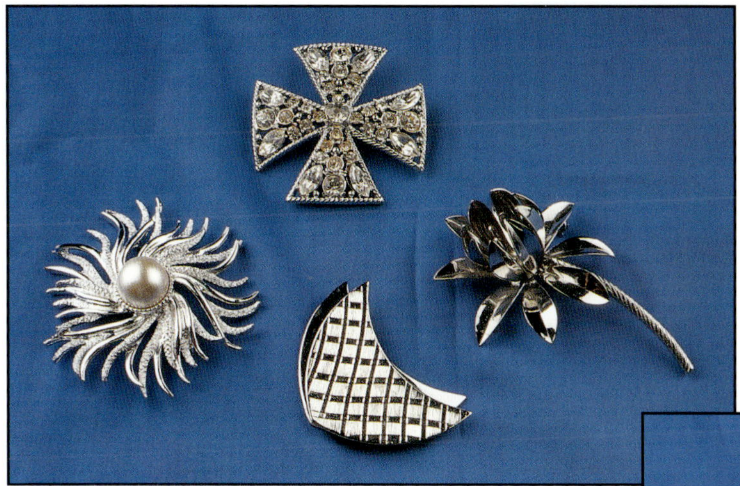

Top: *Unidentified* pin is a stylized cross shape with a variety of crystal rhinestone shapes and sizes. $15-30. **Bottom row, left to right:** *Unidentified* pin is a swirling shape of textured and gleaming silvertone featuring a simulated pearl in the center. $15-30. *Modern Flair* pin (1667, silvery) is from the early 1960s. "A Florentine finish shield, perched on its smooth finish twin, lends the sculptured look so coveted by devotees of modern design. Newer than tomorrow's newspaper achieves a dimensional feeling in jewelry, here interpreted in double wings of goldentone or silvertone." There were also matching earrings. A; $15-30. *Unidentified* 3-dimensional flower on stem looks very life-like and could be attractively worn on any dark costume. $15-30. *Courtesy of Mary Beth Coffman.*

Top row, left to right: *Unidentified* white enameled and golden flower petal pin with simulated pearl center. Notice the intricate design of golden stamens. $15-30. *Unidentified* swirl design of silvertone paved with Austrian crystals pin is definitely striking against a dark costume. $20-35. *Unidentified* golden leaf shape with curved end is very life-like. The combination of gleaming and textured golden finish is dynamic and eye-catching. $15-30. **Bottom:** *Rainbow Star* pin (1610) is from the late 1960s. "A joy to behold, a thrill to own, is our Rainbow Star. As happy and inspiring as a rainbow, you'll feel that you've found the Pot of Gold. Especially pleasing when doubled as a necklace (using Glamour Chain), nestling at your throat." Matching earrings on page 116. A; $20-35. Mary Beth mentioned that this was one of the most popular pieces, and she sold lots of pins and sets. *Courtesy of Mary Beth Coffman.*

Top: *Persian Treasure* pin (1186) is from the 1960s. "Its golden antique finish…flashing glints of blue aurora borealis crystals are mystifying. Three coral-colored cabochon beads with white and golden spots fanning from the height of the motif. With blues it takes on the blue tone, with greens it looks green. With blacks and browns it stands on own color." There were also matching earrings. B; $30-45. **Bottom row, left to right:** *Unidentified* prickly golden pin with turquoise beads give the effect of an underwater urchin. $20-35. *Renaissance* pin (1871) from 1969 is an antiqued golden pin with center turquoise-like cabochon with dark streaks accented by a circle of darker turquoise beads. There were also matching earrings. B; $15-30. *Courtesy of Pat and Gary Wyatt.*

Clockwise, from left: *Dainty Butterfly* pin (1601) is from the early 1960s. "You'll love this graceful butterfly…a delicate filigree" truly small and dainty to look great on "the sheerest blouse and distinctive enough to stand out against heavier fabrics." A; $10-25. *Flutter* pin (1850) from 1969 was identified as "Fashion Variety." This yellow and black enameled golden pin is very dynamic and bold. A; $15-30. *Unidentified* stylized equine is strikingly created from silvertone in a striped effect. Perhaps that makes it a zebra rather than a horse! A unique jewelry design, no doubt from the 1960s. Finding this pin would truly be a collector's treat. $15-30. *Courtesy of Pat and Gary Wyatt.*

Top row, left to right: *Crystal Leaf* pin (1676) is from the early 1960s. "Like a delicate tendril, tipped with dew, a golden furl is capped with shimmering rhinestones. Exquisite as the only accent on a simple black sheath. Equally elegant on white crepe." There were matching earrings as well. A; $20-45. *Unidentified* flower and leaf pin in a slightly textured golden finish is very striking with a cluster of aurora borealis stones in the center. $20-45. *Unidentified* leaf pin created from both textured and gleaming golden gives a light and airy effect. $10-20. *Courtesy of Pat and Gary Wyatt.* **Bottom row, left to right:** *Orbit in Fashion* (1179) is from the 1960s. "Take off on a flight of fancy with Emmons' modern-as-tomorrow Orbit of Fashion…The fashion-free flourish of polished loops circling over the ribbed golden oval provides a chic accent of fashion in your wardrobe to complement suits, woolens, coats, and handbags." A; $15-30. *Sea Flower* pin (1501) is from 1960s. "Straight from Neptune's mysterious ocean deep comes Emmons' Sea Flower…a solitary iridescent pearl (simulated) cradled in wave upon wave of golden colored petals so bright and shimmering." There were matching earrings as well. B; $15-30. *Autumn Echoes* pin (1108) is from the 1960s. "The glint of sunlight on autumn's golden leaves is a never-forgotten sight…richly veined…to conjure such memories." There were also matching earrings. A; $10-20.

On box: *Unidentified* salamander pin. There was a salamander similar in shape with a cluster of green beads on its back, but not these red stones. One representative thought the name might have been Chameleon. This is the only one I have seen, so it will be a collector's find. $20-35. **Bottom row, left to right:** *Unidentified* silvery pin is nearly 3" across. The overlapping open-weave leaves are accented by a fluted center and silvery ball stamens for a very bold and dynamic piece of jewelry, no doubt from the 1960s. $15-30. *White Olive* pin (1512) is from the early 1960s. The gleaming and textured silvery finish with simulated pearls gives an elegant yet simplistic piece of jewelry. There were earrings that matched as well. A; $15-30. *Silhouette* pin is a maple leaf created from gleaming silvery finish. The 3-dimensional effect makes it a very dynamic and yet versatile pin. B; $10-25.

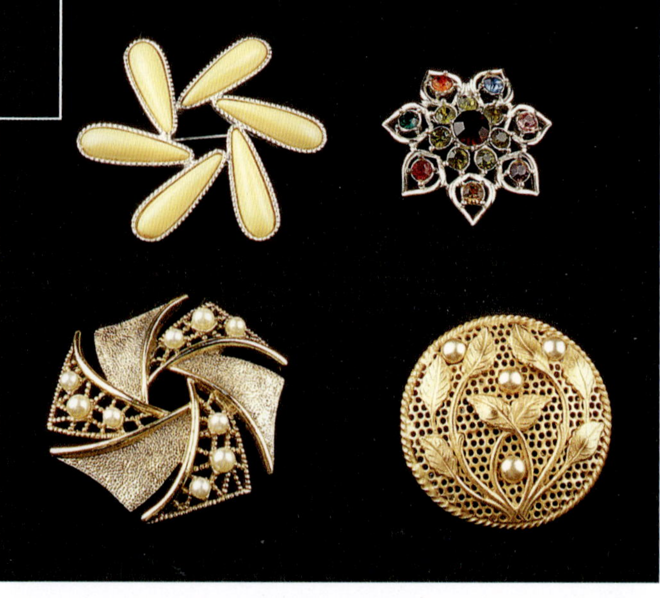

Top row, left to right: *Tutti-Fruitti* pin (1398) is from 1972. It came in lilac and white as well. B; $15-30. *Unidentified* multi-colored Austrian crystal pin. This star-shaped open-weave pin is no doubt from the 1960s with its dazzling array of stones including moss green. $15-30. **Bottom row, left to right:** *Windmill* pin (1270) from 1970 is a unique combination of golden textured and gleaming in a spiraling motion highlighted with simulated pearls. There were also matching earrings. B; $10-25. *Unidentified* circle pin of golden weave accented with overlaid golden leaves, stems, and simulated pearl halves. $15-30.

Top row, left to right: *Unidentified* green enameled pin with yellow center flower on golden stem, no doubt from the 1960s. $10-20. *Unidentified* golden curved leaves pin accented with simulated pearls is from the early years. It also came in silvery finish. $15-30. **Bottom row, left to right:** *Unidentified* large mint green flower pin is 3" across with a textured golden center. A very bold and colorful accessory from the 1960s. $15-30. *Pin Twins* was the name for this pin, which actually came in pairs. "Do you like understated fashion – the light golden touch – single and smooth? Then Pin Twins are your fashion bill of fare. Wear them straight – across or up-and-down – or angle them to follow the cut of your dress or suit." This pin from the early 1960s is still in excellent shape and popular today. A; $8-15.

Autumn Haze pin/pendant (3420) is from 1972 and identified as "Sea Treasures." Symbolic of its name, the translucent amber and green cabochon beads on the golden mounting are very striking. There were matching earrings as well as a tassel of matching colored beads on five short chains for additional pizzazz. The Sand Pebbles ring on page 153 could also be worn as a part of this ensemble. C; $15-30.

Earrings - Emmons Jewelry

Back row, left to right: *Unidentified* pin is a very striking example of Emmons' superb choice in jewelry pieces. The leaf effect of gleaming silvertone is highlighted with a textured, raised strip in the center of each leaf. The leaves and stem draw the eye to the focal point – the prong set blue Austrian crystal offset from the center. This pin seemed to be popular as I have seen several. It is still in excellent condition, even though it most likely is from the 1960s, and yet very appropriate for today's jewelry wearer. $15-30. *Pear Bright* pin (1685) is from the early 1960s. "A jewelry wardrobe becomes that much more exciting with a conversation piece or two…worn on a sweater, or perched on the lowslung beltline of a snappy sweater dress. Mix and match with other earrings and bracelets in the line." Also came in golden. A; $15-30. **Bottom:** *Kaleidoscope* pin (1666) is from the early 1960s. "You'll have a smart array of the season's most popular jewelry items when you shop Emmons. An intriguing combination of colors and shapes form this fascinating pattern." There were matching earrings. B; $20-35.

Top to bottom: *Pearl Wardrobe* earrings (521 ensemble) are a part of a four piece set that was a "Gift for a Royal Queen Hostess" from the early 1970s. These earrings are simulated pearls with matching necklaces in 90", 42" and 18" lengths making the complete set. Matching necklaces on page 146. $10-20. *Autumn Echoes* earrings from 1960s are richly veined golden textured leaves, "the glint of sunlight on autumn's golden leaves are a never-forgotten sight…keep it forever!" As this description states, these earrings were made to be around for many years and over forty is quite a record. Matching pin on page 132. A; $10-18. *Tie 'n Tassel* earrings (2107) in golden, from 1974 through the late 70s. Matching silvery earrings on page 123 and matching pins on page 134. B; $8-15. *Courtesy of Arcadia Historical Society.*

Left to right: **Unidentified** earrings are no doubt from the 1960s. The enamel flower petals are exquisitely designed in gleaming golden. $10-20. **Americana** earrings (2237) are from 1970 and created from a silvery mounting featuring red and white, hence the name. Matching pin on page 122. B; $10-20. **Crystal Lights** earrings (0531) came in pierced and clip on in 1977. Matching necklace on page 126. Total set was originally $27. Current value: $10-20. *Courtesy of Arlena Jordan.*

Top row, left to right: *To and Fro* earrings (2529) are silvery but also came in golden in the mid-to late 1970s. They didn't match any other piece of jewelry, however they could be worn with lots of silvery and golden pieces because of their simplistic, yet exquisite design. B; $10-20. **Unidentified** earrings are a circle golden design with white glass stone prong set in the center. No doubt from the 1960s. $10-20. **Unidentified** earrings are golden weave design with a wing shape effect. Matching bracelet on page 154. $10-20. **Bottom row, left to right: Unidentified** slinky shaped earrings in golden with pierced-look clip. $10-20. **Unidentified** retro design of enameled yellow, white, and blue shapes attached to a crazy curve shape of solid golden. $10-20. *Courtesy of Bill Scheetz.*

Top row, left to right: *Tie 'n Tassel* earrings (2108) are from 1974 through the late 1970s. Matching golden earrings on page 137 and matching pins on page 134. B; $8-15. **Unidentified** earrings are mint green enameled "quote mark" shape in golden mounting. No doubt from the 1960s. $10-20. *Dramatic* earrings (2937) are from 1978 and also came in silvery. C; $10-20. **Center left:** *Multiplicity* earrings from the 1960s were created to also be worn on a silvery chain that could be used as a bracelet or sweater guard. What a versatile use for this jewelry: 1) earrings to coordinate with the bracelet chain, 2) attached to the ends of the bracelet chain, and 3) attached to the bracelet chain to function as a sweater guard. A; $10-20. **Bottom row, left to right:** *Pearl Glamour* earrings (2520) are from 1960s. "Utterly enchanting! The tear-drop styling of this pretend pearl…gives it a soft, delicate look, so attuned to today's fashion." There was a matching necklace and it was created to match many of the pearl and golden pins and bracelets. A; $10-20. **Unidentified** silvery leaf swirl earrings are very delicate and petite. $10-20. **Lemon Twist** (2689) are yellow ball earrings swinging brightly from a trapeze type mounting of golden. A; $10-20. **Unidentified** golden dangle earrings solidly created for a dazzling costume. $15-30. *Courtesy of Bill Scheetz.*

Clockwise, from left: *Icicle* earrings (2278) are from 1972. As the name suggests, these dangle earrings were artfully designed from silvery metal of various geometric shapes paved with Austrian crystals. They were continued for several years, going from pierced-look to actual pierced earrings with surgical steel posts. B; $15-30. *Check Mate* earrings (2220) are from 1969 and created from a textured enameled finish in silvery outline. There was a matching pin. B; $10-20. *Unidentified* dainty antiqued golden earrings with opaque brown cabochon centers may have been from the 1960s clear through the 1980s. Very popular in a pierced design. $10-20. *Unidentified* pink plastic swirl effect earrings with center rhinestones were no doubt from the 1960s. $15-30. *Unidentified* gleaming silvery earrings with shrimp-like ribs may have been from the late 1970s as they were clip style. $10-20. *Twice Is Nice* earrings (2674) were from 1975 and very versatile, as they flipped on a swivel to change from this jet black stone to a silvery engraved and textured surface. There was a matching necklace that also swiveled to change from jet black to the engraved surface. *Courtesy of Mary Elizabeth Snawder.*

Left to right: *Unidentified* mint colored, glass crystal shaped dangle earrings are no doubt from the late 1960s to early 1970s. $10-20. *Love Beads* earrings in yellow with orange spacers (2309), aqua (2310), and lime (2312) are from 1971 and came in clip or pierced. Very colorful to match any costume. A; $10-25. *Courtesy of Mary Elizabeth Snawder.*

Top: *Unidentified* silvery spider web earrings with insects attached were no doubt created in the 1960s to be worn during the fall holidays. Emmons was quite good at designing jewelry intended for the younger generation as well as the young-at-heart older generation. $15-30. Bottom row, left to right: *Unidentified* golden circle dangle earrings are creatively fashioned with three crystal rhinestones of pale yellow, red, and turquoise. They are no doubt from the early 1960s. $15-30. *Spanish Lace* earrings (2257) are from 1970 and created from a repeating open-weave leaf shape. These dangle earrings had surgical steel earwires and were accented by three leaf dangles. B; $10-20. *Golden Odyssey* earrings (2598) are from the mid-1970s. They also came in silvery and had matching bracelets and rings. B; $10-20. *Courtesy of Mary Elizabeth Snawder.*

Top left: *Unidentified* earrings have a slight angle to each of the textured goldentone flower petals nestling a robin's egg blue bead. The simulated pearl in the center completes the gentle yet exquisite design. $20-35. **Bottom row, left to right:** *Unidentified* earrings are similar to sets identified as swingers. Pearlized baroque beads are attached to flattened links for a long dangle effect. $15-30. *Unidentified* earrings have a different look as the chains cascade from the center of the goldentone bead. $10-20. *C'est Belle* earrings from the early 1960s were described as having "delightful swing and sway…'It is beautiful.'" There was a matching necklace as well. A; $10-20. *Confection* earrings (1239) are from the early 1960s. These are pressed pearl (simulated) drop earrings dangling from goldentone clips. There was a matching necklace that could be adjusted to different lengths, also creating a bracelet. A; $15-30. *Courtesy of Mary Elizabeth Snawder.*

Left to right: *Merry Belle* (2353) are silvery earrings from 1973 featuring a unique combination of chain, mesh shapes, and solid balls. They also came in golden. B; $10-20. *Roundabout* earrings (2245) are silvery, but also came in goldentone in 1971. A; $10-20. *Silvery Odyssey* earrings (2599) are from the mid 1970s. Matching golden earrings are on page 139 and there was also a matching bracelet and ring. C; $10-20. *Classic* earrings (2223) are silvery from 1969 and came in golden as well. A; $10-20. *Courtesy of Norma Miles and Mary Elizabeth Snawder.*

Back row, left to right: *Satin Drop* earrings (2242) are from 1971 and identified as "Pearl and Gold…Basic and Classic." A; $10-20. *Regalia* earrings (2172) are from 1969. "Antique Look with Fashion Flair." There was also a matching pin. B; $15-30. *Unidentified* earrings are a dainty pearl (simulated) drop from goldentone flower design. $10-20. **Front row, left to right:** *Temple Bells* (2271) came in pierced and clip style in 1971. There was a coordinating necklace called Scenario, shown on page 147. B; $10-20. *Unidentified* earrings are three simulated pearl drops on chains. $10-20. *Two of Hearts* earrings (2437) are from 1977 and were also available in pierced style. B; $10-20. *Courtesy of Mary Beth Snawder.*

Top: *Tie 'n Tassel* earrings (2427) are from 1972 and are pierced style. They also came in goldentone as well as clip style. There were similar earrings in 1969 called Sophisticates that matched necklaces/sautoirs with attached bracelets. I believe they were interchangeable and used to match various pieces through the years. These earrings were popular so utilizing the same design for several various styles makes sense. Matching pins on page 134. B; $10-20. **Top left:** *Bright Textures* earrings (2848) are silvery hoop earrings with a textured edge. They also came in goldentone in 1978. B; $10-20. **Center row, left to right:** *Buttons* (2163) earrings from 1980 have a gleaming silvery finish. B; $10-20. *Nifty* earrings (2759) were smaller gleaming silvery versions found in 1979. They also came in goldentone. B; $10-20. *Winner's Circle* earrings (2083) in goldentone came from 1979. B; $10-20. *Sassy Hoops* in goldentone (2691) on the pink shoe display and silvery earrings (2590) on the side of the shoe are from 1978. D; $15-30. **Bottom:** *Crescent Moon* earrings (2034) were found in 1979 and had a matching pendant. B; $15-30. *Courtesy of Norma Miles*

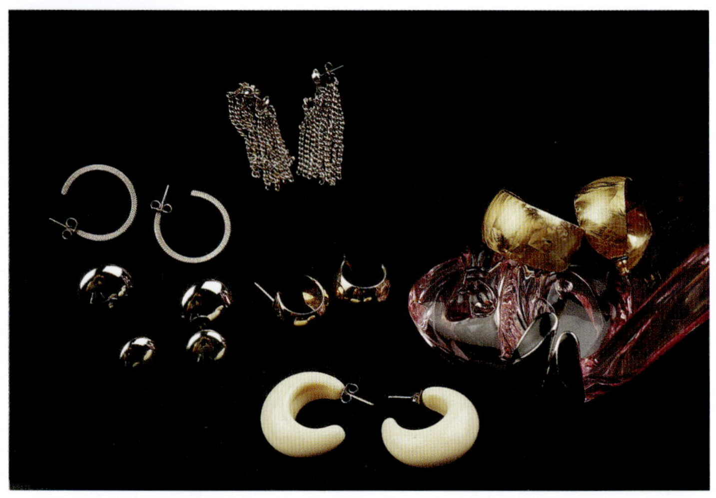

Back row, left to right: *Changing Scene* earrings (2136) are from 1979 and were a very versatile pair of pierced earrings. They can be worn eleven different ways by removing the post and reversing the large and small disk pieces. C; $15-30. *Pearl Love* earrings (2885) are simulated pearls in small goldentone heart shapes attached to 14 kt. posts. Only one earring shown. $15-30. **Bottom row, left to right:** *Casino* earrings (2435) are silvery open geometric shapes with a dangling ball. This is a take-apart piece of jewelry with a smaller similar shape removed. Also came in golden. B; $10-20. *Unidentified* earrings are goldentone with sections of blue, yellow, and white glossy enamel. $15-30. *Courtesy of Norma Miles.*

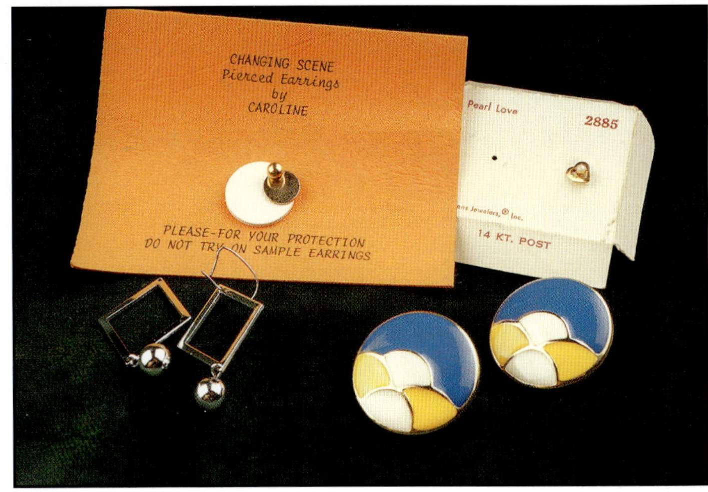

Counterclockwise, from top left: *Avocado* earrings (2678) from the early 1960s have oval green stones nestled in a golden finish circle design. B; $15-25. *Golden Swirl* (2637) earrings are from the 1960s. "Year round pleasure is yours with Golden Swirl. Try snapping out the white center and covering it with fabric to match your outfit of the day. Easily interchangeable – jewelry to perfectly match any dress in your wardrobe." Later there was a pendant called Magic Swirl with a similar interchangeable center to match any wardrobe. A; $10-20. *The Swinger* earrings (golden, 2691; and silvery, 2690) are from the early 1960s. "Here's a ball and chain that's fun to wear…gleaming globes that swing saucily with the faintest tilt of your head or the slightest movement you make. A captivating ear fashion…" B; $10-20. *Unidentified* silvery tie shape earrings are elegantly simple with their flower cut-out effect dangling from the ear. $15-30. **Top right:** These three colors of earrings are interchangeable to match any costume. The surgical steel earwires can be changed from one colored dangle bead to another. $10-20. *Courtesy of Mary Beth Coffman.*

Top row, left to right: *My Favorite* earrings (2641) are from the early 1960s. These are "well-named…wins hearts upon sight. The solitary simulated pearl with its petite rhinestone tip." There was a matching pendant on a chain. A; $10-20. *Ring-a-Lario* earrings (2701) are from the early 1960s. "For a pert appearance, you'll want to wear golden hoops clipped to your ears. A piquant fashion expression, handsomely executed in a smartly styled earring to give a fillip to your sportswear; add a sharp touch to tailored fashions; yet soft enough for dressier apparel." A; $8-15. **Bottom row, left to right:** *Two of Hearts* earrings (2437) are from 1977 and were also available in pierced style. B; $10-20. *Swagger* earrings (2696) from the early 1960s also came in silvery. There were several earrings similar to this set in the 1970s too. The open oval earrings are "perfect companions to any popular pin." A; $10-20 pair. *Unidentified* earrings have two sizes of red beads dangling from golden mounting on clips. $10-20. *Courtesy of Mary Beth Coffman.*

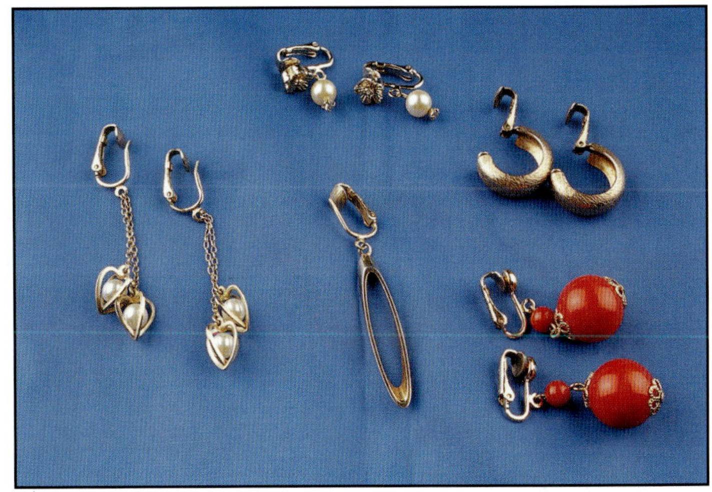

Top row, left to right: *Unidentified* goldentone petaled flower earrings with aurora borealis rhinestone in the center, no doubt from 1960s. $15-30. **Button** textured earrings from the 1970s. $10-20. *Unidentified* diamond shaped silvery earrings are covered with clear iridescent rhinestones. Magnificent earrings for "After 5" wearing. $15-30. **Bottom:** *Unidentified* earrings have a feather-like design with white enamel within gleaming golden design. $10-20. *Courtesy of Pat Wyatt.*

Left to right: *Unidentified* earrings resembling frosted lace are silvery circles of meshed finish. $10-20. *Unidentified* earrings have goldentone leaves surrounding and separating six simulated pearls. $15-30. *Courtesy of Pat Wyatt.*

Left to right: *Teardrop* earrings (2672) are shell finished teardrop designs still in the original box. No date was indicated, but these have to be late 1950s or early 1060s because of the box. $15-30. *Magic Lantern* earrings (1690) are from the early 1960s. "Looking ever-so-much like artistic lanterns." Matching bracelet on page 120. One earring could also be secured to a chain creating its own necklace as well, and many times three earrings were purchased just for this purpose. A; $15-30. *Unidentified* earrings are fashioned from three overlapping open golden leaves with half gleaming, half textured finish. A leaf shaped band of three gleaming rhinestones secures the three leaves together at the base. Very elegant, yet simple. $10-20.

Necklaces - Emmons Jewelry

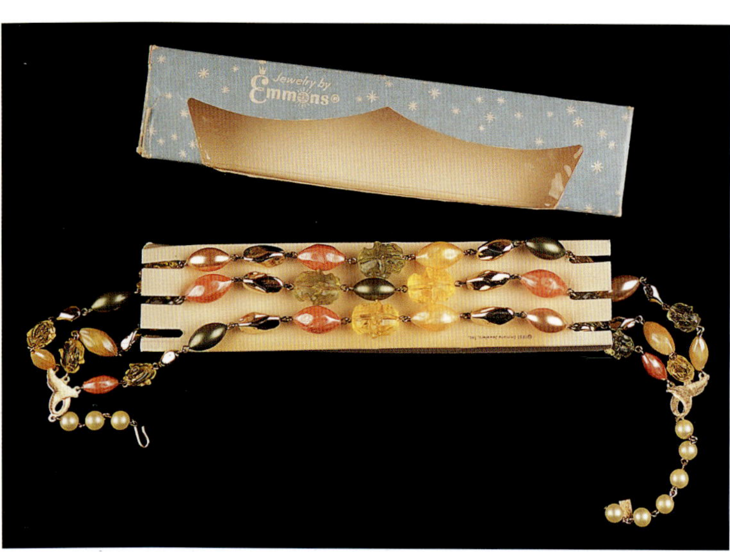

Mardi Gras necklace (3807) is from 1961 and still in its original box. It is a magnificent three strand necklace comprised of plastic beads of various shapes in dark green, salmon, peach, and amber colors. The beads are individually secured to the next with wire. This necklace lives up to its name in brightness and variety. B; $25-35.

Top to bottom: *Unidentified* glass beads are no doubt from the early years. These multi-faceted glass beads are in decreasing size from center to clasp with tiny glass spacers between each bead. These are remarkable beads and most likely had matching earrings. $35-50. *Unidentified* pearl and chain link necklace with pearlized tassel attached. This is no doubt from the 1960s. $10-20. *Fashion Magic Chain* (3798) is from the 1960s. "Look different! Feel different! Be different! This chain of multiple uses will help you create endless jewelry fashions by simply using it with pin, pendants and bracelets of all different types…Be your own designer with 'Fashion Magic'." The chain also came in silvery finish. A; $8-15. *Unidentified* is a bold, silvery finished chain that could be extended by the addition of bracelet length chains or shortened by removing them. A fashionable concept in versatility utilized a great deal by Emmons/Sarah Coventry and their designers. $10-20. *Unidentified* chain with a pink cast has golden beads stationed throughout the length. $10-20. *Courtesy of Bill Scheetz.*

Left to right: *Silvery Chain* from the 1970s is 24" long and coordinated with zodiac pendants or any of the multiple choices available. B; $5-10. *Midi Pearls* (simulated) necklace (3242) was described as "Pearl and Gold…Basic and Classic." B; $10-20. *Bib 'N Bracelet* (3247) was from 1971 and identified as a "take-apart necklace-bracelet." This set came in goldentone and silvery and was described as "Heavy in fashion…Heavier-weight wear." Matching silvery version on page 146. C; $10-20. *Star Spangled Girl* (3896) is a 52" rope "to wear in many ways" with attached small stars. It had matching earrings as well. C; $10-20. *Courtesy of Arcadia Historical Society.*

Left to right: *Unidentified* necklace of goldentone featured a watch pendant set in a filigreed mounting with matching stationed beads on the chain. $20-35. *Ultima II* necklace (3638) from 1977 was originally a two piece necklace with a solid goldentone insert the same shape as this attached independently to a chain. Because they were designed for versatility, the original pieces sometimes do not stay intact. D; $15-30. *Courtesy of Arcadia Historical Society.*

Tangier Simulated Pearl necklace (3313) is from 1971. The box gives the name as Simulated Pearl, however, the actual name is Tangier. The necklace also came with a bracelet section and dangling earrings. "Fashion-Magic at its Beautiful Best." C; $15-30. *Courtesy of Arcadia Historical Society.*

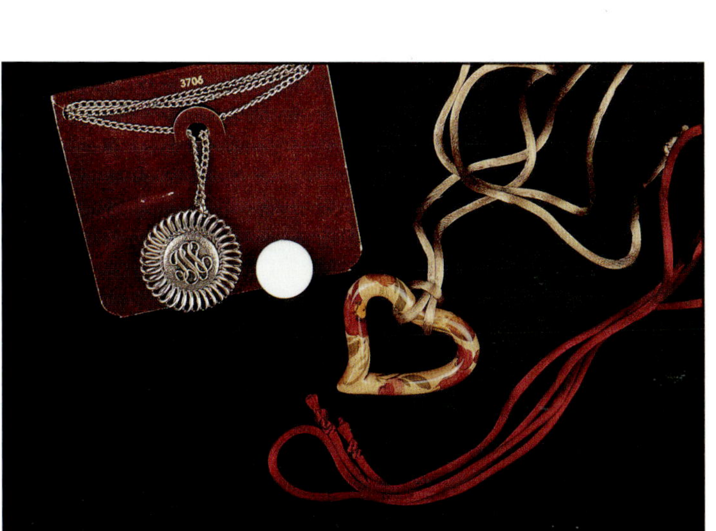

Left to right: *Magic Swirl* pendant (3706) is from 1977. The center punches out so it can be changed from this silvery scroll design to the reverse of plain silver, to the second center of black and white plastic, or covered with fabric – thus able to contrast with or match different costumes. D; $15-30. *Heartstrings* (3404) is a ceramic heart with two coordinating colors of plum and coffee. This unique pendant was from 1981. E; $15-30. *Courtesy of Marjory Ritter.*

Left to right: *Limelight* necklace (3901) is from 1978. The 51" long rope chain has lime green beads stationed throughout and also contains two 7-1/2" sections that become bracelets when removed, thus expanding this ensemble. E; $15-30. *Unidentified* lariat with turquoise-like beads on a long golden chain was one of many lariats created during the 1970s. $15-30. *City Slicker* chain (3745) came in 15", 18", and 24" lengths in silvery as well as golden in the late 1970s. C; $8-15. *Courtesy of Marjory Ritter and Marlene McIlwain.*

Left to right: *Cobra* chain (3316) is from 1980 and came in 15", 18", and 24" lengths in silvery and goldentone. This was a very popular chain that could be worn with many different pendants as well as alone. C; $8-15. *Fashion Bangles Take-Apart Pendant* (3527) from 1974 has a "large silvery bangle removable to wear as bracelet" that has been removed and is not pictured. "Golden bangle removable for child's bangle bracelet" is the pictured outside circle. This versatile necklace in a silvery and golden combination was a very simplistic yet dynamic piece of jewelry. D; $10-20. *Courtesy of Dorothy DeMay.*

Left to right: *Colleen* necklace (3660) is a two piece necklace plus removable tassel from 1976. The oval glass beads in variegated light and dark green are stationed throughout the second chain and at the end of the other with the tassel attached. There were matching earrings as well. D; $15-30. *Fashion Crusader* necklace (3243) is from 1970 and described as having "Colors...Bright and Gay." B; $15-30. *Filigree Flower* pin/pendant (3787) is from 1977 and can be used as a pendant, as shown here, or worn without a chain as a pin. The silvery filigree is accented by a simulated pearl center. C; $15-30. *Golden Veil* pendant (1345) is from the 1960s. "This attractive necklace has all the appeal and sophisticated charm of an heirloom...colored threads intricately patterned on rich black background." There was a matching ring and matching earrings as well. A; $20-35. *Courtesy of Marjory Ritter.*

Left to right: *Cascade* necklace (3724) is a two piece Hi-Lo Necklace indicating the varying style of chain used. One chain, shown with the stationed pearlized beads throughout the 21" length, was combined with a 16-18" chain with three of the pearlized beads in the center. It also came in goldentone (see top photo, next page). The buying special at this time in 1978 was "2 & 4" meaning two items purchased at the regular price allowed one of these items to be purchased for $4. D; $15-30. *Unidentified* pendant is a dainty opal stone set in a filigree golden mounting. $10-20. *Faith* pendant (3242) is a stylized cross of black inlay in goldentone mounting designed for the 1980s customer. C; $15-30. *Sitting Pretty* necklace (3095) from 1978 sports a prong set garnet glass crystal in a goldentone pendant. C; $15-30. *Courtesy of Marjory Ritter.*

Top to bottom: *Cascade* necklace (3724), same as in previous photo (page 144, bottom) but in goldentone. D; $15-30. *Unidentified* necklace is no doubt from the early years. The cream colored oval glass opaque stones are encased in a prong like mounting linked together to create this exquisite necklace. The chain itself is quite unique in style. Locating this piece would be a wonderful find for a collector. $30-45. *Courtesy of Marjory Ritter and Bill Scheetz.*

Below:

Left to right: *Classic Black* necklace (3838) is a 36" rope with black cylinders stationed on either side of an open link silvery chain. C; $10-25. *Honeycomb* necklace (3550) and matching earrings (2550) are from 1974. The necklace is a long 47" rope with the amber colored glass cylinder and round beads stationed throughout the length. The earrings are the same beads and can be converted to pierced dangles. D; $15-30. *Unidentified* cross necklace is a very simple golden cross on a fine chain. $10-20. *Unidentified* is a green bead necklace with chain links through the beads and hooked together in a different style of necklace bead/chain concept. $15-30. *Unidentified* pendant necklace is a golden stylized flower with leaves attached to the adjoining chain. Small amber crystal rhinestones cover the pendant flower. $20-35. *Finesse* necklace (3748) is a two piece necklace with a removable tassel from 1978. The plastic beads are stationed artfully on this goldentone chain and a second chain had the tassel attached. E; $15-30. *Courtesy of Marjory Ritter.*

Top to bottom: *Unidentified* necklace is very similar to several Sarah Coventry ones from the 1960s. The Austrian crystal rhinestones are clear, with a slight yellow tint when hit by light. The golden mounting and links on the rhinestone chain make this a very exquisite necklace and elegant to wear today. $25-40. *Unidentified* teardrop shape pendant in goldentone is dynamically created with a criss-cross textured surface highlighted with tiny garnet rhinestones in a grooved star. The outer edge is also sprinkled with larger garnet rhinestones. This pendant is delightful and I have only seen this one, so the search is on. What a find! $30-45. *Boutique Three* chain (3511) is the chain and tassel part of the take-apart fill in necklace on page 148. C; $10-20. *Courtesy of Pat Wyatt.*

Left to right: *Matinee* necklace (3851) is from 1969. "Simulated, single-strand individually knotted beads." B; $10-20. *Pearl Wardrobe* (521) are three sets of simulated pearls featured in 1971 as "Gift for a Royal Queen Hostess" items. In the front is the 90" pearl rope, in the center is the 42" length, and on right is the 18" length. By combining any of these pearls, many fashionable combinations could be achieved. The earrings on page 137 made the ensemble complete. $10-20. *Courtesy of Norma Miles and Mary Elizabeth Snawder.*

White Magic belt/necklace (3345) is from 1972. As the picture indicates, there were several ways this necklace could be worn and belted. The double strand is a 34" length of simulated fresh water pearls. "Unique buckle hooks are secret to fashion magic belt or necklace." C; $15-30. *Courtesy of Mary Elizabeth Snawder.*

Left to right: *Prima Donna* belt/necklace (3273) is from 1971. The artfully combined chain and pearl beading in this unique necklace/belt is "Fashion-Magic at its Beautiful Best." C; $15-30. *Rope Trick* lariat (3523) from 1974 has attractively simple bell-like ends. There was a clasp about 6-8" up from the end with which to secure the other side. Very versatile. C; $10-20. *Unidentified* belt/necklace is created from golden nugget-like beads spaced with large goldentone links. There is a tassel attached and a hook allows the belt/necklace to be placed in a variety of ways. $15-30. *Bonnie Blue* necklace (3388) from 1972 sports three dark turquoise beads stationed throughout a double goldentone 24" long chain. C; $15-30. *Courtesy of Nina Mooney and Mary Elizabeth Snawder.*

Left to right: *Bib 'N Bracelet* take-apart necklace-bracelet (3246) is from 1969 and described as "Bold…and Beautiful Simplicity." This also came in golden (see top photo, next page). C; $10-20. *Roman Holiday* necklace (525) was a "Gift for Royal Hostesses" during the fall and winter of 1971. It was called a "fill-in necklace" because the combination of two actual necklaces gave a filled-in look. These hostess gifts were available when a show sold over $100 and two additional shows were booked and held. $20-35. *Unidentified* necklace is fashioned from oval glass amber stones encased and prong set in a magnificent goldentone mounting. These sets are stationed on a three strand necklace with a variety of shape and size links. Remarkably exquisite and fashionable yet today. $20-35. *Courtesy of Mary Elizabeth Snawder and Nina Mooney.*

Left to right: *Bib 'N Bracelet* (3247) is a golden finish take-apart necklace/bracelet from 1969. It came in silvery finish as well, as shown in the previous photo (page 146, bottom right). C; $10-20. *Scenario* take-apart necklace/sautoir (3194) from 1969 is a chain with pendant as well as a necklace with pearlized beads stationed between links of chains. B; $15-20. *Confection* necklace (1339) is from the early 1960s. "Tempting indeed is this luscious Sautoir! There's sheer flattery in its pressed pearl (simulated) chain and impressive pendant. Wear it as is, matinee length, or explore the many more exciting features for endless versatility. Detach the links at the top and you have the new shorter length…plus a bracelet to match!" Matching earrings on page 140. B; $20-35. *Finesse* necklace (3748) is a two piece necklace with a removable tassel from 1978. The plastic beads are stationed artfully on this goldentone chain and a second chain had the tassel attached. E; $15-30. *Courtesy of Mary Elizabeth Snawder and Nina Mooney.*

Left to right: *Medallia* long sautoir/adjustable belt (3172) is from 1969. "Antique Look with Fashion flair." A very attractive piece of jewelry to be worn in a variety of ways. B; $15-25. *Chinatown* lariat (3048) in silvery finish is a 36" length of necklace/belt/sautoir to wear many ways in 1978. D; $10-20. *Courtesy of Dawn Michaels.*

Left to right: *Jet Cascade* 54" sautoir/necklace (3195) and earrings (2195) are from 1972. "Silvery Sautoir's Long Cool Look". The three chain sections of the necklace are matched on the earrings, promoting the oval black jet stones mounted in silvery gleaming finish. C; $20-45. *Jet Elegance* sautoir (3500) are two necklaces combined from 1973. The stationed silvery rectangular sections encase the gleaming mounting of the black faceted crystal rhinestone. As a separate necklace or coupled with the linked type chain, this set is a stunning addition to any costume identified as "Elegant Simplicity." C; $15-30. *Courtesy of Nina Mooney and Mary Elizabeth Snawder.*

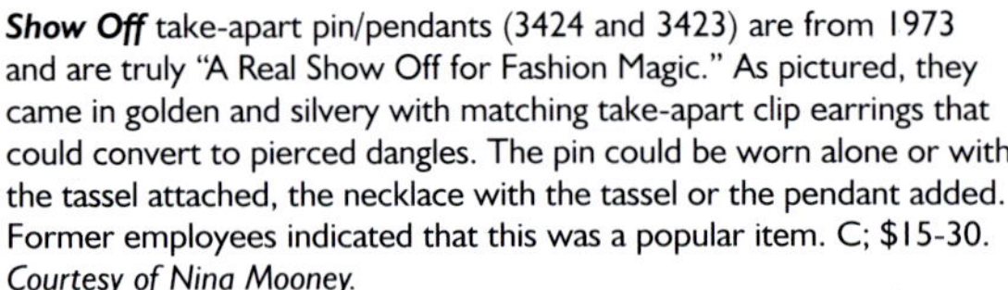

Boutique Three take-apart fill in necklaces (3511, silvery; 3387, golden) are from 1973. These necklaces were actually three separate chains in varying lengths with a locket pendant and tassel. They could be coupled nicely with Golden Odyssey in silvery and golden finish earrings, bracelet, and ring. "Super Fashion Magic." C; $15-30. *Courtesy of Norma Miles.*

Matchmaker necklace (3218) is a double strand of simulated pearls with a saber clasp paved with crystal rhinestones to provide for a variety of wearing positions and fashion magic. Imagination and this necklace created some fascinating styles. C; $20-35. *Courtesy of Nina Mooney.*

Show Off take-apart pin/pendants (3424 and 3423) are from 1973 and are truly "A Real Show Off for Fashion Magic." As pictured, they came in golden and silvery with matching take-apart clip earrings that could convert to pierced dangles. The pin could be worn alone or with the tassel attached, the necklace with the tassel or the pendant added. Former employees indicated that this was a popular item. C; $15-30. *Courtesy of Nina Mooney.*

Left to right: *Medallion* necklace (0529) is one part of a two piece necklace set that could be worn separately or together. This set was a part of a "Boutique Collection," featuring a collection of exquisite high fashion jewelry designs. C; $15-30. *Personality* 3-way necklace (3472) is from 1973. The coding depends on what initial was requested, from A=3459 to Y=3483. The versatility of this necklace allowed the three chains and individual pendants to be worn all together or as single necklaces. B; $10-20. *Courtesy of Norma Miles and Nina Mooney.*

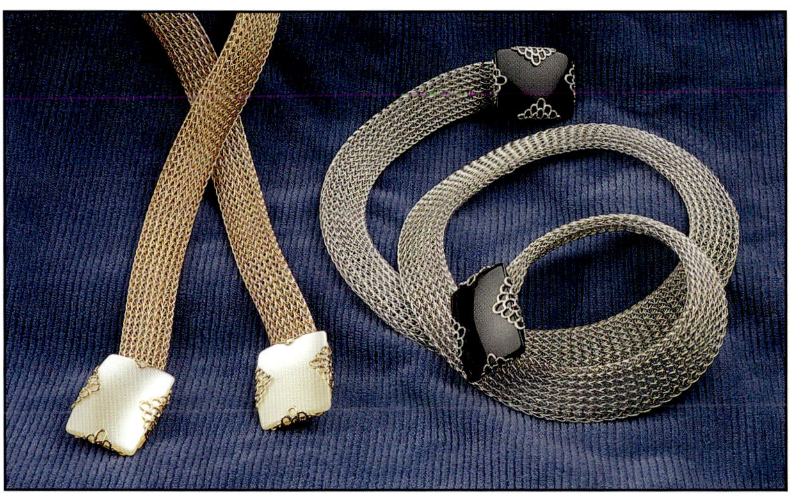

Spellbinder necklace/belt in golden (3219) and silvery (3239). It appears that the golden started in the late 1960s with the silvery added in the mid-1970s. "It's a belt…It's a necklace…It's a Cleopatra arm-bracelet! Soft, smoother mesh metal. Magic hooks hold the clasps wherever it pleases you for 'do your own thing' fashion-magic." The golden version has mother-of-pearl in the clasps, while the silvery version features black onyx. This must have been a very popular piece of jewelry to have continued for so many years. There is a ring to match the golden shown on page 152. D; $15-30 *Courtesy of Nina Mooney and Norma Miles.*

Left to right: *Spirit of '76* pendant (3639) is on a silvery 24" chain and was featured in the 1975 and 1976 catalogs as "Caroline Emmons Salutes America's Bicentennial." D; $15-30. *Twinkling Star* pendant (3411) from 1972 designed in a six pointed star shape features crystal stones faceted in such a way as to catch the colors from surrounding items. B; $15-30. *Soft Touch* necklace (3752) is from 1977. "Starry Nights and Caroline." A slight curve (smile) of crystal rhinestones is attached to a 14-16" silvery chain. B; $10-20. *Courtesy of Mary Elizabeth Snawder.*

Left to right: *Cuff 'n Collar* bracelet/choker (3362, golden) is from 1971. "The latest Fashion Magic news from Caroline Emmons! Chain extender lets you convert from Bracelet to Choker in a flash – it's today!" C; $15-30. *Thunderbird* pendant (3522) from 1975 is a silvery pendant with a turquoise-like center set. C; $15-30. *Silhouette* pin/necklace (3201) from 1969 is a marvelous cameo on an amber oval stone, both encased in a wonderful golden mounting. There were also matching earrings. B; $15-30. *Man Trap* perfume purse pendant (3450) is from 1973. This pendant is reversible and filled with "Essence of Caroline." C; $20-35. *Courtesy of Mary Elizabeth Snawder.*

Left to right: **Unidentified** golden choker has two chains attached to a single chain clasp. $10-20. **Unidentified** antiqued silvery bold chain has a detachable pendant with crest, suggesting that this might have been an item in the men's line of jewelry. $10-20. **Midas Touch** necklace (3320) from 1972 features white beads connected with golden twists and coupled with a golden chain approximately 40" in length for great fashion versatility. C; $10-25. **Sophisticate** necklace with bracelet section (3107) is a golden necklace of eight strands of chain with a detachable tassel. It also came in silvery finish. The detachable bracelet gave added length or a complete fashionable ensemble in 1969 and for several years into the 1970s. The earrings before were called Tie 'n Tassel, and are shown on page 123. They also match the pin with that name on page 134. C; $15-30. *Courtesy of Mary Elizabeth Snawder.*

Left to right: **Unidentified** lariat necklace has silvery finish lump spiral metal bead shapes connected with large silvery links. The long chain tassels on the end of the lariat made for a very versatile necklace to be worn many ways. $15-30. *Courtesy of Mary Elizabeth Snawder.* **Unidentified** necklace/pendant is a magnificent example of the kind of jewelry Emmons created. This is no doubt from the late 1950s or 1960s. The individual sections are black onyx encased in textured and gleaming silvery mountings faceted in such a way as to suggest rhinestones. They are hinged together with chain links and fastened to a bold chain and clasp. The front section is additionally adorned with an upside-down crown shape. I was truly excited to locate this piece. $30-45.

Left to right: **Floral Portrait** pendant (3900) is from 1978. This intricate engraved flower on an oval cream stone is encased in a gleaming golden mounting attached to a 26" linked chain. E; $15-30. **Lovable** necklace (3672) is a delicate golden heart attached to a 16-18" adjustable golden chain. This also came in silvery as well. B; $10-20. **Wind Swept** necklace (3302) from 1981 has three very small textured overlapping leaves on a 16" chain. The pierced earrings were unique in that they came apart and could be worn three ways. The post was attached to the top leaf, which could be worn alone, with the other two leaves behind it in front of the lobe, or behind the lobe. C; $15-30. *Courtesy of Pat and Gary Wyatt.*

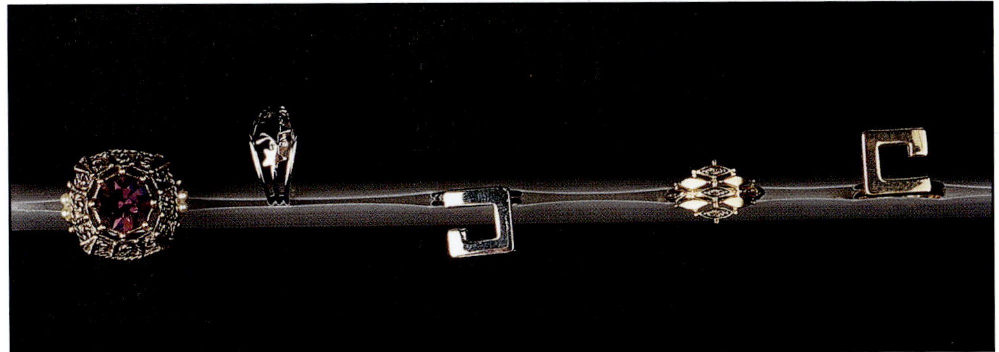

Left to right: *Unidentified* ring is an amethyst glass stone set in a goldentone antiqued mounting. $15-30. *Galaxy* ring (1712) in silvertone is from 1978 and also came in goldentone. B; $10-20. *Twosome* ring (1710) could be worn alone or coupled with the last ring in this row. C; $10-20. *Endearment* ring (1985) is a unique combination of gleaming and textured goldentone. B; $10-20. *Twosome* ring (1710) is the other half of the center ring. A truly different ring. C; $10-20. *Courtesy of Arcadia Historical Society.*

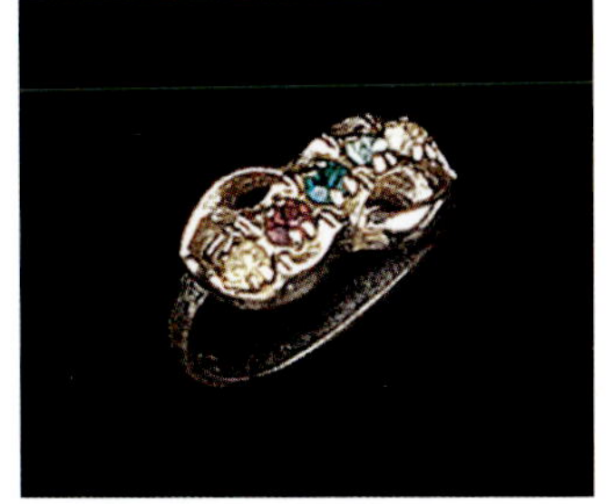

Mother's Ring (1921-1925), featured in 1977, has five stones set in a swirl effect. "Birthstones are custom set to represent birth month of each child. Birthstone is simulated. When setting is not complete, crystal rhinestones are added to Mother's Ring." A color chart was given for identifying the correct stones. There were several different styles of mother's rings featured during the 1970s. D; $10-20. *Courtesy of Brenda Bruzee.*

Left to right: *Legacy* ring (2028) is from 1972. B; $10-20. *Madcap* ring (1005) is from 1971. A; $8-15. *Green Lights* ring (1077) from 1970 has four dynamic prong set light green glass rhinestones. B; $10-20. *Milk 'n Honey* ring (1007) from 1971 is an exquisite white stone encased in a lace goldentone mounting. B; $15-30. *Rapture* ring (1010, golden) is from 1971 and has a simulated pearl center. B; $10-20. *Jet Classic Silver* (1059) and *Jet Classic Golden* (1058) from 1971 have polished jet glass stones to match many of the jet sets of necklaces, pins, and earrings. B; $10-20. *Courtesy of Mary Elizabeth Snawder.*

Left to right: *Spring Reverie* ring (2031) is from 1973. B; $10-20. *Feminique* ring (1014) is from 1971. B; $10-20. *Crimson Rose* ring (1003) is from 1971 and has a unique cluster of red crystals prong set in goldentone. B; $15-30. *Harem Girl* ring (2035) is from 1973. B; $15-30. *Moon Shadow* ring (2026) is an opalescent stone set in antiqued silvery mounting. B; $15-30. *Town N Country* ring (1062) from 1970 has opposite sections of textured and gleaming, suggesting the difference between town and country. "Rings in Bloom for the Season." B; $10-20. *Courtesy of Mary Elizabeth Snawder.*

Top row, left to right: *Pearly Nosegay* ring (1069) is from 1969. B; $15-30. *Milky Way* ring (1076) is from 1971. Matching necklace and earrings on page 119. B; $10-20. *Unidentified* ring is an exquisite faceted blue glass stone encased in golden mounting. $15-30. *Crystal Ball* ring (1078) from 1971 has an imported Bermuda blue crystal aurora glass ball. B; $20-35. *Birthstone* ring (1026) is from the early 1970s. "All stones simulated and prong-set for superior quality and safety, with adjustable shank to fit all finger sizes." B; $10-20. **Bottom row, left to right:** *Dinner Hour* ring (1002) from 1969 has one gray and one clear rhinestone prong set. A; $15-30. *Golden Odyssey* ring (1011) is from the mid-1970s. Matching earrings on page 139. There was also a matching bracelet and the whole set came in silvery as well. B; $10-20. *Garnet Glow* ring (1094) is from 1970. B; $15-30. *White Satin* ring (1097) is from 1971. This ring matched the Spellbinder belt/necklace on page 149. B; $10-20. *Courtesy of Mary Elizabeth Snawder.*

Left to right: *Regency* ring (1004) is from 1972. B; $10-20. *Evening Glitter* ring (1070) is from 1973. B; $15-30. *Sienna* ring (1098) is from 1972. B; $20-35. *Starfire* ring (1936) from 1976 is marked "Caroline." B; $20-35. *Courtesy of Mary Elizabeth Snawder.*

Top row, left to right: *Unidentified* ring is a dynamic combination of brightly colored prong set glass crystal rhinestones. $15-30. *Shalimar* ring (1890) is from 1974. B; $15-30. *Rosebud* ring (1927) is from 1976. B; $10-20. *Unidentified* ring in a snake design. I hate snakes, so this is not a favorite of mine, but it is quite unique. $15-25. **Bottom row, left to right:** *Honeycomb* ring (2036) is a unique butterfly ring from 1973. B; $20-35. *Unidentified* ring has an amethyst glass stone mounted in antique goldentone. $15-30. *Golden Shrimp* ring (1066) is a combination of textured and gleaming goldentone from 1969. B; $15-30. *Courtesy of Mary Elizabeth Snawder.*

Left to right: *Unidentified* ring resembles a love knot design with a simulated pearl in the center. A very exquisite looking ring. $8-15. *Unidentified* green stone ring is prong set with shoulder-like mounting in golden. $8-15. *White Satin* ring (1097) is from 1971. B; $10-20. *Coralette* ring (1934) is from 1975 and introduced with the African Queen set of jewelry. There were also pierced earrings that matched this ring. B; $10-20. *Spring Reverie* ring (2031) is from 1973. This veined stone is artfully surrounded by a filigree golden mounting. B; $10-20. *Cameo* ring (Sardonyx Cameo) is a sized ring from 4-10 dating from 1973. It is also 12 kt. gold-filled as it was part of the Crown Collection utilizing semi-precious stones. There were also matching earrings. D; $15-30. *Courtesy of Mary Beth Coffman and Pat and Gary Wyatt.*

Left to right: *Sand Pebbles* ring (2029) is from 1972, when it was coordinated with the Autumn Haze pin/pendant on page 137. B; $15-30. *Startrek* ring (1008) is a unique ring created from various lengths of tiny golden rods offset and accented with four medium sized crystal rhinestones. B; $15-25. *Lucky Lady* ring (1933) is from 1975 and marked inside as "Caroline." One employee mentioned that periodically the company created pieces of jewelry that bore this signature rather than Emmons. B; $20-35.

Left to right: *Nocturne* ring (1928) is from 1974. C; $15-30. *Portrait* ring (1989) is from 1977. B; $10-20. *Spring Reverie* ring (2031) is from 1973. B; $10-20. *Golden Veil* (1015) is from the early 1960s. "…golden colored 'threads' intricately patterned on rich black background…hard to resist." Matching pendant on page 144 and there were matching earrings too. A; $20-35. *Nostalgia* ring (1975) is from 1976 and identified as "The Beautiful Classics." The center set is a black enameled metal with intricately painted flowers. The antiqued silvery finished mounting gives a Victorian impression. B; $15-30. *Courtesy of Pat and Gary Wyatt.*

Left to right: *Beehive* bracelet (4649) from 1970 sports a beehive charm on this classic chain bracelet. A; $10-20. *Unidentified* charm is one of the many add ons available during the years that Emmons designed jewelry. This one features a cross engraved in the gleaming silvery charm. $8-12. Back of *Caroline Stuart* pin, shown in the pin section on page 132. This pin is a replica of a piece of jewelry C.W. Stuart had made in Syracuse, New York for his wife, Caroline Emmons Stuart, when he owned a jewelry store prior to moving to Newark and starting the many Stuart companies including Emmons and Sarah Coventry. There was no documentation as to the original price but because of its rarity it could bring $35-70 today. *Courtesy of Arcadia Historical Society.*

Little Sweetheart bracelet (4544) is from the 1960s. "Make your little girl a sweetheart with this dainty little ensemble (included necklace). The tiny heart, with a delicate rosebud, is a perfect complement for her. It's perfectly scaled, too, for the tiniest miss as well as the young lady in her pre-teens." A; $15-20. *Courtesy of Mary Beth Coffman.*

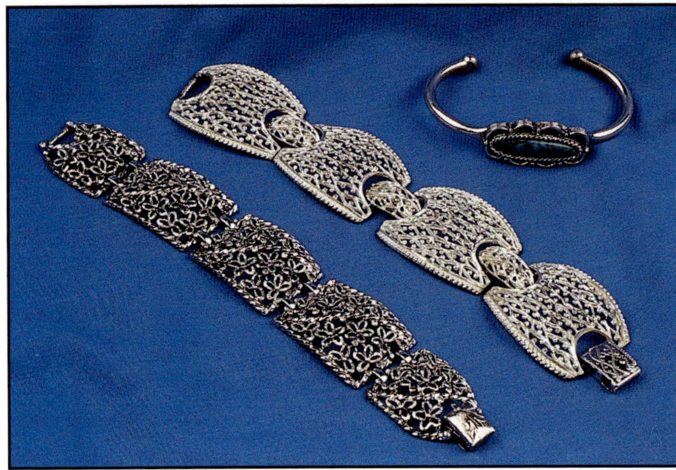

Left to right: *Brocade* bracelet (4528) is from early 1960s. "An exciting pattern of raised design which lends richness to any fabric is called 'brocade.' It gives you the same feeling of luxury and its raised setting of little silvery antique finish flowers is so attractive! The bold, rectangular cut of each link adds to its elegance. How feminine! How charming!" There were matching earrings as well. B; $15-30. *Unidentified* bracelet has a gleaming and textured silvery combination giving a lacy effect on this bold hinged bracelet. $20-35. *Mexicana* bracelet (4818) is a hoop bracelet from 1978 with an elongated turquoise stone set in an antiqued silvery mounting. There was also a matching ring, earrings, and necklace. C; $20-40. *Courtesy of Marjory Ritter.*

Top to bottom: *Fashion Flair* bracelet was a part of an ensemble including necklace and earrings that was not sold, but given as a hostess gift for having a $100 show and booking two additional parties. "Beauty and versatility abound in Emmons' newest special gift to Queen Hostesses. Satiny-smooth strands of golden allure in an intricate design are enhanced by a polished slide bar which features its mobility and lends further prestige and distinction for the most elegant occasion. Adjustable bracelet…is tailor-perfect for daytime wear. So much versatility…so exquisite…" From the early 1960s. $20-35. *Unidentified* bracelet created from smooth and textured links of golden provides an exquisite addition to any costume. $10-25. *Unidentified* bracelet gives the appearance of bamboo sections linked together in gleaming goldentone. $15-30. *Courtesy of Marjory Ritter.*

Two unidentified bracelets. The left one is a combination of golden gleaming and textured metal in a wing effect. There are matching earrings on page 138 and no doubt this piece is a very early one. $10-25. The bracelet on the right is not marked but was definitely identified as an Emmons piece. It is a very early piece, no doubt from the 1950s. The metal is enclosing the stones that are secured through the center and held strongly in place. A very attractive bracelet and one that proves the durability of the jewelry items made and sold by Emmons. Because it is not marked, it will be difficult to locate, but definitely a wonderful find. $50-75. *Courtesy of Bill Scheetz.*

Top to bottom: *Unidentified* bracelet made from white enameled flowers in a dogwood shape with yellow centers. No doubt this is from the early years and had earrings that matched. $15-30. *Gleaming Bows* bracelet (1480) from the 1960s is also shown with the matching earrings on page 132. There was a silvertone set as well. A; $10-20. *Courtesy of Pat Wyatt.*

Left to right: *Unidentified* bracelets in golden and silvery are lightly textured flat ovals linked together to form very simple yet striking pieces of jewelry to be combined with a multitude of other earrings, pins, and necklaces. $8-15. *Luv* bracelet (4384) is a golden bracelet featuring tiny hearts surrounded by links, creating a simple jewelry item. Identified as "The Young Sophisticates…" in 1974. It came in silvery also. $8-15. *Frosty Lace* silvery (4366) and golden (4365) bracelets are truly unique pieces of costume jewelry with a bold oriental style created from thick textured and thin gleaming metal. These pieces could double as a choker necklace by adding a chain to both sides of the bracelet. B; $10-20. *Courtesy of Mary Elizabeth Snawder.*

Left to right: *Simplicity* bracelet (4793) is in goldentone but also came in silvery in 1978. "The Beautiful Classics" could be worn with any combination of pins, earrings, and necklaces. B; $8-15. *Unidentified* bracelet in goldentone is wide with slightly curved filigree sections linked together – very Cleopatra-like. $15-30. *Unidentified* silvery filigree bracelet is medium width with a very simplistic yet rich quality. $15-30. *Courtesy of Pat Wyatt.*

Unidentified bracelets that could be called Jelly given their resemblance to jelly bean colors. The plastic balls in green, hot pink, and black coupled with the silvery bracelet could be worn with many of the similarly colored pins and earrings or multi-colored bead necklaces created by Emmons. These no doubt were from the mid-1960s. $10-20. *Courtesy of Mary Beth Coffman.*

Left to right: *Unidentified* bracelet from the the mid-1960s is a bold white plastic square design set in a gleaming golden finish mounting with unique cross-bars creating the links. $20-35. *Unidentified* multi-chained silvery bracelet from the mid-1960s sports a unique toggle clasp. $10-20. *Petite White* (4659) bracelet is from the mid-1960s. "The popularity of our Channel bracelet in Jet is overwhelming testimony to customer approval of its style and design…What fun you'll have mixing and matching them. So dainty and feminine for everything in your wardrobe…so perfect for all-season wear." B; $15-30. *Jet Petite* (4613) bracelet is from the mid-1960s. "Demure and dainty, this bracelet echoes the real look. The exciting channel design is most effectively carried out in the favorite for all seasons – Jet! A bracelet to please every age – from the teen queen to the sweet grandmother…and all those lucky girls in between, who love fine fashion!" B; $15-30. *Embraceable* bracelet (4616) is from the mid-1960s. "The irresistible charm of bangles never loses its magic spell! This special bangle by Emmons possesses feminine allure with intricate tracery of small, graceful leaves adding to its richness…has a chain guard, too, to keep it forever yours! It's available in both golden and silver finishes to suit your fancy!" A; $15-30. *Courtesy of Mary Beth Coffman.*

Left to right: *Unidentified* solid wide bracelets are from the mid-1960s. The enameled pale blue and mint green set on golden metal has truly lasted the test of time. These could be worn with many of the beaded necklaces and other jewelry pieces to complement the design of clothes in the 1960s. $10-25 each. **Charmettes** bracelet (4521) is from the early 1960s. "Ooh! La! La! In this decade of swing, the swoosh of ruffles and pleats is making a hit from coast to coast. From the strong influence of Paris comes jewelry to complete the look! Emmons designers have created this mood in a lovable bracelet that is bright, gay and devastatingly graceful. You'll love its brilliant hues in a splash of color!" *Courtesy of Mary Beth Coffman and Pat Wyatt.*

Miscellaneous - Emmons Jewelry

A unique collection of items treasured by Bill Scheetz. **Top right:** A plastic top to a jewelry display box used in the early years. **Center row, left to right**: A ring not identified and a unique pin looking for all the world like something out of a space odyssey. Actually it is portraying a light bulb, with the glowing rays symbolized by the rhinestone studded metal wires coming from the sides. Someone in the design department had fun with this one, which could no doubt be one-of-a-kind. **Bottom row, left to right:** *Avocado* pin (1678) and earrings (2678) are from the early 1960s. "The classic circle pin takes on a new look and a rich one. Avocado green with a flash of darker olive through the center creates an interesting pattern of color in the slim oval stones nestled in the round. Matching button earrings, too. Particularly stunning on winter white." B; $20-35. *Unidentified* pin has a feather swirling effect with each swirl centered with a tiny black pearl. $35-45. *Courtesy of Bill Scheetz.*

Left to right: Two pieces from the Emmons Crown Collection. *World's Fair Expo* pin from 1967 was created to commemorate that event, as were many others throughout the years. $30-50. *Zodiac Charm* (Leo – July 24 to Aug. 23) in sterling silver is from the 1960s through 1970s. "Pick your own zodiac sign from among the 12 charms. Each is a beautifully engraved image, set in a laurel wreath. Your choice in brocade gold-plated sterling for your gold charm bracelet; or glistening Brocade Sterling to add to your other Sterling Silver Charms or wear alone." B; $10-20. *Courtesy of Bill Scheetz.*

Two men's tie bars from 1969. **Left to right:** *Tiger Eye* tie tac (859) is from the Crown Collection of semi-precious jewelry. B; $8-15. *Ambassador* tie tac (4857) from the early 1960s. "The man who wears this...will be an ambassador of good will in any circle!...Masterfully crafted in a unique design, 'Ambassador' is truly a symbol of good taste!" A; $8-15. *Courtesy of Norma Miles and Mary Elizabeth Snawder.*

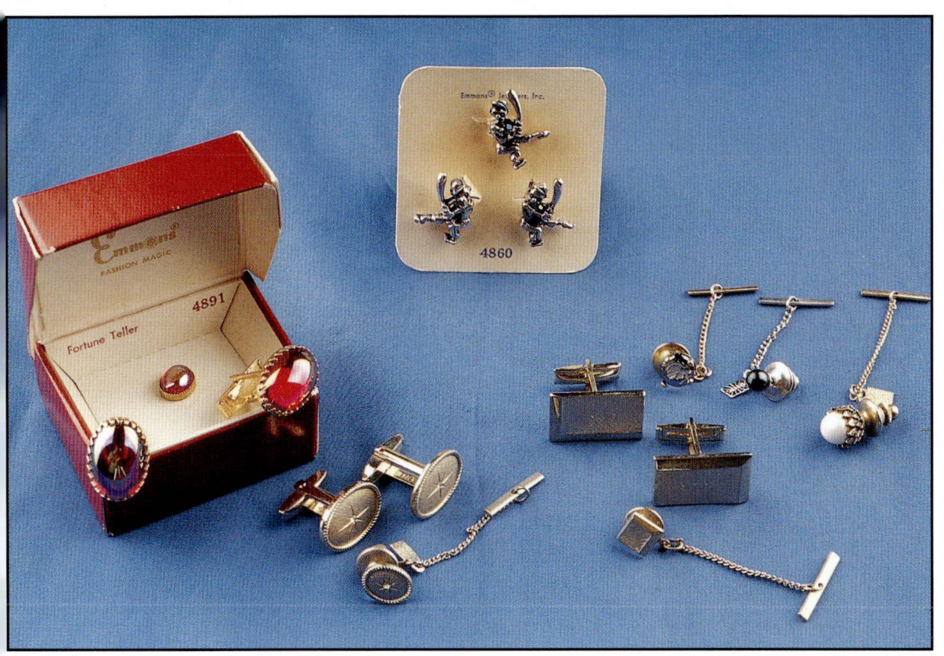

A selection of men's jewelry. **Top:** *Mighty Casey* (4860) cuff links and tie tac are baseball players for the sports enthusiast. " 'Casey at the Bat' is for all generations. Few can recite the legend…today, but we have our modern 'Majesty of the Mets' – a real ambassador of our great American sport. Any little boy would be thrilled to receive Emmons 'Mighty Casey' Tie Bar and Cuff links as a surprise gift. On the Tie Bar, Casey bats left-handed. With the cuff links he bats both ways. Either way, he's the man-of-the-hour with the younger men." B; $20-35. *Courtesy of Pat Wyatt.* **Bottom row, left to right:** *Fortune Teller* (4891) cuff links and tie tac are from the early years, as identified by the box. $15-30. *Unidentified* cuff links and tie tac set are golden textured ovals within a gleaming frame. The star indentation is highlighted with a crystal rhinestone. $15-30. *Unidentified* cuff links are bold rectangular shapes in a textured golden finish, two sides offset with a gleaming frame. Tie tac is the same finish only in a small square shape. $10-20. *Unidentified* tie tac is an intaglio Roman head design in a black circle. $8-15. *Unidentified* tie tac is a black pearl attached to gleaming golden finish. $10-20. *Regal* tie tac (4848) is from the early 1960s. "Fit for a King – Regal is the tie tac supreme. A lone simulated pearl nestles safely protected in its golden colored pinaceous cup. Attached chain guard keeps tie in bounds. For the discerning male…" A; $8-15. *Courtesy of Mary Beth and Chuck Coffman.*

Emmons jewelry came in a wide variety of styles and designs, as shown again in this selection. **Top left:** *Zodiac* neck ring with Aquarius charm from the early 1970s. "Fashion Signs…for Neck and Wrist." There was also a bracelet to wear the charms on. B; $10-20. **Far right:** *Quartet* bracelet (4203, golden) is from 1973. The bracelet combination also came in silvery. B; $10-20. **Bottom row, left to right:** *Unidentified* scarf clips in silvery and golden are no doubt from the early 1970s. These are very simple in textured and gleaming finish to be coordinated with any scarf and other jewelry. $8-15. *Evening Star* pendant (3564) with silvery mounting in black was from the mid-1970s, while the blue enamel was first sold in the early 1960s. "Brightly shines the Evening Star in the celestial sky…so like the guiding Star of old. This beautiful vision is captured in Emmons dainty cross and chain with midnight blue highlights. The girl of any age will appreciate its fine appointments." The same number was carried through to the black star. A (1960s), B (1970s); $10-20. *Midnight Butterfly* stick pin (1024) is from 1979. "You flip your lid over Caroline's Stick Pins which match your favorite Caroline Jewelry items." There was a matching pendant, earrings, and ring. B; $8-15. *Unidentified* charm in golden sand dollar shape from 1970s could be worn as a pendant on a fine golden chain or added to any charm bracelet. $10-20. *Unidentified* pin was recognized by a former employee as a "crown jewel pin." Perhaps this was an award item. Combining simulated pearls and rhinestones against the striking black enamel and golden finish makes for an exquisite jewelry choice. $20-30. *Courtesy of Mary Elizabeth Snawder and Norma Miles.*

Left to right: *Boutique Three* take apart, fill-in necklace (3511) is from 1980. The original included three chains, while only two are shown here. As the name suggests, it can be taken apart and its previous owner apparently did just that. F; $15-25. *Unidentified* pendant is pictured here without any chains. Notice the two loops on the right and also on the left, where chains could be attached creating a unique clasp, pendant on a necklace, or a bracelet. Versatility at its finest. $10-20.

fashion magic costume and Crown Collection semi-precious jewelry
caroline emmons
SHOWCASE

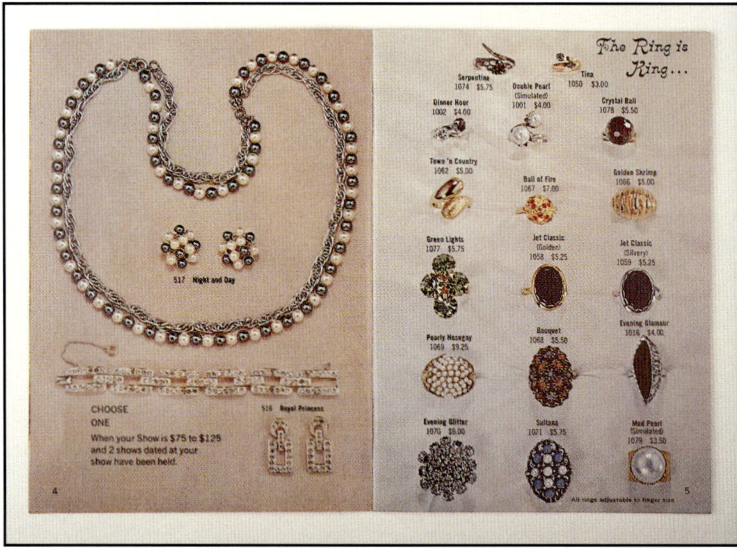

The Ring is King...
Serpentine 1074 $5.75
Double Pearl (Simulated) 1001 $4.00
Tina 1050 $3.00
Dinner Hour 1002 $4.00
Crystal Ball 1078 $5.50
Town 'n Country 1062 $5.00
Ball of Fire 1067 $7.00
Golden Shrimp 1066 $5.00
Green Lights 1077 $5.75
Jet Classic (Golden) 1058 $5.25
Jet Classic (Silver) 1059 $5.25
Pearly Nosegay 1069 $5.25
Bouquet 1068 $5.50
Evening Glamour 1016 $4.00
Evening Glitter 1070 $5.00
Sultana 1071 $5.75
Mod Pearl (Simulated) 1079 $3.50
517 Night and Day
CHOOSE ONE
When your Show is $75 to $125 and 2 shows dated at your show have been held.
516 Regal Princess
All rings adjustable to finger size

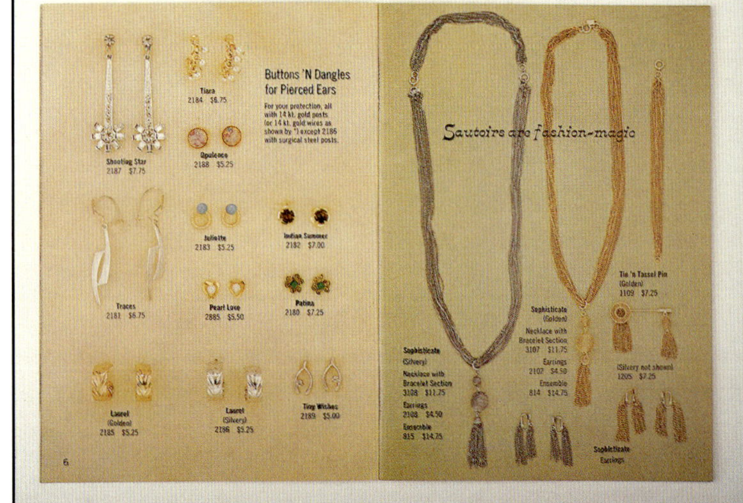

Buttons 'N Dangles for Pierced Ears
For your protection, all with 14 kt. gold posts (or 14 kt. gold wires as shown by *) except 2186 with surgical steel posts.
Sautoirs are fashion-magic
Tiara 2184 $6.75
Shooting Star 2187 $7.75
Opulence 2188 $5.25
Juliette 2183 $5.25
Indian Summer 2182 $7.00
Traces 2181 $6.75
Pearl Love 2885 $5.50
Patina 2180 $7.25
Laurel (Golden) 2185 $5.25
Laurel (Silvery) 2186 $5.25
Tiny Wishes 2189 $5.00
Tie 'n Tassel Pin (Golden) 1109 $7.25
Sophisticate (Golden) 3107 $11.75
Sophisticate (Silvery) 3106 $11.75
Necklace with Bracelet Section 3107 $11.75
Earrings 2107 $4.50
Necklace with Bracelet Section 3108 $11.75
Ensemble 814 $14.75
Earrings 2108 $4.50
Ensemble 815 $14.75
Sophisticate Earrings (Silvery not shown) 2105 $7.25
Sophisticate Earrings

caroline emmons
Hostesses
Build lavish jewelry wardrobes without opening their purses . . .
When you are a Hostess . . .
We give $6 for each Booking at your Show . . . $3 to you, and $3 to each one who books.
You can win a Hostess Gift allowance of $15 to $25.
For 10 orders $10
For Dating your Show 3
For 3 Bookings 9
*HOSTESS CREDIT $22
*$1 for each order at your Show, $1 for each Showcase order, $3 for dating your Show and $3 for each new Booking dated at your Show to be held within 1 month.
PLUS . . . a Door Prize when 10 or more guests attend your show.
AND when you qualify as a ROYAL HOSTESS . . . YOUR CHOICE of a PRINCESS GIFT or a QUEEN GIFT!
Showcase Order Deposit Guide
Paying in advance for your Showcase order will be very helpful to your Hostess. Otherwise, please be guided by our Deposit Schedule.

When Total Retail is: | Suggested Min. Deposit is:
$2.00-3.99 | $2.00
$4.00-5.99 | 3.00
$6.00-7.99 | 4.00
$8.00-9.99 | 5.00
$10.00-14.99 | 7.00
$15.00-19.99 | 10.00

Price $1.00
©1969 Emmons Jewelers, Div. C. H. Stuart & Co., Inc., Newark, New York 14513. Form No. 226. Printed in U.S.A.

514 Portrait in Black
CHOOSE ONE
When your Show is over $125 and 2 shows booked at your show have been held.
513 Jet Fantasy
Gift for a Royal Queen Hostess

The Scarf... So Fashion Important, so Fashion-Magical
Tempo
Scarf Clip Pin
(Golden) 1197 $4.25
(Silvery) 1238 $4.25
Scarf Ring
3209 $3.75
Butterfly
Pussy Cat
Ascot
Hood with Ascot
Off-Shoulder Apache
Head Apache
Scarf Fashion Magic
by caroline emmons
8
Antique look is IN
Cinnabar
Bracelet
4173 $7.25
Earrings
2173 $4.00
Midnight Lace
Pendant 3241 $8.00
Earrings 2241 $4.25
Ensemble 865 $11.25
Cinnabar
Ensemble
834 $10.25
9

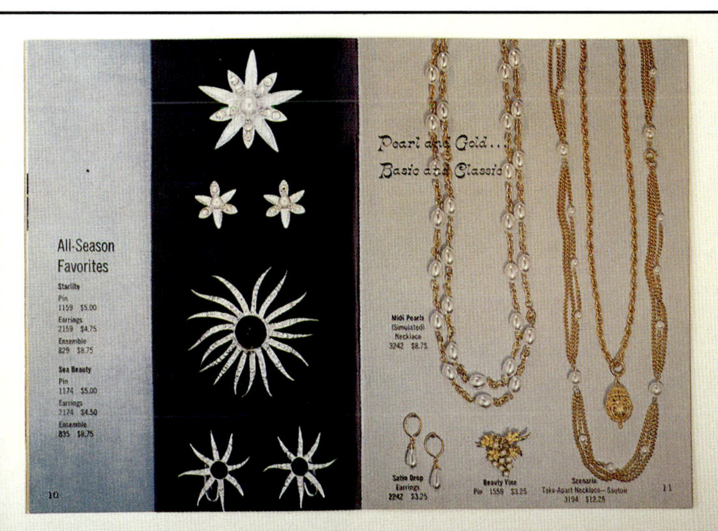
All-Season Favorites
Starlite
Pin
1159 $5.00
Earrings
2159 $4.75
Ensemble
829 $8.75
Sea Beauty
Pin
1174 $5.00
Earrings
2174 $4.50
Ensemble
835 $8.75
10
Pearl and Gold... Basic and Classic
Midi Pearls
(Simulated)
Necklace
3242 $8.75
Satin Drop
Earrings
2242 $3.25
Beauty Vine
Pin 1559 $3.25
Scenario
Take-Apart Necklace—Sautoir
3194 $12.25
11

Pearls...
MATINEE
Simulated, single-strand individually knotted beads.
Necklace
3851 $6.00
Earrings
2851 $3.75
Ensemble
803 $9.00
MATCHMAKER
Long, 48 inch rope of pearls. Unique, rhinestone-studded saber clasp holds rope in any fashion-magic arrangement.
Necklace
3218 $9.25
Earrings
2204 $4.00
Ensemble
858 $12.00
12
SPELLBINDER
It's a belt...
It's a necklace...
It's a Cleopatra arm-bracelet!
Soft, smooth mesh metal. Magic hooks hold the mother of pearl clasps wherever it pleases you for "do your own thing" fashion-magic.
Necklace—Belt
3219 $15.00
Earrings
2219 $6.00
Ensemble
857 $19.50
13

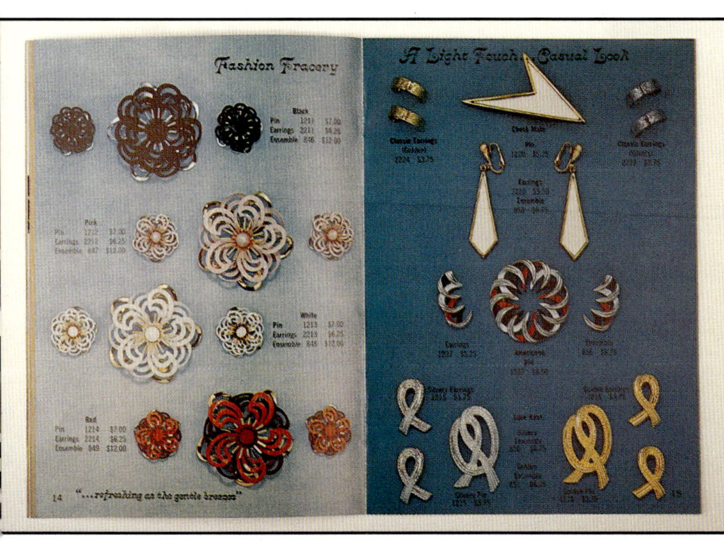
Fashion Tracery
Black
Pin 1211 $7.00
Earrings 2211 $6.25
Ensemble 846 $12.00
Pink
Pin 1212 $7.00
Earrings 2212 $6.25
Ensemble 847 $12.00
White
Pin 1213 $7.00
Earrings 2213 $6.25
Ensemble 848 $12.00
Red
Pin 1214 $7.00
Earrings 2214 $6.25
Ensemble 849 $12.00
14 "...refreshing as the gentle breezes"
A Light Touch... Casual Look
Classic Earrings (Golden) 2224 $3.75
Check Mate
Pin 1220 $5.25
Earrings 2220 $3.50
Ensemble 858 $9.75
Classic Earrings (Silvery) 2219 $3.75
15

caroline emmons
Crown Collection
Semi-precious jewelry
Distinctive . . . quiet good taste . . . for those who prefer real jewelry for themselves and for special gifts.
Crown Collection Jewelry attractively boxed for your gift-giving convenience.
Fish Pin
Genuine Smokey Topaz Quartz & Sterling with Vermeil (gold) finish
1248 $17.00
Cultured Pearl Circle Pin
(Cultured Pearl & 12 kt Gold)
1249 $12.00
Sterling Onyx Man's Ring
(Genuine Onyx & Sterling)
Each $18.50
For proper fit, use our Ring Sizer to determine correct Ring Size
1080 Size 7   1085 Size 9½
1081 Size 7½   1086 Size 10
1082 Size 8   1087 Size 10½
1083 Size 8½   1088 Size 11
1084 Size 9   1089 Size 11½
1090 Size 12
1091 Size 12½
1092 Size 13
Tiger Eye Man's Set
(Genuine Yellow Tiger Eye)
Cuff Links and Tie Tac
Set 859 $20.00
Ivory Bracelet
(Genuine Carved Ivory and 12 kt Gold)
4255 $14.00
Angel Skin Pendant*
(Genuine Angel Skin Coral & Sterling with Vermeil (gold) finish)
3254 $10.00
Cameo
(Sardonyx Cameo & 12 kt Gold)
Pendant* 3251 $12.00
Regular Earrings 2251 $13.00
Pierced Earrings 2252* $13.00
Cultured Pearl
(Cultured Pearl & 12 kt Gold)
Pendant* 3249 $10.00
Regular Earrings 2249 $11.00
Pierced Earrings 2250* $11.00
Jade
(Genuine Jade & 12 kt Gold)
Pendant* 3253 $10.00
Regular Earrings 2253 $11.00
Pierced Earrings 2254* $11.00
6
17

Bold . . . and Beautiful Simplicity
Flutter Pin
1850 $4.00
Fashion Crusader Necklace
3243 $9.00
Colors...
Bright and Gay
Jelly Bean Pin
1240 $6.25
Earrings
2240 $6.25
Ensemble
864   $11.50
Bib 'N Bracelet
Take-apart Necklace-Bracelet Golden
3247 $11.25
Take-apart Necklace-Bracelet Silvery
3246 $11.25
18
19

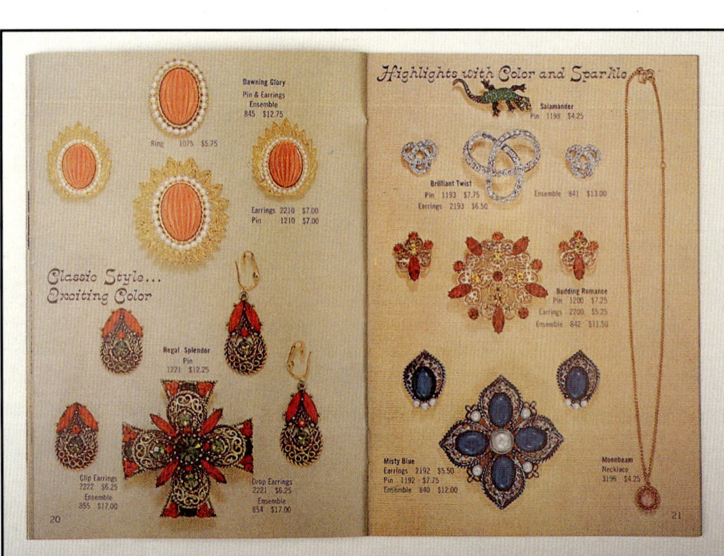

Dawning Glory Pin & Earrings Ensemble
845   $12.75
Ring   1075 $5.75
Earrings 2210 $7.00
Pin   1210 $7.00
Classic Style...
Exciting Color
Regal Splendor Pin
1221 $12.25
Clip Earrings
7222 $6.25
Ensemble
855   $17.00
Drop Earrings
2221 $6.25
Ensemble
854   $17.00
Highlights with Color and Sparkle
Salamander Pin   1198 $4.25
Brilliant Twist
Pin   1193 $7.75
Earrings   2193 $6.50
Ensemble   841 $13.00
Budding Romance
Pin   1200 $7.25
Earrings   2200 $5.25
Ensemble   842 $11.50
Misty Blue
Earrings   2192 $5.50
Pin   1192 $7.25
Ensemble   840 $12.00
Moonbeam Necklace
3195 $4.25
20
21

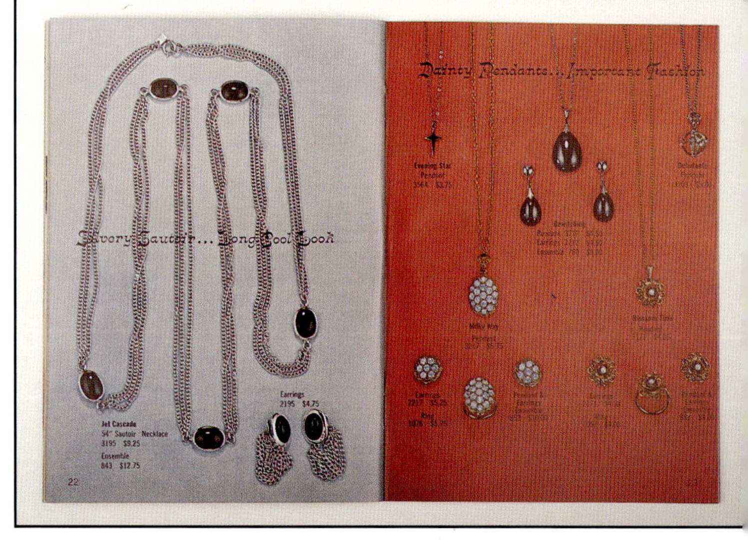

Ivory Saucier... Long Cool Look
Dainty Pendants... Important Fashion
Evening Star Pendant
3964 $3.75
Jet Cascade 54" Sautoir Necklace
3195 $9.25
Ensemble
843   $12.75
Earrings
2195 $4.75
22

Gifts with a personal flavor
Silhouette Pin Necklace
3201 $8.00
To & Fro Earrings (Silvery)
2112 $4.50
To & Fro Earrings (Golden)
2111 $4.50
Ensemble
864 $12.00
Two of Hearts Earrings
2775 $5.00
Silhouette Earrings
2701 $6.25
Birthstone Rings
All stones simulated and prong-set for superior quality and safety, with adjustable shank to fit all finger sizes.
$7.00 each
1022 January—Garnet
1023 February—Amethyst
1024 March—Aquamarine
1025 April—White Sapphire
1026 May—Emerald
1027 June—Alexandrite
1028 July—Ruby
1029 August—Peridot
1030 September—Sapphire
1031 October—Rose Zircon
1032 November—Golden Topaz
1033 December—Blue Zircon
24
25

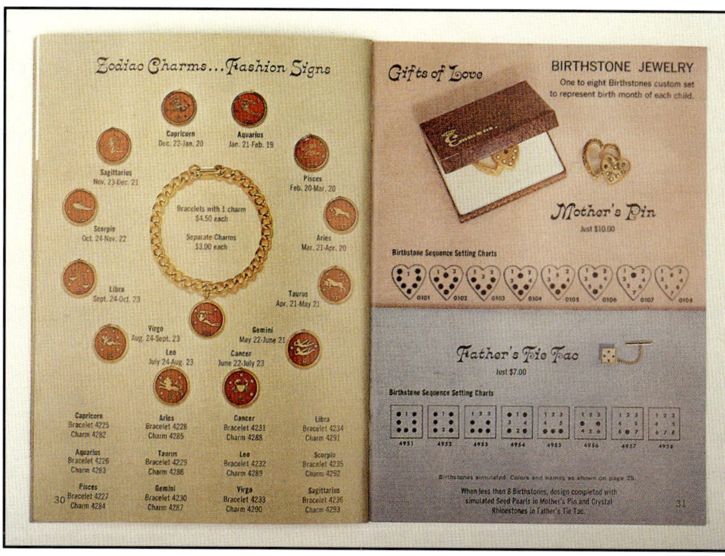
Zodiac Charms...Fashion Signs
Gifts of Love
BIRTHSTONE JEWELRY
One to eight Birthstones custom set to represent birth month of each child.
Capricorn Dec. 22–Jan. 20
Aquarius Jan. 21–Feb. 19
Sagittarius Nov. 23–Dec. 21
Pisces Feb. 20–Mar. 20
Scorpio Oct. 24–Nov. 22
Aries Mar. 23–Apr. 20
Bracelets with 1 charm $4.50 each
Separate Charms $3.00 each
Taurus Apr. 21–May 21
Libra Sept. 24–Oct. 23
Virgo Aug. 24–Sept. 23
Gemini May 22–June 21
Leo July 24–Aug. 23
Cancer June 22–July 23
Mother's Pin
Just $10.00
Birthstone Sequence Setting Charts
0101 0102 0103 0104 0105 0106 0107 0108
Father's Tie Tac
Just $7.00
Birthstone Sequence Setting Charts
4951 4952 4953 4954 4955 4956 4957 4958
Capricorn Bracelet 4225 Charm 4282
Aries Bracelet 4228 Charm 4285
Cancer Bracelet 4231 Charm 4288
Libra Bracelet 4234 Charm 4291
Aquarius Bracelet 4226 Charm 4283
Taurus Bracelet 4229 Charm 4286
Leo Bracelet 4232 Charm 4289
Scorpio Bracelet 4235 Charm 4292
Pisces Bracelet 4227 Charm 4284
Gemini Bracelet 4230 Charm 4287
Virgo Bracelet 4233 Charm 4290
Sagittarius Bracelet 4236 Charm 4293
When less than 8 Birthstones, design completed with simulated Seed Pearls in Mother's Pin and Crystal Rhinestones in Father's Tie Tac.
30
31

Fashion Bracelets... the complete look
Quartet (Silvery) 4202 $5.75
Roundabout Earrings Silvery 2245 $4.50 Golden 2244 $4.50
Roundabout Ensemble Silvery 867 $10.00 Golden 866 $10.00
Quartet Golden 4203 $5.75
Roundabout Bracelet Silvery 4245 $6.50 Golden 4244 $6.50
Beehive Bracelet 4649 $3.50
Charmers for Juniors
Sugarplum Necklace 3191 $3.25
Raggedy Ann Necklace 1375 $3.75
Little Charmer Bracelet 4193 $3.75
Tina Ring 1050 $3.00
caroline emmons
26
27

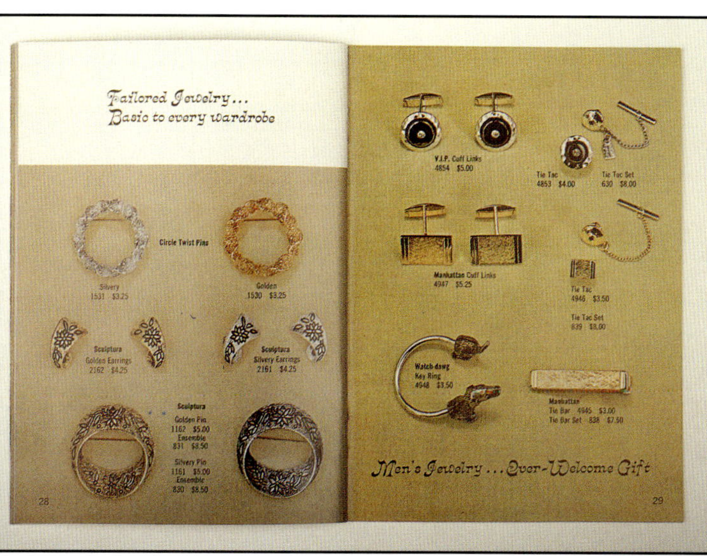
Tailored Jewelry... Basic to every wardrobe
Circle Twist Pins
Silvery 1531 $3.25
Golden 1530 $3.25
Sculptura Golden Earrings 2162 $4.25
Sculptura Silvery Earrings 2161 $4.25
Sculptura Golden Pin 1162 $5.00 Ensemble 831 $8.50
Silvery Pin 1161 $5.00 Ensemble 830 $8.50
V.I.P. Cuff Links 4854 $5.00
Tie Tac 4853 $4.00
Tie Tac Set 630 $8.00
Manhattan Cuff Links 4947 $5.25
Tie Tac 4946 $3.50
Tie Tac Set 639 $8.00
Watch-dawg Key Ring 4548 $3.50
Manhattan Tie Bar 4945 $3.50 Tie Bar Set 638 $7.50
Men's Jewelry ...Ever-Welcome Gift
28
29

THE DESIGN AWARD FOR EXCELLENCE 1969
Award for
Excellence
caroline emmons
fashion magic jewelry

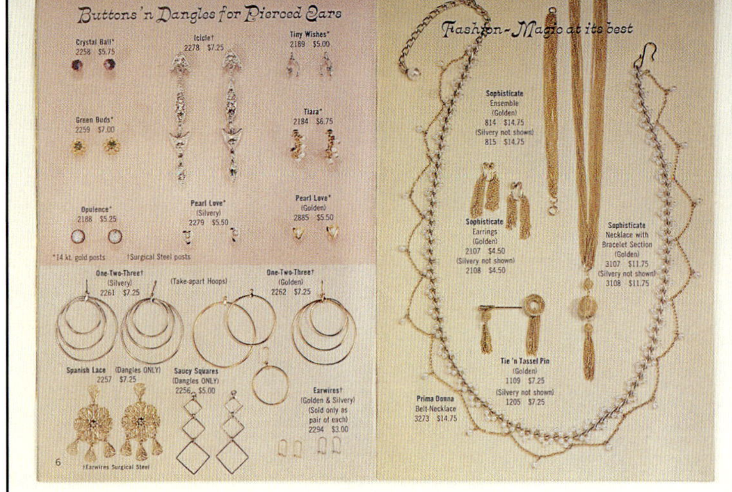

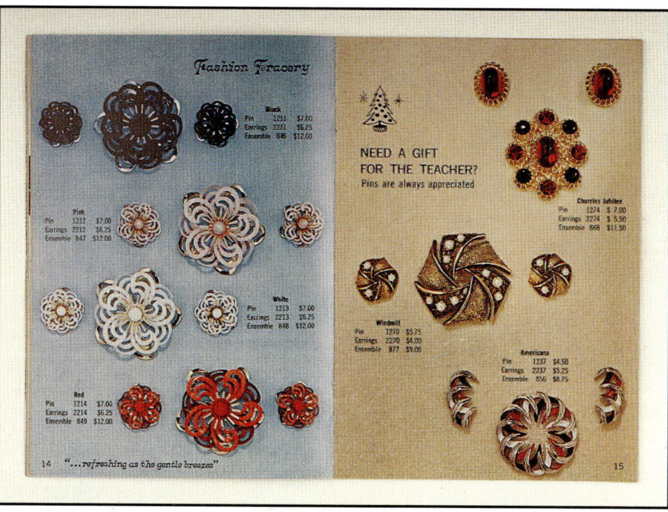

Continued on following pages

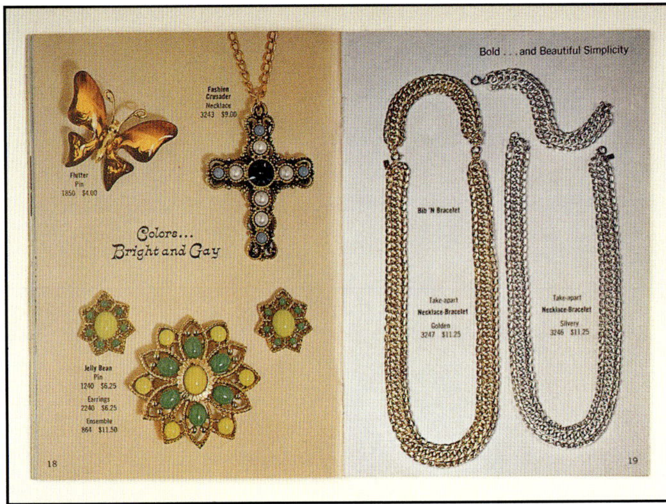

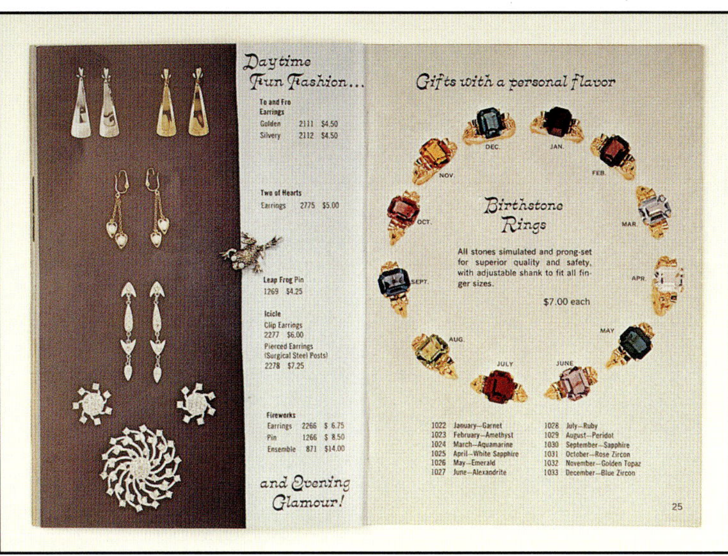

Daytime Fun Fashion...
and Evening Glamour!
To and Fro Earrings
Golden 2111 $4.50
Silvery 2112 $4.50
Two of Hearts
Earrings 2775 $5.00
Leap Frog Pin 1269 $4.25
Icicle
Clip Earrings 2277 $6.00
Pierced Earrings (Surgical Steel Posts) 2278 $7.25
Fireworks
Earrings 2266 $ 6.75
Pin 871 $ 8.50
Ensemble 871 $14.00
Gifts with a personal flavor
Birthstone Rings
All stones simulated and prong-set for superior quality and safety, with adjustable shank to fit all finger sizes.
$7.00 each
DEC JAN FEB MAR APR MAY JUNE JULY AUG SEPT OCT NOV
1022 January—Garnet
1023 February—Amethyst
1024 March—Aquamarine
1025 April—White Sapphire
1026 May—Emerald
1027 June—Alexandrite
1028 July—Ruby
1029 August—Peridot
1030 September—Sapphire
1031 October—Rose Zircon
1032 November—Golden Topaz
1033 December—Blue Zircon
25

Zodiac Charms...Fashion Signs
Chain of Fashion—Magic
Capricorn Dec. 22-Jan. 20
Aquarius Jan. 21-Feb. 19
Sagittarius Nov. 23-Dec. 21
Pisces Feb. 20-Mar. 20
Scorpio Oct. 24-Nov. 22
Aries Mar. 21-Apr. 20
Bracelets with 1 charm $4.50 each
Separate Charms $3.00 each
Libra Sept. 24-Oct. 23
Taurus Apr. 21-May 21
Virgo Aug. 24-Sept. 23
Gemini May 22-June 21
Leo July 24-Aug. 23
Cancer June 22-July 23
Capricorn Bracelet 4225 Charm 4282
Aquarius Bracelet 4226 Charm 4283
Pisces Bracelet 4227 Charm 4284
Aries Bracelet 4228 Charm 4285
Taurus Bracelet 4229 Charm 4286
Gemini Bracelet 4230 Charm 4287
Cancer Bracelet 4231 Charm 4288
Leo Bracelet 4232 Charm 4289
Virgo Bracelet 4233 Charm 4290
Libra Bracelet 4234 Charm 4291
Scorpio Bracelet 4235 Charm 4292
Sagittarius Bracelet 4236 Charm 4293
Endless Fashion 100" Chain
Silvery 3264 $13.00
Golden 3265 $13.00
Multi-strand necklace—Sautoir Belt and Body Jewelry
30
31

Fashion Bracelets... the "complete" look
Tailored Jewelry... Basic to every wardrobe
Quartet (Silvery) 4202 $5.75
Roundabout Bracelet
Silvery 4245 $6.50
Golden 4244 $6.50
Roundabout Earrings
Silvery 2245 $4.50
Golden 2244 $4.50
Beehive Bracelet 4649 $4.00
Roundabout Ensembles
Silvery 867 $10.00
Golden 866 $10.00
Quartet Golden 4203 $5.75
Circle Twist Pins
Silvery 1531 $3.25
Golden 1530 $3.25
Sculptura Golden Earrings 2162 $4.25
Sculptura Silvery Earrings 2161 $4.25
Sculptura
Golden Pin 1162 $5.00
Ensemble 831 $8.50
Silvery Pin 1161 $5.00
Ensemble 830 $8.50
26
27

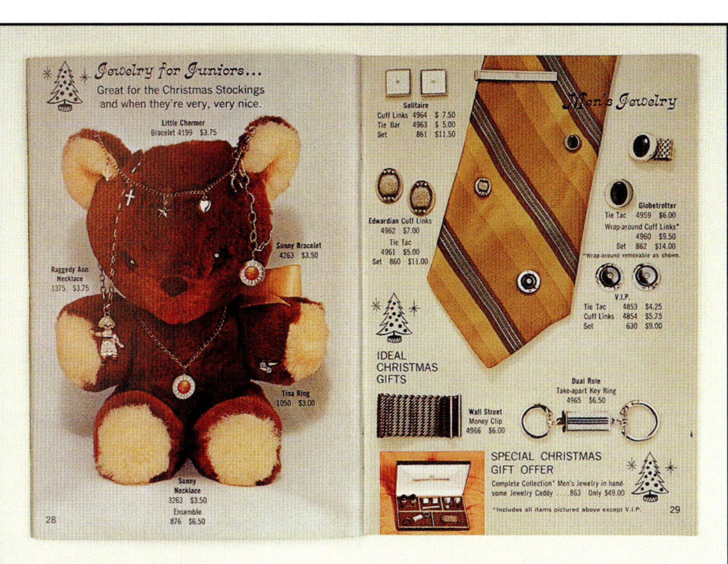

Jewelry for Juniors...
Great for the Christmas Stockings and when they're very, very nice.
Little Charmer Bracelet 4199 $3.75
Sunny Bracelet 4263 $3.50
Raggedy Ann Necklace 1375 $3.75
Tina Ring 1050 $3.00
Sunny Necklace 3263 $3.50
Ensemble 876 $6.50
Men's Jewelry
Solitaire
Cuff Links 4964 $ 7.50
Tie Bar 4963 $ 5.00
Set 861 $11.50
Edwardian Cuff Links 4962 $7.00
Tie Tac 4961 $5.00
Set 860 $11.00
Globetrotter
Tie Tac 4959 $6.00
Wrap-around Cuff Links* 4960 $9.50
Set 862 $14.00
*Wrap-around removable as shown.
V.I.P.
Tie Tac 4853 $4.25
Cuff Links 4854 $5.75
Set 630 $9.00
IDEAL CHRISTMAS GIFTS
Wall Street Money Clip 4966 $6.00
Dual Role Take-apart Key Ring 4965 $6.50
SPECIAL CHRISTMAS GIFT OFFER
Complete Collection* Men's Jewelry in handsome Jewelry Caddy . . . .863 Only $49.00
*Includes all items pictured above except V.I.P.
28
29

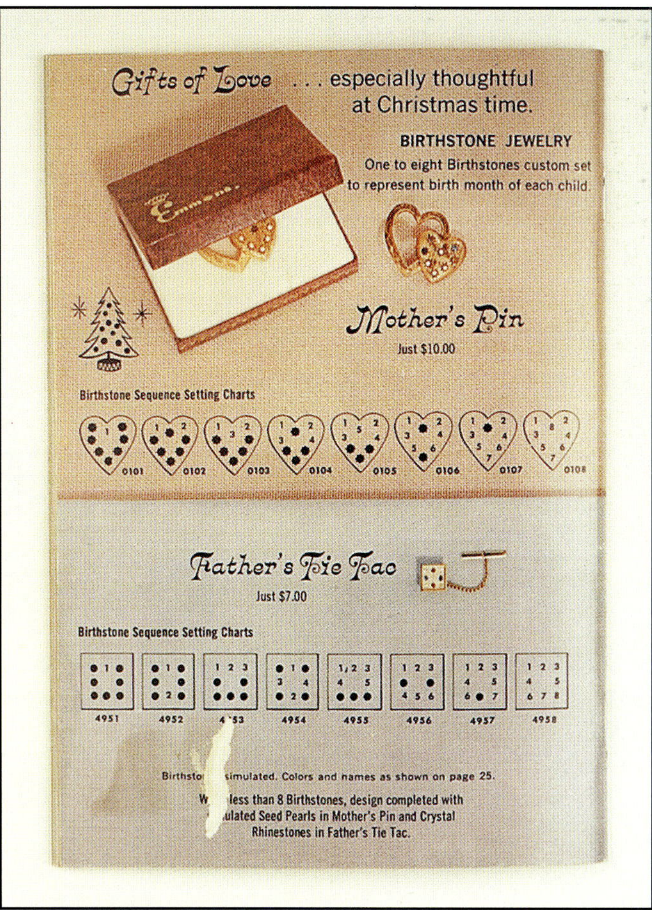

Gifts of Love ... especially thoughtful at Christmas time.
BIRTHSTONE JEWELRY
One to eight Birthstones custom set to represent birth month of each child.
Mother's Pin
Just $10.00
Birthstone Sequence Setting Charts
0101 0102 0103 0104 0105 0106 0107 0108
Father's Tie Tac
Just $7.00
Birthstone Sequence Setting Charts
4951 4952 4953 4954 4955 4956 4957 4958
Birthstones simulated. Colors and names as shown on page 25.
With less than 8 Birthstones, design completed with simulated Seed Pearls in Mother's Pin and Crystal Rhinestones in Father's Tie Tac.

caroline emmons
fashion magic jewelry
Spring & Summer 1974
SAVE UP TO 50%
Caroline's Fabulous 2 & 3 PLAN
BUY 2 ITEMS AT REGULAR PRICES,
PAY ONLY $3.00 FOR THE 3RD ITEM*
*see page 2 for exceptions

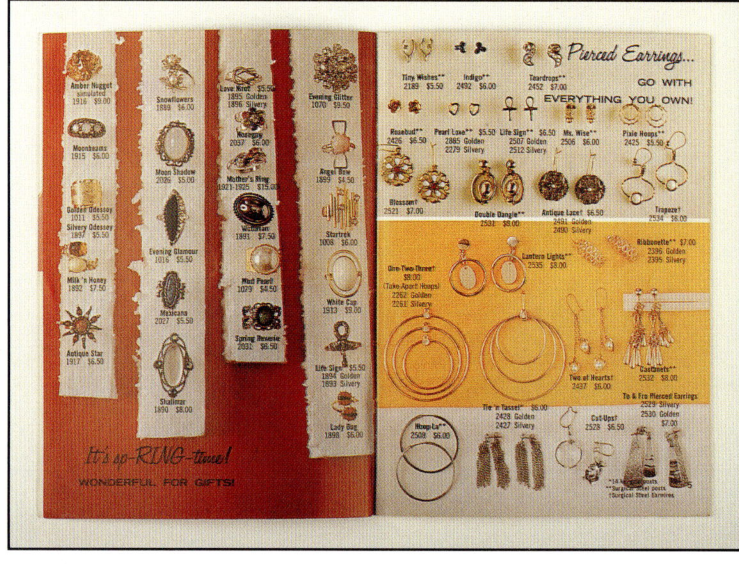

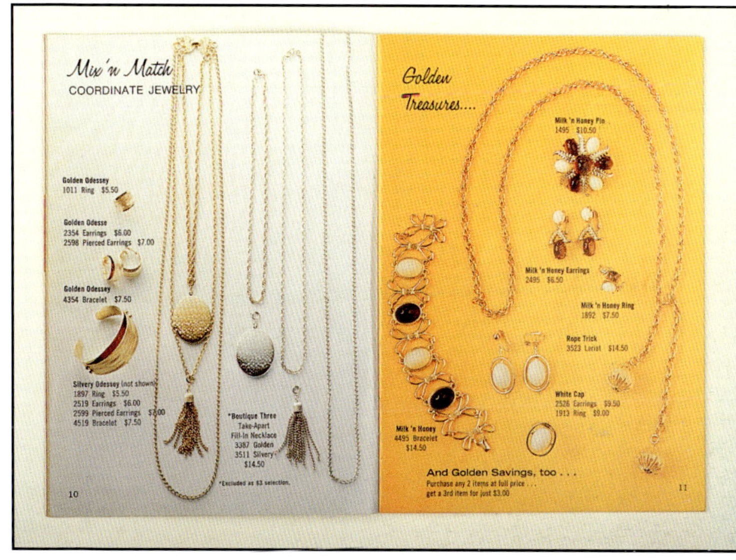

Continued on following pages

All Seasons Favorites...
Wood Chimes
2430 Clip Earrings $5.00
(convertible to Pierced Dangles)
Tie 'n Tassel Pin $8.00
1109 Golden   1205 Silvery
Tie 'n Tassel Clip Earrings $5.50
2107 Golden   2108 Silvery
Tie 'n Tassel Pierced Earrings $6.00
2428 Golden   2427 Silvery
Wood Chimes
3430 Necklace $13.50
Get Wood Chimes Necklace for just $3.00 when you buy on our 2 & 3 Plan!
Flutter Pin
1850 $5.50
16
Gifts of Love
Birthstone Jewelry . . . for the personal touch! Attractively gift-boxed.
MOTHER'S PIN
Just $10.00
FATHER'S TIE TAC
Just $7.00
Birthstone Sequence Setting Charts for Mother's Pin
0101 0102 0103 0104
0105 0106 0107 0108
Birthstone Sequence Setting Charts for Father's Tie Tac
4951 4952 4953 4954
4955 4956 4957 4958
One to eight Birthstones custom set to represent birth month of each child. Birthstone simulated. Colors and names as shown on page 25.
When less than 8 Birthstones, design is completed with simulated Seed Pearls in Mother's Pin and Crystal Rhinestones in Father's Tie Tac.
17

Show Off your own Fashion Ideas...
Show Off Take-Apart Clip Earrings $6.50
2424 Golden   2423 Silvery
(They convert to Pierced Dangles, too!)
SHOW OFF Take-Apart Pin Pendant
3424 Golden   3423 Silvery
$12.00
Take advantage of 2 & 3 Plan and save $9.00 on Show Off Pin Pendant!
18
Love Knot Pin $5.50
1509 Golden   1510 Silvery
To & Fro Earrings $5.50
2111 Golden   2112 Silvery
To & Fro Pierced Earrings $7.00
2530 Golden   2529 Silvery
(with Surgical Steel Posts)
LOVE CHAIN
It's a Necklace!
It's a Belt!
It's a Bracelet!
3499 Take-Apart Necklace $13.00
19

Fashion Bangles* Take-Apart Pendant
3527 $17.50
(Large silvery bangle removable to wear as bracelet, shown below.)
(Golden bangle removable for child's bangle bracelet)
*Excluded as $3 selection.
Lantern Lights
2536 Clip Earrings $8.00
2535 Pierced Earrings $8.00
Lantern Lights
3535 Bib Necklace
$13.00
Silvery Odessey Ring
1897 $5.50
(see matching pieces pg. 10)
Hoop-La
2508 Pierced Earrings
$6.00
Everyday Fashion...
Duchess
Four strand (20") simulated pearl necklace. Wear as a bib (shown) or as 2-strand sautoir.
3525 Necklace $13.00
Valmai Pin
1493 Golden $7.00
1494 Silvery $7.00
Valmai Earrings
2493 Golden $5.00
2494 Silvery $5.00
Times Square
4585 Bracelet $7.50
One-Two-Three Earrings
(Take-Apart Hoops)
2517 Clip Earrings Golden $8.00
2518 Clip Earrings Silvery $8.00
One-Two-Three Pierced Earrings
2262 Golden $8.00
2261 Silvery $8.00
21

Frolic
A burst of color to brighten your spring wardrobe
Wear 2 or 3 or more colors together . . . our 2 & 3 Plan will help you do it
Close-up look on opposite page . . . each one a 36" strand necklace.
3568 Frolic (blue) $5.00
3566 Frolic (white) $5.00
3567 Frolic (red) $5.00
On this page:
3570 Frolic (orange) $5.00
3569 Frolic (brown) $5.00
22
23

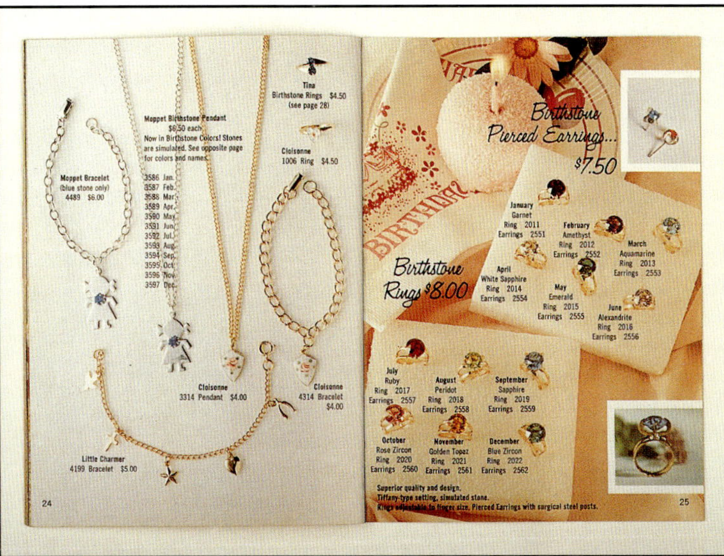

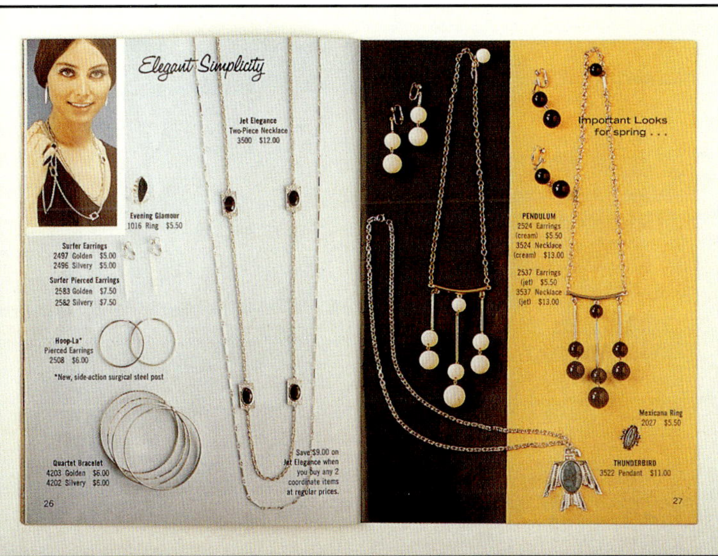

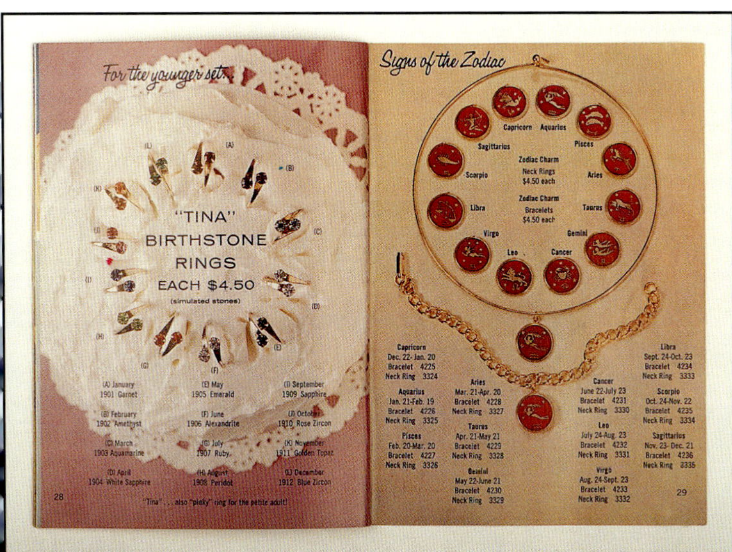

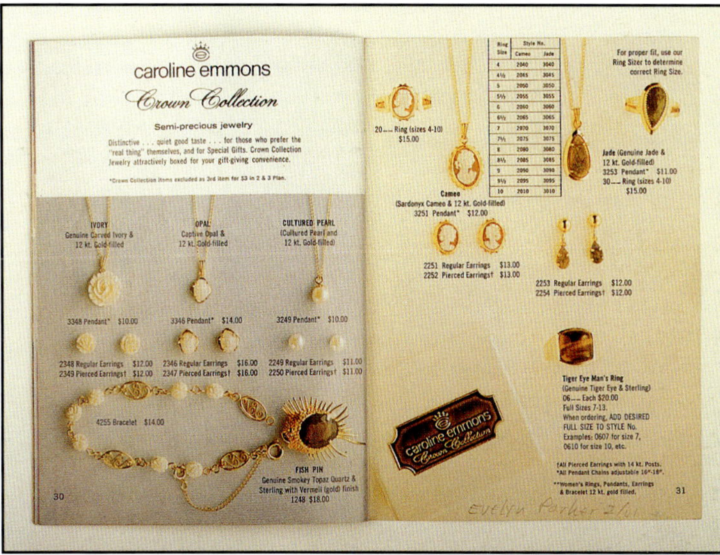

caroline emmons
fashion magic jewelry
1977
SPRING
COMPANION COLLECTION

Mexicana
3818 Pendant $12.50
2818 Pierced Earrings $11.00
caroline emmons
fashion magic jewelry
Silvery Braid
4808 Bracelet $10.50
Golden Braid
4809 Bracelet $10.50
1977
SPRING
COMPANION
COLLECTION
featuring
matching pieces for your
favorite Caroline Jewelry.
Now available for sale
Star Spangled Girl (silvery)
3897 Necklace $12.50
2897 Pierced Earrings $10.50
(Earrings come apart to wear two ways)
Finesse
2748 Earrings $12.00
(they convert to pierced dangles)
ALL items on this page are
available on Caroline's 2
and 4 Savings Plan.
Buy any 2 items at regular
prices and get a 3rd item
for just $4.00.

Collecting Sarah Coventry jewelry became addictive for me, and now I'm wondering if writing will as well. With this being my second book, I'm not sure what that says about me, other than I am a "glutton for punishment."

As I began collecting Emmons jewelry as well and seriously trying to document the pieces, I can't stress enough the hospitality I received from the people in Newark, the Arcadia Historical Society, and the former Fashion Show Directors around the country. Without these people, this book would not have been possible. In my current Style Consultant position with the newly formed Sarah Coventry HPP, I now look forward to putting into practice all of the traits I've found in these wonderful people from the first generation.

Even as I put the finishing touches on this manuscript, I received information from readers of my first book with names of some of the "unidentified pieces" in that volume. Let's continue the communication and let me know what you discover. Enjoy collecting, trading, and keeping in touch.

Glossary

Amethyst. A natural gemstone in shades from lavender to purple. Costume jewelry used imitation rhinestones in these same shades.

Aurora Borealis. A name derived from the colorful aurora lights seen in the northern latitudes. The glass rhinestones have been treated with metals that give the iridescent effect.

Baroque Pearl. A large, bumpy, misshapen pearl, real or man-made.

Bib. A necklace of three or more strands of chain, beads, or simulated pearls in concentric lengths.

Cabochon. An unfaceted form of cutting used for opaque and translucent stones; the stone is given a rounded, convex shape.

Charms. Costume jewelers used the term to refer to the small decorative ornaments fastened to a chain, bracelet, necklace, or earrings.

Chatelaine. Originally, this referred to a chain hanging from the belt of a household employee, on which articles of keys, a watch, a comb, or coin purse were secured. Later, it became a term used for describing a pair of pins that were connected by a chain or perhaps several chains. The two pieces could be worn separately or together.

Cloisonné. Decoration for enamel and metal jewelry in which metal strips are soldered to a piece in a pattern and the enclosed spaces filled by enamel in varying colors. The enamel is then ground and polished.

Costume Jewelry. Jewelry not containing precious jewels or metals. Some Sarah Coventry and Emmons jewelry does not meet this definition as semi-precious stones were used.

Drop. A small decorative object or ornament suspended from a brooch, necklace, hoop, or earring.

Electroplate. Process of coating one metal with a film of another metal.

Emerald Cut. A type of faceted cutting used primarily for emeralds and diamond, square or rectangular in shape.

Enamel. Colored material used for decorative work on jewelry. Can be either melted on or painted on.

Epoxy. Any of several resin compounds having strong qualities of adhesion, toughness, and chemical resistance used in coatings and adhesives.

Filigree. Ornamental work that looks lacy, intricate, and delicate because it is created from intertwining gold, silver, brass, or other fine wires.

Gold-filled. Mechanical means of encasing a base metal with a gold alloy of not less than 10 karat fineness and not less than 1/20 the weight of the piece.

Goldentone. A gold-like finish used for costume jewelry, created by covering metal with an alloy of gold

Intaglio. A design cut or carved into a gemstone, piece of glass, or plastic. Intaglio is the opposite of cameo, which is a raised design.

Jet. A coal fossil lignite of glossy black color. It is usually a cabochon rather than a black glass rhinestone.

Lariat. A long necklace without a clasp giving the open ends the opportunity to be knotted, looped, or held together with a clasp, ring, or pin.

Marked or **Signature**. Refers to when the company's name or mark is identified on the back of the piece, either engraved or raised carving.

Navette. A rhinestone cut in a canoe shape with points at both ends.

Prong set. Metal fingers or prongs used to hold a stone securely in place.

Rhinestone. A cut stone of glass that uses light refraction to create sparkle and could be iridescent. Often backed with foil for additional brilliance.

SarahGlo. High luster finish achieved by a process of covering metal with an alloy of gold. Also shown as goldentone.

SarahSheen. High luster finish achieved by a process of covering metal with rhodium. Also shown as silvertone.

Silvertone. A finish used for costume jewelry, in which metal is covered with rhodium for a lasting finish.

Simulated. An imitation or counterfeit of something that is genuine, as in simulated pearls.

Stationed. To assign to or set in a station or position.

Sterling Silver. An alloy of 92.5% silver and 7.5% other metals.

Bibliography

Arcadia Historical Society, Chris Davis, Executive Director, Newark, New York.

Caroline Emmons Division of C. H. Stuart, Inc., promotional materials and catalogs from former Fashion Show Directors.

Oshel, Kay. *Sarah Coventry Jewelry*. Atglen, Pennsylvania: Schiffer Publishing Ltd., 2003.

Sarah Coventry, Inc., promotional materials and catalogs from former Fashion Show Directors.

Uris, Auren. *The Executive Breakthrough*. Garden City, New York: Doubleday & Company, Inc., 1967.

Personal Collection Sheets

To document your purchases, I recommend the use of Personal Collection Sheets like this one. You can reproduce this chart, then carry with you on your treasure hunting trips to keep track of your finds. Happy collecting!

Description (Name)	Purchase Price	Purchase Date	Reference Information

Index

Overview

Current Value Information, 14
Custom Jewelry, 11
Emmons Jewelry, begins on page 110
Fashion Show Directors, 18, 110, 113, 114
Get Your Charm, 15
Hot Air Balloon, 12
Jewelry Information, 10, 11
Markings, 10
Original Pricing, 14
Promotional Materials, 8, 9
Sarah Coventry, Inc., begins on page 16
Sarah Coventry International, begins on page 85
Sarah Is Home Again, 14, 15
Stuart Company, 5-7
Update on Unidentified Pieces from First Book, 13-14
Versatility, 12-13

Sarah Coventry (USA)

Accessories/Watches/Belts

Bracelet and necklace extenders, 43, 44
Camelot belt, 80
Classic Beauty scarf holder, 80
Disco-Tek belt, 80
Fashion Flair chain belt, 80
Fashion Fortune necklace/belt, 79
Fashion-Hold barrette, 80
French Rope chain belt, 79, 80
Glamour Wardrobe box, 34
Jewelry cleaning cloth, 43
Jewelry red velvet cloth, 42
Key Note key ring, 80
Key-Ringer, 80
Military Brass belt, 79
Mood Mate necklace/belt, 79, 80
Sarah Coventry patch, 42
Shindig pin/barrette, 80
Snow Blossom belt, 79
Surfside belt, 79
Tailored Accent necklace/belt, 80
Trio belt, 80
Watches, 78
White Charmer holder, 80

Awards

Award keys, 66
Crown pin, 35

Bracelets

All Around bracelet, 74
Anniversary Charm bracelet, 75
Antique Rose, 13
Atlantis bracelet, 73, 74
Autumn Leaves bracelet, 74
Avenue bracelet, 75
Betsy bracelet, 72
Bird of Happiness bracelet, 73
Blue Lady bracelet, 75
Boulevard bracelet, 75
Buckle Cuff bracelet, 74
Butterfly Lace bracelet, 72
Classic Cuff bracelet, 75
Classic Elegance bracelet, 75
Coffee and Cream bracelet, 72, 75, 76
Congo bracelet, 74
Cosmopolitan bracelet, 20, 75, 76
Cossack bracelet, 74
Daybreak bracelet, 72
Dazzling Aurora bracelet, 72
Designer's Choice bracelet, 75
Dolphin bracelet, 75
Double Twist Bangle bracelets, 76
Egyptian Temptress bracelet, 72
Embraceable hinge cuff bracelet, 76
Empress bracelet, 74
Evening Sands bracelet, 72, 76
Fancy Free bracelet, 72
Fascination bracelet, 74
Fashion Flirt bracelet, 74
Fashion Rope bracelet, 72
Festoon bracelet, 74
Fiesta bracelet, 73
First Lady bracelet, 72
Florentine bracelet, 74
Four Dimensions bracelet, 73
Frosted Leaves bracelet, 73
Gentle Trio bracelet, 74
Golden Bangle bracelet, 74
Golden Ice bracelet, 76
Golden Leaf bracelet, 76
Golden Nile bracelet, 75
Golden Swirls bracelet, 73
Goldenrod bracelet, 73
Highlight hinged cuff bracelet, 72
Identity bracelet, 11
Inca bracelet, 73

Infinite bracelet, 73
Jet Set bracelet, 74
Little Love bracelet, 72, 73
Milky Way bracelet, 73
Mural bracelet, 74
Panda Bear charm, 73
Posie hand painted cloisonné bangle bracelet, 76
Roundabout bracelet, 74
Sabrina Fair bracelet, 72
Scandia bracelet, 74
Snow Princess bracelet, 75
Spangle-Bangles bracelet, 74
Star Attraction bracelet, 73
Sultana bracelet, 72
Swingalong bracelet, 73
Tailored Accent bracelet, 73
Tailored Cuff bracelet, 74, 75
Tempo bracelet, 72
Tourister bracelet, 74
Town and Country bracelet, 72
Tri Twist bracelet, 76
Turn-a-bout bracelet, 74
Two-Tone Bangle bracelets, 75
Victorian Blue bracelet, 72
Wisp bracelet, 74
Wrist-O-Crat bracelet, 74

Brooches

Accent pin (1968), 33
Accent pin (early 1960s), 34
Anniversary pin, 36
Bold Gypsy, 35
Butterfly Duo pin, 35
Butterfly scatter tac, 35
Changing Times stick pin, 34
Christmas Holiday, 33
   Angel pin, 33
   Holly Bell, 33
   Santa Claus, 33
Crescent pin, 34
Crown pin, 35
Demi pin, 34
"Dogwood" Jet Black pin, 35
Elegance stick pin, 35
Evening Snowflake, 15
Family Parade pin, 34, 36
Fan Bar pin, 35
Feather pin, 35
Fashion Rite pin, 35
First Lady pin, 36
Floral Delite pin, 34
Flower of the Month pin, 34
Golden Scepter pin, 19
Gypsy pin, 36
Heart Delight stick pin, 36
Jacqueline pin, 36
Lite Touch pin, 36
Misty Morning pin/pendant, 35
Moonmist stick pin, 35
Mother's Pin Family Tree, 34
Multiple Choice Pins – Sarah's ABC, 34
Nature's Pearl pin, 33
Night Owl pin, 36
Norwegian Ice pin, 36
Nova pin, 36
Octagon pin, 36
Oriental pin, 35
Overture pin/pendant, 35
Precious pin, 34
Puppy Love pin, 36
"S" pin, 34
Sarah's A.B.C.'s pin, 11
Silhouette pin, 33
Silvery Maple pin, 34
Sincerely Yours initial pin, 11
Slow Poke pin, 35
Snow Blossom pin, 35
Snowfall pin, 36
Solitude pin, 35
Squeaky pin, 36
Starburst Pin, 35
Swan Scatter Tac, 36
Sultry pin, 36
Sweetwater Magic pin, 36
The Sting pin, 36
Tic-Tac-Toe pins, 34
Tinsel Twist pin, 33
Ultima pins, 33
Victorian pin, 36
Vintage pin, 36
Waltz Time pin, 35
Whimsical pins, 33
Windfall pin, 34

Catalogs, 83-84

Charms

#1 Drop, 79
Cherub Christmas charm, 79
Christmas Tree charm, 42
Little Love charm, 79
Owl drop, 79

Pineapple charm, 79
Puffed Heart drops, 79
Sail Boat charm, 22
Sailing drop, 79
Three Wise Men charm, 79
Young Sailor drop, 79
1979 Limited Edition charm, 79

Christmas

Gabrielle Christmas drop, 45
Ornaments, 82

Crosses

Mythology cross, 49
Romanesque cross, 43
Sterling Faith cross, 58
Tiger Eye cross, 77

Earrings

Accent earrings, 39
Angel Pink earrings, 39, 41
Anniversary earrings, 40
Any Thing Goes clip earrings, 27
Atlantis earrings, 41
Autumn Trio earrings, 40
Azure Skies earrings, 39
Basic Hoop earrings, 42
Birds in Flight earrings, 38
Blue Champagne earrings, 39
Blue Cloud earrings, 39
Blue Note earrings, 38
Carousel earrings, 37
Chan-Di-Lites earrings, 37
Classic Partners Going Steady earrings, 40
Cleopatra earrings, 39
Coffee Break earrings, 38
Colleen earrings, 38
Confetti earrings, 40
Coraline earrings, 38
Crystal Snowflakes earrings, 39
Crescent earrings, 38
Daisy Time earrings, 41
Dancing Jet earrings, 40
Debutante earrings, 38
Delicious earrings, 38
Duchess earrings, 38
Easy Going earrings, 40, 42
Evening Snowflake earrings, 40
Fashion Frost earrings, 54
Fashion In Motion earrings, 37
Fiesta earrings, 73
Flair earrings, 41
Flower Flattery earrings, 38
Golden Mum earrings, 42
Golden Swirl earrings, 37
Holiday Circles earrings, 40
Indian Maiden earrings, 39
Indian Treasures earrings, 38
Jet Flight earring, 37
Legend earrings, 38
Madame Butterfly earrings, 38
Military brass earrings, 37
Moonlight Madness earrings, 38
Multi-Swirl earrings, 37
Nocturne earrings, 37
On Stage earrings, 39
Orbit earrings, 39
Over the Rainbow earrings, 40
Papillion earrings, 40
Pastel Parfait earrings, 39
Pastel Parfait pierced earrings, 40
Pearl Flight earrings, 37
Pink Radiance earrings, 19
Portrait earrings, 37
Pyramid Treasure earrings, 41
Primrose earrings, 37
Reflector earrings, 40
Roman Coins earrings, 38, 41
Royal Crown earrings, 40
Sabrina Fair earrings, 37
Scandia earrings, 41
Scarlet tears earrings, 38
Sea Urchin earrings, 40
Show-stopper earrings, 42
Showtime earrings, 41
Silvery Fern earrings, 41
Simplicity earrings, 38
Spanish Moss earrings, 38
Springtime earrings, 40
Stargazer earrings, 38
Swingalong earrings, 41
Tahitian Flower earrings, 38
Teahouse earrings, 41
Touch of Elegance earrings, 37
Town and Country earrings, 39
Two-Timer earrings, 39
Ultra Fashion earrings, 37
Vienna earrings, 37
White Velvet earrings, 39
World's Fair earrings, 37
Young and Gay earrings, 38

Fashion Show Director

Michael, Dawn , 18

Lady Coventry

Amethyst Oval pin, bracelet, earrings, 30
Aqua Treasure ring, 77
Carved Tiger Eye earrings, 38
Filigree Onyx earrings, pendant, bracelet, 77
Flowered Circle pin, earrings set, 77
Genuine Crystal Heart pendant, 77
Genuine Jade pendant, 77
Genuine Tiger Eye choker, 77
Golden Scarab bracelet, 77
Heather pendant, 77
Jade 'n Pearl ring, 66, 70
Jade Oval bracelet, earrings, pin, 77
Lord and Lady ring, 77
Mother of Pearl Cameo ring, 69, 70
Onyx Tears pin and bracelet, 77
Opal Treasure bracelet, 77
Roxanne ring, 77
Silvery Moonstone pendant and earrings, 77
Solitude necklace, 77
Star Bright necklace, 77
Sterling Locket, 77
Sterling Locket pendant, 77
Tiger Eye cross, 77
Togetherness ring, 77
Unidentified ring in goldentone, 77
Unidentified ring with jet black set, 77
Wedding band ring, 77

Men's Jewelry

Aztec choker, 81
Cossack bracelet, 74
Dare Devil bracelet, 81
Daytona choker, 81
Devotion pendant, 81
Eric ring, 82
Explorer bracelet, 81
Gaucho bracelet, 81
Goldenwood necklace, 81
Indian Head pendant, 81
Italian Horn pendant, 81
Lumberjack choker, 81
Men's I.D. bracelet, 81
Modern Trio bracelet, 81
On the Square tie tac, 81
Tiger Eye ring, 82
Togetherness ring, 82
Unidentified button covers, 82
Wrist-O-Crat bracelet, 74

Necklaces

Amulet pendant, 54
Angel Pink pendant, 44
Austrian Crystal lariat, 51
Autumn Beauty pendant, 47
Autumn Trio pendant, 61
Beau-Time choker, 55
Bernie the Frog pendant, 63
Bird of Paradise pendant, 61
Birthstone Heart pendant, 52
Black Beauty pendant, 62
Bold and Beautiful necklace, 48
Cameo Lady pendant/pin, 50
Caramel Twist choker, 60
Career Girl necklace, 48
Caress necklace, 50
Chain Reaction necklace, 51
Chan-Di-Lites necklace, 43
Change of Heart choker, 48
Cinema necklace, 51
Cinnamon Swirl necklace, 63
Cleopatra bib-necklace, 46
Concord necklace, 44
Copenhagen pendant, 49
Cord necklace/belt, 60
Coronation necklace, 56
Cosmopolitan pendant, 63
Country Roads necklace, 51
Coventry Cameo pendant, 48, 58
Creamy Shell pendant drop, 54
Crystal Fire necklace, 42
Danish Modern pendant, 56
Daybreak choker, 53
Debut necklace, 32
Deep Burgundy, 59
Desert Scene pendant, 44, 55, 64
Devotion pendant, 64
Dew-Drop pendant, 63
Dream Weaver chain, 53
Duo Heart choker, 48
Elegant Trio necklace, 51
Egyptian choker, 55
Egyptian Goddess necklace, 65
Emberglo necklace, 52
Enchantment choker, 55
Encore pendant, 45
Essence pendant, 48
Evening Mist necklace, 47
Expressions pendant, 54
Exquisite Lady necklace, 54
Fancy Free necklace, 22
Fantasia pendant, 54

Fashion Basic chain, 54
Fashion Braid choker, 48, 59
Fashion Frost necklaces, 54
Fashion Tie-up, 56
Festival Beads, 51
Festive necklace, 52
Field Flower necklace, 61
Fifth Avenue choker, 48
Fine "C" chain, 65
First Love necklace, 42
First Love pendant, 44,
First Star pendant, 56
Fly Away necklace, 50
Frolic pendant, 42
Front Row pendant, 52
Frostfire necklace, 58
Gala choker, 53
Gentle Moods choker, 63
Glacier necklace, 50
Going My Way necklace, 60
Gracious Lady pendant, 57
Glamour necklace, 45, 53
Golden Coin pendant, 63
Golden Braids choker, 47
Golden Gypsy necklace, 44
Goldenwood necklace, 81
Hawaiian Fantasy pendant, 60
Headliner necklace, 62
Heiress lariat, 61
Hidden Pearl necklace, 44
Hi Lo Elegance necklace, 13
Hi 'N Low lariat necklace, 62
Hi-Style choker, 55
Holiday Beads, 42, 55
Holiday Lites choker, 48, 56
Image pendant, 61
Imagination necklace/belt, 52
Indian Pride necklace, 59
Indian Summer necklace, 62
Infinity Chain, 56
Instant Fashion necklace, 62
Intrigue necklace, 62
In the Swim pendant, 54
Jealous Heart, 58
Jet Ice necklace, 46
Jet Set necklace, 43
Jet Set Versatile pendants, 53
Jewelfish pendant, 54
Jug of Wisdom drop, 54
Krackle Beads, 64
Lavender 'n Lace necklace, 53
Lilac Time choker, 44
Lites pendant, 46
Lotus Blossom pendant, 52
Love Knots choker, 44
Lovely Lady choker, 50
Lucky Lady necklace, 59
Lucky Lady necklace, 63
Magnolia Locket pendant, 54
Mahogany necklace, 49
Melissa choker, 49
Melon Accent choker, 49
Mint Delight lariat, 63
Mirage choker, 44
Misty necklace, 42
Monterey necklace, 53
Moon Cloud necklace, 59
Morning Blossoms pin/pendant, 45, 62
Mushroom pendant, 54
Nature's Treasure necklace, 53
necklace extenders, 43, 44
New Design choker, 49
New Image drop, 54
New Polonaise choker, 60
New Sarah Coventry Collection
    Flight pendant, 65
    Genuine Jade apple charm, 65
    Genuine Tiger eye heart, 65
    Gold – 10 Karat Plumb Gold, 78
    Gold – 14 Karat Gold, 78
    Snowflake charm, 65
    Unidentified blue lapis stone butterfly charm, 65
New Summer Magic necklace, 55
New Yorker choker, 47
Nile Queen pendant, 57
Old Vienna necklace, 47
On The Move necklace, 46, 59
Oriental Lanterns necklace, 60
Oriental Mood choker, 44, 58
Outer Space pendant, 47, 53
Our Secret pendant, 56
Paradise choker, 51
Park Avenue choker, 49
Party Hearts necklace, 48
Pastel Parfait Beads, 54, 55
Pink Lady pendant, 47, 53
Pink Parfait necklace, 42, 64
Pirouette lariat, 55
Pizzazz choker, 56
Plain and Fancy necklace, 43

Plum Lustre Triple Strand necklace, 57
Premiere necklace, 57
Preview choker, 49
Primrose pendant and necklace, 65
Promenade necklace, 63
Protestant pendant, 56
Puppy Love Poodle pendant, 42
Queen of Hearts choker, 59
Rajah drop, 57
Rapture necklace, 47
Raspberry Ice necklace, 57
Reflections necklace, 51
Rendezvous pendant, 43, 61
Rock Trio-hoop necklace, 56
Rose Cameo pendant, 50
Rosette pendant, 47
Royal Flair pendant, 54
Royal Lace bib-necklace, 48
Safari Necklace Beads, 59
Samantha choker, 57
Sand Dune choker, 61
Sarah's Birthstone pendant, 48
Sara-Zade necklace, 64
Saturn drop, 54
Scandia choker, 49
School Days Initial pendants, 57
Sea Shell Lariat, 50
Seashore pendant, 48
Sensation choker, 50
Serenade necklace, 54
Sierra necklace 2-151
Sierra choker, 54
Sierra pendant, 62
Silhouette Perfume pendant, 48
Silver Nugget choker, 56
Silverspin choker, 51
Silvery Sunset necklace, 43
Spangle-Bangles pendant, 56
Sparkle Beauty necklace, 58
Splendor necklace, 61
Spring Beauty pendant, 52
Spring Fever necklace, 52
Spring Bouquet pendant, 45, 46
Spring Song pendant, 44
Starlite choker, 60, 61
Summer Scheme necklace, 42, 49
Surfside necklace, 61
Sweetheart Locket, 51
Tailored Lady necklace, 55
Tapestry necklace, 63
Teahouse pendant, 48
Teen Heart Locket, 50
Three Cheers pendant, 55
Three-Timer necklace, 45
Tiara pendant, 45
Timeless pendant, 11, 47
Timely necklace, 54
Tinkerbell necklace, 60
Touch of Elegance necklace, 43
Trade Winds necklace, 65
Trinity necklace, 54
Two-Tone Butterfly pendant, 44
Umber Tones necklace, 53
Victorian Bouquet pendant, 63
White Elegance necklace, 49, 57
White Magic choker, 49
White 'N Bright choker, 49, 57
Wire Wrap pendant, 46
Zulu choker, 56

Overview, 16-19

Rings

Age of Aquarius ring, 71
Alexandria ring, 70
Ambrosia ring, 71
Antique Bouquet ring, 71
Autumn Haze ring, 66
Aztec Treasure ring, 70
Ballerina ring, 70
Birthstone Duet ring, 66
Blue Feather ring, 70
Blue Lady ring, 66
Blue Moonlet ring, 69, 70
Blue Night ring, 71
Buckle ring, 70
Camelot ring, 68, 70
Cameo Lady ring, 67, 69, 70, 71
Capri ring, 69
Caress ring, 69, 70
Carnelian Cameo ring, 69
Charity ring, 70
Citation ring, 70
Cleopatra ring, 69
Cleopatra Perfumed ring, 67
Confetti ring, 71
Contessa ring, 67, 70
Continental ring, 71
Coraline ring, 67, 68
Coronation ring, 68
Crimson ring, 69
Curved arrow ring, 70

Dainty Combo ring, 66
Danish Modern ring, 67
Dazzler ring, 68, 69
Debutante ring, 68
Deep Purple ring, 70
Desire ring, 68
Duo Fashion ring, 71
Dusk ring, 71
Elegant ring, 67
Elite ring, 68, 71
Ember Beauty ring, 70
Enchantment ring, 68
Festive ring, 69
Fieldflowers ring, 69
Fire Lite ring, 70
First Choice ring, 67
First Lady ring, 66
Galaxy ring, 68
Garland ring, 66
Gay Pretenders ring, 71
Genie ring, 67
Genuine Opal ring, 66
Genuine Solalite ring, 70
Gleaner ring, 69
Golden Embers ring, 71
Golden Ice ring, 68
Golden Nugget ring, 68
Hemisphere ring, 68
Heritage ring, 69
Illusive ring, 68
Images ring, 69
Indian Maiden ring, 69
Indian Princess ring, 67, 71
Ingrid ring, 69
Jade 'n Pearl ring, 66, 70
Jet Navette ring, 68, 69
Jet Set ring, 68
Jonquil ring, 67, 68
Julia ring, 71
Kathleen ring, 66
Lagoon ring, 68
Locket ring, 66, 69, 71
Love Story ring, 69, 71
Lover's Knot ring, 70
Marie ring, 69
Mediterranean ring, 71
Melissa ring, 70
Michelle ring, 67
Misty ring, 70, 71
Moon Cloud ring, 70
Moon Glo ring, 67
Moon River ring, 70
Moonmist ring, 69
Morning Glory ring, 70
Natasha ring, 67
Night Lights ring, 68
Odyssey ring, 70
Oriental Melody ring, 70
Over the Rainbow ring, 69
Pink Lady ring, 68, 71
Princess ring, 68
Regina ring, 69, 70
Rosette ring, 71
Roxanne ring, 68
Royal Crown ring, 69
Sarah Coventry's Family bouquet ring, 71
Sarah's Birthstone ring, 70
Sarah's Traditional Birthstone ring, 70
Satin Elegance ring, 68
Scandia ring, 69
Sea Treasure ring, 67, 68
Serenity ring, 71
Shell ring, 70
Spanish Lites ring, 69
Sport ring, 69
Spring Fever ring, 71
Star Shine ring, 69
Stardust ring, 68
Starry Nights ring, 68
Starstruck ring, 67
Sterling Pearl ring, 67
Sugarplum ring, 70, 71
Sultana ring, 71
Suzette ring, 71
Sweet Briar ring, 71
Taffy ring, 71
Tapestry ring, 69
Trulove ring, 67
Two-Tone Stackable ring, 68
2 Ct. Cubic Zirconium ring, 67
Victorian Blue ring, 66
Vintage ring, 71
Vogue ring, 69
Wildflower ring, 69
Wings of Fashion ring, 71
Yesterday ring, 67, 68, 70
Zuni ring, 71

Sets

Americana pin and earrings, 23

Aqua Fleur pin and earrings, 32
Aquarius pin, earrings, ring, 24
Aztec pendant and earrings, 25
Bewitchery necklace and earrings, 29
Black Charmer necklace/pin and earrings, 31
Caged Pearl earrings and necklace, 22
Catherine pin and earrings, 24
Celestial Spray bracelet and pin, 13
Centurion pin/pendant and earrings, 32
Chinese Modern necklace and earrings, 32
Cleopatra bracelet, earrings, ring, 26
Contessa pendant/pin and earrings, 26
Contessa pin and earrings, 13
Coraline pin and earrings, 29
Coronation necklace and bracelet, 29
Cosmopolitan bracelet and belt, 20
Cosmopolitan necklace, earrings, bracelet, 21
Czarina earrings and pendant, 20
Debutante necklace and earrings, 21
Double Choice chain and earrings, 31
Duchess necklace and earrings, 29
Dynasty pendant and earrings, 32
Embraceable necklace and bracelet, 23
Empress necklace and earrings, 25
Enchantress necklace and earrings, 26
Evening Comet pin and earrings, 23
Fascination pin and earrings, 21
Fashion Frost necklace and earrings, 54
Fashion in Motion pin and earrings, 24
Fashion-rite necklace and earrings, 31
Fashion Mobile necklace and earrings, 31
Golden Brocade bracelet and earrings, 19
Golden Cluster bracelet and pin, 30
Golden Ice bracelet and earrings, 26
Golden Rope pendant and earrings, 25, 31
Golden Scepter pin and Pink Radiance earrings, 19
Gracious Lady necklace and bracelet, 32
Heritage necklace/pin and earrings, 25
Hi-Fashion necklace and earrings, 27
Hong Kong earrings, necklace, bracelet, 32
Indian Maiden pendant, earrings, ring, 28
Magic Spell choker and pierced earrings, 32
Matinee Elegance necklace and earrings, 29
Mini-Midi-Maxi necklace and earrings, 27
Moonlight pin and earrings, 28
New Polonaise necklace and earrings, 60
Northern Lights bracelet, earrings, ring, 25
Operetta pin and bracelet, 28
Perfection necklace and Anything Goes clip earrings, 27
Polonaise pendant and earrings, 21
Primrose pin and earrings, 24
Rope of Fashion necklace and earrings, 20
Rustic Charmer necklace and earrings, 26
Safari necklace and earrings, 32
Sea Scroll bracelet and earrings, 29
Sea Star bracelet and earrings, 33
Sea Urchin pin and earrings, 25
Shell-Cor choker and shell earrings, 20
Silvery Moon necklace and Blue Moon choker, 25
Slim Line earrings, necklace, bracelet, 22
Sparkle Circle pin and earrings, 24
Summer Flirt necklace and earrings, 27
Sunburst pin, earrings, bracelet, pin/pendant, 33
Sweetheart Chatelaine pin and earrings, 22
Taffee Tones pendant and bracelet, 27
Tassel Magic necklace/bracelet and earrings, 30
Tawny Shadows bracelet and earrings, 20
Tea Garden enameled bracelet and glass pin, 33
Turn-a-bout earrings, bracelet, necklace, 21
Venetian Treasure necklace and bracelet, 27
Victorian Bouquet pendant, earrings, ring, 30
Vienna pin, earrings, bracelet, 21
White Charmer necklace/belt and earrings, 27
Windfall necklace, earrings, bracelet, 32

Sarah Coventry International

Accessories/Watches/Men's
Fashion-Hold barrette, 94
Kilt Holder clip, 94
Romanesque Clasp, 94

Bracelets
Antique Rose bracelet, 13
Caprice bracelet, 94
Chain Reaction bracelet, 94
Hocus Pocus bracelet, 94
Kismet bracelet, 93
Textured Links bracelet, 93

Brooches
Austrian Lites pin, 88
Beau-Tie scarf pin, 87
Blitzen pin, 89
Candy Apple pin, 89
Caprice pin, 88
Carousel stick pin, 89
Changing Times stick pin, 89
Colonial pin, 87
Coraline pin/pendant, 89
Cupid stick pin, 89

8" Ball pin, 87
Gillian, 88
Golden Era pin, 87
Golden Snowflake pin, 89
Heritage pin, 87
Heritage tac pin, 89
Isabella pin, 88
Lady Coventry Mother of Pearl pin, 87
Lion charm holder pin, 91
Mandolin pin, 88
Mr. Sea Gull pin, 88, 89
Petit Point pin, 87
Pitter Patter pins, 87
Reefer pin, 87, 89
Regal pin, 88
Saffron pin, 87
Sea Swirl pin, 88, 89
Silvery Sunburst pin, 89
Spring Bouquet pin, 88
Warm Heart pin, 87
Whirlwind scarf clip, 87
Who's Who? pin, 88

Catalogs
Australia, 108-109
Canada, 95-104
Scotland, 105-107

Earrings
Gillian earrings, 88

Necklaces
Avanti pendant, 90
Blue Cloud necklace, 91
Chain Reaction necklace, 92
Charisma necklace, 92
Coraline pendant, 89
Crusader pendant, 92
Fashion-Rite necklace, 92
Florentina pendant, 89
Heirloom locket, 92
Hocus Pocus necklace, 90
Imperial, 92
Interlocking Love Accessory pendant, 88
Jet Set necklace, 92
Lightning pendant, 88
Madame Butterfly pendant, 90
Magic Moods necklace, 91
Malibu pendant, 91
Night Owl pendant, 92
Polka pendant, 92
Rajah Elephant pendant, 91
Roman Holiday pendant, 92
Rose-Marie necklace, 92
Talisman of Love pendant, 92
Textured Links pendant, 92
The Littlest Angel pendant, 94
Two Timer necklace, 91
Woodland Flight, 89

Overview, 85

Rings
Butter Finger ring, 93
Isabella ring, 93
Jubilee ring, 93
Rose Garden ring, 93

Sets
Blue Twilight pin and bracelet, 86
Chateau pendant and earrings, 86
China Lady necklace, earrings, bracelet, 85
Fashionaire pin and earrings, 86
Garland bracelet and earrings, 86
Light 'n Lovely necklace and earrings, 85
Norwegian Wood ring, pin, earrings, 86
Rainbow pin and earrings, 85
Silvery Sunburst pin and earrings, 88
Sunspray pin and earrings, 86

Caroline Emmons

Accessories
Twin Key key chain, 11
Unidentified scarf clips, 157
Zodiac neck ring, 157

Awards
Elephant pin, one-of-a-kind, 110
Jewelry cases, 115

Bracelets
Beehive bracelet, 153
Bib 'N bracelet, 143
Brocade bracelet, 154
Charmettes bracelet, 156
Cuff 'n Collar bracelet and choker, 149
Embraceable bracelet, 155
Fashion Flair bracelet, 154
Frosty Lace Golden bracelet, 155
Frosty Lace Silvery bracelet, 155
Gleaming Bows bracelet, 154
Jet Petite bracelet, 155
Little Sweetheart bracelet, 153
Luv bracelet, 155
Mexicana bracelet, 154
Petite White bracelet, 155
Quartet bracelet, 157
Simplicity bracelet, 155
Sophisticate necklace with bracelet section, 150
Zodiac charm, 156

Brooches
African Queen pin/pendant, 133
Autumn Echoes pin, 132, 136
Autumn Haze pin/pendant, 137
Beauty Vine pin, 135
Calypso pin, 134
Camellia (white) pin, 132
Caroline Stuart signed pin, 132
Caroline Stuart signed pin (back), 153
Crystal Leaf pin, 136
Dainty Butterfly pin, 136
Double-Take pin, 135
Fireworks pin, 132
Flutter pin, 136
Gibson Girl pin, 135
Highlights pin, 133
Jelly Bean pin, 133
Kaleidoscope pin, 134
Locket/pin, 134
Love Knot pin, 133
Midnight Butterfly stick pin, 157
Misty Blue pin, 133
Modern Flair pin, 135
Mother's Pin, 132
Orbit in Fashion pin, 136
Pear Bright pin, 137
Persian Treasure pin, 135
Pin Twins pins, 137
Rainbow Star pin, 116, 135
Renaissance pin, 135
Sculptura Silvery pin, 133
Sea Flower pin, 136
Signature pin, 11
Silhouette pin, 136
Sorcery Lavalliere pin, 134
Springtime pin, 11
Starburst pin, 134
Starfish pin, 133
Starry Night pin, 134
Tie 'n Tassel pins, 134
Tutti-Fruitti pin, 136
Twinkling Butterfly pin, 133
Victorian Lace pin/pendant, 133
White Olive pin, 134, 136
Windmill pin, 134, 136
World's Fair Expo pin, 156

Catalogs
1969, 158-161
1970 Fall and Christmas, 162-165
1974, 166-169
1977 Companion Collection, 170

Earrings
Americana earrings, 138
Autumn Echoes earrings, 137
Avocado earrings, 141
Bewitching earrings, 139
Bright Textures earrings, 140
Button earrings, 141
Buttons earrings, 140
Cameo regular earrings, 127
Casino earrings, 141
C'est Belle earrings, 140
Changing Scene earrings, 141
Check Mate earrings, 139
Classic earrings, 140
Confection earrings, 140
Crescent Moon earrings, 140
Crystal Lights earrings, 138
Dramatic earrings, 138
Golden Odyssey earrings, 139
Golden Swirl earrings, 141
Icicle earrings, 139
Lemon Twist earrings, 138
Love Beads earrings, 139
Magic Lantern earrings, 142
Merry Belle earrings, 140
Multiplicity earrings, 138
My Favorite earrings, 141
Nifty earrings, 140
Pearl Glamour earrings, 138
Pearl Love earrings, 141
Pearl Wardrobe earrings, 137
Regalia earrings, 140
Ring-a-Lario earrings, 141
Roundabout earrings, 140
Sassy Hoops earrings, 140
Satin Drop earrings, 140
Silvery Odyssey earrings, 140
Spanish Lace earrings, 139
Swagger earrings, 141
Teardrop earrings, 142
Temple Bells earrings, 140
The Swinger earrings, 141
Tie 'n Tassel earrings, 123, 137, 140
To and Fro earrings, 138
Twice Is Nice earrings, 139
Two of Hearts earrings, 140, 141
Winner's Circle earrings, 140

Fashion Show Directors
Coffman, Mary Beth, 110
Miles, Norma, 114
Williams, Ginny, 113

Men's Jewelry
Ambassador tie tac, 156
Fortune Teller cuff links and tie tac, 157
Mighty Casey cuff links and tie tac, 157
Quartet bracelet, 157
Regal tie tac, 157
Tiger Eye tie tac, 156
Unidentified black pearl tie tac, 157
Unidentified intaglio Roman head tie tac, 157
Unidentified ovals cuff links and tie tac set, 157

Necklaces
Bib 'N Bracelet take-apart necklace/bracelet, 143, 146, 147
Bonnie Blue necklace, 146
Boutique Three chain, 145, 157
Boutique Three take-apart fill in necklace, 145, 148
Cascade necklace, 144, 145
Chinatown lariat, 147
City Slicker chain, 144
Classic Black necklace, 145
Cobra chain, 144
Colleen necklace, 144
Confection necklace, 147
Cuff 'n Collar bracelet/choker, 149
Evening Star pendant, 157
Faith pendant, 144
Fashion Bangles take-apart pendant, 144
Fashion Crusader necklace, 144
Fashion Flavor necklace, 116
Fashion Magic chain, 142
Filigree Flower pin/pendant, 144
Finesse necklace, 145, 147
Floral Portrait pendant, 150
Golden Veil pendant, 144
Heartstrings necklace, 143
Honeycomb necklace, 145
Jet Cascade necklace, 147
Jet Elegance sautoir, 147
Limelight necklace, 144
Lovable necklace, 150
Magic Swirl pendant, 143
Man Trap perfume purse pendant, 149
Mardi Gras necklace, 142
Matchmaker necklace, 148
Matinee necklace, 146
Medallia long sautoir, adjustable belt, 147
Medallion necklace, 149
Midas Touch necklace, 150
Midi Pearls (simulated) necklace, 142
Pearl Wardrobe necklace, 146
Personality 3-way necklace, 149
Prima Donna belt/necklace, 146
Roman Holiday necklace, 146
Rope Trick lariat necklace, 146
Scenario take-apart necklace-sautoir, 147
Show Off take-apart pin/pendants, 148
Silhouette Pin/necklace, 149
Silvery Chain, 143
Sitting Pretty necklace, 144
Soft Touch necklace, 149
Sophisticate necklace with bracelet section, 150
Spellbinder necklace/belt, 149
Spirit of '76 pendant, 149
Star Spangled Girl necklace, 143
Syncopation pin/pendant, 123
Tangier simulated pearl necklace, 143
Thunderbird pendant, 149
Twinkling Star pendant, 149
Ultima II necklace, 143
White Magic belt/necklace, 146
Wind Swept necklace, 150
Zodiac charm, 156
Zodiac neck ring, 157

Overview, 110-116
Promotional Materials, 111-114

Rings
Birthstone ring, 152
Cameo ring, 152
Coralette ring, 152
Crimson Rose ring, 151
Crystal Ball ring, 152
Dinner Hour ring, 152
Endearment ring, 151
Evening Glitter ring, 152
Feminique ring, 151
Galaxy ring, 151
Garnet Glow ring, 152
Golden Odyssey ring, 152
Golden Shrimp ring, 152
Golden Veil ring, 153
Green Lights ring, 151
Harem Girl ring, 151
Honeycomb ring, 152
Jade ring, 127
Jet Classic Golden ring, 151
Jet Classic Silver ring, 151
Legacy ring, 151
Lucky Lady ring, 153
Madcap ring, 151
Milky Way ring, 152
Milk 'n Honey ring, 151
Moon Shadow ring, 151
Mother's Ring, 151
Nocturne ring, 153
Nostalgia ring, 153
Pearly nosegay ring, 152
Portrait ring, 153
Rapture ring, 151
Regency ring, 152
Rosebud ring, 152
Sand Pebbles ring, 153
Shalimar ring, 152
Sienna ring, 152
Spring Reverie ring, 151, 152, 153
Starfire ring, 152
Startrek ring, 153
Town N Country ring, 151
Twosome ring, 151
White Satin ring, 152

Sets
African Queen pin/pendant and two bracelets clipped together, 121
Americana pin and earrings, 122
Avocado pin and earrings, 156
Aztec Princess pin with Tie 'n Tassel earrings, 123
Bewitching pin and earrings, 126
Blossom Time necklace and earrings, 125
Bluebell pin and earrings, 122
Budding Romance pin and earrings, 122
Capriccio necklace, earrings, ring ensemble, 119
Champagne necklace and earrings, 126
Chantilly necklace, earrings, bracelet, 118
Cinnabar bracelet and earrings, 118
City Slicker chain and pierced earrings, 127
Classic Beauty pin and earrings, 129
Cleopatra necklace, earrings, bracelet, 118
Cloisonné necklace and ring, 127
Cobra chain and pierced earrings, 127
Coco necklace and earrings, 125
Crimson Beauty choker, 126
Crimson Glory pin and earrings, 123
Crystal Light Rhinestone Chain necklace, 126
Cultured Pearl pendant and earrings, 127
Czarina pendant and earrings, 126
Daughter of the Nile necklace and bracelet set, 124
Delicate Spiral necklace and earrings, 126
Ducks in Flight pendant, bracelet, earrings, 126
Fashion Tracery pin and earrings, 121
Festival pendant and earrings, 126
Fireworks pin and earrings, 122
Gay Marguerita pin and earrings, 120
Genuine Carved Ivory pendant and earrings, 127
Gleaming Bows bracelet and earrings, 132
Golden Scroll pin and earrings, 119
Heart Throb Take-apart Heart pendant and earrings, 126
Her Majesty Ensemble, 129
Ice Bouquet pin and button earrings, 123
Interlude necklace and earrings, 130
Jade pendant and earrings, 127
Jet Cascade 54" sautoir necklace and earrings, 147
Jet Splendor bracelet and earrings, 131
Lady Love pendant, earrings, ring, 125
Legacy ring, bracelet, earrings, 124
Love Story necklace and earrings, 125
Magic Lantern bracelet and earrings, 120
Midnight Lace pendant and earrings, 123
Midnight Magic necklace, pendant, earrings, 124
Milky Way pendant and clip earrings, 119
Nostalgia necklace, bracelet, ring, 131
Olympiad tac pin and pendant, 117
Opal pendant and pierced earrings, 127
Pearly Pinwheel pin and earrings, 132
Portrait in Black bracelet and earrings, 128
Queen of Fashion necklace, earrings, bracelet, 124
Rainbow Star pin and earrings, 116
Regal Splendor pin and clip earrings, 118
Rhapsody in Blue pin and earrings, 123
Roundabout bracelet and earrings, 125
Royal Princess bracelet and earrings, 125
Sculpture pin and earrings, 122
Sea Beauty pin and earrings, 122
Shimmering Lace pin and earrings, 129
Solid wide bracelets 4-180
Spectator pin and earrings, 129
Starburst pin and earrings, 132
Starburst pin and earrings, 131
Starlite pin and earrings, 120
Victoria pin and drop earrings, 122
White Camellia pin and earrings, 130
Zigzag Golden pin, 123
Zigzag Silvery pin and earrings, 123